WORKING
Sociological Perspectives

ROBERT A. ROTHMAN

University of Delaware

Prentice-Hall, Inc., Englewood Cliffs, New Jersey 07632

Library of Congress Cataloging-in-Publication Data

Rothman, Robert A., (date)
   Working : sociological perspectives.

   Bibliography: p.
   Includes index.
   1. Work—Social aspects. 2. Industrial sociology.
3. Quality of work life. 4. Industry—Social
aspects. I. Title.
HD4904.R655 1987   306'.36   86–22540
ISBN 0–13–965252–3

To Cathy, Anne, and Patty
who give me hope for the future

Editorial/production supervision and
  interior design: Marjorie Borden
Cover design: Ben Santora
Manufacturing buyer: John B. Hall

Printed in the United States of America
10 9 8 7 6 5 4 3

ISBN 0-13-965252-3   01

Prentice-Hall International (UK) Limited, *London*
Prentice-Hall of Australia Pty. Limited, *Sydney*
Prentice-Hall Canada Inc., *Toronto*
Prentice-Hall Hispanoamericana, S.A., *Mexico*
Prentice-Hall of India Private Limited, *New Delhi*
Prentice-Hall of Japan, Inc., *Tokyo*
Prentice-Hall of Southeast Asia Pte. Ltd., *Singapore*
Editora Prentice-Hall do Brasil, Ltda., *Rio de Janeiro*

Contents

9 Occupational Prestige 213

10 Job Dissatisfaction and Work Reform 231

PART FOUR: OCCUPATIONAL CAREERS

Preface

Sociological analysis of work is undergoing dramatic change. Traditional and artificial academic boundaries between Industrial Sociology and Occupational Sociology have blurred, leading to a more general focus upon the nature of work. Long-ignored forms of work, such as domestics and housework, have begun to be examined. Conflict and Interactionist approaches have added a whole new dimension to the study of the division of labor. The field has been enriched by the contributions of social historians and anthropologists who have added a much needed temporal and cross-cultural perspective to the study of modern occupations.

There is, simultaneously, continuous attention to refining and elaborating certain basic issues and problems. The social organization of work roles, professionalization and deprofessionalization, occupational inequality, socialization practices, and career patterns form a central core of analysis.

The workplace itself is in a state of flux. Broad social, demographic, and economic forces—shifting work values, attempts at restructuring work, the decline of smokestack industries and the growth of the service sector, the dramatic increase of women's participation in the paid labor force, and widespread structural unemployment—are having a profound impact on the way people experience work.

Such patterns dominate the environment in which workers (individually and collectively, alone and as members of groups) confront the problems of breaking into nontraditional jobs, seek to derive meaning from their jobs and careers, negotiate career along career paths, establish working relationships with mentors, cope with the reality of joblessness, struggle over pay equity, or face the dilemma of blowing the whistle.

This book integrates these emerging issues with the classic concerns of the field. It has been written specifically for students about to enter the world of work.

Robert A. Rothman
Newark, Delaware

ONE

Sociological Perspectives on Work

INTRODUCTION: THE SOCIAL AND TECHNICAL DIMENSIONS OF WORK

Work is often thought of as a set of physical and mental activities. The government-prepared *Dictionary of Occupational Titles* (U.S. Employment and Training Administration, 1977) lists and defines over 20,000 specific jobs. Many are well known, and formal descriptions merely confirm common-sense observations. Thus, cocktail waiter/waitress becomes

> **Waiter/Waitress, Bar** (hotel & restaurant)
> waiter/waitress, cocktail lounge.
> Serves beverages to patrons seated at tables in bar or cocktail lounge. May take orders for and serve meals and hors d'oeuvres. May compute bill and accept payment. When working in establishment serving only beer and wine, is designated **Waiter/Waitress, Tavern** (hotel & restaurant).

And the job of a nurse is described as:

> **Nurse, General Duty** (medical service)
> Renders general nursing care to patients in a hospital, infirmary, sanitarium, or similar institution. Administers prescribed medications and treatments in accordance with approved nursing techniques. Prepares equipment and aids **Physician** (med. serv.) during treatments and examinations of patients. Observes patient, records significant conditions and reactions, and notifies su-

pervisor or **Physician. . . .** takes temperature, pulse, blood pressure and other vital signs . . . (and) may prepare rooms, sterile equipment, and supplies, and handling, in order of use, to assist **Surgeon** or **Obstetrician. . . .**

Such manual and mental operations may be called the *technical dimensions* of work roles. These are the activities typically profiled in newspaper want ads and listed in job descriptions distributed to new employees. However, a focus exclusively upon the technical dimensions of jobs ignores their history and isolates them from the sociocultural, economic, and political environments that shape them. Moreover. no job is simply a bundle of technical tasks. As Richard Neff (1977:41) has put it, work is "overwhelmingly a public and social activity," drawing attention to social behaviors such as details of dress and grooming, styles of speech, and ability to relate to superiors and coworkers, all of which may be more important to success than is the ability to perform a given technical operation. In addition, most workers function as members of work groups that define the nature of work. To gain acceptance, people must be willing and able to learn group norms and values, and even accept (or appear to accept) the group's systems of belief and opinion. These may be referred to as the *sociological dimensions* of work roles. The key elements in this approach may be organized into five categories: interpersonal relationships; intergroup dynamics; work groups and subcultures; organizational environments; and the sociocultural context.

Interpersonal relationships.   Work is seldom, if ever, a solitary activity. Rather, work is regularly carried out through face-to-face interaction with coworkers, customers, superiors, and countless others. Unraveling the complex network of interpersonal relationships between the cocktail waitress and customers, bartenders, bosses, dishwashers, and other waitresses is more important to an understanding of the work than any analysis of the routine of taking orders, making change, and serving patrons. Workers generally have some freedom to negotiate and define the way they do their jobs, but they are simultaneously subject to constant pressure to conform to the expectations and demands of those with whom they must interact. A recurrent struggle for individual autonomy underlies and articulates much workplace behavior.

It is also necessary to recognize that work roles touch social relationships beyond the workplace. Dual-career families must work out accommodations that allow both partners to pursue their occupations. Frustrations caused by customers or supervisors can strain family relationships and, if they persist over time, can permanently injure family life (see, for example, Meer, 1985).

Intergroup dynamics.   The configuration of technical tasks that characterize work roles at any point in time can be understood, at least in part, by conceptualizing occupations as self-conscious social groups evolving, changing, cooperating, and competing with other occupations for the right to do certain things. The innocuous phrase "aids physician" in the description of the role of the nurse conceals a long, sometimes acrimonious disagreement between nurses and physicians over the appropriate roles of the various participants in the health-care system. Tradition, custom, and expertise all enter into the formation of occupational roles, but the formation of such roles is also influenced by the relative power of participants to expand and protect their domains.

Work groups and subcultures. Workers usually perform as members of groups, either formal or informal. Informal work groups usually emerge when people must work together for any length of time. Shared experiences, working conditions, or problems, or interdependence of tasks can create a bond among workers, fostering the development of shared perceptions of their work and its meanings, and common understandings of appropriate behavior. The term *subculture* can be applied to these distinctive behavioral systems. Subcultural norms defining appropriate levels of effort, output, and quality have been found among work groups in virtually every type of job. They can be viewed as collective responses to the demands of the work situation, usually functioning as a buffer against the environment.

The concept of subculture may, in many instances, be applied to entire occupations. Police officers, musicians, coal miners, accountants, scientists, physicians, and others identify themselves as members of distinctive and select groups, distinguished by a unique language, a configuration of values and beliefs, special symbols, and codes of conduct. Those who aspire to admission to such occupations undergo a process of socialization that requires them to learn to conform to the group's expectations and accept its belief systems.

The organizational context. Work in industrial societies is likely to be performed within an organization. Employers are in a position to define the technical aspects of work roles, sometimes in extraordinary detail. For example, in 1984, a left-handed grocery clerk was forced to quit after being ordered to operate the cash register with her right hand (Haitch, 1985). Rules of employee conduct recently promulgated by a large corporation (Exhibit 1:1) outline the range of required and proscribed activities that are typical of American industry.

Careers, in the sense of advances in income, prestige, and responsibility, are measured largely in terms of organizational designations. The career opportunities available to workers are a structural attribute and may be limited or open. Consequently, whole categories of the work force may be denied the opportunity to advance by the structure of the organization rather than by lack of aspiration. This has long been true of assembly line

EXHIBIT 1:1   Organizational Code of Conduct, United States, 1985

Rules Governing Employee Conduct

Employees are expected to treat each other with respect, to respect the property of others, and to carry on their assignments with care and diligence. The following acts constitute unsatisfactory work performance which will subject an employee to disciplinary action which may include discharge. In all cases where performance is unacceptable, the facts and merits of the case will be considered before disciplinary action is taken.

1. Unsatisfactory job performance, including a serious act of negligence in the performance of the job, a series of less serious acts or omissions, serious violation of safety rules, and excessive absences or tardiness.
2. Dishonest acts and falsification of records, including the giving of false information when hired.
3. Engaging in a fight on site property, or in activity that could provoke fighting.
4. Acts of "horseplay" on site property.
5. Use or possession of weapons, ammunitions, explosives, intoxicants, illicit drugs or narcotics on site property.
6. Smoking in unauthorized areas.
7. Reporting for work under the influence of drugs or intoxicants.
8. Insubordination or deliberate refusal to comply with reasonable requests or instructions.
9. Absence from work without notice or permission from supervision unless the cause of absence prevents giving notice.
10. Obscene or other conduct which violates common decency or morality.
11. Using or divulging, without permission, any confidential information acquired through employment with the site.
12. Theft or unauthorized removal of site property or property belonging to site employees, contractors, or vendors.
13. Sleeping during work periods.
14. Physical, mental, or sexual harassment of fellow employees including threat to do bodily harm.
15. Intentional damage to site, employee, contractor, or vendor property.

It is not intended that the foregoing covers all acts or series of acts which could result in discipline including discharge. The list, however, indicates misconduct which is contrary to the best interests of all and which will not be tolerated.

---

workers, for example, (Chinoy, 1955) and clerical workers (Kanter, 1977). Within some limits, organizations also control the criteria and standards for promotion (and demotion), timetables and routes of advancement, and the rewards that accompany advancement. Individuals must decipher the intricacies of organizational career paths, be willing to accommodate organizational structures and demands, establish working relationships with superiors and subordinates, and adjust to success or confront failure.

Sociocultural systems. The meanings attached to work and the rewards derived from it are formed by the sociocultural context of particular societies at specific points in time. Our society's limitation of the application of the very term *work* to tasks performed in exchange for monetary remuneration—thus excluding housework and unpaid volunteer activities—can be traced to societal developments accompanying industrialization. People's feelings about their own work and that of others reflects the value systems—religious, social, and economic—and prestige rankings of society.

In the United States and elsewhere, garbage collection is commonly considered "dirty work," depreciated by society and thus personally degrading to those who earn their living by collecting refuse. In other societies, it may be butchers or leather workers who suffer this fate. It is often possible to rehearse the history of discrimination against racial, religious, or ethnic minorities by tracing their allocation into the least desirable forms of labor. "Dirty work" in the factories of Australia, for example, has been performed by successive waves of Italians, Greeks, Yugoslavs, Turks, Lebanese, Chileans, and now Vietnamese (Game and Pringle, 1983: 38).

JOBS, OCCUPATIONS, AND WORKING: TOWARD CONCEPTUAL CLARITY

There is no agreement within sociology about the definitions of basic concepts used in this book. Therefore, it is appropriate to identify the way in which key terms are used. The most basic term is *work*, activity performed to produce goods or services of value to others (Hall, 1986: 13). Work occurs within society, its meaning and value determined by social values and beliefs. Unpaid work, which has no monetary measure, is defined in social relationships with others.

A *job* (or, *work role*) is a specific set of technical and social activities located within a specific context. An example of a job would be sales clerk at Saks Fifth Avenue. Each job is somewhat unique because workers have the ability to define and redefine jobs in interpersonal relationships with superiors, coworkers, and subordinates. The term *occupational role* focuses on the common features of all jobs with the same general title, such as sales clerk, nurse, plumber, medical technician. There is often a good deal of variation in occupational roles in different settings—sales clerk is a very different job at Saks than it is at Sears or K-Mart stores—but the similarities are clear. All sales clerks, for example, are expected to show deference to customers. One way to describe an occupation is simply to refer to the collection of people who engage in a particular set of technical and social activities; in that sense occupation is an aggregation of all specific jobs. Although there is merit to that approach, *occupations* are more correctly understood as collective enterprises with members usually sharing values and perspectives, and feeling a sense of shared identity. Occupations, sometimes represented by formal bodies (unions and professional associations), act collectively to establish the form and content of occupational roles, and in turn, jobs. Control over the technical dimensions of work emerge within this context as occupations compete for the right to perform desirable and remunerative tasks.

Working, for individuals, is a complex and demanding activity. It starts with the dynamics of selecting occupations, getting jobs, and learning how to perform them. Work roles are not limited to technical operations, but also demand learning how to think and act and look like a member of the occupation (in ways that may have no apparent relationship to the work being performed) and require the formation of complex and subtle social relationships with superiors, subordinates and peers. As time passes, individuals must accommodate to successes and promotions, failures and the lack of progress, each calling for personal adaptations and a restructuring of social relations.

TYPES OF WORK: BASIC PATTERNS OF SOCIAL ORGANIZATION

The analysis of work roles is typically organized around broad categories of occupations. Unfortunately, there are no self-evident categories. Sociologists and others who study work have utilized a number of alternative classification systems, depending upon their research objectives and theoretical orientations.

Labor-Force Data

Most labor-force analysis in the United States ultimately depends upon categories created by the Bureaus of Labor Statistics and the Census, largely because they have been the only constant sources of reliable data over time. The single most serious shortcoming is that this data is limited to "gainfully employed" persons, thus excluding many important forms of unpaid work.

Occupational information has been included as part of the decennial census in America since 1850. Originally, there were only five categories: agriculture, proprietors, clerical employees, skilled workers, and laborers. Beginning in 1930 and continuing through the 1970s, a systematic series of revisions were introduced, culminating in the classification of all "gainfully employed" persons into eleven broad categories. Pre-1930 data was, when possible, reclassified using the new system, and social scientists doing occupational analysis generally conceptualized and recorded their data using the same system. These broad groupings, such as "professional," "sales," and "clerical," generally reflected common understandings of the nature of work in modern industrial societies, although there were some anoma-

EXHIBIT 1:2 Occupational Classifications, United States, 1982

OCCUPATIONAL GROUPS, 1970 SYSTEM	% OF WORKERS	OCCUPATIONAL GROUPS, 1980 SYSTEM	% OF WORKERS
Managers, officials, and proprietors	11.7	Executive, administrative, managerial	10.7
Professional, technical	17.4	Professional specialty	13.0
—		Technicians, and related support	3.1
Salesworkers	6.8	Sales	11.7
Clerical workers	18.6	Administrative support	16.5
Private household	1.1	Private household	1.1
—		Protective service	1.6
Service workers	12.7	Service occupations	10.9
Farm workers	2.7	Farming, forestry, fishing	3.6
Craft workers, and foremen	12.1	Precision production, craft, repair	11.6
Operatives	9.1	Machine operators, assemblers, inspectors	7.5
Transport equipment operatives	3.4	Transportation, material moving	4.2
Non-farm laborers	4.4	Handlers, cleaners, helpers, laborers	4.5

Source: Gloria P. Green et al., "Revisions in 'Current Population Survey' Beginning in January 1983," *Employment and Earnings* 30 (Feb. 1983), 10.

lies. "Laborer," for example, placed simple physical laboring jobs in the same category as lumbering and fishing, which require high levels of skill and elaborate systems of teamwork.

A modified method of coding was developed for the 1980 census (Green, et al., 1983). New categories were created and specific occupations were shifted among existing categories. One goal was to create categories that more accurately reflected skill levels and working conditions. Unfortunately, in the process of modernizing the system, much of the current data has been rendered incompatible with earlier data, thus making historical comparison much more difficult. Even these new categories have some limitations, because they continue to combine dissimilar jobs. Both systems must be employed at various points, but it should be remembered that the two are not strictly comparable. The distribution of the labor force in 1982, calculated using both methods, is shown in Exhibit 1:2. It provides a broad overview of the basic distribution of paid work in America. The transition does not produce large shifts when broad categories are compared.

Trends in the Shape of the Work Force

Occupational trends. Meaningful historical trends in the composition of the paid labor force are evident from even a cursory examination of the

EXHIBIT 1:3   The Shifting Shape of the Work Force*

Occupation	PERCENTAGE OF PAID WORKERS				
	1900	1920	1940	1960	1980
Professional	4.3%	5.4%	7.5%	11.4%	16.0%
Managerial	5.8	6.6	7.3	10.7	11.2
Clerical	3.0	8.0	9.6	14.8	18.6
Sales	4.5	4.9	6.7	6.4	6.3
Service	3.6	4.5	7.1	8.9	12.6
Private household	5.4	3.3	4.7	2.7	1.2
Crafts	10.5	13.0	12.0	13.0	12.9
Operatives	12.8	15.6	18.4	18.2	14.2
Laborers	12.5	11.6	9.4	5.4	4.6
Farmworkers	37.5	27.0	17.4	7.9	2.8
Labor force (millions)	29.0	42.2	51.7	65.7	99.3
Rates of participation					
Females	20.6%	23.7%	25.8%	34.5%	51.5%
Males	n/a	n/a	n/a	83.3	77.4

Sources: U.S. Bureau of the Census, Commerce, *Historical Statistics of the United States, 1975* (Washington, DC: Government Printing Office, 1975); U.S. Department of Labor, *Handbook of Labor Statistics* (Washington, DC: Government Printing Office, 1985); and U.S. Department of Labor, *Employment and Earnings,* vol. 47 (Jan. 1981).
Note: Labor force data is not strictly comparable over time due to changes in methods of enumeration.

data in Exhibit 1:3, which cover this century. Possibly the single most obvious pattern is the transition from a basically rural society, with one-half the population engaged in agriculture, to an urban industrial system. In the process, America has become an organizational society, which is reflected in rapid expansion of both the managerial and clerical sectors. The explosion of new knowledge has created a whole host of new and esoteric "professional specialties," organized around narrow areas of expertise, supplementing law. medicine, and the clergy, which formed the bulk of this elite group in the nineteenth century.

Service work, including food preparation, personal services such as barbering, and maintenance work, has become an increasingly significant sector of the economy and, by all estimates, promises to offer the greatest number of new jobs in the future. Domestic work, once an occupation engaged in by many, has continued to shrink.

Work in the industrial sector has fluctuated a great deal over the last century. In the high-skill "craft" occupations (such as the construction trades, printing, and machine work), a period of expansion until about World War II was followed by a more recent contraction in the size of this group. A more important development, which is masked by these broad categories, is the dramatic changes in the composition of craft work; entirely new occupations (such as that of auto mechanic) have been created, and older occupations (like tailoring) have been almost entirely eliminated by mechanization. The changing shape of the economy is also evident in the general decline in the demand for less skilled forms of blue-collar work. Unskilled labor, which was an integral part of the early industrialization process, currently provides jobs for less than 5 percent of the labor force.

Men and women in the labor force. Most men are in the paid labor force, but their relative rates of participation have been declining since about 1960. In that year, over 83 percent of adult males were working for pay, but that percentage has slipped to a current figure of about 76 percent (U.S. Bureau of Labor Statistics, 1985:422). In contrast, the participation rate for white females has generally been increasing, and has grown markedly since the 1960s; labor-force participation rates for black women have generally been 40 percent to 50 percent for this entire century (Dill, 1983). The most rapid influx of women into the labor force has apparently occurred in the last two decades: The rates have risen from about 25 percent in 1940 to 34 percent in 1960, and to a current rate over 52 percent. The same pattern has been reproduced in several other industrial nations, including Sweden, Canada, Australia, and Great Britain.

Several factors have contributed to the changing patterns of labor-force participation. Improving public and private social welfare programs, in the form of disability benefits, Social Security, and pensions, have made it financially feasible for men to withdraw from paid employment. Also a factor is the popularity of early-retirement programs. At the same time, for both economic and social reasons, women have been moving into paid employment. Financial considerations have always been a motivation, especially in households headed by women and in families with husbands in lower-paying, unstable blue-collar occupations. Rising divorce rates since World War II have swelled the number of female-headed households; they now constitute 16 percent of all households (U.S. Bureau of Labor Statistics, 1984a: 3). Complex social changes and legal breakthroughs have increased the likelihood that more women will pursue paid work for the same configuration of reasons that motivate men.

THE SOCIAL ORGANIZATION OF WORK ROLES

The Bureau of Labor Statistics' categories are useful, but they tend to focus exclusively upon the technical dimensions of work. The challenge facing the sociologist attempting to analyze the social organization of work roles is to identify occupations that share salient social, structural, and technical characteristics, yet remain consistent with the basic government coding system. The following typology is an attempt to capture the basic forms of work in modern industrial society. These forms are identified in Exhibits 1:4 through 1:8, along with representative occupations and some preliminary data on the gender and racial composition of the work force.[1]

Self-regulating Professions

Professions are grounded in a body of expert knowledge acquired through a prolonged period of specialized training. They may be arrayed along a continuum of self-regulation. *Self-regulation* measures the extent to which occupations have translated expertise into control over the conditions of work (Larson, 1977). Architecture, dentistry, law, and medicine are among the occupations that enjoy the highest levels of what may be called *autonomy* and *monopoly* (Freidson, 1976). At the group level, *autonomy* means that the professions, acting through associations, have been able to win control over the content of training, the right to practice, licensing procedures, and internal discipline of incompetent members. *Monopoly* refers to the exclusive right to do certain types of work, such as the legal right of physicians to prescribe controlled drugs, or the right of lawyers to represent others in court for pay. Autonomy and monopoly are never without some limits, and the professions may be ranked along a continuum of freedom from external control.

About 13 million workers (13 percent of the paid work force) are classified as belonging to a "professional specialty." Approximately 75 percent of them are employed in organizations (Becker, 1984); they include engineers, scientists, nurses, and even some lawyers and physicians. This creates the potential for an interesting structural anomaly. As professionals, they have developed expectations of self-control and self-regulation, but they are subject to the same supervisory authority and general set of rules as other white-collar employees.

Approximately one-half of all professional workers are women, but they have long been concentrated in elementary school teaching, nursing, and library work, and have been underrepresented in medicine, engineering, and science. Such patterns of occupational segregation, which are shifting (in some cases slowly, and in others, such as law, quite rapidly) reflect the interaction of gender socialization, choice, and allocative processes.

The Administrative Hierarchy

Between 10 and 15 percent of the labor force can be defined as white-collar workers concerned with operations and administration—managing,

---

[1]Those familiar with Bureau of Labor Statistics' categories will find that this typology does not exactly coincide with that system. The deatils involved in creating the present categories are reported in footnotes to the text and exhibits.

EXHIBIT 1:4   The Self-Regulating Professions, United States (1985)

Occupation	Total Employed	PERCENT OF TOTAL		
		Women	Black	Hispanic
Professional Specialty	**13,680,000**	**49.1**	**6.3**	**3.0**
Architects	130,000	11.3	3.1	4.6
Engineers	1,683,000	6.7	2.6	2.6
Physicians	492,000	17.2	3.7	3.9
Registered nurses	1,447,000	95.1	6.8	2.1
Teachers	3,523,000	73.0	9.2	3.1
K and Pre-K	329,000	98.8	11.9	5.4
Elementary	1,360,000	84.0	11.1	2.7
Secondary	1,175,000	54.0	7.6	3.2
Social workers	438,000	66.7	17.6	5.6
Lawyers	642,000	18.1	3.0	2.3
Designers	484,000	51.1	3.0	3.6

Source: "Employed Civilians by Detailed Occupation, Sex, Race, and Hispanic Origin," *Employment and Earnings*, 52 (Jan. 1986), table 22, 175–79.

directing, and supervising the work of others in organizations. Their tasks range from the highest level of executive responsibility to the supervision of a few production or clerical workers. Responsibilities may extend to hiring, training, monitoring, motivating, and evaluating personnel, as well as to defining the very tasks involved in subordinates' jobs. Such tasks coexist and interact with whatever substantive responsibilities the particular job entails. School superintendents, for example, exercise some degree of authority over teacher and staff activity, as they concurrently perform technical tasks such as budgeting, public relations, and presiding over curricula matters. Despite the diversity and the vast differences in power encountered when jobs ranging from the top to the bottom of the administrative hierarchy are combined, they are grouped together for the compelling reason that all roles wield some authority over others by virtue of their position within the organizational hierarchy.

Administrative authority may be exercised within industrial, commercial, governmental, military, educational, or religious organizations, but certain critical issues transcend the substantive context. In an abstract sense, authority derives from organizational position; in other words, it resides in the role or office, not in the person. It is often clearly compartmentalized in neat organizational charts. In practice, however, authority must constantly be negotiated and legitimized with subordinates, peers, and superiors, for they are seldom powerless, even when their only power rests in their ability to resist or to fail to cooperate, if they are willing to risk the consequences. This is a crucial, but often overlooked, consideration. Subordinates also derive power from the fact that superiors are de-

EXHIBIT 1:5 The Administrative Hierarchy, United States (1985)

Occupation	Total Employed	PERCENT OF TOTAL		
		Women	Black	Hispanic
Executives	Data not available			
Managers*	12,221,000	35.6	5.3	3.5
Marketing, advertising	419,000	23.8	3.9	2.5
Medicine, health	106,000	59.2	8.1	4.6
Purchasing managers	99,000	24.4	4.0	2.7
Supervisors†	6,792,000			
Sales supervisors	3,316,000	31.2	3.8	4.0
Clerical supervisors	712,000	53.4	12.3	4.5
Protective services	134,000	5.8	9.5	4.0
Food service	284,000	67.0	11.0	7.6
Construction trades	602,000	1.3	3.4	4.9

*Managers: executive, administrative, and managerial categories.
†Supervisors: supervisors aggregated from all categories.
Source: "Employed Civilians by Detailed Occupation, Sec, Race, and Hispanic Origin," *Employment and Earnings*, 52 (Jan. 1986), table 22, 175–79.

pendent upon them to accomplish their own tasks and are evaluated on the basis of subordinate performance. An example of this is enacted every day in the world of professional sports: When teams lose because of poor player performance, it is usually the coach or manager who is fired.

Administrative positions must be differentiated along hierarchical lines.[2] *Executives* occupy the top levels of organizations—presidents and vice-presidents, chief executive officers, chairpersons of boards of directors. This is a difficult category to identify with precision, because "executive" is included within the larger "executive, administrative, and managerial" category in official statistics. They are often called "general managers" to indicate that, by virtue of these positions, their authority is generalized over the entire organization, rather than limited to a specific area.

Manager is the general label applied to a wide variety of positions located below the vice-presidential level. These workers have such titles as personnel director, production manager, plant superintendent, dean, and countless others that are organization-specific. It is characteristic of American organizations for such personnel to have specialized training and functions and, as a consequence, the scope of their authority is more limited.

[2]There is no agreed-upon definition of *executive* in the literature. One possibility is to follow the work of Eric Olin Wright (1982) who, using a neo-Marxian model, estimates that approximately 2 percent of the work force (which would translate into about 2 million executives) qualify as "employers," in that they own or control productive capacity, employ workers, and have authority over them.

About 60 percent of the persons classified as "executive, administrative, and managerial" are men. Within more specific substantive areas, men are more likely to hold managerial positions in finance, public relations, and construction, while women are more likely to manage in health care or personnel.

First-line supervisors are the lowest level of administrative personnel. Their formal authority is limited to overseeing the performance of a relatively small number of workers. The scope of their authority is circumscribed, seldom extending to decisions about the job structures or expected rates of production. Such decisions are generally made at higher levels. Rather, their responsibilities are primarily interpersonal, centering on the allocation of specific persons to specific jobs, monitoring the quality of the product or service, and ensuring that workers meet production quotas. It frequently has been noted that supervisors are in a position of structured conflict, caught between the production expectations of higher-level management and workers' expectations of autonomy and tendency to resist demands for levels of output that exceed their own individual and group norms.

Supervisors are not ordinarily aggregated in government data, but rather are included in the same category as the type of worker they supervise. Combining these numbers yields approximately 6 million first-line supervisors of all kinds. Women occupy over one-half of the general office supervisory positions, and nearly two-thirds of the food-preparation positions, both of which tend to involve the supervision of other women. Women are rare in the typically male construction and protective-service (police, fire fighter, and guard) occupations.

Administrative Support Work

Within organizations there a large number of workers who are defined as providing "administrative support." The largest single group are the 15 million, overwhelmingly female, *clerical workers*. The proliferation of communications in the twentieth century has created the demand for vast numbers of people to record, process, store, file, or facilitate this vast flow of information. Clerical workers include stenographers, typists, file clerks, office-machine operators, timekeepers, key punchers, and bookkeepers. Most of these occupations have been filled by women since the early part of this century. Some occupations, such as secretary or keypuncher, require a high level of expertise or skill, while others are the white-collar equivalent of semiskilled blue-collar work, in the sense that the technical tasks required to run an addressing machine are no more or less complex than those involved in running a shoe-sewing machine. However, working conditions are better and generally safer. The definition of clerical work as administrative support is of great significance, both organizationally and

EXHIBIT 1:6   Administrative Support Workers, United States (1985)

Occupation	Total Employed	PERCENT OF TOTAL		
		Women	Black	Hispanic
Clerical Workers*	16,597,000			
Computer operators	774,000	66.5	13.5	5.9
Secretaries	4,059,000	98.4	6.5	4.3
Receptionists	679,000	97.6	6.7	6.2
Mail carriers	255,000	17.2	11.7	4.7
Shipping clerks	491,000	25.5	13.1	10.6
Bank tellers	484,000	93.0	6.0	6.6
The Technostructure†	3,255,000	47.2	8.9	4.0
Dental hygenists	56,000	99.5	2.0	2.0
Drafters	297,000	17.4	3.9	5.5
Airline pilots, navigators	77,000	2.6	1.0	.1
Computer programers	534,000	34.3	6.4	2.5
Legal assistants	148,000	75.6	7.3	4.6

*Clerical: Administrative support, minus supervisors.
†Technostructure: Technicians and related support.
Source: "Employed Civilians by Detailed Occupation, Sex, Race, and Hispanic Origin," *Employment and Earnings,* 52 (Jan. 1986), table 22, 175–79.

socially. *Support* implies and reinforces the notion of inferiority and subordination. It has drawn a significant barrier to social interaction between administrative and support personnel, and it has blocked mobility from clerical work into administrative work.

There is also, within the support component, a group of jobs that can be identified as the *technostructure*. These occupations require extensive educational training. Some 3 million workers are identified by the Bureau of Labor Statistics as "technicians"—computer programmers, legal assistants, dental technicians, drafters, and electronic technicians. The very fact that the Bureau of Labor Statistics has created this category reflects the demand for more skilled work—at the expense of blue-collar jobs. The technical disciplines, like the professions, are organized around specialized areas of expertise; in recent years, many have sought to professionalize, creating jurisdictional disputes with established groups.

The Blue-Collar Hierarchy

Blue-collar occupations involve technical operations performed on, or with, tangible physical products and machines, rather than people or information. The distinction between blue-collar and white-collar work illustrates the symbolic meanings that can become attached to technical tasks.

CASE STUDY: WHITE COLLAR VERSUS BLUE COLLAR

Probably the oldest and most fundamental distinction between blue-collar and white-collar work is based on the type of product created or service offered. The origins of a dichotomy between blue-collar and white-collar work can no doubt be traced to the infancy of industrialization, when employers and office help dressed more sedately and formally than did the men and women who worked the factories, mills, and mines. Clothing symbolized differences in wages, working conditions, and tasks between those who directed operations and those actually engaged in the production. There was a certain logic to the distinction; it reflected the relatively simple division of labor in a fledgling industrial economy.

Over the years, the term *blue collar* has generally been applied to work roles involved in manufacturing—the creation of products. It is sometimes presumed to require only manual or physical labor, usually summarized as "working with their hands." Electricians, carpenters, truck drivers, machine operators, and laborers are joined in this designation. In contrast, *white collar* has been used to refer to the work of managers, teachers, salespeople, and office workers. Phrases such as "intellectual" and "mental" tasks, "working with people," or ideas or information (rather than things) are commonly encountered.

Some have claimed that the white-collar/blue-collar distinction is more than simply a classification system—that it reveals deep-seated, fundamental ideas about the nature of work. Adriano Tilgher (1930) argues that Western societies inherited from the ancient Greeks a view that physical, manual work was a curse imposed by capricious gods. Hence, manual labor was to be avoided whenever possible, and preferably relegated to slaves. Work using the mind and the intellect became a cultural ideal, a claim to respectability, a status distinction. Some residual of disdain for manual work persists into modern societies, with white-collar work tending to enjoy more social prestige than blue-collar work. Some white-collar workers feel that it is somehow demeaning to work with one's hands (Sennett and Cobb, 1972). Skilled manual workers certainly do not share such judgments, typically exhibiting fierce pride in their craft and likely to depreciate white-collar workers who "shuffle papers" or "work with their mouths" (LeMasters, 1975). The terms may have originated merely as a convenient way of organizing labor-force data, but they have clearly taken on symbolic meanings attached to different forms of work.

Internal divisions within blue-collar work are based on skill and autonomy. *Craft work* (now called "precision production, craft, and repair") requires a high degree of expertise and manual dexterity. Some of these occupations are modern descendants of ancient forms of work—tailors, stone masons, and printers—while others are products of the industrial revolution—machinists, electricians, and auto mechanics. It is their skill that both allows these workers to exercise control over the work process

EXHIBIT 1:7   Blue Collar Work, United States (1985)

Occupation	Total Employed	PERCENT OF TOTAL		
		Women	Black	Hispanic
Craft* work	11,102,000			
Mechanics, repairers	4,209,000	3.1	6.9	6.8
Construction trades	4,143,000	2.1	7.2	7.2
Carpenters	1,259,000	1.2	4.8	6.4
Brick, stone masons	173,000	.5	17.1	9.3
Concrete finishers	85,000	.2	26.5	21.4
Metalworkers	914,000	6.3	5.5	7.8
Butchers	286,000	19.3	13.1	13.2
Operatives†	15,449,000			
Machine operators	5,191,000	41.9	15.0	12.5
Lath operators	68,000	9.6	5.9	8.2
Sewing machines	760,000	90.8	14.9	19.9
Assemblers	1,047,000	41.8	16.4	11.4
Heavy truck drivers	1,838,000	2.1	12.9	5.9
Unskilled work‡	9,066,000			
Construction laborers	686,000	3.1	16.7	13.0
Stock handlers	818,000	22.1	11.9	6.9
Hand packagers	304,000	65.2	15.3	10.6
Building services	2,049,000	29.4	24.0	10.9
Farm workers	1,786,000	18.3	11.9	15.6

*Craft: precision production, minus supervisors.
†Operatives: machine operators, minus light motor vehicle operators.
‡Unskilled: handlers, equipment cleaners, helpers, plus farm workers, and building cleaning workers.
Source: "Employed Civilians by Detailed Occupation, Sex, Race, and Hispanic Origin," *Employment and Earnings,* 52 (Jan. 1986), table 22, 175–79.

and forms the basis of the emergence of powerful subcultures. The history of the crafts can be written as a struggle to guard skills and attendant autonomy from encroachments of industrialization and attempts to rationalize the organization of factories. The underrepresentation of women and minorities in many crafts is a contemporary legacy of this historic struggle.

Unskilled work ("helpers, equipment cleaners, and laborers") is assumed, by definition, to utilize virtually no abilities or skills beyond those found in the general population. Early industrialization generated the demand for heavy physical labor in factories, railroads, and coal mines. Many were subsequently eliminated by mechanization and automation, but there remain hundreds of thousands of jobs that involve moving stock, driving, packing, general cleaning up, harvesting, and clearing fields.

Between the skill extremes are occupations that require some measure of training and skill, referred to as "machine operators, assemblers, and inspectors." The term *operative* has long been used and probably remains the most descriptive label. Most operatives work on factory machines of one kind or another—metalworking lathes, sewing machines, stamping presses, woodworking machines, and furnaces. Operators must have some knowledge of the materials they process and must be able to maintain and adjust their machines. Many operate some kind of industrial vehicle—large-rig trucks, tractors, bulldozers, graders, and forklifts. Another group are the *assemblers*, who put together the complex manufactured products (such as electronic devices) that demand the use of a variety of skills and tools. The remainder are inspectors, checking on the work of others.

Direct-Service Work

A direct-service category can be created by combining the "sales worker," "private household," and "service" categories, plus some workers in the "protective" class. The rationale for this combination is that all are organized around providing services in a direct, face-to-face interaction between worker and customer. Skill variations are found within service work, and the occupations may be conveniently divided into small self-employed entrepreneurs (frequently found in the personal-grooming occupations) and employees (most restaurant servers, bartenders, and so on). However, skill considerations may contribute less to an understanding of the nature of the work than the interaction between customer and worker. Customers, who are to be served, control important rewards, and are thus in a position to influence workers' behavior. Much effort is therefore devoted to negotiating this relationship. Analysis of these negotiations reveals consistent, patterned attempts by workers to neutralize the power of the consumer and to direct the relationship to their advantage.

Salespersons act as intermediaries between seller or producer, and consumer. Stockbrokers, realtors, insurance agents, and newspaper vendors are in this category, along with millions of retail salespersons. Most are employees or agents for the seller or producer and are therefore strongly encouraged to maximize sales; for both the employer and the salesworker, "sales" is the criterion by which job success is measured. As a consequence, the salesworker-customer relationship often takes the form of an attempt to control and direct the behavior and actions of potential consumers. In some instances, the relationship takes the form of formalized strategies of manipulation.

Cab drivers, waiters, waitresses, barbers, hairdressers, some janitors, and airline attendants form a *personal-service* component. Service is directed to an individual client, either as a representative of a company or on an individual fee-for-service basis.

Also in this category are *domestic workers*, or "private household workers." It is tempting to think that the luxury of employing full-time "ser-

EXHIBIT 1:8   Direct Service Work, United States (1985)

		PERCENT OF TOTAL		
Occupation	Total Employed	Women	Black	Hispanic
Sales Workers*	9,357,000			
Retail sales	5,682,000	68.5	8.2	5.6
Wearing apparel	465,000	82.7	7.8	5.5
Motor vehicles	275,000	7.7	4.2	4.8
Home furnishings	161,000	51.0	4.2	4.2
Cashiers	2,174,000	83.1	12.1	6.4
Sales representatives	2,099,000	41.0	3.4	2.7
Real estate	659,000	51.6	2.3	2.7
Financial	266,000	24.6	2.2	1.2
Personal Service†	10,852,000			
Restaurant work	5,094,000	62.5	12.0	8.3
Personal grooming	2,049,000	80.9	11.0	6.8
Barbers	91,000	15.5	12.9	7.2
Hairdressers	707,000	89.9	8.2	7.0
Flight attendants	65,000	78.8	13.2	4.8
Taxi-cab drivers	183,000	10.9	23.8	11.0
Domestic Work**	1,532,000			
Child care	399,000	96.9	8.9	4.3
Maids, housemen	583,000	83.5	30.8	12.7
Cleaners, servants	550,000	95.8	42.3	13.3
Protective Work‡	1,356,000			
Law enforcement	412,000	5.7	9.5	4.4
Corrections	711,000	20.6	17.0	5.6

Sales: sales, minus supervisors.
†*Personal Service:* service occupations, minus supervisors, cleaning and health services; plus taxi and bus drivers.
***Domestics:* Private household workers, plus maids and housemen.
‡*Protective:* Protective, minus supervisors.
Source: "Employed Civilians by Detailed Occupation, Sex, Race, and Hispanic Origin," *Employment and Earnings,* 52 (Jan. 1986), table 22, 175–79.

vants" is a thing of the past, or is limited to a handful of relatively wealthy families. The evolution of the job of "servant" has its own interesting history, but the apparent disappearance of this role should not obscure the fact that many middle-class families continue to employ people to clean, prepare meals, and care for their children in their homes on a regular basis. Over a million workers—and they are overwhelmingly female, and often black—do some form of private household work. Here too, the social relationship between domestic worker and consumer is a key to understanding the work.

In retail sales and service and in domestic occupations, the dominant feature is the process of interaction between worker and customer. Some protective occupations (especially law-enforcement officers and guards in correctional facilities) can also be analyzed using the same perspective. Obviously, their service is not directed toward "customers," in the usual sense of the word, but it is clearly concerned with directing and controlling face-to-face encounters with citizens as well as with those accused of criminal behavior.

Family Farm Work

A small but significant number of people own and operate small family farms. Their number has declined dramatically and continuously as industrialization has transformed our society into a primarily urban population. Nearly 75 percent of all Americans lived on farms in 1820, compared to only 3 percent today. (Actually, only about 700,000 qualify as full-time farms since many people depend upon other occupations to support themselves [Dentzer, 1985].) Officially included in this number are about 250,000 unpaid family workers, mostly young men under the age of 25 and adult women (Daly, 1982). The figure may well be much higher because children under the age of 16 are not included, and because the worker must report 15 hours of work per week directly related to the farm, and women may underreport activities that contribute to the farm but are not directly related to it.

Work on family farms reveals an intricate and complex social organization (Boulding, 1980). The farm itself is an economic enterprise, and the bulk of activity is directed toward maintaining it. At the same time, individual family members may engage in self-contained economic activity. Children may have their own animals, for example, that they breed, care for, and sell for their gain. Women may maintain gardens for the express purpose of selling the produce. In addition, a large number of farm family members engage in nonagricultural employment to supplement family incomes. Finally, unpaid housework is performed by women and children. Family members may thus occupy as many as four work roles: farm oriented, individual, paid nonfarm, and unpaid housework.

Operation of the family farm reveals it as *multiperson career*, a job requiring the collaborative efforts of at least two persons. (Only 8 percent of all family farms are headed by a single adult male or female.) The vast array of tasks that must be carried out, especially during peak periods of planting, harvesting, or birthing, are beyond the capabilities of a single worker. Consequently, wives, children, and extended family members form a work unit directed toward the maintenance of the farm.

A farm wife devotes an estimated average of six hours a day to the farm, in addition to the eight hours devoted to housework (Boulding, 1980). The most common responsibilities are driving farm machinery, bookkeeping, feeding animals, and acting as a "gofer." ("Gofer" refers to running errands, such as "going for" replacement parts when machinery malfunctions.) Tasks tend to be segregated along gender lines, but the active role taken by farm wives in the operation of the farm is a major source of satisfaction for them. The most frequently mentioned feature of an agricultural life is the "togetherness" of a husband-wife partnership. Love of nature, independence, and a sense of creating something for the future are ranked next. Participation in the operation of the farm also translates into participation in the decision-making process. Unilateral decisions made by husbands are apparently rare; the more typical pattern finds men, women, and other family members welded into an independent unit in which responsibilities, risks, and rewards are shared (Rosenfeld, 1986).

Unpaid Work

Not all work is done in exchange for salary or wages. Countless people work on an unpaid basis. The government lists 350,000 unpaid workers in addition to those already noted as working on family farms (Daly, 1982). The vast majority (85 percent) are women helping families by record keeping, doing clerical work, and aiding in the operation of stores and restaurants. The two largest categories of unpaid work deserve special mention.

The occupation of *homemaker*, loosely described as operating a home and caring for dependent children, is probably the most complex of occupations in terms of technical tasks. It is organized around a variety of technical tasks, ranging from skilled professional (child care) to unskilled (dishwashing). Moreover, the demands of the role change, often quite dramatically, over the life cycle. There are no "official" statistics, but it is usually estimated that there are 30 million *full-time* homemakers, making it the largest single category of work. In the United States, homemaker is often a second occupation for a woman (usually) or man who is also part of the paid labor force.

The other major form of unpaid work is *volunteer work*. Millions of persons do significant amounts of free work. Schools, charities, churches, political organizations, hospitals, and social welfare agencies depend upon such work and probably could not function without the assistance of volunteers (Daniels, 1985). Again there is little verifiable data, but a question about volunteer work, posed by a 1981 Gallup Poll, revealed that 47 percent of all men and 56 percent of all women had done some work "to help others for no monetary pay" (Gallup Organization, 1981). This estimate does not, of course, distinguish between people who donate a few hours to a charity and those who are extensively involved in community activities, but it does hint at the scope of voluntary activity.

Deviant Work

Although they are not always evident in official statistics, there are a number of "deviant" occupations that must be included in any analysis of work in an industrial society. One obvious reason is that some unknown number of people earn their livelihood in this way. Moreover, the work exhibits the same social, technical, career attributes that characterize more conventional work. Criminal activities, such as prostitution in most American jurisdictions, fencing stolen goods, burglary, and counterfeiting, are in this category. Also included are occupations that operate on the margins of society; although these occupations are technically legal, they violate the social codes and values of some relevant segment of society. Stripping, gambling, carnival work, and begging all deviate from community standards to some extent. The stigma that results influences both the organization of the work and relations with the public.

CONCLUSION

Work in modern industrial society may be divided into a number of major categories, each characterized by a different pattern of social organization. This classification system does not accommodate every occupation, but it does provide an introduction to a sociological approach to working.

Working involves a set of technical operations (either physical or intellectual, or some combination of the two). Work roles are a process shaped by technological developments, and forged in interaction and competition with other workers. The process occurs both at an individual level, as persons negotiate their specific work roles, and at a collective level, as members of occupational groups struggle to define and protect their work. With a few rare exceptions, work is a social activity, enacted with reference to other persons and groups that define the nature, content, and meanings of work. This is most clearly illustrated by work subcultures as distinctive configurations of norms, values, and beliefs.

Several broad historical trends are evident (Hall, 1986: Ch. 1). At a structural level, the tendency has been toward *specialization*, with work roles become more narrowly focused over time. Witness the evolution over the nineteenth century of the role of the general-practitioner physician into a vast number of specialties, or the evolution of auto assembly from a single occupation to hundreds of distinct operations. Specialization, stimulated by the unprecedented growth of technology and information, has produced a proliferation of new occupations, some of which did not even exist a decade ago.

Many new occupations, such as computer programer, are highly skilled, but technological advances combined with organizational principles of job design can produce a *deskilling* of work. The same technology that generated the computer programer occupation has also created countless unskilled, repetitive, "keyboard" jobs. At another level, practitioners of formerly proud, highly skilled craft occupations, such as printers and machinists, are being reduced to machine operators or monitors.

Work has shifted from small-scale entrepreneurial or independent activity to *organizational* employment. In the process, individuals have had to surrender to the organization the right to make decisions about the nature and pace of work. Moreover, advancements in income and responsibility have become dependent upon the ability to move along in preexisting hierarchical structures.

The decline in opportunities for self-employment is itself an important issue in the analysis of work roles. The ideal of self-employment, of being an independent businessperson, looms large in American culture. Countless people aspire to having their own small business, and many risk it, although the failure rate is high. The lure of money is an important factor, but the opportunity to "be my own boss" is probably the prime motivator. A study of truck and cab owners confirmed "independence" as the single most important reason given for purchasing their own vehicles (Peterson, et al., 1982). To these people, ownership signaled freedom from the direct supervision experienced by other blue-collar workers. Self-employment involves risks and imposes burdens, but it frees the individual from direct supervisory authority, which is a trade-off many are obviously willing to make.

As a counterpoint to these changes in the structure of work, workers (both collectively and individually) have consistently sought to protect their *skill* and *autonomy* from external control. Through strikes and in countless everyday acts, they have demonstrated an interest in meaningful work and in some right to make independent decisions about how it is performed.

In order for the overall division of labor and the social organization of occupations to be understood, they must be conceptualized within an external environment of groups and occupations. Attempts by any occupation to expand or protect its preogatives can place it in competition with other groups that are pursuing their own interests. Occupations evolve over time in response to shifting patterns of power and influence.

TWO

Power and Negotiation
in the Division of Labor

INTRODUCTION: THE SOCIAL AND POLITICAL CONTEXT

Occupations are commonly viewed as merely a logical configuration of technical tasks within an overall economic division of labor. When occupations are viewed in a broad social context, however, it is apparent that form and content are emergent and dynamic, reflecting the outcome of negotiations, competition, conflict, bargaining, and accommodation with external groups. Individuals and occupational groups act self-consciously to enhance their own interests and rewards. They seek to define their roles so as to increase their autonomy, maximize intellectual challenge, and improve their social and economic rewards (Rothman, 1979). Such efforts often place them in competition with other occupational groups pursuing different interests and objects. In short, work roles are shaped within a complex social and political network.

This approach to work roles combines the perspectives of conflict and interactionist theories. *Conflict theory* addresses questions of inequality and power, competing interest groups, and social change. Therefore, occupations can be understood as *organized interest groups* (acting through labor unions and professional associations) in competition with other occupations, and work roles can be understood as "the temporary outcome in a past, present, and future struggle between groups who are interested in the acquisition of power, prestige, and reward even at the expense of others"

(Krause, 1971:82). The *interactionist theory* emphasizes the social and interpersonal processes involved in the creation and maintenance of social roles by people sharing a common situation. Thus, work roles are a "process of social interaction in the course of which the participants are continuously engaged in attempting to define, establish, maintain, and renew the tasks they perform and the (social) relationships . . . (related to) the tasks . . ." (Freidson, 1976:311).

Consider police work using this perspective. The police, like other occupations, seek to enhance their prerogatives and rewards. However, the fundamental nature of the occupation locates it in relation to courts, legislatures, the legal profession, informants, criminals, and the public. Each group can, in one way or another, influence the way in which the police do their work. Courts and legislatures set legal limits on the treatment of suspects and prisoners; lawyers define the manner in which records are kept and evidence collected; and the public places heavy demands upon police for services not related to the control of crime—activities such as resolving domestic altercations, controlling drunks, and providing emergency medical care. Police work thus evolves at the point of convergence of the activities and competing demands of a number of external groups.

Occupational roles are shaped both by deliberate attempts by members of groups to impose control upon an occupation and the unintentional, unanticipated consequences of contacts between groups. Attempts to control are "deliberate" in the sense that they are articulated as conscious efforts at control, such as when the courts impose limitations on police activity. The term should not be construed to imply that actions are always concerted and coordinated group efforts, for the sum of individual actions can be an equally powerful force, such as in the case of citizens demanding courteous treatment. Unintentional and unanticipated consequences develop when groups take some apparently neutral action that helps them achieve their own goals, but that impacts the way in which work must be performed. The British "bobby," for example, long famous for being unarmed, has had to accommodate to widespread terrorism and the use of weapons by criminals.

RESOURCES, POWER, AND SOCIAL CONTROL

The success of any group in expanding or protecting its prerogatives resides in the command of resources. *Resources* may be defined as "any attribute, circumstance, or possession that increases the ability of its holder to influence a person or groups" (Rogers, 1974:1425). External groups with resources will be in a position to define tasks, limit areas of expertise, enforce deference and subordination, and control the evolution of specific roles in many other ways. Currently, for example, a number of occupa-

EXHIBIT 2:1   The Distribution of Resources in the Occupational Sphere

EXTERNAL GROUPS	RELEVANT RESOURCES
Customers or clients	Earnings
	Referrals
	Malpractice suits
Allied occupations	Cooperation
Employers	Earnings
	Employment
	Promotions
Government	Laws/regulations
	Funding
The public	Income
	Prestige
Political parties	Employment
Vendors	Products/raw materials

tions—pharmacists, medical doctors, physicians' assistants, nurses, ophthalmologists, and dentists—are competing for the legal right to prescribe and dispense drugs. The outcome—the issue of which occupations in addition to medical doctors will be able to perform this specific technical task—will be largely a question of resources and power.

Many external groups control relevant resources, as shown in Exhibit 2:1. Obviously, members of any given occupation do not interact with every one of these groups, but each has been shown to have the potential to influence work roles in some situations. It should also be noted that the linkages between groups may take the form of direct contacts or may be mediated through a third party. The way in which these resources are utilized is best illustrated by focusing upon the dynamics of interaction among the most salient of these groups.

CLIENTS OR CUSTOMERS

Any occupation involved with direct provision of goods and/or services invests some resources in the hands of its clients or customers. The idea of patronage in the arts is an extreme example of consumer control. When the relationship is conducted on a face-to-face, fee-for-service basis (as is the case with dentists, prostitutes, barbers, and auto mechanics) consumers will have three primary resources at their disposal: *income,* in the form of withholding the decision to purchase; *referrals* of other customers; and the threat of *malpractice suits.*

Direct fee-for-service practitioners must attract and maintain a clientele. Each customer is important both as a source of income and as a possible reference for other clients. William Goode put it well when he noted that

> Client choices are a form of social control. They determine the survival of a profession or specialty, as well as the career success of particular professionals (Goode, 1957:198).

People seeking services and help frequently depend upon what Eliot Freidson (1960) identified as "lay referral systems"—informal networks of friends, relatives, and neighbors who provide information, leads, and evaluations of practitioners. Therefore, customers (whether they realize it or not) are in a position to influence the manner in which occupational tasks are performed.

Concessions to clients may involve no more than attempts to display a pleasing demeanor. Or, such concessions may be more consequential if client expectations can determine the form and content of tasks. Customers' wishes define some of the tasks of prostitutes (Bryan, 1965), salespersons (Miller, 1964), masseurs (Velarde and Warlick, 1973), waitresses (Karen, 1962), and physicians. It has been argued that certain common medical practices, such as the prescription of vitamin injections, antibiotics, and tranquilizers, are dictated more by patient demand than by therapeutic considerations (Freidson, 1970:306). The same may be true for some surgical procedures: It has been reported that patients request—and receive—hysterectomies as a method of contraception. The demands may extend to pressure toward illegal behavior: Stockbrokers may employ illegal tactics or use forbidden information to increase their client's profits (Evan and Levin, 1966).

CASE STUDY: HOSPITAL HOSPITALITY

Hospital routines evolved to facilitate the work of medical personnel (Lorber, 1975). "Good patients" were those who followed orders and did not disrupt standard operating procedures. More than one hospital, confronted with a more educated clientele and dwindling revenues created by the trend toward outpatient services and declining government support, has responded by developing a new philosophy toward patient care. Antiseptic technical impersonality has been supplanted by campaigns directed toward treating patients like "guests" rather than merely case studies in illness.

A leader in this area was the Albert Einstein Medical Center in Philadelphia, which in 1983 turned to a group of hotel managers for advice on how to make the hospital more attractive to potential patients (Carey, 1985). Some of the changes were of the cosmetic variety—name tags, more palatable food, and attention to attractive decor. More significantly, though, seminars on patient courtesy became mandatory, and house rules for patient contacts were established. For example, staff members were told, "Make eye contact. Introduce yourself. Explain what you're doing." Although such changes met with some initial resistance, they have helped to produce alterations in the fundamental nature of the relationship between the patient and the health care professional. It is not mere common courtesy; it is a matter of more interaction and more information passing from doctor to patient, which is a reversal of the tendency of "experts" to distance themselves from the less knowledgeable.

Recognition of the consumer's potential for control may stimulate attempts at the neutralization of client resources. It may be observed that occupations "mystify" and obscure their expertise by the creation of an esoteric jargon, or by deliberately limiting the information available to clients. Such techniques seem designed to minimize the client's ability to evaluate the practitioner's behavior.

A somewhat different response is found in direct attempts to manage and control the client. The goal may be directly financial (increasing sales, tips, or commissions), or it may take the form of a struggle to be free from constraints imposed by clients (Mennerick, 1974). There is evidence of such a struggle among taxi drivers (Henslin, 1967, 1968; Davis, 1959), attorneys (Reed, 1969), milk deliverers (Bigus, 1972), employment counselors (Martinez, 1968), waiters and waitresses (Whyte, 1946; Butler and Snizek, 1976), and even fortune-tellers (Tatro, 1974). Attempts are made to direct the relationship by initiating the interaction, defining the role of the client, and setting limits on the services to be provided. Dentists, for example, wear uniforms, display their educational credentials, and learn to manifest a calm, self-possessed style which conveys the image of authority. Further, they direct the interaction with questions and directions as the patient reclines amid the technical paraphernalia of the dental office. And, of course, dentists ultimately control the conversation because they can terminate it at any point by approaching the patient's mouth with some instrument (Linn, 1967). Members of service occupations may even cultivate "friendships" with clients, hoping that they will express their regard by purchasing "extras" or paying their bills on time (Bigus, 1972:153). When these techniques are successful, the service worker is freed from subordination to the consumer.

Workers employed by organizations are more insulated from the direct influence of customers, but they are not immune, because dissatisfaction is expressed to the employer. People lodge complaints about treatment by the police, or about buses being behind schedule (Slosar, 1973), or about the speed of table service (Whyte, 1946). Workers obviously cannot ignore clients, but not all clients receive the same treatment. Postal clerks (Goodsell, 1976), medical personnel (Sudnow, 1967), and bus drivers (Toren, 1973) respond differently to different types of people. In most cases, clients who seem to be higher on the socioeconomic scale receive more care, better service, or more deferential treatment. One interpretation of this is that these are the customers perceived as the most likely to file complaints with employers; hence, they are accorded special treatment.

Malpractice suits are another type of resource at the disposal of clients. The legal right to bring suit is not new; what *is* new is the scope of lawsuits, especially against physicians and lawyers. In California in 1984, 14 percent of the lawyers were defendants in malpractice suits—double the rate of six years earlier (Galante, 1985:25). Malpractice claims against physicians have increased 300 percent in the ten years between 1975 and 1984 (ABC News, 1985). A more recent development is the extension of this strategy against a whole range of new groups. "Educational malpractice" suits have been filed against schools for failing to provide students with basic skills, and although all cases have been dismissed on grounds that it is impossible to firmly fix blame, they have been one source of the pressure that has produced state laws defining minimum competency standards (for graduation) and renewed emphasis on teacher competence. Even members of the clergy have become targets. In 1985, a clergyman was sued when a young man he had counseled committed suicide. Again, the case failed, but such cases have the potential to cast a subtle "chilling effect" on the performance of these roles (Woodward and Luck, 1985).

Malpractice suits have had more direct and measurable consequences for the shape of professional practice. In health care, reaction to malpractice claims has resulted in the practice of "defensive medicine," with an emphasis upon detailed record keeping, more comprehensive assessments and tests, and a reluctance to innovate or to adopt new procedures (Hershey, 1973). One estimate places the cost of defensive medicine at $15 billion to $40 billion a year in the United States (ABC News, 1985). Among lawyers, concern about malpractice claims will probably mean that certain common practices, such as representing both parties in property transfers and uncontested divorces, will be abandoned because they leave the attorney vulnerable to "conflict of interest" suits.

ALLIED OCCUPATIONS

Most occupations are strongly dependent upon allied occupations. Relationships among occupations may be either casual or highly formalized, but such ties invest power in the allied occupations. The most fundamental of all resources is simple *cooperation*—the willingness to help people. The use of this resource is most apparent when it is exercised by workers who are nominally subordinate. Machine-maintenance workers can be powerful, because their willingness or unwillingness to service or repair equipment determines which machines will run and, hence, determines levels of productivity and earnings (Crozier, 1964; Burroway, 1983). The power of nonprofessional attendants in psychiatric hospitals has derived from the fact that professionals depended upon them to control the behavior of patients. Subordinates may demand no more than respectful treatment, but the desire for respect is a powerful motivator, and the reliance of professionals on the cooperation of subordinates enables them to earn more deference than they would otherwise be able to command by virtue of their lowly position in the hierarchy.

Dependence upon allied occupations can be illustrated by the career of a burglar. As Neal Shover (1973) has noted, burglars who hope to improve their skills and enhance their incomes face several problems that render them vulnerable to external control. First, the need to master the esoteric skills and techniques of theft requires the novice to obtain the tutelage of an experienced and successful burglar, who will expect some demonstration of proper character as a prerequisite to the sharing of the "tricks of the trade." Second, there is a need for a system of "contacts" or "tipsters" who can supply information about potential victims. Bartenders, delivery persons, and custodians, who are some of the more common sources of information, elicit payoffs in return for their information. In other cases, the burglar must learn the skills of deception to gain this information from unsuspecting security personnel. Third, burglars sometimes reluctantly depend upon the cooperation of partners with specialized expertise in alarms, lock boxes, or transformation. Partners enforce norms prohibiting informing on other criminals by scorn, avoidance, or even physical violence (Inciardi, 1975:69–70). A fourth problem involves the disposal of stolen merchandise, which brings the burglar into contact with pawnshop owners and "fences" who can determine which items are stolen by making their needs known. The final category of people are those in the criminal justice system—bail bondsmen, defense attorneys—who can influence burglars' careers if and when they are arrested.

EMPLOYERS

A major historical trend has been a contraction of the proportion of the labor force employed as independent entrepreneurs and craft workers. Most occupations are comprised of employees of public or private organizations. The nature of employment in a market economy places the major resources in the hands of the employer. The primary resources are *employment, earnings, promotions,* ownership of the *facilities of production* (raw materials, equipment, tools, and so on), and the *product* and/or control of the *clients* to be served. Even such previously independent, fee-for-service occupations as medicine have come to depend on clinics, hospitals, and laboratories that possess the diagnostic and therapeutic equipment necessary for modern health-care delivery. Consequently, it is virtually impossible to practice without access to such organizations.

The division of labor in profit-oriented organizations has generally been guided by the quest for efficiency and reduction of labor costs. In American industry, this quest has placed a high premium on two organizing principles: the standardization of tasks and narrow specialization. The origins of this administrative ideology can be traced to a school of thought often called *Taylorism*, which flourished in the early part of this century.[1] At the center of this philosophy was the idea that complex operations should be broken down into smaller units of specialized activity, primarily because it was argued that workers became more efficient and productive when their attention was limited to a small number of tasks. The result has been the creation of a large number of blue-collar and clerical occupations organized around one or a few routine, repetitive operations performed under close supervision. Telephone operators are called upon to repeat predetermined speeches while supervisors listen (Langer, 1970); assembly-line workers repeat exactly the same task on an endless procession of objects passing before them.

It is often assumed that the nature of work is dictated by available technology—a kind of *technological determinism*. The invention of sewing machines creates sewing-machine operators, for example, or the assembly-line leads logically to the idea of assembly-line workers. Technology does not inevitably create work roles; it merely defines the range of possibilities.

> A new method of production does not have to be technologically superior to be adopted; innovation depends as much on economic and social institutions—on who is in control of production and under what constraints control is exercised (Marglin, 1974:36).

Thus, the ultimate reason for adopting a technological or social innovation may be to enhance the potential for social control, or to neutralize the potential power of workers.

This approach has been applied to the evolution of factory work in the latter part of the nineteenth century by Katherine Stone (1974). Employers were confronted with the threat of the homogenization and "proletarianization" of the work force, manifested in militancy, strikes, slowdowns, and an expanding labor movement. It was a situation with the potential for worker organization and collective action on a large scale. Partly to counter this trend, employers fostered the proliferation of narrow, specialized occupations, plant-specific jobs, job ladders, and wage incentive systems that resulted in divisions among workers and weakening of their collective power. Jobs that were simple, specialized, and limited to a single plant rendered workers easily replaceable and neutralized the threat of strikes and other job actions. Piece-work wage incentive systems, overtly

---

[1]Taylorism is discussed in more detail in a later chapter.

designed to increase output, also generated internal competition among workers and created social distance between the "efficient" and "inefficient" workers. Further, occupations were arranged in "job ladders," with slight increases in prestige and pay along a chain of potential promotions. Stone argues that career ladders did not reflect any true increase in complexity, but rather were a technique to create a sense of vertical mobility and to throw workers into competition with one another for advancement. Thus, organization-based division of labor may represent an attempt to impose social control or to weaken the power of occupational groups, as well as a consideration of efficiency and effectiveness.

The employer's ability to exert control is modified by a number of factors. As a general rule, occupations with craft, entrepreneurial, or professional roots tend to enjoy greater autonomy than do occupations originating within organizations. In this category are scientists, printers, and physicians. All share, to some extent, certain features, a specialized expert knowledge, a sense of occupational community, and a training period that inculcates an emphasis upon autonomy and individual, internalized standards of performance and accountability. Practitioners bring such orientations to their employment, where they tend to come into conflict with the organizational emphasis on hierarchy, coordination, and standardized procedures.

PUBLICS

In this context, *publics* may be defined as aggregates of people who are affected by an occupation's activities and are able to take some action to collectively register their response. The response may be the sum of voting patterns, letter writing, lobbying legislatures, buying (or refusing to buy) books or tickets to performances. Publics are the ultimate consumers, but the relationship is usually more remote and impersonal compared to the relationship between publics and members of direct-service occupations. Nevertheless, the sum of these individual acts can influence the structure of such occupational roles as professional athlete, performing artist, political officeholder, journalist, and novelist.

All members of these occupations must—to some extent—cater to the preferences of their publics and/or attempt to influence them. The American sports industry offers many instances of responses to perceptions of public demand. Professional hockey is currently dominated by the belief that fans want aggressive play punctuated by fistfights, and the players have moved in that direction. The dramatic increases in attendance that have accompanied increases in violence seem to validate the public's appreciation of the new role of the hockey player (Gammons, 1977). Likewise, the commercial success of particular books, films, plays, newspapers, or performances influences the manner in which these artistic and support occupations are subsequently performed.

While members of such occupations must be somewhat sensitive to their publics, there is a tendency for them to believe that the public lacks an understanding of the finer points of their work; to some extent, this is an accurate observation. It reflects the fact that practitioners, as a result of their long, esoteric training, often hold different values and standards from those held by the public. Practitioners typically attempt to have their standards prevail, usually with the assistance of certain allied occupations such as critics and teachers. All three typically share the same standards and attempt to impose their standards upon the public through their domination of the public media and the classrooms. In the following passage, a critic lectures the public that it is not enough for them to merely *enjoy* a musical composition; they must abide by the standards he imposes:

> On its highest level the appreciation of art is as elitist as the creation of art. Those listening to a Beethoven symphony, content merely to let the music wash over them, are operating at a very low level. It is necessary for the music to mean something more than a collection of pleasant sounds, to know something about the composer, his place in history, the place of a particular work in his total output, the place of the total output in relation to the music of the time, the technique of the composition, the technique of the performance (Schonberg, 1978:19D).

It seems clear that, as a *New York Times* drama critic put it, the critic's role is to form the critical judgment of the reader (Elder, 1978:17).

Some occupational groups are especially sensitive to a generalized public. School teachers have always had to be concerned with public response to their demeanor both in the classroom and in private. Earlier in this century, public response extended to prescriptions on dress, residence, and life-styles. More recently, teachers complain that widespread public awareness of child abuse has produced a generalized "suspicion" of everyone who cares for children and has made teachers reluctant to even touch students for fear that it will be construed as misconduct (Associated Press, 1985).

Occupations typically respond to general publics by attempting to physically obscure their behavior from view. Classroom doors are closed, literally or symbolically, as are the doors of massage parlors. Legislators' decisions are made in the privacy of the caucus room or the cloakroom. The idea of "executive sessions" shield public administrators from the public.

Generalized public responses to occupational performance often stimulates the creation of groups specifically designed to constrain behavior. Public education is a frequent target, and attacks seem to have sharpened since the 1970s. Books chosen by teachers and librarians are often challenged, and in over half the cases they are removed from class lists and library shelves in response to public pressure. In 1982 the most likely victims were *Go Ask Alice, Catcher in the Rye, Our Bodies, Ourselves, Forever,* and *Of Mice and Men* (Associated Press, 1982). Disputes over the teaching of Darwin's theories of evolution have directly caused curriculum revisions, and have even impacted book publishers, resulting in a 30 to 80 percent decline in the textbook coverage of *any* theories of evolution (Hechinger, 1984). Teachers and administrators worry that these acts represent a form of censorship.

GOVERNMENT

Many agencies of government at the local, state, and federal levels may define certain aspects of occupational roles. Control is accomplished both by direct, deliberate *legal intervention* (via statutes, licensing, judicial rulings, and so on) and more indirectly by the *allocation of government funds* (including grants, contracts, and reimbursements). In theory—and sometimes in practice—the government functions to protect the public welfare. In other cases, special interest groups attempt to utilize the powers of the state to their own advantage. When that happens, governmental involvement in occupational affairs merely represents an indirect form of social control by some third party. The fact that nurses and pharmacists are legally prohibited from prescribing drugs is certainly a reflection of the continuing power of organized medicine enacted through legislatures.

Statutory controls.   Legislatures set criteria for work, mandate minimum performance standards, and establish procedures for the handling and processing of products, all of which impact occupational roles. For example, food-handling regulations define the tasks of cooks, butchers, and restaurant workers, while safety regulations define the schedules and tasks of truck drivers, airline pilots, and coal miners. Enforcement of such laws is always problematic, because statutes designed to protect either workers or citizens may be circumvented when other groups have sufficient resources. For example, Sherrill (1977) argues that truckers drive unsafe vehicles and work unsafe hours because the power of the trucking industry in Washington prevents effective safety enforcement.

Licensing boards.   A surprisingly large number of occupations are licensed by the states. This includes such diverse groups as pharmacists and plumbers, masseurs and morticians, cab drivers and certified public accountants (CPAs). The primary motivation is to establish standards when the public safety is at risk. Hence, licensing boards control access to the occupation, and establish and enforce educational requirements and rules on advertising, fee splitting, confidentiality, and scope of practice. In addition, periodic renewal provides a recurring opportunity for reexamination and reevaluation of qualifications. Many states require CPAs, dentists, optometrists, pharmacists, and veterinarians to enroll in some form of continuing education in order to qualify for relicensure.

In practice, the history of licensing boards reveals that they are the focus of a struggle for occupational control. It is common for the "regulated" group to win control of these boards, as is generally the case in medicine and law (Cohen, 1975, 1980). Licensure is sometimes initiated by a segment of an occupation that seeks to utilize the power of the state to control entry, impose standards, and eliminate marginal practitioners. A number of medical occupations have followed this pattern, with the professional associations playing a central role in the establishment of licensing statutes. In other cases, those regulated have been able to gain control of membership of the boards, and hence to limit external involvement in internal matters. Most licensing legislation has apparently been passed without much consideration of the "conflict of interest" created by placing control in the hands of those to be regulated. Some states have recently moved to rectify this situation; New Jersey, for example, requires lay members on every licensing board.

Courts.   The courts are playing an increasingly decisive role in defining the parameters of occupations. The occupation of accounting, for example, has seen its tasks and obligations expand over the last decade because of a series of court decisions dealing with the interrelationships between corporate clients and the investing public. Rulings now in effect hold that CPAs must go beyond their traditional, narrowly circumscribed technical tasks of examining financial statements to ascertain whether generally accepted accounting practices have been followed; they must now concern themselves with the fairness of such disclosures, and they have a right and obligation to delve into corporate matters not previously included in annual audits (Business Week, 1976). It is clear that the courts have redefined the accountant's role, asserting that the primary responsibility is to the investor, not the client.

One of the single most profound and far-reaching court actions occurred in 1975, when the U.S. Supreme Court decided that lawyers were not automatically exempt from the Sherman Antitrust Act by virtue of being a self-regulating "learned profession." It ruled that the standard fee schedules that had been in use in the legal profession since 1795 constituted a "classic illustration of price-fixing" (Kohlmeier, 1976). Although the Court stopped short of eliminating all distinctions between professions and other business activities, it is clear that many traditional patterns in law, medicine, architecture, and engineering will be open to judicial review.

Whatever the outcomes, it is apparent that the courts will be determining a number of important aspects of professional roles.

Government funding. Government funds in the form of grants, subsidies, contracts, and fellowships are a significant source of income in the sciences, medicine, and the arts. The scope of this funding can be quite dramatic. The National Institute of Health supports 75 percent of all biomedical research in medical schools and 40 percent of all university research (Gustafson, 1975:1060). The implications of this are neatly elucidated by Krohn (1972:65–66) in his analysis of science, but they may apply to any occupation that depends upon government money:

> The dangers in a unique dependence on government support seem . . . obvious; how can a science retain a critical measure of autonomy, self-discipline, and a sense of direction? It is probably safe to say no government has yet supported science on a modern scale and allowed it broad and intellectually autonomous development. The United States certainly does not seem to be immune to a narrow and direct use of science on government's terms.

At a subtle level, the competition for government funds may influence scientists (consciously or not) to modify their work or their methods to conform to perceptions of governmental objectives. In one study of academic social scientists, a majority admitted altering their research topics and techniques in response to shifts in government priorities (Useem, 1976:154).

A more clearly defined form of governmental control is exercised when eligibility for public funds is made contingent upon the adoption of certain tasks. This is nowhere more evident than in the health-related occupations. In New York, the state Board of Health made participation in continuing education a requirement for dentists if they wished to treat Medicare patients. In 1971, the Public Health Service Act required that the curriculum in colleges of pharmacy place greater emphasis upon clinical work in order to qualify for federal assistance (Ruane, 1975).

POLITICAL PARTIES

Political parties continue to exert influence upon some occupations. Their power lies in control of nominations for elective and/or appointive office. The role of political parties is readily evident in the competition for access to the standard political careers (legislators, governors, mayors, and so on), as well as in quasi-political positions in the diplomatic corps, or in various regulatory bodies, or in cabinet appointments.

Politics may also intervene in "nonpolitical" occupations such as police administration. In many large cities, the election of a new mayor means the appointment of a new police commissioner and a subsequent reshuffling of top-level police administrators. Judicial selection is also a political process in many states, and many people favor the election of judges because it frees candidates from dependence upon the continued good will of party leaders. At the national level, senators have traditionally had the right to nominate or veto appointments to the federal bench in their states. Considerations other than legal expertise may thus enter into the screening process, which in turn has the potential to influence the behavior of judicial candidates.

VENDORS

Vendor is a general term referring to any of a number of organizations or groups that supply raw materials, products, or components to members of an occupation. Included are manufacturers and their sales representatives, distributors, wholesalers, and the like. Each exerts control over some item necessary to the performance of a work role. The plight of small businesspersons (such as movie theater operators and book store owners) who must merchandise a whole range of marginal items in order to acquire one high-volume product exemplifies deliberate manipulation of a situation by wholesalers.

The relationship between auto manufacturers and dealers is a case in point, according to Harvey Farberman (1975). Dealers obviously depend upon the manufacturer for the cars they sell and service, and are thus vulnerable to their actions. Based on the "economics of scale," auto makers have a vested interest in a high volume of sales. They accomplish this by setting low profit margins on the sale of new cars, thus effectively forcing dealers to devote their attention to promoting sales of new cars and to deemphasize used cars. Moreover, it generates pressures on dealers to exploit customers in repair bills in order to supplement small profits. Rackets, such as billing for work not actually done, replacing parts unnecessarily, and charging for new parts while using materials that are actually "rebuilt," are common.

Manufacturers and suppliers may make more impersonal decisions based upon criteria such as efficiency or profit; these decisions also serve to define occupational roles. Retail pharmacists, for example, are strongly impacted by the actions of pharmaceutical firms. Developments such as prepackaging of pills, standardized dosages, and direct promotion of drugs to physicians have eroded the image of the retail pharmacist and has reduced them from compounders of prescriptions to dispensers of prepackaged items (Shaw, 1972).

Role Conflicts

When these external groups are considered together, they form what Robert Merton (1957) has called the *role set*—the total complement of groups that interact with members of a particular role. It is evident that these multiple partners can—and often do—confront the individual with the potential for *role conflict* in the form of contradictory and/or competing expectations. Managers of publishing firms find themselves caught between employers' expectations of profit and authors' demands for the publication of work on the basis of literary merit, regardless of sales potential (Lane, 1970). School superintendents must balance the demands of students, teachers, parents, school boards, and others (Gross, et al., 1958). The academic department chairperson is typically caught between the expectations of the faculty that they act as advocates and defenders of academic freedom, and the demands of administration for cost effectiveness.

Role conflicts are apparently common, with one study reporting that approximately one-half of all workers experienced conflict situations (Kahn et al., 1964). There is a good deal of evidence showing that role conflict produces undesirable consequences. People may become anxious and frustrated because of their inability to meet or reconcile these pressures (Kahn et al., 1964; Gross, et al., 1958). Role conflict contributes to feelings of stress and to job dissatisfaction. One study even found an increase in the incidence of coronary disease associated with role conflict (Sales and House, 1971).

Not all of the consequences of role conflict are negative. There may also be some benefits that may serve to neutralize all but the more disruptive problems (Seiber, 1974; Marks, 1977). Compensatory rewards are structured into such positions. Chairpersons often have salary increments, reduced teaching loads, and institutionalized contact with high-status persons (such as deans and vice-presidents). These roles can also offer an added element of challenge, for they require (and reward) tolerance of discrepant viewpoints, provide exposure to a variety of stimuli, and demand flexibility in adjusting to the demands of diverse role partners. Thus, role conflict can, in some cases, produce satisfaction as well as stress.

Responses to Role Conflicts

Individuals develop a number of strategies for coping with the problems of role conflict (Gullahorn and Gullahorn, 1963; Merton, 1957; Gross, et al., 1958). These diverse techniques lend themselves to organization into three broad categories.

Redefinition. One way of dealing with competing demands is to work actively at negotiating a new and less demanding set of expectations. Such negotiation may involve any of the following: attempting to eliminate the demands of some groups, bringing contradictory demands into better alignment with one another, isolating the competing groups, redefining the manner in which the demands are met, or reordering the sequence of events. Nurses in hospitals are able to devote more time to patients if they can convince physicians to reduce their expectations for the nursing staff (Strauss, et al., 1963). These different strategies have in common the fact that the individual perceives the conflict, directly confronts the conflict, and seeks to alter the conflict-producing situation. When they are successful, role conflict is reduced or eliminated.

Avoidance. An alternate strategy is to try to avoid the situation. This may involve actual physical avoidance of a conflict-laden situation. Thus, people often refuse roles like assembly line supervisor (Chinoy, 1955), prison welfare officer, (Priestly, 1972), and academic department chairperson (Hoult, 1970) because they are associated with a great deal of inherent conflict. Those in jobs with high levels of role conflict are the people most likely to be thinking about leaving (Senatra, 1980).

A psychological form of avoidance is the "defense mechanism" of withdrawal. Withdrawal is manifest in ambiguity, apathy, and indecisiveness. Some may turn to alcohol or drugs (Trice and Roman, 1972). The problem is that this makes individuals less effective workers and less satisfied with their jobs. A more sociological response is evident when people limit interaction with those seen as producing the conflict. Attempts are made to reduce conflict by the minimizing involvement in conflict situations. This leaves the individual isolated from coworkers.

Selective conformity. The third possible response is behavior that responds to the demands of one or more of the competing groups. There are two possibilities: conformity to the expectations of one group, at the expense of others, and attempting to conform to some of the expectations of all the competing groups. This can only be accomplished by extra effort and the ability to compartmentalize the conflicting demands.

Three variables must be considered in attempting to predict which response will occur: the relative *resources* of the various groups, the *legitimacy* (perceived right to make demands) of their expectations, and the degree of attraction or *commitment* to each. All other factors being equal, conflict will be resolved in favor of conforming to the demands of the groups or individuals with the greatest resources, legitimacy, and attraction. Selective conformity has been shown to follow this pattern among workers as diverse as school superintendents in Massachusetts (Gross, et al., 1958) and local government officials in Nigeria (Magid, 1977:226). These, of course, are the easiest situations to deal with for conformity represents the most logical, rational course of action. In contrast, avoidance is apparently the modal response when all of the groups have some elements of power, legitimacy, or attraction, and the worker is relatively powerless. Attempts at redefinition are most likely to occur when the worker has some power, allowing some room for negotiation.

CONCLUSION

The evolution of occupational roles reflects the interplay between members of an occupation and groups external to it. These groups, acting to enhance their own advantages, interests, and objectives compete and cooperate with one another. The work roles that emerge from this process, reflect the relative power of specific groups at specific points in time; thus work roles and whole occupations are constantly changing.

For members of an occupation, the activities of external control agents will create role conflict if the demands are discrepant and inconsistent. Role conflict can generate stress, anxiety, frustration, and deviance, and it can weaken patterns of mutual cooperation. There are three types of responses to role conflict—redefinition, avoidance, and conformity. The kind of response is determined by the configuration of power, legitimacy, and attraction of the control agents.

Several basic issues are consistently contested at both the individual and collective levels. *Income* and *prestige* are relevant, but apparently no issue is more important than *autonomy.* "Autonomy is the prize sought after by virtually all occupational groups, for it represents freedom from direction from others, freedom to preform one's work the way one desires" (Freidson, 1976:368). Freedom to make decisions about work is rated "very important" by most workers (Quinn, et al., 1974), and they resist encroachments upon it. Workers meticulously manage the time it takes to do a total job as a strategy to allow themselves freedom in the performance of specific tasks within the sequence. They establish informal norms restricting output as a means of gaining some discretion.

Individuals also rate *challenging tasks* among the most strongly desired attributes of their jobs. Industrial workers trade jobs in order to alleviate the boredom and monotony of routine, repetitive work. At the group level, occupations consistently attempt to gain control over more interesting and challenging aspects of work, while sloughing off the routine. In medicine, physicians have willingly delegated the routine of taking patient histories to nurses and physician's assistants, while jealously guarding the right to diagnose.

THREE

Occupational
and Work Subcultures

INTRODUCTION: THE EMERGENCE OF SUBCULTURES

People who work together for any appreciable length of time tend to develop distinctive patterns of thinking, acting, and feeling. These unique perceptions of the world, shared values and symbols, special languages, and behavioral norms distinguish members from nonmembers and legitimately characterize these groups as *subcultures*.[1] Probably the most famous accounts of work subcultures emerged from the Hawthorne studies in the 1930s (Roethlisberger and Dixon, 1939). Observations of workers producing telephone equipment uncovered the existence of *quota restrictions*—informal norms setting upper and lower limits on output. The Hawthorne workers also had their own social rituals and private system of job rotation. New recruits had to learn the subculture and become integrated into it if they hoped to become effective workers.

Subcultures reflect a collective adaptation to the social and physical working conditions. The basic model shown in Exhibit 3:1 isolates the key elements in the process (see Arnold, 1970). Individuals who do the same kind of work are exposed to a common set of experiences; they confront

---

[1]The term *work subculture* is used here to refer to those systems that develop in physical work settings and encompass members of different occupations. *Occupational subculture* is reserved for systems existing among members of specific occupations, such as dentistry or printing.

EXHIBIT 3:1. The Development of Work Subcultures

similar problems, interact with the same kind of people, and enjoy similar rewards. Coal miners and soldiers in combat operate in an environment of constant danger; industrial work groups face bureaucratic pressures for productivity; waitresses' encounters with customers have common elements. Shared experiences, reinforced through face-to-face interaction, foster the creation of a common bond and a feeling of solidarity or cohesion among workers. As they work, they accumulate specialized knowledge, develop a common language, and devise informal rules for dealing with collective problems. Some patterns are invented by the group, while others are externally imposed. For example, fledgling nurses must master the delicate etiquette of social interaction with physicians who are in positions of authority. Common objects that are part of the work may take on new, often symbolic, meanings as a consequence of being shared. Specific items of work clothing, for example, may become symbols of group membership or exclusion, as among coal miners, among whom an orange hard hat identifies a person as a rookie (Vaught and Smith, 1980).

This distinctive cognitive and behavioral perspective is transmitted to new members through formal and informal socialization and enforced by social sanctions. Railroaders spend the greater part of a year mastering the esoteric language of the rails (Kemnitzer, 1973). Eager and energetic new maintenance workers must be taught about what constitutes a fair day's work (Dalton, 1974). Those who violate such norms run the risk of being labeled "deviant." The Hawthorne telephone equipment workers who's output rose above the group standard found themselves cast as "rate busters"; those who produced too little were called "chiselers." If peer disapproval proves ineffective, more direct deterrents may be invoked. Professional athletes have developed their own enforcement system. Baseball players who are overly aggressive will find a pitch sailing near their heads the next time they come to bat. In any occupation, coworkers will have one powerful sanction at their disposal—the ability to withhold their support and their cooperation, thus isolating the deviant. Cases abound in the lore of police work, mining, and construction work of people being driven out of the field because they failed to live up to group expectations.

Socialization and social control link each succeeding generation of worker to the perspectives of the group, foster group solidarity, and encourage common motivations, reactions, and habits (see Turner, 1971:1). The norms and values of the group may be *internalized* (in other words, they may become the values and norms of the individual), and may become the standards by which they judge themselves and their peers. Ironworkers who have violated subcultural expectations have been known to put down their tools and quit on their own without outside pressure (Haas, 1977).

Subcultural perspectives tend to isolate individuals from other groups and from the larger society. It is not uncommon to find occupations in which this segregation extends beyond the workplace to include social and leisure activities. Members may form *occupational communities,* in the sense that they associate with and make friends with people in the same occupation to the exclusion of outsiders (Salaman, 1974:21). The people they work with are also the people they drink with, play golf with, and visit at home. They form a socially self-contained unit both on the job and away from it.

THE FUNCTIONS OF SUBCULTURES

Subcultures comprise a distinctive system of attitudes, behaviors, and meanings shared by members of a work group or an entire occupation. The key to understanding the origin and survival of subcultures lies in the analysis of their social functions both for individuals *and* for the group. As in all cases employing functional analysis, it is important to keep in mind that this perspective does not imply or deny deliberate planning, nor even an awareness of the process on the part of participants.

Subcultures are *instrumental,* providing members with a means of accomplishing the technical and social goals of work. Language, tools, technical norms, and values may be seen as historically evolved techniques for getting the work done. Subcultures may be viewed as a way of maintaining and passing on the accumulated experience and wisdom of the group. For the newcomer, the subculture provides a preexisting fund of knowledge and techniques which would otherwise have to be learned by a process of trial and error.

From the perspective of the group, the presence of shared work patterns ensures *predictability* and *reliability.* The acquisition of group standards allows individuals to anticipate how other members of the group will behave in work situations. This is especially vital in occupations in which individuals are dependent upon teamwork.

Subcultures are *protective,* sheltering members and their collective interests from a social and physical environment perceived as malevolent. The challenge may be to physical safety, group autonomy, prestige, income, or group integrity. "Rate busters" are never popular, for they threaten the integrity of members by "showing up" other workers, disrupting individual control over the work process, causing more work, and inviting external control (Dalton, 1974). Consequently, individual and group response to deviants will be strong and direct when they are perceived as a threat to the group.

Subcultures are *integrative,* with common perspectives and symbols linking members together and producing a feeling of solidarity. The shared uniforms, symbols, traditions, and rituals of the military help to weld the members together into a cohesive and highly integrated group.

Finally, subcultures determine *self-image* and *social placement,* within both the subgroup and the larger society. Qualification as a member of a subculture can foster a sense of pride and accomplishment, as is evident in the pride with which lawyers and electricians announce their status through language and dress. Subcultural membership also confers social status which may be either degrading (as in the case of a prostitute) or dignifying (as it is with a clergy member). This, in turn, influences relationships and responses from outsiders and contributes to the shaping of self-images. Within the group, conformity and deviance with respect to subcultural standards and expectations influence internal prestige and power.

THE CONTENT OF SUBCULTURES

Subculture, as a general concept, encompasses a number of elements shared by participants in a common work situation. A convenient way of classifying the content of subcultures is outlined in Exhibit 3:2, along with examples which will be analyzed in more detail. Not every subculture manifests all the elements incorporated in this classification. Soldiers, police,

EXHIBIT 3:2   The Elements of Work Subcultures

DEFINITION	ELEMENT	EXAMPLES
Forms of verbal and nonverbal communication	**Language**	Argot Gestures Posture
Objects having functional/symbolic meaning	**Artifacts**	Tools Grooming Uniforms
Definitions of social or physical reality	**Beliefs**	Knowledge Myths Stereotypes
Abstract priorities	**Values**	
Expectations of apropriate behavior	**Norms**	Technical norms Interpersonal norms
Standardized ceremonies	**Rituals**	Magic Rites of passage Naming Expulsion ritual

miners, fishers, printers, musicians, scientists, journalists, executives, and athletes are among the groups about which the most is known.

Language: Verbal and Nonverbal

Every type of work seems to have its own spoken language. Distinctive vocabularies, usually called *argot,* emerge in part from the need for terms to describe the tools, roles, and circumstances unique to the work. Circus and carnival argot offers countless colorful terms for which there is no ready equivalent in conventional English.

> *slum:* cheap items distributed as prizes in games of chance
>
> *patch:* a person who acts as a mediator of complaints against the show (also known as fixers or menders)
>
> *louse:* a person who follows the show from town to town, but has no official function
>
> *sticks:* local individuals hired to win prizes, thus inducing others to gamble
>
> *reader:* a person responsible for checking the show area prior to departure, ensuring that no equipment is left behind
>
> *grinder:* an announcer who talks continuously outside a show to attract customers (adapted from Maurer, 1981; Easto and Truzzi, 1974).

Each of these words names, summarizes, and succinctly conveys complex ideas and relationships. Thus, an occupational language may be merely a technical vocabulary, a means of communication among coworkers, which is a universal function of language.

However, occupational argot extends beyond this to include words that seem to be no more than synonyms for common terms:

> *ace:* dollar bill
>
> *chump heister:* ferris wheel
>
> *dentist's friend:* candy apples
>
> *crack:* (verb) to speak
>
> *dip:* pickpocket
>
> *goffer:* circus owner (also governor)
>
> *trick:* any carnival or circus
>
> *mitt:* a palmist (abbreviation for "mitt-reader")

Some of these terms reflect the history of the group. Thus, a meal ticket is an "Annie Oakley," named for the famous rifle woman who could toss a playing card into the air and shoot holes in it resembling the punches in a meal card.

Occupational language has meanings and functions beyond that of a technical vocabulary. The key may be that a nonstandard and semisecret argot distinguishes members from nonmembers. Access to, and mastery of, the lexicon confirms "insider" status, while ignorance and exclusion signifies nonmember, "outsider" status. A shared language creates and strengthens a sense of identification, promotes group solidarity, and affirms the history and traditions of the group. The status-conferring value of language is evident in the manner of usage in intergroup and intragroup interaction. It has often been noted that members of high-prestige occupations will tend to ostentatiously employ their jargon in conversation with outsiders as an expression of individual and collective pride and exclusiveness. In contrast, jargon is seldom used by members of deviant or low-status occupations, in which identification with the work has the potential to degrade.

The dynamics of internal-language use can be extremely subtle and complex, as illustrated in Kemnitzer's (1973) analysis of railroading. The argot of this occupation, having a century of tradition, has evolved at three levels. A formal language is found in the official publications of railroading. For example, the process of relocating a car from behind a locomotive to the front by moving them onto different tracks is described as a "flying switch." In everyday discourse railroaders use a technical language that designates this operation as a "drop." This word is also used in written communication, such as newspapers, union publications. and grievances. A kind of slang or informal language is also used among senior workers, where "flip" or "wiggle" apply.

The different forms predominate in very specific contexts and among specific categories of railroaders:

flip: used in interaction among veterans, or interaction between veterans and officials

drop: used in interaction between veterans and rookies

flying switch: used in interaction between railroaders and officials in *conflict* situations

Informal language dominates in conversations among veteran railroaders and in work-related interaction with officials who have been promoted from the ranks, expressing acceptance and symbolizing equality. Technical language is the usual form between veterans and inexperienced workers. Newcomers are thus constantly reminded of their inexperience and lack of acceptance into the inner circle of senior workers. It is only in conflict situations that formal language surfaces—in conversations between officials and railroaders when rule infractions are at issue, or in formal disciplinary hearings, or during union negotiations. The exaggerated formality of the discourse underscores the status differences.

Language also includes nonverbal *gestures*. Construction workers have an elaborate system of hand signals to communicate among themselves over long distances. One of the most interesting examples of this is the "police officer's stare" (Rubinstein, 1973: 220–21). The authority of the role invests officers with the right to violate the usual norms of eye contact with civilians. Fixed, direct staring is unsettling, borders on rudeness in American society, and, at least among males, is taken as a challenge. But a police officer may do so with impunity. An angry "Who are you looking at?" may be countered with a quiet "You." The stare is not ridicule or an abuse of authority but rather a valuable tool in police work because responses are used in evaluating people in suspicious circumstances. Those who calmly return the stare are judged as having nothing to hide, but failure to meet the glance suggests the need for further investigation. Also judged as suspicious are persons who attempt to withdraw too quickly, for they may be in possession of illegal weapons or drugs. Thus, subcultures may involve a complex repertoire of nonverbal gestures and meanings which must be learned in order to function effectively.

Posture can also appropriately be included as part of the subcultural language of communication. The rigid stance of the soldier and "the stroll" of the street prostitute must be mastered just as surely as the more technical tasks of the jobs. Assuming the proper posture is not unlike donning a costume:

> A (ballet) dancer sits slouched down in a chair with her feet propped up against a window. She arises and walks into the studio. Upon entering, she lifts her head, pulls in her stomach and walks with feet turned slightly outward, glancing in the mirror as she takes her place at the barre. (Hall, 1977:201).

In such instances, posture acts as confirmation of membership in an exclusive occupational group for the individual, colleagues, and the public.

ARTIFACTS

The physical objects utilized in the work process may be called *artifacts*. Included here are tools, work uniforms, and ritual objects. Subcultures define the selection, use, and care of artifacts. Moreover, subcultures invest them with meanings not inherent in their physical characteristics. Some, such as the uniform and badge of the police officer or the hairstyles of corporate executives and popular entertainers, derive their significance from their symbolic meanings. Others, such as the tools of the electrician or the surgeon, play a more direct part in the performance of work tasks, but even these have symbolic meanings. Proper use of artifacts, as subculturally defined, is thus essential to understanding the work, effective performance, and interaction with coworkers. In many instances, appropriate handling of artifacts is a prerequisite to group acceptance.

Tools.   All work requires the use of tools, ranging from the wrenches of a plumber to the scalpel of the surgeon to the word processor of the journalist. Rarely is it merely a matter of picking up an implement and setting to work. There are countless lessons to be learned. Apprentice electricians typically start by carrying an elaborate and disparate array of hand tools (Riemer, 1980). Gradually, extraneous tools are discarded, and those which are retained tend to be of the same brand as that favored by veterans, which is an indication of emersion in the subculture. Apprentices learn which tools are used and how to make one tool take the place of another. Certain brands are perceived as superior by veterans, and adoption of these brands is taken as a mark of technical sophistication.

Policing provides interesting insights into the subculture of tool use. Guns and nightsticks are key ingredients in police work. The nightstick, also called a baton or "the wood" (argot), obviously functions as a weapon, but rookies must overcome natural tendencies and learn effective usage. To raise the stick overhead signals one's intentions and leaves the body vulnerable to a counterblow; short, sharp blows to the knees, elbows, and thighs are the most effective means of disabling a person. Aiming for a person's head is also inappropriate, for the stick can inflict serious injury. Police who persist in the latter tactic earn the disapproval of their peers and are labeled "headhunters."

Equally important is learning the symbolic value of the baton. It is an emblem of authority and a deterrent. As one police academy instructor puts it:

> The most important thing is to always remember to take your stick with you when you get out of your car. . . . You don't always need it but people really respect a stick. They see you coming with it and they think, Oh, oh. (Rubinstein, 1973:278).

The baton's symbolism of implied threat also extends to interaction with coworkers. Even in station-house horseplay, officers seldom use it as a toy. An officer will jab another with a stick only if there is a clear and strong relationship and only in situations where it is impossible to misconstrue the act as a threat.

Police use of handguns is severely circumscribed by department regulations. There are differences among cities, but as a general rule guns are to be drawn and fired only for self-preservation or to bring down a fleeing felon (Rubinstein, 1973). There is obviously a great deal of discretion involved in determining whether the situation calls for the use of the weapon. It is in the making of such decisions and the handling of resulting situations that the subculture is most evident. Anyone who is careless with the weapon (not keeping it pointed down when running, for example) is subject to immediate reprimand by other officers. An officer who reaches for his or her weapon in response to an obscenity or a verbal threat conveys the impression of being unable to control feelings of fear and is likely to be branded "unreliable." Partners who cannot agree upon when a drawn pistol is appropriate will not long work together.

Uniforms.   Distinctive and standardized costumes are components of countless occupations. Soldiers, firefighters, miners, judges, athletes, airline pilots, clergy, prison guards, police, medical personnel, waiters and waitresses, and ballet dancers are among the most readily recognized. A few groups, such as the police, have been able to win a legal monopoly over their display. Then, too, there are what might be called "quasi-uniforms," which are distinctive and standardized variations of more conventional clothing (Joseph and Alex, 1972). Most British architects claim they can identify another member of their profession by outward appearance (Salaman, 1974:101). The usual elements of the architect's costume are grey suit, colored shirt, bow tie, bright socks, and suede shoes or boots. It would thus seem appropriate to classify the three-piece suit of corporate executives in the 1980s, the conservative dark suits and ties of funeral directors, and the jeans and western hats of long-haul truck drivers as uniforms, just as surely as the lab coat of the scientist, for they serve the same functions.

The uniform is, above all else, a symbol of group membership. In dealing with outsiders it serves as visible and unequivocal identification of occupational membership. It thus supports claims of deference and prestige among members of high-status occupations (such as judges and physicians). For others—waitresses, domestics, airline attendants—it symbolizes subservience and inferiority. Uniforms are usually worn by members of occupations that are seeking to maintain some kind of authority relationship with the public. Police, physicians, and guards all depend upon their uniforms to legitimate their authority to control and direct the behavior of others. For example, when police in Menlo Park, California reinstated their traditional blue uniforms in 1977 after experimenting with blue blazers and gray slacks, there was a decline in assaults directed at officers. The same study also showed that citizens responded more positively to the conventional uniforms (Mauro, 1984).

Uniforms are also symbols of subcultural acceptance and membership for the people who wear them. Every individual must earn the right to don the distinctive dress. Prerequisites are usually formal and extensive, as is evident in the case of pilots, physicians, and members of other high-technology fields with extensive educational requirements. This form of control usually resides with the employing organization or the government, but work groups may also control access to uniforms. Miners who demonstrate that they have adopted the group's norms (which are discussed next) are required to adopt the quasi-uniform of the true miner—the orange hard hat must be painted over in some other color (Vaught and Smith, 1980:170).

Grooming.   Even the manner in which people wear their hair can be included as part of the material elements of a subculture. Distinctive grooming is associated with the occupational roles of military officers, police, managers, and rock musicians. Like posture and uniforms, grooming expresses group membership to outsiders, but there is also a more subtle dimension. As Erving Goffman (1961) has noted, hairstyles are an expression of individuality and personality—part of each person's private "identity kit"—and they are perceived in that manner *within* the context of work subcultures. Personal grooming is often interpreted as an outward reflection of underlying personality orientations. Organizational managers rely upon outward manifestations such as hairstyles (along with dress and demeanor) as a clue in judging whether or not aspiring executives have the right attitudes and perspectives for advancement (Kanter, 1977). Rightly or wrongly, senior people associate conservative hairstyles with character traits such as reliability, dependability, stability, and good judgment. The result is the well-known "corporate executive look" found in countless "dress for success" books.

BELIEFS

Shared ideas about the nature of reality may be called *beliefs*. Beliefs define for participants in the subculture the manner in which the world is perceived, experienced, and organized. Symbolic interactionists note that objects, people, and events have no intrinsic characteristics or meanings independent of those created in the process of human interaction. There are multiple realities. Workers, like other groups in a society, develop shared ideas about reality which can differ from ideas prevailing in other occupations.

Beliefs that are assumptions about the nature and functioning of salient components of the work process may be called *knowledge*. This includes beliefs about the physical environment, people (clients or customers), or the work process. "Knowledge" need not be validated by objective evidence. In fact, it may run counter to the best available scientific research. The men and women who work the underground mines commonly hold certain beliefs about the threat of cave-ins. It is felt that rockfalls can be prevented by judicious use of wooden props (Gouldner, 1954). Miners frequently recount stories of narrow escapes made possible by a single prop holding back a rockfall. Moreover, they believe advance warning of cave-ins will be signaled by the sounds of shifting rock. They like to say the roof will "talk to you," providing time for escape (Fitzpatrick, 1980). Mining engineers report that serious cave-ins are unlikely to be prevented by wooden braces, nor are they always preceded by audible warnings. Despite the evidence, miners cling to such beliefs; when they are contradicted by events, miners seem genuinely surprised, which suggests that the beliefs are deeply ingrained.

One of the ways in which "knowledge" is perpetuated is through *myths*, those stories of the legendary exploits of figures from the history of the occupation. Miners usually have elaborate stories of persons who displayed extraordinary strength in preventing cave-ins. In the telling and retelling of these tales, the miners beliefs are validated.

Thus, the importance of beliefs is not in whether or not they can be confirmed by some objective standard; rather they must be understood as a means of molding perceptions, as guides to conduct, and as a justification for behavior. For example, occupations requiring interaction with customers develop *stereotypes*—shared beliefs about the motives and morals of people. This is nowhere more evident than in some (but not all) areas of retail sales, in which newcomers are taught to regard potential customers as con artists who are devious and not too bright—"out to make or save a buck in any way they can" (Miller, 1964; see also Bogdan, 1972). They, in turn, are perpetuated by myths about bad customers. It follows then that this belief will selectively shape perceptions of customers. Salespersons will be sensitive to any act that confirms the belief and will tend to ignore disconfirming behavior. This belief also calls for certain kinds of behavior on the part of the worker in order to be effective. If consumers are ignorant and opportunistic, salespersons must depend upon misrepresentation and deception to make a sale, lending credence to customers' stereotype of the "used-car salesperson."

The internalization of such beliefs provide justification for behavior that diverges from conventional norms of interpersonal conduct. It also frees the individual from feelings of guilt. It is not easy to determine whether such beliefs emerge from collective experience in dealing with people or are a rationalization for manipulative, exploitative behavior.

SUBCULTURAL VALUES

Values are preferences—collective expressions of what is good or bad, important or unimportant, commendable or deplorable. In short, they define goals; professional athletes place great value on winning, construction workers value fine workmanship, and journalists strive for objectivity. Values can probably be best described as abstract and relative priorities (or goals or guidelines) to be employed in making decisions in concrete cases. Because they are abstract, values are often vague formulations. The goals of "covering the news" or "objectivity" pursued by journalists are very general ideals, difficult to define and not easily measured.

CASE STUDY: DECIDING WHAT IS THE "NEWS"

Journalists working for the major American television networks and national news magazines offer an enlightening case study of subcultural values. As Herbert Gans (1979:39ff) argues, the definition of "the news" inevitably reflects the value system of journalism. News reporters are confronted with an endless array of events and occurrences. Some items out of the daily myriad of violence, disaster, conflict, political activities, social causes, and bizarre events are chosen as "newsworthy" and disseminated to the public. The selection of some events as newsworthy (while others are ignored) and the manner in which they are handled led Gans to make inferences about the value system of journalists.

Ethnocentrism.   All other things being equal, domestic events supersede foreign events, even when they are comparable by some objective standards. For example, foreign disasters must be more serious than equivalent American ones; any plane crash in America claiming more than a few lives is likely to receive network coverage, but there must be a substantial loss of life in a foreign crash for it to be newsworthy, unless, of course, Americans are involved. The suggestion is that human lives are not equal. This ethnocentrism is evident in an old British scale of value for measuring the importance of disasters: one thousand wogs, fifty frogs, or one Briton (reported in Gans, 1979:338).

Altruistic democracy.   Journalists generally believe that the public is interested in news of domestic politics (Tuchman, 1972). Therefore, the activities of political figures and governmental bodies are the focus of attention. The activities most likely to become "news" focus on corruption and bureaucratic malfunctioning becuase they violate the ideal of altruistic democracy that "politics should follow a course based on the public interest and public service" (Gans, 1979:43). Hence, nepotism, patronage, log rolling, waste, financial corruption, and exorbitant expenses are newsworthy because they violate the public trust. This helps to explain why political scandals—from Teapot Dome to Watergate—are usually pursued with such zeal.

Responsible capitalism.   Corruption and bureaucratic malfunctioning in business and industry are disapproved, and although the range of tolerance is greater than it is for government, unreasonable profits and exploitation of workers or customers violate the journalists' value system. Thus, the plight of migrant workers is a continuing media issue, as are industrial hazards (such as mine safety and toxic wastes), inferior product lines (such as the controversy over Ford's Pinto in the late 1970s), and the endless cost overruns and the extravagant prices charged by defense contractors in the 1980s.

Small-town pastoralism. The selection and coverage devoted to some apparently minor events suggests a residue of anti-industrialism/urbanism, and an idealization of nature and the small rural community. Small towns in Maine or Vermont that resist urban land developers are news. The media notes with regret the demise of symbols of an idealized pastoral past: the final trip of a steam locomotive, the close of a hand-crafted shoe factory, or the razing of an architectural landmark. The mating habits of pandas in a Washington zoo earn prime-time coverage. Likewise, the failures or urban society—power blackouts, massive traffic jams—are used to underscore the flaws of modern life.

Individualism. The choice of news items is strongly influenced by a concern with individual freedom and autonomy hedged against the encroachments of nature, society, or government. The news pinpoints acts of heroism during disasters, people who conquer nature without harming it (explorers, astronauts, mountain climbers), people who overcome poverty or personal handicaps, and people who resist pressures for social conformity. Stories that dramatize individual rather than group accomplishments are celebrated. For example, the space program is a massive organizational and technological endeavor, but it is the feats and the faces of the astronauts that gain the widest coverage.

Moderation. The idealization of the individual is not without limits. Excesses, and violations of law, mores, or traditional values are met with criticism. It may be subtle, in keeping with the norms of objectivity and neutrality, but it often surfaces in the choice of labels. Protestors become "rioters," those who contest selective service are "draft dodgers" or "evaders," rather than "resisters" or "objectors." Those who maintain extraordinary political, cultural, and religious positions are negatively referred to as "extremists" or "radicals." Endorsing moderation emphasizes maintenance of stability and a preference for evolutionary, as opposed to revolutionary, change.

Gans (1979:206–8) believes that these values are shaped by the complex social, political, and organizational environment of modern journalism. In part they are a form of self-protection, for acting as advocates for extremist positions would be likely to open journalists to criticism, and they are aware of the repressive measures taken against the press in other times and places. Acting as a watchdog over responsible government and business may be traced to their historic role as the fourth estate. Other values may be extensions of attributes they themselves desire in their work. Individualism in others may be celebrated because it is that to which they aspire—freedom from unnecessary editorial and governmental control.

SOCIAL NORMS

Subcultures invariably involve expectations—*norms* of conduct appropriate for members of the occupation or the work group. One category of norm deals with the *technical* aspects of work by providing "unofficial" but accepted ways of doing the job. Included here are norms defining the pace and sequencing of work, levels of acceptable output and quality, and the like. Subcultural norms may contradict formal descriptions, requirements, and rules. For example, it is the common and accepted practice in most organizations for work to trail off and stop somewhere between 15 and 30 minutes before the official quitting time. Technical norms reflect collective adaptations to the complex demands of the work situation—the pressures of time, uncertainty, limited resources, and role conflict.

In a public defender's office, Sudnow (1965) encountered the concept of "normal crimes," which illustrates how prosecutors and public defenders evolved norms of plea bargaining to enable them to handle an impossible caseload, yet ensure "justice." Certain defendants were allowed to plead guilty to lesser offenses than those with which they were originally charged. To qualify for this, public defenders selectively organized and classified the events to determine whether they fit a normal pattern. Molesting a minor, for example, has a statutory definition, but in determining whether the case qualified as eligible for a plea bargain, other informal rules applied—namely, did it conform to the standards of a "typical case"? The typical child-molesting case involved middle-aged strangers or lower-class fathers, a bad or unsatisfactory marriage, mild touching or fondling without actual physical penetration, and multiple instances of the same offense. More serious sexual crimes against children did not receive such lenient treatment. But if these factors were present—although legally irrelevant—the defendant was allowed to plead guilty to the lesser crime of loitering around a school yard, although the crime may actually have taken place elsewhere. A young and inexperienced public defender who objected to this classification was admonished, "Fella, you don't know how to use that term; he might as well have 'loitered'—it's the same kind of case as the others."

These now discarded subcultural rules for "normal crime" were apparently developed by public defenders as a means of achieving their goals without without violating their sense of justice. It enabled them to deal with an impossible case load, and by guaranteeing a guilty plea, they were assured that the defendant would not escape retribution by being found innocent in a trial. The punishment for the reduced charge was a penalty deemed appropriate to the defenders' perception of the seriousness of the crime and the history of the criminal. This subcultural rule indicates not that they condoned the crime, but merely that they were aware of the vagaries of the legal process, and they evolved this system to ensure that defendants would not escape punishment.

A second category of norms define appropriate behavior as it relates to coworkers. *Interpersonal norms* proliferate whenever the conduct of any one worker impacts other workers. Most work involves some degree of interdependence, but it is most pronounced when the tasks involve shared danger (as among miners or police officers) or when cooperation is essential (teamwork in operating rooms or airplane cockpits). The primary function of interpersonal norms is to ensure predictable, reliable, dependable behavior.

The subculture of miners again aptly illustrates a normative system in an occupation in which predictability and reliability are paramount because of the hazards. Shared danger is inherent in the very nature of the work; the regular use of heavy equipment and explosives in cramped quarters, combined with the ever-present threat of cave-ins, floods, and toxic fumes. Irresponsible behavior by one worker can easily endanger the lives of others. Miners' norms are thus aimed at ensuring behavior and attitudes that reduce the risks and instill cooperative reactions in crisis situations.[2]

"Act responsibly."   Individuals are expected to display mature, responsible demeanor in the face of the everyday annoyances of the job—cables snapping, explosives failing to detonate, equipment failures. Outbursts of anger, panic, and frustration are interpreted as a sign of inability to manage emotions. "If you ever (get the warning) don't panic. Just get out as fast as you can, but don't lose your head." Loss of control suggests the possibility of "doing something crazy," which could cause harm. A more important function may be to teach miners to react calmly in a crisis, when dependence on others for assistance is imperative.

"Act with moderation."   Miners are expected to avoid both excessive risk and excessive safety. The work is admittedly dangerous, and management exerts pressure to maximize output, which can lead to miners' taking shortcuts with safety in order to produce more ore. But, they are warned, "These contractors get in a hurry, they get hurt." However, rigid adherence to considerations of injury will slow the production process. "You couldn't make a dime if you're always going to be safe," observes one miner. "You've got to do some dangerous things." An example that illustrates the compromise between safety and risk is the practice of storing explosives and blasting caps together below ground, a clear violation of safety rules. It is deemed acceptable because it expedites the work cycle and because it is believed that caps will not detonate unless struck with powerful force. (This also illustrates how norms and beliefs interact.) Explosives and caps must be separated in other situations, such as moving equipment down a shaft, because it is recognized that the potential for an accident is greater in such cases.

"Accommodation to personal fears."   Miners value the ability to overcome fear, but this norm imposes limits by allowing for individual idio-

---

[2]This analysis is adapted from Fitzpatrick, 1980. All quotes are from that source, except as otherwise noted.

syncrasies. Miners must respect coworkers' fears of specific situations or tasks. As one explains, "(We all) have hang-ups, . . . myself, I don't like to load holes with prell (explosives). It scares me. . . . If a guy doesn't want to do something 'cause he thinks it is dangerous, they don't make him." A certain logic and an implicit understanding of psychology underlie this prescription. Fear makes people nervous and careless, which increases the risk of an accident.

"Informal cooperation."   Probably the key element in the miners' code is the obligation to assist others and the right to call upon others for help. This is a general (not specific) norm of reciprocity. Workers are expected to be available to aid those who have fallen behind schedule, or tire, or are in a precarious position. They do this in anticipation, not that *that* specific miner will repay the favor, but rather that *any* other miner can be relied upon to return the favor at any time in the future. This norm engenders a cooperative spirit which enhances everyone's safety, and can be counted on in the event of a real disaster.

Adherence to this norm is a prerequisite to acceptance into the mine subculture. And miners withhold their cooperation as a means of showing their disapproval or, in more extreme cases, as a way of expelling the unreliable. When asked how they cope with a consistently careless worker, the reply was, "We make it so hard for him he quits. . . . We don't help him even when he needs it. We don't talk to him." (Gouldner, 1954:134).

"Look out for the other fellow."   Miners must not only assist coworkers as the occasion arises, they also have the obligation to actively protect the welfare of other members of the subculture. The obligation is first to one's partner, then to the novice miner, then to the rest of the crew, and finally to miners on other shifts. Thus, miners must be sensitive to threats to the safety of the persons digging next to them and also to the people on the next shift. Miners will never leave a dangerous situation unattended at the end of a shift, for it could endanger the next, unsuspecting worker.

This norm enables the group to transcend personal animosity among miners. It is enforced even among those who personally dislike one another; thus the concept of safety is isolated from the potentially disruptive influence of personality conflicts. To be sure, partners who are unable to get along will eventually be separated, but they will actively protect one another as long as they must work together.

RITUALS

Emile Durkheim was among the first social scientists to become sensitive to the role of ritual in group situations. At a strictly behavioral level, *rituals* are standardized ceremonies usually involving the manipulation of some symbolic objects. Rituals are most commonly associated with religious activity; take, for example, baptism, marriage, and communion. The key to understanding the purpose of the ritual obviously is to be found not in the overt behavior, although strict conformity is important, but rather in the act of participating in the ritual and in the ideas, values, and beliefs symbolized by the conventionalized behavior. Rituals are an integral part of many subcultures and serve important functions for the members.

Magic. Magic is based on the premise that performance of a ritual will produce control over unpredictable events. In everyday language, such practices have connotations of "superstition" and "luck." Baseball magic is evident in the unwillingness of players to mention the fact that a pitcher has a "no-hitter" in progress, or in the practice of wearing the exact same uniform (sometimes without washing it for fear of washing out the luck) during a winning streak. The little good luck charms that countless players have do not qualify as subcultural because they are idiosyncratic rather than shared.

Situations of high risk or unpredictability foster the emergence of magic and consequently are most commonly found in occupations such as fishing, athletics, mining, and lumbering—any occupation in which workers perceive themselves as at the mercy of unpredictable forces or unusual danger. Magic has meaning only within the subculture.

Solidification rituals. Everyday interaction among workers is frequently punctuated by apparently trivial or frivolous activity. Donald Roy's (1960) description of the elaborate daily routine of machine operators in a clothing factory has become a classic. At midmorning, one worker, Sammy, announced "peach time" before sharing his fruit with other operators. A coworker named Ike complained of the quality of the fruit, leading to prolonged banter between the two. About an hour later, Ike stole a banana from Sammy's lunch box and yelled "banana time" before eating it, which led to prolonged denunciations by Sammy and another worker. Ike later retaliated by opening a window, causing a draft on Sammy. Still later in the afternoon, Ike and another worker took a break for a snack of pickled fish provided by Ike. Sammy was not invited to share it. Finally, late in the day, the workers took turns buying cold drinks and making the trip to the vending machine. What is unusual about this interaction is that it was repeated with unvarying regularity. Every day, Ike shared a peach, stole a banana, opened the window, and ate pickled fish!

The activity clearly had significance and meaning to members of the work subculture that they themselves may not have planned or even understood. Roy has argued that the rituals served to relieve the monotony of their dreadfully boring and repetitive jobs. These verbal byplays were an excuse for momentary interruptions of the routine and provided bench-marks for measuring the passage of time. But there are also the pleasures of sharing a joke and feelings of camaraderie, of being a member included in group-based activities, that serve to create and maintain a sense of solidarity.

Many rituals in traditionally male occupations center on physical punishment and have sexual connotations. Many miners' rituals involve the invasion of the genital area of the "victim," which can only be accomplished by the group physically restraining the person. One social function is, no doubt, to reemphasize the primacy of the group over the individual in a highly dangerous setting, but it is also a test of the American version of masculinity and is generally understood in that context by the participants (in other words, "men" are expected to "resist like a man" and "take it like a man"). Women miners who are subjected to the same ritual, but who are not members of the male subculture, are likely to be degraded and violated by the experience. At the same time, men are unlikely to be able to under-stand such responses. This is but one of the many subtle problems inhibit-ing the entry of women into nontraditional occupations.

Rites of passage.   An integral part of subcultural ritual is the initia-tion ceremony. This ceremony has been identified as a *rite of passage* be-cause it marks the transition (or passage) from "outsider" to accepted mem-ber of the group (Van Gennep, 1960). Rites of passage may be either simple, brief acts or complex symbolic ceremonies. Among paratroopers, the fifth successful jump culminates with the platoon sergeant rolling the trainee's chute, placing it in the truck, and extending a handshake (Weiss, 1967). For miners, it involves being held down and spanked with a clip board (Vaught and Smith, 1980). Admission to the subculture of construc-tion work is no more than the simple act of including the newly accepted member in the horseplay and joking relationships of the group (Roy, 1954; Graves, 1958).

Some ceremonies are rich with imagery and meaning. The initiation of male smokejumpers (forest service fire fighters who parachute into the fire area) is such a rite of passage (McCarl, 1976). Those who successfully complete a month of rigorous physical conditioning and training qualify for actual practice jumps from a plane. Late in the night before the first jump, rookies are dragged from their beds, taken into the woods, stripped, bound with plastic tape, and doused with soapy water followed by a spray of fresh water. After the rookies are released, the same ritual is turned upon senior smokejumpers.

Each element in the initiation has symbolic meaning. The individual's nakedness is that of a newborn infant, here representing rebirth in a new role. It is also the imagery of a corpse, indicating the demise of an earlier phase of life. The helplessness in the face of powerful external forces (fire, nature) connoted by nakedness is further reinforced by the binding, which is done with a nylon filament tape used in all phases of fire fighting. Cleansing with soap and water suggests baptism and preoccupation with the suppression of fires with water. Finally, the rookies' reliance upon their friends to set them free at the conclusion of the initiation emphasizes dependence upon the cooperation and assistance of other members of the group.

Rites of passage can serve many functions for both the group and the individual. For the smokejumper they reemphasize group values and norms (for example, accepting harassment with grace evidences self-control in difficult situations) and facilitate the creation of a self-image as a smokejumper. Possibly the most important activity in the ceremony is the turning of the initiation back on the senior fire fighters, which symbolizes group acceptance and a shared fate. Rituals are also functional for other members of the subculture. Participation reaffirms group values, and sharing the experience promotes solidarity among members.

Ritual of naming.   The ritual of naming is a subtle and virtually universal process within subcultures. Subculture argot almost always has a designation for the inexperienced and uninitiated. Many are occupation-specific (miners are "snowbirds," steelworkers are "punks") but others are merely adaptations of conventional terminology connoting a lack of experience (for example, "rookie," "bird," "boy," or "girl"). To be freed from such appellations symbolizes acceptance. An extension of this practice is the bestowal of nicknames, such as were found in one coal mine: Possum George, Alice (for a male), Maggot Mouth, Plunger Lip, Hook Nose, Grandma, and Big Bertha Butt (Vaught and Smith, 1980). Nicknames have meaning only within the work context, and symbolize group acceptance.

Rites of expulsion.   Scattered subcultures also have ritualistic ways of dismissing the deviant. Rites of expulsion appear to be limited to very tightly knit occupations that have stringent requirements. For example, a paratrooper may resign at any time because it is a voluntary assignment, but to quit is to admit failure and, more importantly, to reject the group and its values and goals. Those who quietly indicate a desire to drop out are immediately sent to another outfit, sometimes without being given time to pack. Members of the group immediately shun them. Those who quit in front of other recruits are exposed to public humiliation. The paratrooper-unit patch is ripped from the uniform and the laces of the jump boots are cut (Weiss, 1967), thus symbolically stripping individuals of membership and labeling them a disgrace to the uniform and what it stands for to those who remain.

CONCLUSION

Subcultures can exert a powerful influence upon individuals, shaping the way they perceive and experience their world and how they behave in it. Those who fail to master the subculture may be destined to forever remain "outsiders." Some subcultural elements are found in virtually every stable work group. Most notable is the quota restriction uncovered among the Hawthorne workers, which turns out to be not at all unusual and can be found flourishing among industrial workers in every conceivable setting. In fact, it was this very practice (then called "soldiering") among others that started Frederick W. Taylor (1911) along the path toward "scientific management." The more fully developed and integrated subcultures are most likely to be found in a more limited range of occupations. There seem to be several factors that stimulate their emergence and elaboration and that contribute to their survival.

Interdependence.   Occupations in which the performance of individuals is dependent upon the active cooperation and collaboration of others place a premium upon predictability and reliability. In work such as policing, music, or team sports, a successful endeavor is built upon the contribution of every performer. In such instances, individual motivations must be suppressed in favor of the interests of the group.

Uncertainty.   Uncertainty in the form of shared danger or the inability to control the environment is also likely to promote the emergence of work subcultures. The high-risk occupations, such as police work, mining, fire fighting, the military, and high steel construction trades, are all characterized by strong subcultures emphasizing group solidarity and conformity to collective expectations. It is in these subcultures that failure to conform to group expectations produces social isolation and powerful pressures designed to expel the unreliable.

Isolation.   Work situations that isolate members from the larger society separate them from competing social contacts and enhance the importance of the subgroup as a source of recognition, social support, and status. Language and symbols of membership and group solidarity proliferate in such situations, and the threat of expulsion becomes an extremely powerful sanction. Isolation is often simply physical, as in the case of the military or forestry or railroading, where workers are segregated from others by the location of their employment. When there are barriers to social interaction, isolation may be symbolic. The worlds of carnival workers and prostitutes are separated from society by their tarnished images, and police work by a wall of public ambivalence toward authority in a democratic society.

FOUR

Professionalization
and Deprofessionalization

INTRODUCTION: DEFINING THE PROFESSIONS

The term *professional* has several common meanings (see Freidson, 1977). It is frequently used to differentiate between those who earn income from an activity and those who work without any direct monetary remuneration. This distinction separates the paid professional athlete from the unpaid amateur. The label *professional* is employed by the government in labor-force analyses to identify occupations requiring specialized knowledge, skills, or experience. Using this criterion creates a list including accountants, actresses, clergy, musicians, physicians, and surveyors. A third use of the term is as a form of self-identification used by certain occupations seeking to create a positive public image. Truck drivers, realtors, janitors, and domestics have all made claims to the title of "professional."

Sociologists employ the term in still another way to identify occupations enjoying, or seeking to enjoy, a unique position in the labor force of industrialized countries. In this context, the term *professional* is reserved for those occupations that have been able to establish exclusive jurisdiction over certain kinds of services and to negotiate freedom from external intervention and control over the conditions and content of their work (see

Freidson, 1977:22–23). It is thus *self-regulation,* taking the form of monopoly and autonomy, which distinguishes the professions from the great majority of other occupations.

Monopoly. Monopoly prevails when members of a group have exclusive rights to do certain kinds of work. Individuals who lack certification are expressly excluded from these activities. In the United States, with few exceptions, it is only a licensed physician who may prescribe drugs, perform surgery, certify that a child has been born, or certify that a person has died and identify the cause of death. Only a licensed lawyer may represent another person in court or prepare legal documents. Occupations vary in the extent of their monopoly; physicians, architects, and lawyers have control over a wide range of activities, while dental technicians have exclusive jurisdiction over a narrow spectrum of work.

In most instances, monopoly is a legal concept embodied in licensing statutes that are enacted and enforced by the individual states in the United States or by the federal government in other countries. However, monopoly may also be combined with what might be called "voluntary compliance." While lawyers have statutory monopoly over the representation of clients in most courts, it is unlikely that many people would turn to nonlawyers when faced with a criminal prosecution or a major liability claim, even if they could. It is also uncommon for people to rely upon anyone except an accountant to maintain complex financial records or perform audits. Yet this is strictly "voluntary compliance" since there are few legal restrictions that prevent nonaccountants from keeping and interpreting others' financial records.

Autonomy. *Autonomy* refers to freedom from external social control over internal affairs and individual behavior. One dimension involves collective authority to establish and enforce membership criteria. Thus, in most states it is physicians who determine initial admission to practice as well as the minimum standards required for continued certification. Autonomy also involves the discretion to define the content, pace, and scope of their work (Freidson, 1970). It is manifested in interpersonal relationships whenever professionals are tacitly granted the right to handle cases without client interference. In criminal cases, most defendants rely upon their attorney's judgment in the preparation, conduct, and disposition of their cases (Grossman, 1969). Again, as in the case of monopoly, autonomy is a combination of formal (legal) and informal (voluntary) rights.

Neither monopoly nor autonomy is ever without some limits. Many external groups impose limits on the activity of professionals. It has been noted that government regulations, client preferences, and the activities of other occupations constrain professional practice. Therefore, it is important to treat self-regulation as a matter of degree.

THE PROCESS OF PROFESSIONALIZATION

Medicine, law, religion, and teaching have long histories, but the idea of self-regulating professions may be traced to the nineteenth century. Their present organization evolved out of an attempt to accommodate to and fashion a place in the social, political, and economic forces changing the face of industrializing societies. A review of the history of occupations that had achieved some degree of professional status, carried out by Harold Wilensky in 1964, suggests a sequential development progressing through several identifiable stages, some of which can be documented by specific events. Exhibit 4:1 provides a summary of major benchmarks in the evolution of selected professions in the United States. Each event has important symbolic, social, or political meaning in the quest for professional status.

The major events in the professionalization process cluster near the last half of the nineteenth century and the early part of this century, and tend to occur in a particular order. It is during this period that the concept of self-regulation slowly, haltingly became institutionalized (Larson, 1977). Those occupations that have emerged more recently, sensitive to the advantages of professional status, have undertaken a more direct approach and have thus altered and shortened the process.

Origins as a full-time occupation. An obvious first step toward professional status is emergence as a full-time occupation. For definitional purposes, an occupation can be said to originate at the point when poeple begin to earn a livelihood from the work. Those that are marked by a specific innovation can be specified with a high degree of confidence. Chiropractic can be dated from 1895, the year in which Daniel David Palmer formulated principles of skeletal manipulation based on the theory that illnesses may be traced to unrelieved pressure or tension on the nervous system. In a strict sense, Palmer rediscovered and elaborated on medical practices known and used by ancient Greek physicians. Accounting first appeared in the American colonies in 1718, when Mr. Browne Tymms of Boston became the first individual known to maintain the financial records of merchants and shopkeepers (Previts and Merino, 1979:9).

Most occupations emerged without benefit of a dramatic event, however, and hence are more difficult to locate in time. Many evolved as unique occupations by unifying a configuration of tasks that had previously been scattered among members of other occupations. Funeral directors followed such a pattern of growth by synthesizing the functions of embalming technicians, clergy (in charge of bell tolling and grave digging), stable keepers (provision of carriages, hearses), cabinet-makers (building coffins), and midwives or nurses (preparation of the dead for burial) (Mitford, 1963:199). Others evolved by a process of specialization from more gener-

EXHIBIT 4:1 The Process of Professionalization in the United States

	BECAME FULL-TIME OCCUPATION	FIRST TRAINING SCHOOL	FIRST UNIVERSITY SCHOOL	FIRST LOCAL PROFESSIONAL ASSOCIATION	FIRST NATIONAL ASSOCIATION	FIRST STATE LICENSING REQUIREMENT	CODE OF ETHICS
Law	17th century	1784	1817	1802	1878	1732	1908
Medicine (M.D.)	17th century	1765	1779	1735	1847	1780	1912
Dentistry	17th century	1840	1867	1844	1840	1868	1866
Pharmacy	1646	1821	1868	1821	1852	1808	1850
Insurance brokerage	1750s	1927	—	1869	1890	1911	1929
Accounting	1718	1853	1882	1882	1886	1896	1917
Nursing	1790s	1839	1909	1886	1897	1903	1893
Funeral directing	1860s	1874	1914	1864	1882	1894	1884
Psychology	1880s	1888	1888	1892	1925	1945	1952
Optometry	1880s	1892	1910	1896	1897	1901	1935
Chiropractic	1895	1898	—	—	1926	1913	1966

Source: Harold L. Wilensky, "The Professionalization of Everyone?" *American Journal of Sociology*, 70 (Sept. 1964), p. 143. © 1964 by the University of Chicago Press.

al, comprehensive work. Modern pharmacy, as the work of compounding and dispensing drugs, evolved from broader commercial and medical practice. Druggists in the colonial period practiced medicine and dispensed a wide range of products, such as spices, tea, paint, and building materials (Kronus, 1976).

Some occupations, such as law and medicine, predate industrialization, but in a very different form. Until well into the nineteenth century, only a liberal education was required for entry into these fields, and there were no systematic professional curricula or qualifying examinations. In the United States, members of the early professions often lacked even formal training, depending instead on apprenticeships. For example, it is estimated that only 5 percent of all colonial physicians held degrees (Shryock, 1960:9). Their practice was competitive, and the distinction between medicine and other forms of business was vague, as indicated by the extensive litigation by clients protesting fees and colonial legislatures regulating price structures (Shryock, 1960:14).

Specification of a particular year can be misleading because it directs attention to a single event rather than to the context in which that event occurs. New occupations cannot proliferate within a market economy unless there is a demand for the goods and services being offered. Whatever else they may be, "professions were and are a means of earning an income on the basis of transacted services" (Larson, 1977:9). At one level of analysis, the genesis of demand can be traced to impersonal social, economic, and demographic developments in the larger society—the same trends that transformed Western societies from agrarian to industrial. Beginning in the nineteenth century, the proliferation of a broad urban middle class provided a potential market for the skilled services of practitioners in law and medicine (pharmacists, physicians, dentists). Obviously, the needs for health care and legal advice predate the nineteenth century, but demand was generally limited to a small elite who could afford the luxury of these services.

The demands of industrial capitalism fostered the expansion of technical occupations such as engineering, architecture, and information-managing professions (such as accounting). The proliferation of hospitals stimulated the need for a trained staff of nurses. Problems encountered in operating large, complex organizations called for managerial professions (such as hospital administration). Shifting values and perceptions of the motives underlying human behavior later created the need for the counseling professions (psychiatry, psychology, sex therapy, social work). The very complexity of professional expertise can proliferate to a point requiring new specialized occupations to emerge out of work previously performed by general practitioners (consider, for example, physical therapy and dental hygiene).

---

*CASE STUDY: THE PROFESSIONALIZATION OF SEX
THERAPY*

The relatively new role of sex therapist offers a specific illustration of the social and scientific context of an emerging profession. Sex therapists counsel individuals and partners on the physical, psychological, emotional, and interpersonal aspects of sexual relationships. In 1976 there were some 5,000 practicing therapists offering counsel and advice on sexual matters to individuals and couples (Brody, 1976). The income potential is great: The fee for 15 hours of therapy ranges between $2,500 and $4,000 (Lo Piccolo, 1977:64).

Some number of people have probably always felt dissatisfied with their sexual relationships, but the conditions for emergence of a paid occupation dedicated to providing advice was dependent upon certain social changes that occurred in the United States after World War II. One factor was the evolution of new attitudes toward sex and a willingness to openly discuss such matters with others (Lo Piccolo, 1977). Another was the emergence of the belief that sexual relations were not simply recreational or procreational, but rather demanded standards of performance. "Sexual adequacy" became something to be worried about and worked at, as is evidenced by public adoption of terms such as "frigidity" and "impotence" and the proliferation of sex technique manuals. Finally, beginning in the 1960s, meaningful scientific research began to accumulate, culminating in the highly publicized work of Masters and Johnson.

These trends slowly combined to generate a demand for expert advice. Couples first tried self-education and sought advice from physicians, social workers, clergy, and general psychotherapists, but by the 1960s they were willing to turn, in large numbers, to members of a new occupation that was proliferating. Estimates suggested as many as 5,000 sex therapy clinics (Holden, 1974:331). Membership in the new occupation was unrestricted; hence it drew a broad range of practitioners, including those with medical, psychological, and sociological training. In addition, though, people who lacked any formal training in the dynamics of sexuality—masseurs and hairdressers, for example—were known to have established themselves as sex therapists (Brody, 1976). Consequently, more responsible members lobbied for educational credentials and licensing regulations, a clear step toward professional status.

Social conditions can create only the potential for employment. Initial public response to new occupations may range from grudging, reluctant acceptance to outright hostility. The prestige typically enjoyed by modern professions is notably absent in the early stages of development. During most of the seventeenth century, most Americans handled their own law, if they could, which was consistent with the Puritan concept that justice was a theological or moral concept, rather than a legal one. This was compounded by a general suspicion that lawyers encouraged interpersonal disputes as a means of stimulating business for themselves. John Quincy Adams, writing in 1787, articulated a common view of lawyers:

> The mere title of lawyer is sufficient to deprive a man of public confidence . . . (and) prevails to so great a degree that the most innocent and irreproachable life cannot guard a lawyer against the hatred of his fellow citizens (quoted in Lieberman, 1979:47).

Thus, there are pressures upon members to take some action if they hope to expand the market for their services and enhance their social standing.

Expert Knowledge: Establishing Programs of Formal Education

The creation of a training school is usually the first organizational event. Until that point, new recruits are self-taught or are the products of apprenticeship programs under the tutelage of established practitioners. The stimulus for the formation of a training school may originate within the profession or may come from outside groups. Some schools were established by advocates of some new, innovative approach to the work, such as Florence Nightingale and her emphasis on hospital sanitation and hygiene. More typically, it is simply the accumulation of knowledge combined with the uneven quality of apprenticeship programs that provide the impetus for the creation of formal training schools.

Regardless of the stimulus, training schools have important social consequences. Completion of the curriculum serves as certification of special competence. Diplomas symbolize this expertise and are freely displayed. A formal education program thus serves to differentiate members of the emerging profession from the lay public. This was a major distinction during the nineteenth century, when, as late as 1900, less than 8 percent of the adult population had completed high school. The shift in the locus of education from training schools to universities serves to further emphasize claims of special expertise.

Expert knowledge plays a central role in the development of self-regulation. It becomes the basis of claims to both exclusive jurisdiction and freedom from external control. Professionals are able to argue, with some justification, that their special training means that their clients lack the ability to make substantive judgments or qualitative evaluations of professional performance. Clients, because they are relatively "ignorant," are encouraged to accept the professional's authority and advice. It is also appropriate, they point out, considering their expertise, that they alone should be able to provide these services. In short, the group must be able to persuade society that "no one else can do the job, and that it is dangerous to let anyone else try" (Goode, 1969:279).

Expert knowledge does create a genuine gap between members of the profession and the lay public, but it is also evident that professionals intentionally or unintentionally act to maintain the relative ignorance of outsiders. This can take the form of attempts to "mystify" their knowledge through the use of esoteric subcultural argot, or to limit client access to the intricacies of practice. Lawyers have a record of opposition to writing contracts and laws in plain, nontechnical language (Business Week, 1978), and have been reluctant to discuss legal matters with clients (Reed, 1969). A 1930s state bar association's official advice to lawyers illustrates this strategy:

> Get at the client's problem immediately and stick to it. Don't bother to explain the reasoning process by which you arrive at your advice. The client expects you to be an expert. This not only prolongs the interview, but generally confuses the client. The client will feel better and more secure if told in simple straightforward language what to do and how to do it, without an explanation of how you reached your conclusions (Rosenthal, 1974:19).

The Role of Professional Associations

Among the older professions, associations tended to develop at a local (community, metropolitan area, or regional) level, with these units subsequently nominating delegates who met to found national associations. The newer professions—those which emerged after the development of modern systems of communication and transportation—have been just as likely to organize on a national level first. Associations provide a forum for the exchange of ideas and information, but they are also political entities concerned with the organization of the profession and relations with external groups. Once formed, professional associations have consistently pursued specific goals, including self-regulation, educational reform, boundary maintenance, professional-image maintenance, licensing, and creation of codes of ethics. Such activities can be variously interpreted. Advocates argue that they represent sincere efforts to upgrade the quality of professional work and protect the public, while critics claim that they are deliberate attempts to enhance professional prerogatives at the expense of the public and other groups. It is not easy to unravel the motives, but it is possible to describe the activity.

Self-regulation.   Civil authorities have long imposed restrictions on occupations that provide services considered essential. Colonial legislatures were enforcing admission criteria for physicians as early as 1652. In fact, America's first medical society was formed in an unsuccessful attempt to establish the authority to certify physicians (Shryock, 1967:18). The Litchfield Society, composed of thirty Connecticut physicians, petitioned the legislature in 1767 for the right to examine and "license" physicians. The first success occurred later, in New Jersey. Judges of the state supreme court originally held authority to examine physicians, but in 1780 this power was delegated to the professional association. These early attempts do not meet the modern criteria for compulsory licensing since unlicensed practice was neither prohibited nor punished.

Claims for self-regulation center on the issue of expertise. Nonprofessionals—whether clients or governmental regulatory agencies—are portrayed as lacking the knowledge and background to evaluate and judge professional performance. It is only other members who possess this ability.

Educational reform and regulation.   Problems with the nature of professional education have repeatedly been a major factor in the formation of associations, especialy major national associations such as the American Bar Association (Auerbach, 1976), the American Medical Association (Stevens, 1971), and the American Nursing Association (Levi, 1980). The late nineteenth century was a period in which schools of all kinds proliferated. The number of medical schools grew from 100 in 1880 to 160 in 1903 (Larson, 1977:281). Levels of training were uneven at best, and in some cases, clearly substandard. State regulation was weak. This was a special problem in the health fields, where unqualified practitioners represented a real threat to the public. Attempts to improve and standardize professional education led these groups to endorse curricular reform, recommend higher admission standards, and establish programs for the accreditation of schools.

Less altruistic motives may also operate, along with a sincere desire to improve the overall quality of professional practice. It is frequently suggested that the regulation of educational opportunities also serves to restrict the supply of practitioners, reduce the potential for competition for clients, and thus guarantee artificially higher incomes.

Boundary disputes.   The quest for professional status is often marked by controversy over the boundaries between the particular profession's work and that of other occupations. Attempts to gain control over work tasks may be grounded in the professionals' belief that they are better qualified, or may be motivated by a desire to secure the economic and symbolic rewards associated with specific services. These disputes must usually be settled in the state legislatures. The long-standing contest between pharmacists and physicians for the right to prescribe drugs is a prime example of a boundary dispute (Kronus, 1976).

In the colonial period, the tasks of prescribing, compounding, and selling drugs were shared by both physicians and pharmacists (then called apothecaries). During the time of the Revolution, physicians began an effort to regulate pharmacists and limit their right to prescribe drugs, on the grounds that because of their university educations, in contrast to the guild-like apprenticeships of apothecaries, they were better qualified. It is also possible that physicians wished to disassociate themselves from the crass, commercial aspects of drug sales, while retaining the more prestigious task of prescribing. By 1821, those who established the first school of pharmacy accepted the principle that pharmacists should be limited to compounding and selling drugs. The matter was far from settled, however. Improvements in the education of pharmacists enabled the founders of the American Pharmaceutic Association (1852) to adopt a code of ethics that challenged the absolute prohibition against recommending drugs. The code stated that members "should avoid prescribing for diseases when practicable, referring applicants for medical advice to the physician" (Kronus, 1976:29). The growth in the power of the medical profession eventually led to more absolute monopoly by physicians. The pharmacists' 1922 code of ethics reflected this: The pharmacist should make "no attempt to prescribe or treat diseases, . . . even when urgently requested to do so (by customers)." Although far from being permanently resolved, physicians continue to defend this position.

The professional image.   In countless subtle and blatant activities, the associations strive to improve the profession's public image. Primary attention is devoted to elevating professional practice to a level above simple commercialism. Educational reform represents progress in this direction, but it also necessitates a shift in the style and substance of behavior. Consider the following advice to optometrists published during the post–World War I period of professionalization:

> Continuing to remember the public point of view, how are we to enter the professions? The following method is obvious, necessary and somewhat drastic. Let your shops to tradesmen and occupy a private house in a professional quarter. Instead of exhibiting spectacles behind a plate of glass, hang up a plate of brass. Describe callers as patients instead of customers or clients. Require callers to press a bell-push to gain admittance instead of allowing them to walk right in. Transform shops into waiting rooms in which optical apparatus is not displayed, and "sight-testing rooms" into consulting rooms without glass showcases. Let the diagnosis be the main consideration, glasses only remedies for physical deformities, and charges according to the value placed upon services rendered in correcting errors of refraction. Do all this or remain forever a *tradesman*. There can be no half-way between the two (Turville, 1920:109).

Associational formation may be the decisive organizational development in this process. Resistance—whether active or passive—to professional recognition may come from competing occupations, an unresponsive public, or reluctant legislatures and must be overcome. Collective effort is a prerequisite to success in these struggles. Moreover, professional associations have proven to be the moving force in producing ethical codes and securing exclusive jurisdiction through licensing statutes.

Licensing

The official legal rationale for licensing is the protection of the public against unethical and incompetent work, as stated in the 1888 United States Supreme Court ruling upholding exclusive licenses,

> The power of the State to provide for the general welfare of its people authorizes it to prescribe all such regulations as will secure . . . them against the consequences of ignorance and incapacity as well as deception and fraud. As one means to this end it has been the practice of different States . . . to exact in many pursuits a certain degree of skill and learning upon which the community may confidently rely . . . (quoted in Marks and Cathcart, 1974:195).

Licensing laws originate in one of two ways (Cohen, 1973). They may be instituted by civil authorities as a means or protecting the public from the hazards of the incompetent or unscrupulous. The first licensing requirements for lawyers, physicians, and pharmacists were established by colonial legislatures. and vested responsibility for examination in the hands of public officials, probably reflecting the low public opinion of such practitioners. One must remember that colonial medicine was primitive and dangerous during this period and that professional training was unsystematic and unstandardized.

Licensing may also originate at the instigation of members of the profession. In some ways licensing is probably the most important victory in the evaluation of a profession because it grants the profession exclusive jurisdiction supported by the authority in the state. "Voluntary licensing" means that only certified practitioners may use a particular title. This certification by civil authorities has great symbolic meaning, for it implies that licensed professionals have some special expertise that the unlicensed do not possess. (This may or may not be accurate in any absolute sense since unlicensed personnel may have the same or equivalent training, or more practical experience.) The practical value of voluntary licensing is that it may foster an informal monopoly by discouraging the public from using the services of uncertified practitioners.

"Compulsory licensing" formalizes monopoly and utilizes the authority of the state to enforce exclusive jurisdiction. Representatives of the American medical profession had pursued this goal since the seventeenth century but were unable to accomplsih it until the end of the nineteenth century. Innovations in medical science were the decisive factor in enabling them to legitimate claims for exclusive jurisdiction (Kronus, 1976:25–26; Stevens, 1971:39; Shryock, 1960:126–148). The use of anesthetics and antiseptics improved the success of surgical procedures; instruments such as the stethoscope, ophthalmoscope, and thermometer-aided medical examinations; drugs such as morphine and quinine proved to be effective in the treatment of illness; important developments in bacteriology by Koch and Pasteur pointed in the direction of preventative medicine. This allowed the medical societies to stress the increasing need to protect the public from unschooled lay persons and from physicians representing several "unorthodox" systems that were flourishing in America at the time.

By the turn of this century, most states had licensed physicians, pharmacists, attorneys, and dentists. Between 1900 and 1960, licensure was granted to another twenty occupations, including accountants, nurses, realtors, funeral directors, and chiropractors (Roederer and Shimberg, 1980:1). The usual procedure was to vest responsibility for the administration of the licensing laws in a relatively autonomous board composed of members of the profession and having broad authority over internal affairs. Their powers encompassed the preparing and grading of admission examinations, defining qualifications for licensing, establishing standards of practice and behavior, and exercising disciplinary control over practitioners. In short, licensing statutes granted the professions both exclusive jurisdiction over a range of services and broad autonomy in the conduct of professional affairs.

Professional dominance in the political arena is achieved through a combination of circumstances (Begun and Feldman, 1981:11–12). Associations tend, of course, to be active advocates through lobbying, providing legislative testimony, creating advisory committess, and preparing model legislation, and are able to justify their advocacy on the grounds that they have special expertise which deserves protection in the public interest. Their chances of success are enhanced because of the nature and dynamics of the process. Licensing statutes have generally been issues of interest only to the group seeking licensure (with the exception of cases in which competing occupations are actively seeking to protect or defend their own interests). Until more recently, licensing was not considered a salient issue by the legislators or their constituents; hence they were willing to acquiesce to the pressure of professionalizing occupations. In addition, the issues involve technical matters of some complexity, in which legislators are not expert. The information they do have generally originates with the groups involved, not from "objective" sources. It is, in short, a favorable situation for the professionalizing occupation.

Codes of Ethics

Ethical codes define general principles of conduct. As such, they may be traced back in history as far as the Hippocratic oath of ancient Greece. Modern codes of ethics are of more recent origin, having been adopted in the second half of the nineteenth century, and having been subject to periodic revisions since then. These codes define the responsibilities of members to the profession, to clients, to society, and to colleagues. Violation of these standards can lead to expulsion from the profession. Among older professions such as accounting, architecture, engineering, law, medicine, nursing, and optometry, it is the final event in the professionalization process. For new professions, it is more likely to precede licensing, and it has been used as a rationale for licensing.

CASE STUDY: NURSING AND ETHICAL STANDARDS

The origin of codes of ethics in nursing can be traced to the Nightingale pledge, formulated in 1893 at the Farrand School of Nursing in Detroit. Although named for Florence Nightingale, she was not involved in its creation. It exhorts dedication to patient care and demands an exemplary personal life, consistent with nineteenth-century cultural conceptions of womanhood. Nurses are reminded of their role in maintaining the standards of the profession, and the importance of patient confidentiality is recognized.

The American Nurses' Association adopted its first formal code of ethics in 1950. Confidentiality and professional obligations are reaffirmed. Standards of personal behavior are spelled out in much more detail, extending even to the obligation to vote. In item 10, it is noted that professionals do not accept "tips."

The code was revised in 1960, and again in 1976, by which time the personal lives of the members were no longer considered a matter of ethics. The emphasis has clearly shifted to an enumeration of the many facets of quality of patient care.

In almost all cases, codes of ethics follow the establishment of professional associations, for it is these organizations that promulgate and enforce them. Ethical codes usually define responsible behavior in at least four areas: conduct of practice, behavior toward clients, interaction with colleagues, and relationships with allied professions. Codes change in response to changing conditions, but the same four general areas of behavior continue to be singled out for regulation. Codes of ethics serve a number of functions that may or may not reflect deliberate intent by the framers of such documents.

EXHIBIT 4:2   The Nightingale Pledge

I solemnly pledge myself before God, and in the presence of this assembly: to pass my life in purity and to practice my profession faithfully. I will abstain from whatever is deleterious and mischievous, and will not take or knowingly administer any harmful drug. I will do all in my power to maintain and elevate the standard of my profession and will hold in confidence all personal matters committed to my keeping and all family affairs coming to my knowledge in the practice of my calling. With loyalty will I endeavor to aid the physician in his work and devote myself to the welfare of those committed to my care.

Source: Agnes G. Deans and Anne L. Austin, *The History of the Farrang Training School for Nurses.* Detroit: Alumnae Association, 1936, p. 58.

EXHIBIT 4:3   American Nurses' Association, A Code for Professional Nurses

1. The fundamental responsibility of the nurse is to conserve life and to promote health.

2. The professional nurse must not only be adequately prepared to practice, but can maintain professional status only by continued reading, study, observation, and investigation

3. When a patient requires continuous nursing service, the nurse must remain with the patient until assured that adequate relief is available.

4. The religious beliefs of a patient must be respected.

5. Professional nurses hold in confidence all personal information entrusted to them.

6. A nurse recommends or gives medical treatment without medical orders only in emergencies and reports such action to a physician at the earliest possible moment.

7. The nurse is obligated to carry out the physician's orders intelligently, to avoid misunderstanding or inaccuracies by verifying orders and to refuse to participate in unethical procedures.

8. The nurse sustains confidence in the physician and other members of the health team; incompetency or unethical conduct of associates in the health professions should be exposed, but only to the proper authority.

9. The nurse has an obligation to give conscientious service and in return is entitled to just remuneration.

10. A nurse accepts only such compensation as the contract, acutal or implied, provides. A professional worker does not accept tips or bribes.

11. Professional nurses do not permit their names to be used in connection with testimonials in the advertisement of products.

12. The Golden Rule should guide the nurse in relationships with members of other professions and with nursing associates.

13. The nurse in private life adheres to standards of personal ethics which reflect credit upon the profession.

14. In personal conduct nurses should not knowingly disregard the accepted patterns of behavior of the community in which they live and work.

15. The nurse as a citizen understands and upholds the laws and as a professional worker is especially concerned with those laws which affect the practice of medicine and nursing.

16. A nurse should participate and share responsibility with other citizens and health professions in promoting efforts to meet the health needs of the public—local, state national, and international.

17. A nurse recognizes and performs the duties of citizenship, such as voting and holding office when eligible; these duties include an appreciation of the social, economic, and political factors which develop a desirable pattern of living together in a community.

Source: *American Journal of Nursing* 50 (July 1950), p. 392.

Protecting the client public.   The official rationale prompting ethical codes is to guarantee the highest standards of service. In fact, people often define professionalism in terms synonymous with the ideals embodied in these statements. Ethical admonitions demand and, to the extent that they are enforced, guarantee honesty, good character, competence, and dedication to the client's best interests. Such behavior is essential because clients are extremely vulnerable in dealings with experts, whose services cannot be adequately judged. For example, professional codes early in this century

EXHIBIT 4:4   American Nurses' Association Code for Nurses

1. The nurse provides services with respect for human dignity and the uniqueness of the client unrestricted by considerations of social or economic status, personal attributes, or the nature of health problems.
2. The nurse safeguards the client's rights to privacy by judiciously protecting information of a confidential nature.
3. The nurse acts to safeguard the client and the public when health care and safety are affected by the incompetent, unethical, or illegal practice of any person.
4. The nurse assumes responsibility and accountability for individual nursing judgments and actions.
5. The nurse maintains competence in nursing.
6. The nurse exercises informed judgment and uses individual competence and qualifications as criteria in seeking consultation, accepting responsibilities, and delegating nursing activities to others.
7. The nurse participates in activities that contribute to the ongoing development of the profession's body of knowledge.
8. The nurse participates in the profession's efforts to implement and improve standards of nursing.
9. The nurse participates in the profession's efforts to establish and maintain conditions of employment conducive to high quality nursing care.
10. The nurse participates in the profession's effort to protect the public from misinformation and misrepresentation and to maintain the integrity of nursing.
11. The nurse collaborates with members of the health professions and other citizens in promoting community and national efforts to meet the health needs of the public.

Source: *Code for Nurses with Interpretative Statements.* Kansas City: American Nurses' Association, 1976.

prohibited advertising and all other forms of price competition on the grounds that such activities would encourage shoddy and cut-rate service by less principled members of the profession. The American Optometric Association declared

> all advertising of price . . . is fundamentally fraudulent . . . (and) the method of charlatans, whose only purpose is mercenary, and therefore a sinister practice, in that the public is deceived which results in injury to vision and health (Begun and Feldman, 1981:9).

When the early codes originated this was a valid and especially important consideration because of the uneven quality of education and the frequently lax admission standards. Disciplinary committees were established, and in some instances (such as law and medicine), the codes have been incorporated into state legal codes.

Trust-building.   The ethical ideals can also be expected to inspire a special kind of trust which can differentiate the client-professional relationship from other kinds of transactions. In a strict sense, clients employ professionals to provide services, but the norm of *caveat emptor*—let the buyer beware—which typically underlies transactions with television repairers and cab drivers is replaced by the idea of *credet emptor*—let the buyer trust (Hughes, 1963). It is a belief that the client's interests will be paramount, taking precedence over any personal or commercial interests. Trust, combined with special expertise and internal regulation, justifies autonomy, but probably most importantly severs the link between the provision of professional services and the pursuit of economic gain.

Group solidarity. Sections of codes devoted to colleague relations are consistently organized to minimize internal competition and promote solidarity and cooperation. Solidarity is a prerequisite to mobilizing the membership to protect the group from external regulation. It is also vital that members place group interests above personal interests, especially when individual behavior might reflect badly on the entire profession. This objective is usually manifested in direct language; realtors, for example, are warned not to seek "unfair advantage over other realtors and to avoid controversies with other realtors" (Shenkel, 1978:109).

In a less direct way, strictures on advertising and price competition accomplished the same goal (Berlant, 1975:55). Professionals were prevented from competing among themselves for clients by the usual commercial strategies of soliciting clients by advertising or cutting prices . This also reinforces building the element of trust into the client relationship.

It has frequently been alleged that the restriction of advertising raises consumer costs by reducing competition. Economic analysis offers some support for this position. A study of the cost of eye examinations and eyeglasses in cities prohibiting commercial practices by optometrists averaged $94.46, compared with an average cost of $70.72 in less restrictive communities (Bond, et al., 1980:5). There was no appreciable difference in the quality of service in the two situations.

Prestige. The prestige value associated with ethical behavior cannot be overlooked or underestimated. It is clear that advocates of ethics were, and are, sensitive to such considerations, as is evident in this statement from the American Bar Association committee which produced the first national code:

> We cannot be blind to the fact that, however high may be the motives of some, the trend of many is away from the ideals of the past, and the tendency more and more to reduce our high calling to the level of a trade, to a mere means of livelihood, or personal aggrandizement. . . . much as we regret to acknowledge it, we know such men are in our midst, . . . (and) they not only lower the morale within the profession, but they debase our high calling in the eyes of the public (Auerbach, 1976:41).

Formal proclamation of the notion that professional conduct is ethical or moral helps to elevate the prestige of the entire profession.

SUMMARY: THE PROFESSIONAL MODEL

By the 1970s, a number of occupations had moved toward self-regulation, as defined by exclusive jurisdiction over work tasks and freedom from external control. Monopoly took the form of licensing, granted on the grounds of expert knowledge and the need to protect the public from exploitation or abuse at the hands of unqualified practitioners. Autonomy took the form of control over certification and discipline, granted on the grounds that nonprofessionals lack the expertise to evaluate the work of professionals. The interests of the public are assumed to be ensured by peer review and by ethical standards which guarantee competence and the protection of the client. It was the culmination of a process that depended, at least in part, upon deliberate, self-conscious social and political activity.

Professionalization must be viewed as a continuum, upon which occupations are arrayed according to the criteria of monopoly and autonomy. It is a relative term, since no occupation is without some restraints upon its activities. Moreover, the current status of any group is merely one point in a continuous process stretching back into the past and extending into the future, a history characterized by fluctuations in the nature and conditions of work.

One method of measuring professionalization is to examine state licensing laws, which define the parameters of monopoly and the structure of regulation. For purposes of comparative analysis, licensing regulations in the state of Delaware in 1981 are summarized in Exhibit 4:5. Four factors are considered.

Licensing.   All occupations are licensed, but there are two forms of licenses. *Compulsory licensing* limits practice to those certified by the state; unlicensed persons are prohibited from doing certain kinds of work. This is the most comprehensive form of legal monopoly and describes the situation of physicians, dentists, optometrists, pharmacists, and veterinarians in this state and in all others. Significantly less restrictive is *voluntary licensing*, which limits the use of a title (like that of cosmetologist) to persons holding a license, but unlicensed persons are not prevented from working in the field. The value of voluntary licensing is primarily social rather than legal, serving to confirm and symbolize special qualifications when competing with unlicensed practitioners.

Work domain.   The scope of exclusive jurisdiction can be broad or narrow, as illustrated by comparing three professions responsible for vision

EXHIBIT 4:5 The Organization of Occupational Licensing: The State of Delaware, 1981

	MONOPOLY		AUTONOMY			
			Board: Practitioner/Total	Functions Controlled		
Profession	Compulsory Licensing	Work Domain		Admission	Qualification	Discipline
Physician	Yes	*Protected:* investigation and diagnosis of any physical or mental ailment, condition, or disease of any person, living or dead; sale, prescription, suggestion, recommendation of any drug; surgery, medicine, appliance for the prevention, cure, or relief of any symptom, disease, wound, fracture, or deformity *Exceptions:* family remedies; emergency first aid; the application of eyeglasses; massage; ritual circumcision; manicuring; spiritual healing; the licensed work of physical therapists, psychologists, optometrists, pharmacists, chiropractors, cosmetologists, barbers, dentists, oral hygienists, and nurses	11/14	Yes	Yes	Yes
Dentist	Yes	*Protected:* diagnosis and treatment of diseases or lesions of human teeth, jaws, and oral tissues mechanically, surgically, or by radiograms, X rays, or fluoroscopic methods; attempts to correct malpositions; taking impressions for replacement of teeth; writing prescriptions				

(continued)

EXHIBIT 4:5 *(Cont.)*

Profession	MONOPOLY		AUTONOMY			
	Compulsory Licensing	Work Domain	Board: Practitioner/Total	Admission	Functions Controlled Qualification	Discipline
		Exceptions: physicians or surgeons may extract teeth and treat pathological conditions of the mouth, teeth	5/5	Yes	Yes	Yes
Optometrist	Yes	*Protected:* examination and diagnosis of the human eye; prescribing and application of corrective lenses or physical therapy for correction of abnormalities *Prohibited:* use of drugs or surgery during eye examination *Exceptions:* work of physicians	3/3	Yes	Yes	Yes
Podiatrist	Yes	*Protected:* diagnosis and medical, surgical, mechanical, manipulative, or electrical treatment of human foot and leg *Prohibited:* administration of general anesthetic; amputation	4/4	Yes	Yes	Yes
Chiropractor	Yes	*Protected:* locating and removing any interference with the transmission of nerve energy *Prohibited:* use of drugs, surgery, osteopathy, obstetrics, dentistry, optometry, or chiropody	3/3	Yes	Yes	Yes

Occupation	Yes	Yes	Ratio	Yes	Yes
Funeral director	Yes	*Protected:* care, disinfection, embalming, transportation, burial, or cremation of human dead *Prohibited:* receiving commissions from cemetery in connection with the transfer of property; operating a funeral service establishment within confines of a cemetery	5/7	Yes	Yes
Pharmacist/Druggist/Apothecary	Yes	*Protected:* compounding, dispensing, or sale of drugs, chemicals, or poisons upon prescription of physicians, dentists, veterinarians; owning or managing a place of business where such activities are conducted; substitution of generic drugs when permitted by prescriber *Exceptions:* physicians and dentists may compound and dispense medicines; sale of nonpoisonous domestic remedies, patent medicines, or proprietary preparations	5/6	Yes	Yes
Physical therapist	Yes	*Protected:* treatment of any bodily or mental conditions by use of physical, chemical, electrical, or manipulative means only upon prescription, direction, and supervision of licensed physician *Prohibited:* X-ray or radium diagnosis or treatment; cauterization	3/3	Yes	Yes

(continued)

EXHIBIT 4:5 *(Cont.)*

| Profession | MONOPOLY | | AUTONOMY | | | |
| | Compulsory Licensing | Work Domain | Board: Practitioner/Total | Admission | Functions Controlled | |
					Qualification	Discipline
Registered nurse	Yes	*Protected:* the observance, care, and counsel of the ill, injured, or infirm for compensation; the maintenance of health or prevention of illness of others; supervision and teaching; administration of medication as prescribed by a licensed physician or dentist *Prohibited:* diagnosis or prescription of therapeutic or corrective measures *Exceptions:* gratuitous nursing by family, friends, or domestics; nursing services during epidemics or national disasters	5/7	Yes	Yes	Yes
Certified public accountant	Yes	*Protected:* giving opinions on financial statements	4/5	Yes	Yes	Yes
Speech pathologist	Yes	*Protected:* measurement, testing, evaluation, prediction, counseling, instruction, habilitation, or rehabilitation relating to speech development and disorder *Exceptions:* physicians and teachers in schools may deal with speech problems	4/5	Yes	Yes	Yes

Profession		Description			
Real estate broker	Yes	*Protected:* negotiation to (or actual) purchase, sale, lease, rental, or exchange of real estate for others for compensation *Exceptions:* owners, leasors (and their employees), attorneys, or executors may engage in real estate transactions	5/5	Yes	Yes	Yes
Oral hygienist	Yes	*Protected:* removal of calcific deposits and stains from teeth; instrumental examination of teeth for cavities; applying preventative chemicals to the teeth *Prohibited:* operations on hard or soft tissue; working without the direction, supervision of a licensed dentist	0/5	Yes	Yes	Yes
Insurance agent	Yes	*Protected:* solicitation and negotiation of applications for insurance or annuity contracts on behalf of an insurance company; the right to earn compensation from the insurance company	None	No	No	No
Securities broker-dealer	Yes	*Protected:* effecting transactions in securities for others or self	None	No	No	No
Licensed practical nurse	Yes	*Protected:* care, in return for compensation, of ill, injured, infirm under the direction of a registered professional nurse, physician, or dentist	2/7	Yes	Yes	Yes
Cosmetologist	No	*Protected:* none	4/5	Yes	Yes	Yes

care. Ophthalmologists (MDs), members of a medical specialty, have the broadest monopoly; they may perform vision examinations, prescribe optical aids, diagnose and treat eye diseases, prescribe drugs, and perform surgery. Optometrists (ODs), graduates of optometry schools, may only perform examinations and prescribe optical aids. Opticians may grind prescribed lenses and fit and adjust eyeglasses. There is a clear hierarchy here. As a rule, the most successful monopolies are those most broadly and generally drawn, as in the case of law.

Another indication of successful monopoly is the exclusion of self-help or services performed by lay (unlicensed) persons. Funeral directors, for example, have exclusive rights over the care of the dead; neither friends nor relatives can legally engage in any such care. In contrast, registered nurses, as an occupation, control physician-prescribed care and medication administration, but uncompensated nursing services by family, friends, and even domestics such as housekeepers are allowed. Another exception is nursing care during emergency situations. Thus, nurses have not been able to make themselves indispensable.

Domination of regulatory boards. One form of autonomy is professional control of the agencies or boards responsible for the administration of licensing statutes. Domination prevails in those cases in which the profession has exclusive representation (podiatry, for example) or majority membership (as is the case in pharmacy). Minority membership (as in licensed practical nursing) or nonrepresentation (as in securities brokerage) suggests external control over the regulation of the group.

Functions. A second element of autonomy focuses on the functions under the jurisdiction of this board. Self-regulation is greatest when professionally controlled boards have responsibility for establishing qualifications, granting admission, and internal discipline, as is the case with physicians. External control is greatest when any or all of these functions are under the control of some other state agency, such as the Securities Commissioner.

Applying these criteria suggests a ranking of occupations along a continuum of professionalism ranging from dentists, physicians, and lawyers at one extreme to licensed practical nurses, realtors, and cosmetologists at the other. Those most highly professionalized enjoy a broad (and generally unrestricted) monopoly and wide latitude in the conduct of professional affairs. The least professionalized have special titles and state-recognized certification but are without exclusive jurisdiction or subject to external regulation, or both. This does not mean that the least professionalized have no influence upon the legislatures in matters that concern them; it means merely that they have been unable to institutionalize their positions.

DEPROFESSIONALIZATION: THE EROSION OF MONOPOLY AND AUTONOMY

Professional dominance evolved over a period of time extending from the nineteenth century into the twentieth century, probably culminating in the 1960s and 1970s (see Larson, 1977; Starr, 1982). However, a variety of social, political, and economic changes have combined to significantly alter the environment that facilitated the emergence and dominance of the modern knowledge-based professions, and modified the professions themselves.[1] Some changes reflect the long-term trends, while others are of more recent origin. These changes have disrupted the internal structure of the professions, challenged institutionalized relationships with clients and civil authorities, and highlighted discrepancies between professional ideals and actual practice. The result has been a weakening of traditional claims to special privilege. This, in turn, has articulated the process of *deprofessionalization*, which may be described as the erosion of autonomy and monopolistic privileges. All professional occupations are exposed to these forces and are affected by them to a greater or lesser extent, although some of the most dramatic changes can be illustrated by focusing upon the experiences of the legal profession in America.

A series of developments both in the larger society and within the professions have contributed to the deprofessionalization of law. Internal trends include changes in the nature of the knowledge base, the composition of the profession, and employment patterns. External trends include changes in the client population, consumerism, and encroachment by other occupations.

Narrowing of the competence gap. The concept of the expert professional was institutionalized during a period when the general educational attainment of the population was relatively low, and when specialized training could produce an exclusive cadre of learned professionals. This discrepancy, labeled a *competence gap* by Parsons (1970), has been eroded by the rising educational level of the population (Haug, 1975). It must be remembered that at the turn of the century, less than 8 percent of the population had graduated from high school, compared to a current rate of over 70 percent. Education can mean greater sophistication about professional activities, some actual sharing of the intricacies of professional expertise, and greater skepticism about the certainties of professional practice (Wilensky, 1964). Members of the public have become more knowledgeable about their rights and about the kinds of services to which they are entitled. Moreover, the courts have mandated the concept of "in-

---

[1]This approach was originally developed in Robert A. Rothman, "Deprofessionalization: The Case of Law in America." *Work and Occupations*, 11 (May 1984), 183–206.

formed consent," and the threat of malpractice for violation of these norms seems to have encouraged professionals to actively involve clients in the process. This new relationship represents a challenge to the idea of unquestioned professional authority. For example, a growing public awareness of the basic principles of nutrition and simple pharmacology seems to have weakened the expert role of the physician in the areas of diet and the treatment of insomnia and anxiety. It has also become more difficult to claim exclusive control over the handling of client problems and to demand trust and passive acceptance of professional judgment. A recent study of personal injury cases involving predominately well-educated clients confirms this: Over one-third either sought a second legal opinion or made active demands about the conduct of their cases (Rosenthal, 1974:31).

Routinization of expert knowledge.   Concurrent with the public's increasing knowledgeability have been internal changes in the body of knowledge upon which the professions are founded. As knowledge and practice accumulate, some tasks have become so well understood and predictable that they are susceptible to routinization and standardization (Toren, 1975). Services that had once depended upon esoteric knowledge and professional judgment are reduced to simple, straightforward procedures. This is the problem that confronted community pharmacists in the 1950s and 1960s, when emergence of standard dosages and bulk packaging transformed them from compounders of drugs to dispensers of prepackaged products (Denzin, 1968).

Many of the tasks ordinarily handled by lawyers qualify as routine. This has long been true of most residential property transfers, wills, and small claims litigation; more recently, uncontested no-fault divorce and personal bankruptcy can be added to the list. All involve simple procedures and utilize preprinted forms, although their basic nature had generally been obscured from public view by the mystification of the legal process. This was first brought to wide public attention by the publication of Norman Dacey's 1967 best-seller *How to Avoid Probate*, which contained several hundred pages of forms and instructions for the preparation and handling of wills. It should be noted that the book met with strong opposition from the organized bar, which was apparently sensitive to its implications. The New York County Lawyers Association sued to prevent publication on grounds that Dacey was engaging in the unauthorized practice of law, and the case reached the highest state court before he won publication rights (Lieberman, 1979:124). Many other "do-it-yourself" legal manuals have followed, and in 1986, one firm began marketing software that enables people to compose wills at home on their personal computers (Lewyn, 1985:4B).

The result is that many lay persons are now undertaking tasks previously reserved for professionals, thus informally narrowing the range of exclusive jurisdiction. One instance is the trend toward self-administered law. It has been estimated that 20 percent of all divorces in California in 1976 were carried out without the aid of an attorney (Cavanaugh and Rhode, 1976:10). The same situation can be observed in the health field, in which the market for consumer health-aid products exceeded $100 million in 1985, and might reach $500 million by 1990 (Bauer, 1985). Included are devices such as cancer screening kits, blood pressure monitoring devices, home pregnancy tests, and stethoscopes sold in retail stores and by mail. Professionals and public health officials are concerned that consumers will not use these devices properly or will misinterpret the results. There is also the danger that reliance upon self-help products may delay consumers from seeking expert help beyond the point when it is required. Recent advances in electronic data processing have been it possible to further routinize a wide range of activities (Haug, 1977). The full text of federal legislation, and state and Supreme Court decisions are stored on disk, indexed, and quickly retrievable. This significantly reduces the resources required for legal research, but the more significant implication is that it opens the previously esoteric and complicated area of legal research to anyone with access to a computer terminal. There has also been experimentation with computer-generated legal documents such as wills, complaints, and trusts, which are automatically completed when case-specific data are entered. Preliminary screening of prospective jurors has also been partially computerized. Perfecting such information has the potential to significantly reduce reliance upon legal advice concerning prospective litigation.

Developments in the routinization of legal expertise threaten to reduce some aspects of the practice of law to the status of mere clerical work, not a condition likely to justify the advantaged position of the profession since self-regulation and autonomy were founded upon a base of specialized competence. The standardization of knowledge may also narrow the scope of their monopoly by opening legal data to bankers, realtors, and accountants.

Specialization.   Not all components of expert knowledge are becoming standardized; a countertrend is the expansion and proliferation of esoteric new knowledge. Expansion generates pressure toward internal specialization (Freidson, 1977:27). It becomes increasingly difficult for the generalist to assimilate and keep abreast of developments in all areas of the field. As a consequence, specialties have begun to emerge on a large scale, first informally as individual adaptations and later as formally recognized subfields with their own curricula and certification criteria. Specialization has the potential to create internal divisions and threaten the integrity of the group. Practitioners serve different classes of clients, depend upon different skills, and have different objectives. Internal stratification based on income, task, prestige, or type of client may emerge. In such a situation, it is more difficult to maintain normative, cognitive, and attitudinal consensus.

Specialization within the legal profession began in the late nineteenth century. An urban elite of advisers and counselors to corporate and financial interests became differentiated from general practitioners, who continued as generalists handling a broad range of legal matters ranging from real estate transactions, criminal law, and personal injury to family law (divorce, wills) and small claims (Handler, 1967:4–5). Esoteric areas, such as patents, trademarks, and admiralty, were the only nineteenth-century exceptions. More precise specialization in these areas, along with newer areas such as regulatory law, tax law, and labor law, grew slowly until the process was accelerated by the proliferation of government activity, especially after World War II. Over 40 percent of American lawyers recently defined themselves as specialists (Heinz and Laumann, 1983).

The American Bar Association acknowledged de facto specialization as early as 1953, but attempts at formal recognition and regulation failed for two decades. The first specialty certification plan was implemented in California in 1973, and most state bars are now at least considering such plans. It appears that the prolonged resistance to this development centered on its potential for disrupting group solidarity (Fromson, 1977). It was argued that specialization would create competition between generalist and specialist, and generalists expressed the fear that claims of specialized competence would downgrade their role and stature. Formal specialization has now become a reality and can be expected to contribute to greater diversity within the profession.

A study of the Chicago bar suggests the impact of specialization (Heinz and Laumann, 1983). Specialty is related to the type of clientele (socioeconomic status), character of practice (routine versus complex), type of practice (solo versus firm), prestige within the profession (with divorce at the bottom and securities at the top), and income. This study offers some confirmation of the fear earlier expressed by some segments of the profession that specialization would accelerate the decline of homogeneity within the profession. Research on other professional groups suggests that such segmentalization is associated with a low level of effectiveness in dealing with legislatures (Begun and Feldman, 1981).

Consumerism.   It was during the 1960s that consumerism flourished as a broadlybased social movement. Allegations of consumer fraud, abuses, and unfair trade practices became the subject of wide public discussion. The origins of this movement can be traced to Rachel Carson's 1962 attack on the irresponsible use of pesticides, *Silent Spring,* or to Ralph Nader's 1965 exposé of the auto industry, *Unsafe at Any Speed.* In fact, these were merely two of a series of events serving to highlight problems facing the public—many of which implicated the professions. Jessica Mitford, for example, publicized allegations of misleading practices and fraud in the funeral industry in *The American Way of Death* (1963). The American Medical Association was engaged in organized opposition to national health insurance at a time when the health-care problems of the poor were a major public issue (Stephens, 1971). The organized bar opposed "no-fault" auto insurance during a period of soaring repair costs (Green, 1976). Huge malpractice settlements suggested widespread undetected professional incompetence. One major consequence of these developments was to stimulate public awareness of the potential for narrow self-interest on the part of the professions and the need for new and closer scrutiny of professional performance.

Individual consumers, consumer groups, state legislatures, and the federal government began to scrutinize the professions and challenge traditional prerogatives. A suit initiated by a private individual challenging that legal fee schedules constituted illegal price-fixing was won by a unanimous vote in the United States Supreme Court (Goldfarb versus Virginia State Bar, 1975). The Federal Trade Commission and the Justice Department, after a long history of noninvolvement in the affairs of the professions, turned activist in the late 1970s. The Justice Department filed suit against the American Bar Association in 1976, charging that the advertising provisions of the ethical code violated federal antitrust laws. Two years later, the Supreme Court outlawed Arizona's prohibition against advertising the fees lawyers charged clients for routine legal services (Bates versus State of Arizona, 1977). In both instances the Court intervened in areas previously left to self-regulation within the profession. Possibly more significant in the long run is the fact that the Court affirmed that the practice of law was a form of "commerce," thus effectively weakening the crucial symbolic separation from other forms of market exchange traditionally used to justify the concept of *credet emptor*.

Encroachment by allied professions. Some professions have established exclusive jurisdiction over an area of work only after confrontation with other professions laying claim to the same activity, as was the case with the struggle between pharmacists and physicians for control of the right to prescribe drugs. The professional monopoly is tenuous, and must constantly be protected from encroachment by competing groups.

The 1970s and 1980s have witnessed a proliferation of aspiring professions seeking to enhance their own prerogatives and rewards by expanding into areas previously dominated by existing or more established professions. These groups have employed the same tactics that were successful for the very professions they now challenge. Professional associations are formed. Specialized expertise and training are emphasized. Codes of ethics are promulgated, and there is a push for state licensing. This phenomenon has been most pronounced in the field of health care, in which groups such as nurse practitioners, physical therapists, clinical pharmacists, and midwives, which had had narrowly prescribed and subordinate roles in the patient-care system, have sought to win the right to do work formerly reserved for the established professions. For example, in 1986 Florida's pharmacists gained the right to prescribe 30 different medicines for the treatment of minor illnesses, thus encroaching on the monopoly of M.D.s (Du Bois, 1986).

CASE STUDY: DENTISTS VERSUS DENTURISTS

A case of successful encroachment is provided by the case of "denturists" in Oregon (Rosenstein, et al., 1980; Waldman, 1980). Dentists have traditionally had a monopoly over the provision of dental plates and related devices, although the dentures were actually constructed by "dental technicians," who followed a written prescription provided by the dentist. It was the dentist who examined and diagnosed the patient, took bite impressions, and inserted the dentures. For a number of years, technicians in low-income areas had been illegally providing dentures to clients who could not otherwise afford them. Beginning in the 1970s, some technicians began to organize, renamed themselves "denturists," and lobbied for legalization and licensing. The Oregon Dental Association successfully opposed the "illegal dentistry movement," arguing that denturists lacked the training necessary to provide comprehensive oral health care and thus jeopardized the health of the public. Eventually, denturists—supported by consumer groups—were able to place the issue on the ballot and win a statewide referendum. Since 1980, denturists who have completed a two-year course have been able to provide dentures directly to clients.

This type of intrusion upon the activities of established professions, which is being repeated on many fronts, is successfully narrowing the legal monopoly of the established professions. For the legal profession, competition has traditionally come from accountants, bankers, title insurers, tax consultants, and realtors, who perform work that deals with questions of law and thus impinges upon the self-defined legal monopoly. The legal profession was able to successfully protect itself from those engaging in the "unauthorized practice of law" by lobbying, litigation, and negotiation between the 1920s and the 1960s.

State and local bar associations lobbied for the passage of general, broad statutes limiting the "practice of law" to members of the bar. Individuals who did engage in tasks that might be considered legal practice were brought to court by the organized bar; at least 248 such cases were recorded between 1921 and 1958 (Christensen, 1980:192) for charges such as "giving said legal advice" and "preparing legal documents." The American Bar Association sought to avoid direct confrontation in a number of cases by negotiating formal agreements with allied professional associations (such as accountants, realtors, and underwriters) in which the groups agreed not to encroach upon one another's territory. There were, at one time or another, 20 such agreements.

Encroachment has intensified, however, and allied professions have more recently met with considerable success in breaching traditional monopolies. They clearly have been aided by the tide of consumerism. Realtors in Arizona won the right to draft property-transfer documents by placing the issue on the ballot for a public referendum and mobilizing public support (Christensen, 1980:199). Title insurers in Virginia won the right to make title searches by challenging the bar in federal court.

Organizational employment.   Members of professions such as law, medicine, dentistry, and pharmacy which established themselves as primarily self-employed, fee-for-service practitioners have been confronted with special problems arising from expanded employment in "bureaucratic organizations" (Haug, 1973; Toren, 1975). As has frequently been noted, professional and bureaucratic principles of organization can be inconsistent, or even contradictory (Hall, 1986:48–50). Individual independence, initiative, and judgment may be circumscribed by organizational priorities and by a bureaucratic structure stressing centralized authority and standardized procedures. Of course, the extent to which the bureaucratic model is articulated varies widely among organizations or classes of organizations, but it is instructive to note documented challenges to traditional sources of autonomy that arise from organizational employment.

Eisenstein's (1978) study of Department of Justice attorneys is illustrative. The agency is in part influenced by political and public relations considerations, resulting in the assignment of high or low priority to the prosecution of certain types of cases. Organized crime cases, for example, receive high priority because of the favorable publicity they generate. The actual conduct of prosecution is dictated by a 56-page operating manual produced in an attempt to standardize procedures in all jurisdictions. Conduct is further limited by a centralized decision-making apparatus controlling personnel, disbursement, and the disposition of major cases. Each of these situations places limits on the traditional prerogatives of lawyers to exercise professional judgment.

It is this kind of threat to autonomy that confronts the organizational lawyer, and the shift toward this type of employment is readily apparent. Many young attorneys choose government employment as a means of gaining valuable legal experience. Salaried private-sector job opportunities are increasing at an unprecedented rate due to increases in government regulation and consumer litigation. AT&T alone employed 900 lawyers during the legal battle over break-up (Galluccio, 1978). In 1980, 27 percent of all lawyers were salaried employees (Curran, 1984).

Demographics of the professions. There have been a number of changes in the composition of the professions within the last two decades which suggest a shift toward greater heterogeneity. The most dramatic change has been a trend away from domination of law, medicine, and engineering by white males. Minority enrollments in law schools have remained stable at about 4.3 percent to 4.4 percent, but matriculation for women has increased from 4.0 percent in 1964 to 37.7 percent in 1983 (Sylvester, 1984:43). These groups have also begun to move into the mainstream of the legal profession. The percentage of women in the largest, most prestigious law firms has, for example, increased from less than 1 percent in the 1960s to 20.1 percent in 1982 (Sylvester, 1984:1). These changes have contributed to attitudinal diversity; surveys of lawyers evidence that females are more favorably disposed than males to public issues such as international human rights, nuclear arms, and gay rights (Law Poll, 1978). Black lawyers favor greater participation by the bar in public policy issues than do white lawyers. Women also place significantly less emphasis than men on the protection of traditional elements of professionalism, such as enhancement of the status of the profession and prevention of the unauthorized practice of law (Heinz and Laumann, 1983).

It is difficult to measure group solidarity retrospectively, but there is some indication that the legal profession, at least in metropolitan areas, exhibits a degree of diversity that contrasts with earlier perceptions of a homogeneous professional community. Specialization, organizational employment, demographics, and the relaxation of anticompetitive rules all point toward increasing diversity. One sure indication of a decline in group solidarity is the emergence of unionization among some segments of the profession. Four thousand legal-aid attorneys are members of a national union (Waldman, 1986), and staff lawyers for the California Bar Association have gone on strike over wages (Galente, 1986), emphasizing the special needs of these subgroups within the profession. The organized bar has historically opposed unionization as a violation of the code of ethics, probably because, as Haug and Sussman (1973) have noted, unionism is a conflict-oriented strategy which is inconsistent with the ideology of professionalism.

The Consequences of Deprofessionalization

Deprofessionalization processes have combined to affect all professions, sometimes causing significant internal changes and altering traditional relationships with government, clients, and other external groups and in turn weakening the advantaged position of the professions.

Autonomy. The authority of professionals in relationships with clients has been undermined by a weakening of previous sources of legitimacy. The narrowing of the competence gap and the routinization of knowledge have placed limits on claims to superior expertise. A general skepticism fostered by the consumer movement, combined with revelations of incompetence and shoddy practice, has called *credet emptor* into question. This new attitude was perhaps best illustrated by the comment of Supreme Court Justice Blackmun, which could apply not just to law, but to any of the professions: "The belief that lawyers somehow are 'above' trade has become an anachronism" (Bates versus State of Arizona, 1977). Freedom to advertise has blurred the distinction between the professions and other commercial endeavors. One measurable result is that public confidence in the professions is on the decline. Manifestations of this new, more skeptical attitude show up in competitive shopping for fees, seeking of second opinions, reluctance to accept professional advice, and, dramatically, in the proliferation of formal complaints. For example, in 1984, 8,402 complaints were lodged against lawyers in New York State (Johnson, 1986).

The concept of unrestricted self-regulation by the professions is no longer inviolate. As previously noted, the courts have begun to invalidate professional regulatory norms such as fee schedules and advertising. In the Goldfarb case, minimum fee schedules were invalidated as an instance of "price-fixing" and thus in violation of antitrust statutes. In Bates versus State of Arizona, rules prohibiting advertising were struck down as an abridgment of the First Amendment right to free speech. The position of the courts is clear—self-regulation within the professions must be oriented toward the protection of the public, not solely toward the protection of the interests of the profession itself.

Self-regulation in the form of control over the mechanics of licensing and discipline has also been challenged because of a somewhat belated recognition of the potential conflict of interest inherent in placing regulation in the hands of the regulated. One alternative has been to restructure the composition of regulatory boards to include nonprofessional members. It is not yet clear what impact this will have since public members are usually a minority of the total membership. A related development has been the creation of "sunset" legislation since 1976, that requires the termination of programs and laws unless they are specifically reenacted by the legislature. Licensing boards have been included in sunset legislation in over 30 states (Martin, 1980:67). The codes vary, but in many instances licensing boards are required to explicate the public benefits of regulation. Both sunset laws and structural reform of regulatory boards reflect a demand for greater accountability to the public on the part of self-regulating professions, another legacy of the consumer movement. It may also signal a decline in the power of the professions.

Monopoly. The concept of exclusive jurisdiction over a core of expert work remains firmly entrenched in the law, and is a form of voluntary compliance for the established professions of engineering, law, medicine, and architecture. The scope of this monopoly appears to be narrowing, however, due to the general demystification of the nature of expert knowledge and the routinization of many tasks. The proliferation of "self-help" books on legal problems, diets, pharmacology, and general health reflects a trend toward self-reliance and away from dependence upon experts. It is difficult to document the extent of such activity. It is certain that lawyers are no longer able to depend upon the old practice of formal agreements on the division of labor with such groups to discourage encroachment; the American Bar Association has had to rescind them in response to pressure from the Justice Department, which argued that they violated the antitrust laws.

CONCLUSION

The self-regulating professions, which emerged in their modern form in the nineteenth century and flourished in the first six decades of this century, appear to be in a state of flux. Autonomous, monopolistic professions may indeed have become an anachronism—a form of social organization rendered obsolete by changing conditions, as were the medieval guilds. Although the process of deprofessionalization is likely to continue, it is difficult to anticipate the form of the professions of the future. Professionalism may be replaced by a narrower, more clearly circumscribed client-expert relationship which permits the exercise of skill and judgment within a context of accountability to client and public.

Perhaps the proliferation of the so-called no-frills clinics or storefront firms provides a glimpse into the future. They are an innovation of the 1970s, with Hyatt Legal Services, founded in 1977, pioneering in the legal field. Professionals of all kinds—physicians, dentists, opticians, lawyers—have located offices in suburbs, urban neighborhoods, shopping malls, and even in department stores. These firms advertise aggressively, seeking to bring direct, low-cost service to clients at rates lower than those charged by conventional arrangements. Depending upon volume to reduce costs, they offer standardized fees for consultations and, in the case of law, preparation of routine wills, bankruptcies, and divorces.

"Storefront" legal services have proved to be popular with the public. Hyatt Legal Services has become the second largest law firm in the United States, employing over 550 attorneys in 200 offices around the country in 1986 (Trigoboff, 1986). They are not without their critics, including former Chief Justice Burger, who worries that they are undignified, unprofessional, and border on "sheer shysterism." Cases of extravagant promotion have been cited, but state courts retain control over the form and content of advertising. There is the potential for abuse, but research has concluded that competition benefits clients by lowering prices and that, overall, there is no compromise in quality, at least for common legal problems. In addition, they may have the added benefit of making legal services more readily available.

FIVE

The White-Collar Hierarchy

INTRODUCTION: ORGANIZATIONAL WORK SYSTEMS

> Every day a large proportion of all Americans don their figurative white collars and go to work in offices, where they take their stations in the administrative machines that run large organizations (Kanter, 1977:15).

These people are the executives, managers, secretaries, clerks, supervisors, and technical experts whose work is concerned with designing and maintaining the flow of operations in organizations. In hundreds of thousands of small companies, offices are staffed by a handful of people able to handle the planning and paperwork necessary to run the operations. At the other extreme are the giant industrial, commercial, and government agencies requiring thousands of specialized workers.

Some organizations publish elaborate organizational charts which neatly compartmentalize every job or class of occupation. Certainly, not every company or firm has a formal document, and even those that do may not be able to capture the actual dynamics of the firm. The point is that formal plans are merely a convenient representation of the way in which white-collar work is organized. Even if they do not exist on paper, they do exist in the workers' cognitive structures and are manifested in the relations of workers to one another.

One purpose of organizational charts is to locate every job within an overall division of labor. At least theoretically, each position has specific

EXHIBIT 5:1 Organizational Chart, United States Information Agency

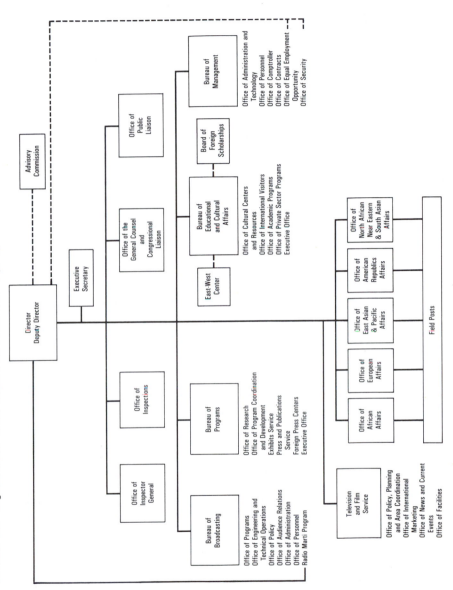

Source: U.S. General Services Administration, *United States Government Manual, 1984/85* (Washington, DC: Government Printing Office, 1984), p. 860.

substantive tasks that fit into the overarching objectives of the organization. The other important purpose of organizational charts is to locate positions within a hierarchy of authority. The arrows which radiate across the chart specify the positions that report to others and the offices that are responsible to others. According to the theory behind organizational charts, "authority" resides in positions and clearly defines relationships; in practice, however, authority may have to be constantly negotiated and legitimized with subordinates, peers, and superiors, for they are not without the ability to resist the exercise of authority. Moreover, it is clear that the exercise of "power" and "influence" often follows routes not shown on any chart.

There is no agreement on terminology to describe various forms of control or direction in social relationships. For convenience, *authority* will be defined as the legitimate right to direct the behavior of subordinates. In the organization, this right is embedded in the hierarchical organization of roles. *Power* implies coercion, based on control of resources. To fine or suspend a worker or to threaten dismissal involves the exercise of power. *Influence* depends upon personal persuasion to convince a subordinate to comply. In any given situation, the three forms of control tend to interact.

Work within the administrative part of the white-collar hierarchy can usefully be approached from the perspective of *responsibilities* and *relationships*. The former are substantive tasks related to the functioning of the organization. The latter are associations, both formal and informal, with peers, superiors, and subordinates. In some instances, relationships and responsibilities extend across organizational boundaries to external individuals and groups.

EXECUTIVE ROLES

Executive is the term used to identify positions at the top of organizations. In corporate America, the positions usually included in this category are presidents, chief executive officers, and vice presidents. In federal and state government, they are cabinet-level personnel and directors of agencies. School superintendents, hospital administrators, and city managers are also in this category.

Most descriptions of executive work are vague and focus on the idea of abstract decision making; "Management does not do things. It decides what should be done," explains one observer (Abrams, 1951). Such statements conjure up an image of impeccably groomed and superbly organized individuals, usually found in richly paneled rooms, calmly announcing crucial long-term judgments subsequently articulated through a smoothly functioning bureaucratic system. An accumulating body of research on the actual behavior of executives suggests a very different picture (Mintzberg, 1973; Kotter, 1982).

Executive Responsibilities

By virtue of their position at the apex of organizations, executives assume responsibility for the current and future functioning and performance of the organization. Many groups and individuals—including stockholders, boards of directors, and employees—may be in a position to evaluate how well they handle these responsibilities. They are often judged on the basis of some criterion of organizational performance, such as profits, although financial success is not fully under their control and direction. Performance is ultimately the cumulative outcome of the efforts of countless subordinates and employees, and will be influenced by factors that no one in the organization is able to either predict or control.

The most useful approach to executive work roles is to build upon the most fundamental distinction that they themselves use—time frames. Every executive assumes some responsibility for the long-term survival of the organization. They are required to develop what can be called an *organizational strategy*, which requires setting basic goals and priorities that address the products or services to be produced, questions of expansion versus concentration, and structure of the organization (Kotter, 1982:11). The organizational strategy is a vision of the future; it may be projected anywhere between five and twenty years hence, depending upon specific circumstances.

Time perspectives tend to be longer when organizations operate in stable, homogeneous environments. American auto executives enjoyed such a situation during much of the 1950s and 1960s, and they were consequently able to focus on long-term planning. In contrast, unpredictable and rapidly changing environments force executives to limit their concept of the future to a maximum of only a few years. This is evident in organizations which employ technologies that are evolving rapidly (such as computers), or which are affected by shifts in governmental regulation (like airlines).

Because every organization has limited resources (money, personnel) and many competing needs (research, plant maintenance, sales, marketing), executives are confronted with *tactical responsibilities*. Meeting such responsibilities requires a balancing of priorities on a more immediate basis, making projections one to five years into the future. For example, the executive may have to determine how much money to allocate to research on new products without stifling the sales force, which is marketing current products.

Some responsibilities must be classified as *short-run problem-solving*. This time frame is measured in months, weeks, or even days. A managing partner of a professional-services corporation laments, "Sometimes this job is just a never-ending supply of little problems" (Kotter, 1982:15). "Little" does not mean unimportant or minor; it means immediate! In executive terminology, this problem solving is usually referred to as "fighting fires," and it is an apt analogy. Any unexpected problem that disrupts the functioning of the organization requires a swift response. It might be something as dramatic as a wildcat strike, or as common as a bottleneck in a shipping department.

Some "fires" are referred upward because they can only be resolved at a policy-making level. Union negotiations would be in this category. Other problems are passed upward because there are honest differences of opinion or strategy. In one actual case of delayed shipments, subordinates had differing perceptions of the problem and of appropriate solutions. One traced it to the inept performance of specific personnel; others felt there was a mechanical flaw in the production process; still others argued that the marketing department was at fault for promising unrealistic delivery dates (Kotter, 1982:15). Problematic situations may come to the attention of general managers because subordinates perceive them as too risky to make a decision about, and thus "pass the buck" upward.

American executives are confronted with a predictable and recurrent goal, which has come to be accepted as a short-term problem—quarterly profits. Quarterly dividends are certainly an imperfect indication of corporate viability or progress toward long-term goals, but profits are closely monitored by powerful external groups—institutional investors and financial analysts who are in a position to affect the company's ability to raise money. Executives also typically earn bonuses based on current profits. It is not uncommon, therefore, for American corporate executives to allow short-term profit considerations to dominate, at the expense of longer-term objectives. As a consequence, they have been unwilling to risk the resources for basic research, building service networks, and capital investment necessary for long-run profitability and survival.

Executive relationships.   "Making decisions is easy, but getting them implemented is sometimes nearly impossible. I have to work through so many people . . ." (Kotter, 1982:17). This comment by the vice chairperson of a billion-dollar industrial corporation emphasizes executives' dependence upon a vast network of people and groups in the process of managing their organizations. There are four basic types of relationships, involving various groups of people and patterns of formal authority. A five-week study of several executives revealed the scope of relationships shown in Exhibit 5:2.

Executives have formal authority over several levels of *subordinate* managers. The executives are responsible for evaluating the subordinates' performance, managing their careers, resolving conflicts among them, and motivating and directing their activities. Executives enjoy the right to command (formal authority) but, of course, cannot operate by minutely directing subordinate behavior. They must depend upon subordinates' judg-

EXHIBIT 5:2   Work Relationships in the Executive Role

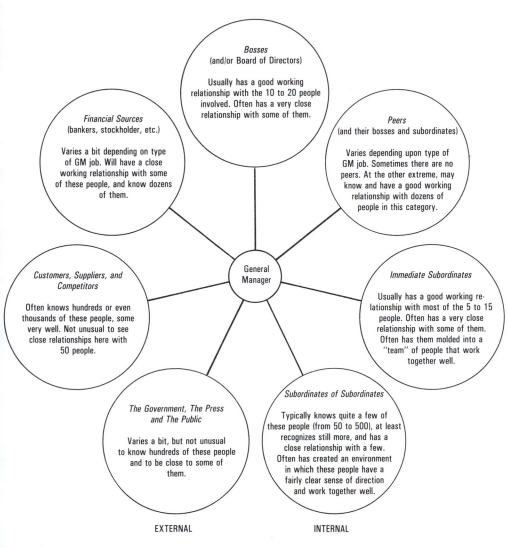

Bosses
(and/or Board of Directors)

Usually has a good working relationship with the 10 to 20 people involved. Often has a very close relationship with some of them.

Financial Sources
(bankers, stockholder, etc.)

Varies a bit depending on type of GM job. Will have a close working relationship with some of these people, and know dozens of them.

Peers
(and their bosses and subordinates)

Varies depending upon type of GM job. Sometimes there are no peers. At the other extreme, may know and have a good working relationship with dozens of people in this category.

General Manager

Customers, Suppliers, and Competitors

Often knows hundreds or even thousands of these people, some very well. Not unusual to see close relationships here with 50 people.

Immediate Subordinates

Usually has a good working relationship with most of the 5 to 15 people. Often has a very close relationship with some of them. Often has them molded into a "team" of people that work together well.

The Government, The Press and The Public

Varies a bit, but not unusual to know hundreds of these people and to be close to some of them.

Subordinates of Subordinates

Typically knows quite a few of these people (from 50 to 500), at least recognizes still more, and has a close relationship with a few. Often has created an environment in which these people have a fairly clear sense of direction and work together well.

EXTERNAL   INTERNAL

Source: Reprinted with permission of the Free Press, a Division of Macmillan, Inc. from *The General Managers* by John P. Kotter. Copyright © 1982 by the Free Press.

ment, ability, competence, and cooperation. Moreover, when called upon to invoke a decision opposed by a subordinate, it has consistently been observed that executives seldom rely exclusively upon their right to command, but rather are more likely to negotiate, attempting to convince, persuade, cajole, or even entice cooperation by exchanging favors.

This characteristic of executive behavior points to two often neglected aspects of superior-subordinate relationships at the top of organizations. The most obvious is that formal bureaucratic authority does not guarantee the power to command obedience. Subordinates can always disobey if they are willing to suffer the consequences. Moreover, subordinates may have the power to resist because they have developed alliances or their own sources of power. In addition, reliance upon specific commands will usually tend to elicit only minimal compliance, not active cooperation.

General managers must also *manage upward*. It is tempting to think of executives as being at the pinnacle of the organizational hierarchy, but, in fact, executives deal with the superior authority of executive committees, boards of directors, and chief executives. Superiors have formal authority, including control over salary and employment, and are responsible for the distribution of resources among competing units. A good deal of any executive's time must be devoted to these critical relationships. Recent history in corporate America is littered with the names of displaced executives who were unsuccessful in their dealings with boards of directors (O'Toole, 1984). Lee Iacocca, prior to his highly visible success at Chrysler, was forced out at Ford because of disagreements with chairman Henry Ford (Iacocca, 1984).

Executives are also dependent upon *lateral relationships* with people within the organization over whom they have no formal authority. This is most common in a multidivisional corporation such as General Motors, which is composed of several relatively autonomous manufacturing divisions. It is also not uncommon for executives to have to struggle with corporate advertising departments who demand unreasonable favors for important customers (Kotter, 1982:17). Thus, executives must somehow generate cooperation and accomplish goals despite resistance and conflicting objectives.

Finally, there are *external relationships* with individuals and groups outside the organization. Unions, major customers, suppliers, and bankers are all part of the environment in which the organization must function. Executives obviously have no authority over these groups, who may in fact be powerful enough to disrupt the realization of corporate goals.

Executives are thus confronted with a wide variety of responsibilities, ranging from solving immediate problems to anticipating potential problems in the distant future. The problems are shaped in a complex network of individuals and groups having various amounts of power, as well as by impersonal social and economic forces. Policy-making decisions consist of solutions and compromises among competing groups and priorities. To implement any decisions, executives must work through this network. Formal authority extends only to subordinates within the organization, and even then has apparent limits.

Uncertainty

If there is any one dominant attribute of the executive role, it is uncertainty (Thompson, 1967; Kanter, 1977; Kotter, 1982). Executives operate in an environment of unknowns, unpredictability, and uncontrollable events, actors, and processes. This uncertainty is most dramatically illustrated in the countless "fire-fighting" problems that compete for their attention. Such problems may be as minor as an unexpected equipment failure or as devastating as the sudden American boycott of the 1980 Olympics, which cost the NBC television network hundreds of millions of dollars in lost revenues.

Uncertainty also plagues the executive seeking to develop a long-term agenda. Much of the information required for future planning is unknown and unpredictable. For example, even the most elaborate data-gathering and forecasting systems will be unable to provide definitive answers to the following list of crucial long-term planning questions:

1. What technological breakthroughs will affect the manufacturing/service process?
2. What will the inflation rate be, and how will it affect consumer demand and the ability to finance operations?
3. Will any major new competitors (domestic or foreign) enter the field?
4. How will consumer preferences change?
5. Which party will win the elections, and how will this affect government regulation of the industry, or government priorities, or budget allocations?

All social relationships involve some degree of uncertainty. Both external and lateral relationships involve independent groups with their own goals and sources of power. Relationships with superiors cannot always be managed with complete certainty. Downward relationships are also problematic, because subordinates always have some spheres of independence and discretion. It is impossible to anticipate and direct the actions of people, despite having formal authority over them. Thus, executive role behavior can usefully be understood as occurring within an environment of uncertainty.

Some observers of Japanese industry have suggested that a fundamental difference between the two cultures lies in perceptions of uncertainty (see, for example, Pascale and Athos, 1981:139—41). Japanese industry is characterized by a greater tolerance of uncertainty, imperfection, and ambiguity. Predictability is sought, but uncertainty is more likely to be accepted as an "immutable fact of life," to be responded to or reduced as much as conditions permit. In contrast, American culture instills the idea that uncertainty is intolerable, a condition to be mastered and overcome by decisive action. To the extent that this is an accurate description of cultural conditioning, it helps to explain why American executives allow immediate problem solving to dominate their roles.

EXECUTIVE WORK PATTERNS

The modern organizational executive does not have a neatly defined role. Rather, as noted by Kanter (1977:55), it is appropriate to view the role as the pursuit of a complex set of long- and short-term objectives through a vast and complex set of relationships within a context of uncertainty. John Kotter's (1982) study of fifteen general managers is instructive. Although each brought his or her own personal style to the job, there were some similarities which can be viewed as common responses to the demands of the role.

Communications.   Possibly the most striking pattern of executive work behavior was the amount of time devoted to interpersonal communication. The executives interviewed spent about 60 hours a week on the job, and an average of 75 percent of that time was spent talking and listening to people in meetings, on the phone, in the hallways, in the office, and at lunch. Some executives spent as much as 90 percent of their work time communicating. This pattern serves to emphasize the importance of the interpersonal network for the executive's role, for it is this network of people that general managers depend on to formulate and implement their plans.

Extensive networks.   The executive's contacts regularly extend beyond his or her direct subordinates and superiors. Kotter found that it was not unusual to observe conversations with a boss's boss or a subordinate's subordinate, or even with outsiders who had no apparent relationship to the organization. These managers had "close" working relationships with scores of people with whom they interacted on a more or less regular (daily or weekly) basis, and less regular but periodic contacts with literally hundreds of others inside and outside the organization. This suggests the vast scope of interpersonal relationships necessary to direct a large organization. It is also clear that executives do not depend upon the formal chain of command to accomplish their goals and gather information.

Information gathering.   During the course of the conversations observed, executives were constantly posing questions. It was apparently not uncommon for executives to ask hundreds of questions about people and operations. These executives were obviously depending upon the interpersonal network for information of all kinds, much of it related to the organizational environment, which allowed them to constantly reappraise and reevaluate their tactics and strategies. A good deal of effort was also devoted to short-term problem solving. Much of the information solicited in this manner produced conflicting interpretations of problems and competing solutions, and thus called for action by the executive.

Unstructured contacts. A glance at an executive's daily calendar will reveal a schedule of meetings and conferences. Contrary to popular opinion, however, the major part of the manager's day was not meticulously planned in advance, but rather evolved in response either to contacts initiated by others or to the flow of events. Subordinates alerted managers to potential problems; discussions of issues led to other issues in an apparently haphazard manner; chance encounters in elevators became opportunities to seek out information. Moreover, little time was devoted to any one topic; a discussion of one topic rarely lasted even ten minutes (Kotter, 1982:81). Rather, most encounters ranged over a wide variety of points in the space of a few minutes.

These patterns confirm the importance of a continual flow of data, opinions, and information beyond that contained in computer printouts and reports. More than one observer has concluded that the attribute that distinguishes the successful executive from the unsuccessful one is the ability to sort through this vast array of seemingly unrelated pieces of information, choosing the topics that require attention while ignoring the others.

Extraneous interaction. Not all the interaction focused upon the work of the organization. In fact, executives will privately claim that they "waste" a lot of time on apparently extraneous matters. Subordinates may want to share family or vacation photographs, or a secretary may want to discuss decorating her new apartment, or a customer may want to talk baseball. Such items may, on the surface, appear irrelevant to the functioning of an organization, but they are vital at an interpersonal level. Maintaining cordial and cooperative relationships with people demands attention to their nonwork activities as well as their work behavior.

Humor. Another facet of maintaining cooperative work relationships was manifest in the constant joking, story telling, teasing, and kidding that was an integral part of these interactions. Anthropologist Radcliffe-Brown (1952:90–104) has noted that humor is frequently used in social situations involving the potential for conflict and hostility. Interaction among superiors and subordinates in bureaucratic organizations clearly carries the potential for conflict, in the form of power differentials, promotion rivalries, and competing ideas. Overt conflict would certainly be disruptive, but laughter helps to defuse such situations by dispelling frustration and by allowing unacceptable hostility to be displaced onto others in the organization.

Influence and authority.   During the innumerable encounters that took up the executives' days, it was rare to find the direct exercise of formal authority. They seldom gave direct orders to their subordinates. Explicit orders were given in situations that required immediate attention or in which irreconcilable differences persisted among subordinates. More often than not, executives attempted to influence subordinates by offering suggestions, making requests, persuading, or other indirect means. This may be a misleading observation, for it ignores a subtle aspect of the exercise of control by people who have formal authority; subordinates may accept "suggestions" and ideas as orders and may act upon them in the same manner as other, more explicit directives. However, the infrequency of direct orders also suggests the executives' recognition that subordinates have their own goals, objectives, limitations, and sources of power. An executive often must be responsive and allow them to determine the flow of events. This feature of the executive role, combined with the uncertainty of the environment, serves as a reminder that executives have less power and authority to control their organizations than is implied by their formal position.

Executives, by virtue of their positions, must assume responsibility for making a vast array of decisions about the structure and function of their organizations, and Kotter found that all the general managers approached their jobs in roughly the same way.

Agenda setting.   The first few months were devoted to developing an overall corporate agenda. Interestingly enough, long-term corporate strategy tended to be quite vague, involving general income projections, ideas about product lines, and notions about the kind of organization they envisioned. The typical agenda was more a loosely connected set of general ideas than a formal, clearly articulated plan.

In contrast, more specific organizational tactics were much more clearly defined. Each executive developed a plan that he or she hoped could be implemented within one to three years. These lists included such items as specific new product lines, sales and revenue goals, and reorganization plans for particular departments. They created a more immediate agenda for the next few months, which focused on such objectives as promotion or replacement of particular individuals, or precise profit goals. The process was continuous and constantly shifted in response to the situation.

Network building.   At the same time, executives devoted much time and effort to developing cooperative relationships with the people involved in the realization of their agendas. This activity built upon preexisting relationships and extended to the people identified as crucial to the realization of the goals. As a general rule, the more dependent a manager was upon a particular person, the more time was spent cultivating the relationship. Key personnel were hired, fired, and shifted during the network-building period. Lee Iacocca reports having dismissed some 33 high-level managers in his first few weeks at Chrysler (Iacocca, 1984).

Execution.   The initial phase was a period of intense activity aimed at gathering and assimilating vast amounts of information, formulating an agenda, and creating an interpersonal network. This period was followed by a shift toward employing the network needed to implement the agenda. Attention tended to shift to more specific items and personnel, and activity was much more specifically goal directed.

MANAGERS

"Systems of Tension"

Middle management, or simply *management,* as the term is used here, is one of the most ambiguous categories of work. By general agreement, the label is applied to positions below "executive" positions having organization-wide responsibilities, and above "supervisory" positions, which are concerned with the completion of specific tasks at the production level. Thus, upper levels of management may extend to vice-presidents in functional areas (such as finance or personnel), middle ranges of management include departmental directors and plant managers, and the lower levels often have vague titles such as "assistant manager," or "specialist." It sometimes appears that management is a residual category comprising positions not located at the extremes of organizational hierarchy. Organizations may recognize dozens of levels of management, but titles and tasks are usually organization-specific, making it difficult to compare positions in different firms.

A simple diagram can aid in conceptualizing managerial roles within the structure of American organizations. Each position is located along two axes—the vertical, corresponding with the hierarchical level of tasks, authority, rewards, and prestige, and the horizontal, defined by the specific department or functional area (Exhibit 5:3).

It was this model which led Leonard Sayles (1966:218) to describe organizations as "deliberately created systems of tensions." Managers are subject to tension that has its source in the demands and expectations of superiors, subordinates, and interdepartmental colleagues. Managerial roles in American organizations are characterized by two key features—specialization and interdependency.

EXHIBIT 5:3   The Functional and Hierarchical Location of Managers

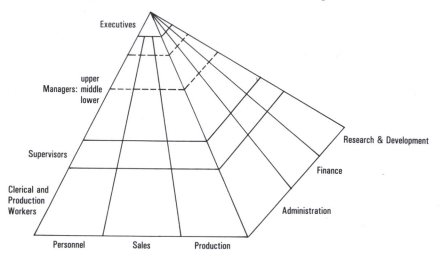

Specialization

Managers tend to be specialists in functional areas of administration. Business schools typically describe executives as "generalists," in contrast to managers, who are referred to as "specialists." Beginning with undergraduate business education, which recognizes marketing, finance, operations, and other majors or departments, and continuing through careers that usually focus on particular areas of business, management has tended to emphasize specialization.

Specialization of managerial roles has coincided with the specialization of organizations into functional *subunits*, which are defined as segments of the whole. Subunits are expected to make relatively specific contributions to the goals of the organization. The three types of responsibilities that have been used to define executive roles apply here, but are more clearly divided among the various levels of management. Upper management has primary responsibility for long-term subunit strategy, translating a broad corporate vision into more concrete goals and objectives. Linkages between organizational and subunit goals are not always smooth. Research suggests that upper managers feel they lack sufficient input into the decisions that affect their units (Hale, 1983). Managers at the upper levels have the added responsibility of competing for the organization's scarce resources by acting as advocates for their departments.

Tactical responsibilities (balancing priorities, but *within* units) usually reside with middle managers who direct departments or divisions or plants. Representative titles include production managers, sales representatives, personnel managers, accountants, and maintenance superintendents (Hall, 1975:148). They may have some input into subunit goals, but they are generally responsible for implementing quotas and decisions made by upper management. They are thus occupied with scheduling, designing work flow, and coordinating the internal activities of their units. The position of plant manager, for example, has several tactical components: (1) formulating production plans consistent with corporate goals, (2) scheduling the completion of various aspects of the overall plan, (3) monitoring the work and progress of individuals (engineers, supervisors) and units, and (4) readjusting plans and schedules, ironing out problems, and coordinating (Miller and Form, 1980:332).

Lower-level managers have the most clearly specialized responsibilities and tend to focus directly on a single task. A production coordinator, for example, will be charged with meeting explicit quotas, and work will be organized around the smooth functioning of a segment of the manufacturing process. They must, of course, be technical experts, for success depends upon anticipating and avoiding problems or expeditiously solving problems as they arise.

Interdependency

A second characteristic of managerial work roles is interdependency. Specialization inevitability imposes the need for coordination among various subunits. Virtually any objective can cut across functional areas. The introduction of something as simple as a new data-processing system involves operations, personnel, maintenance, and other units during the process of implementation. Even activities that seem self-contained within a specialized unit typically require the participation of other units. A sales manager seeking to improve volume cannot hope to succeed without help from the production, advertising, distribution, and service units. In extreme cases, weak integration among corporate subunits can produce dramatic and costly failures. Analysts note that Coleco's abortive attempt to enter the personal-computer field in 1982 floundered when the production, distribution, and service functions failed to meet the demand created by the marketing unit.

Managers are expected to think and act in terms of coordination and integration. Some organizations deliberately transfer staff across functional lines in order to promote an understanding of the perspectives and problems of other parts of the organization. Yet the ability to elicit the cooperation of other units remains problematic. Managers frequently complain that they encounter inertia, lack of cooperation, resistance, and even outright opposition from the managers in other units. The origins of this form of internal disunity are partly structural. The mere fact that subunits must compete for limited resources creates a zero-sum situation. A fixed pool of resources means that a gain by one unit must be at the cost of other units.

Another structural source of disunity centers on the issue of functional importance. Managers tend to overestimate the importance of their own activities and units relative to others. A study of 663 Italian managers revealed that members of every subunit defined their units as being "key" departments more frequently than other unit managers would grant this status (Derossi, 1982:54–55). The most dramatic discrepancy was found among personnel managers, 60 percent of whom claimed that their departments were "key" units, although very few others concurred with this evaluation. Only in the area of production is there much consensus on which are key departments.

There is also a discrepancy between perceived importance and participation in corporate level decision making. Only 20 percent of the managers participate (by their own admission) in policy formation. Managers thus have a clear tendency to feel that they make a key contribution to the organization and yet do not have sufficient input into the process of decision making. It is to be expected that specialists in any area would consider their role to be central to the organization's functioning. To do otherwise would depreciate the value of their work.

There is also an element of vertical interdependency which cannot be overlooked. Managers must act as integrators between executives, who define the basic organizational agenda, and the workers, who are actually in touch with the production process (Schlesinger and Oshry, 1984). Information, ideas, and grievances flow in both directions via managers. Working downward, they interpret and implement executive policy; working upward, they focus attention on problems and concerns originating with the work force. Some managers feel they have become mere messengers, acting as a conduit for the flow of communication.

The difference in organizational structures between the U.S. and Japan has attracted a great deal of attention. The Japanese are prone to deliberately deemphasize the notion of specialization in careers and training. This may reflect deeper cultural ideals supporting collective, rather than individual, goals.

Managerial Relationships: Politics and Power

Managers must function in a complex structural situation, and it is interesting to examine how they view their relationships with others. It is clear that managers are most satisfied with their relationships with their *subordinates* (Breen, 1983;20). This level of satisfaction is to be expected because managers have authority over subordinates and, as a result, are in a position to exert some control over their activities. But it is not simply that managers admire obedience; rather, managers claim that they consult subordinates (80 percent) and value "determination" and "dependability" in their subordinates (Schmidt and Posner, 1982). They seem to want to be able to rely on them to finish the tasks they undertake.

Relationships with *superiors* are, relatively, the most unsatisfactory (Breen, 1983). Managers look to their superiors for leadership, understanding, and encouragement (Schmidt and Posner, 1982), but executives do not live up to these expectations very well. One of the most commonly mentioned faults is a lack of honesty and openness; only one-third felt that executives had these traits. Both men and women managers felt the need for improved upward communication, an effective appraisal system, and a more structured network for the dissemination of information. Women managers consistently placed more emphasis on each of these items, suggesting that they may be more socially isolated from the dynamics of organizational life and power relationships.

Satisfaction with *lateral relationships* falls somewhere between the other two variables, with most reporting generally satisfactory working relationships. More than anything else, they value people who are cooperative and responsive. It has long been noted that managers feel that success depends upon traits such as "tact" and "agreeableness" (Porter, 1964), skills that emphasize lateral interpersonal relationships. For the manager, the ability to accomplish goals may become a question of politics—handling opposition, building coalitions, and enlisting the support of allies (Kanter, 1982). In such situations, the ability to get things done is often a matter of power.

Managers must function at the center of a complex set of horizontal and vertical forces, and they must have power in order to function effectively. This is evident in the recent success of popular manuals that emphasize the cultivation of personal "power" (Biggart, 1983). Politics and power in the organizational context of middle management should be understood as a tool for accomplishing goals in the absence of bureaucratic authority. This does not mean that some managers do not seek power for its own sake or that power may not be a form of self-aggrandizement. Rather, following Kanter and others, power must be viewed in an instrumental sense, as a resource necessary for anyone to function in a managerial role in complex, hierarchically structured organizations. When conceptualized in this manner, power is not a function of personality, but a structurally imposed requirement of the managerial role.

One consequence has been that managers have frequently resisted attempts to grant more participation and decision making to the work force. An executive complains, "Middle managers just won't buy into this QWL (worker participation) stuff" (Schlesinger and Oshry, 1984). Any power or influence delegated downward is perceived as a threat to their ability to function in their own roles. Top management will continue to expect results, but their ability to influence the process is reduced, resulting in feelings of ambiguousness, confusion, powerlessness.

THE TECHNOSTRUCTURE: EXPERTS IN ORGANIZATIONS

The Evolution of the Technostructure

Business, industry, and government depend heavily upon experts, including accountants, auditors, computer programmers, engineers, lawyers, scientists, social workers, and teachers among them. John Kenneth Galbraith (1971) has referred to this group of occupations as the *technostructure* of industrial societies, providing the fundamental expertise necessary for the functioning of complex organizations. Some are technicians, but most members of the technostructure are simultaneously professionals and participants in organizations. Thus, to identify a person as a "Mayo Clinic nurse" incorporates both employer and profession. Thus the individual can have both an external reference group and values or standards of performance which transcend the specific organization.

The widespread employment of technicians and professionals in organizations has followed a number of paths. Some professions have always practiced in organizations as salaried employees. It is not an exaggeration to argue that some occupations were created to meet the technical needs of organizations. Civil engineering is a case in point (Layton, 1969). It is estimated that there were less than 30 practical mechanics (engineers) in the United States at the beginning of the seventeenth century, working either as independent craftspersons or on limited-term projects. By 1850, the census first took note of some 2,000 members of the new profession of civil engineering. The stimulus to the emergence of this occupation was the wave of large-scale public works such as railroads and canals. Engineering schools responded to the demand for a cadre of engineers by developing standardized training programs, and the first national professional society began in the 1850s. Thus, Layton notes, "the engineering profession in America was called into being and shaped by the needs of large . . . mostly private organizations."

A different pattern of growth has been found among members of groups that have traditionally been fee-for-service professionals. Lawyers in corporate law departments or physicians in government are two of the most commonly noted examples of this arrangement. The key attribute of this pattern is that much of the history of these professions was dominated by a concern for protecting the autonomy of practitioners from external encroachment. It is epitomized by the notion that a physician is to have final control over the care of a patient, free from intrusions even by other physicians. The result is that socialization for the profession anticipates individual and group autonomy, making submission to organizational authority difficult.

Another form of professional employment involves firms made up of, and managed by, professionals. Law firms, engineering consultants, medical clinics, and accounting firms usually follow this pattern. More than 5 percent of all physicians in the United States are in group practice with 25 or more other doctors (Kleinfield, 1985). Some of these organizations are quite large. All five of the largest accounting firms in 1981 had approximately 2,000 partners (Wayne, 1982). The scale and size of such organizations means that some centralization and bureaucratic procedures must be instituted to coordinate the vast array of activities, but the top executives are members of the same profession.

Incompatible Expectations

Members of the technostructure can occupy an ambiguous position within the structure of organizations. They are described as occupying "staff" positions, as opposed to having "line" authority. They are viewed as providing advice, specialized information, or services, but not as having responsibility for making policy decisions. Symbolically, organizational charts link them into the unit with broken lines to identify their unique position in the authority structure. Some staff members may have specific areas of authority and, of course, the managers of such units (research directors, for example) are a part of the line structure.

Preparation and socialization for technical and professional work begins in the schools and tends to instill certain perspectives and orientations. The process and scope of training are certainly not uniform across all groups, but there are some common educational features. They are, first and foremost, trained to be *experts*, devoting many years to formal, post-secondary education. This education is a continual screening process, exposing them to ever more specialized and esoteric knowledge and, at the same time, weeding out those defined as less competent. At the conclusion of the process, they are publicly certified with a B.S., Ph.D., M.D., D.V.M., or other degree. Certification usually legitimizes the social-psychological transformation into an "expert" that has been evolving over the course of the training. Physicians are likely to remember the first time a patient refers to them as "doctor," confirming their new social role of expert (Merton, et al., 1957).

The role of expert encompasses more than substantive knowledge; it also implies *independence,* the competence to practice without constant supervision. Independence is an explicit part of the formal definition of the Ph.D. dissertation, which is a prerequisite to certification in some occupations. The dissertation must be a piece of original research, initiated, designed, and executed by the student. Faculty act as "advisors," offering advice and council, but the ultimate responsibility for completion of the project rests with the student. It is the final requirement, to be completed after grades in course work have demonstrated mastery of the subject matter. A few students will always remain "ABDs" (All But Dissertation), trapped in a kind of academic limbo reserved for those who somehow cannot demonstrate the capacity for independent research. Expertise and independence usually combine to produce heightened expectations of *autonomy*.

Some members of the technostructure will also be subject to ethical standards imposed by their associations. Although codes of ethics may have elements of self-interest, they are also designed to protect clients and the general public if there are questions of public trust involved. Members of society, individually and collectively, place professionals in a position of trust—for their physical and mental health, education, protection of their rights and freedom, the creation of useful knowledge—and they consequently must be governed by standards that extend beyond the principle of *caveat emptor* that prevail in the commerce for other goods and services.

Finally, members of the technostructure may be tied into a national or international occupational community. Individuals are linked together at a structural level through professional associations, conferences, and journals, but they also share an identity. Research shows that colleagues outside the organization are a salient reference group (Wilensky, 1964). Evaluations by this subculture may be more important than the judgments of bureaucratic superiors or even clients. Individuals in scientific communities depend upon the originality of their research to win prestige and recognition among their peers. Occupational communities are not as well developed in professions such as nursing and pharmacy as they are in law, medicine, and science; nevertheless, all professionals can be members of social groups beyond the boundaries of the organizations that employ them.

In any of these arrangements, there is the potential for some degree of incompatibility between organizational demands and professional expectations. For example, experts dedicated to the practice of their craft seem to be universally surprised and dismayed to learn that administrators have to accommodate to considerations like reducing operating costs and political realities. The issue is not merely one of internal competition for scarce resources, however. There may be more fundamental disagreements over organizational goals, issues of autonomy and ethics, and problems of career development. Incompatibility may generate stress or overt role conflict.

Focusing upon areas of incompatibility is a useful way of analyzing the nature of work among members of the technostructure. This is not to suggest that there is no common ground or mutual interests. Physicians and administrators in clinics work out schedules and procedures for chart review without encroaching upon medical prerogatives (Goss, 1961). At an absolute minimum, workers will have an interest in the survival of the organization, which will ensure continuity of their employment. Minimal standards of productivity, efficiency, and quality are likely to be another area of agreement. The level of incompatibility that does exist varies extensively, depending upon the specific profession (and its history, organization, and power) and the type of organization (governmental or industrial). In this section, broad areas of incompatibility will be identified and illustrated in order to describe the full range of potential conflicts confronting members of the technostructure who have a dual orientation to their organizations and their professions.

Skill Utilization

Technical personnel trained outside the organization in esoteric areas of expertise have made a substantial investment in their education and have acquired a high level of skill and knowledge. Probably the most frequently cited source of dissatisfaction is the perceived underutilization of their capabilities. Almost every study of engineers, scientists, organizational physicians, teachers, and nurses confirms this feeling. It is often most evident early in careers, when new professionals may be assigned narrow, routine tasks until they demonstrate the competence and dependability necessary to assume greater responsibility. As the career unfolds, more enduring forms of underutilization may emerge. A shortage of adequate support staff, such as technicians and lab personnel, may require that professionals perform what they consider routine and undemanding tasks. This was the complaint most often repeated in a study of industrial chemists, for example (Cotgrove and Box, 1970:93). Alternatively, professionals may be expected to devote a significant proportion of their time to the supervision of support personnel. Both patterns generally prove to be unsatisfactory because they deflect time and effort from the core tasks for which the professional is trained.

Underutilization of skills within organizations may also reflect the realities of power at the professional level. Many pharmacists and nurses, for example, have long believed that the knowledge, skills, and judgment acquired during their professional training is circumscribed by the power of the medical profession to maintain legal control of diagnosis and the prescription of therapy. Pharmacists, for example, although highly trained in biochemistry and pharmacology, have often been relegated to the role of dispenser of drugs prescribed by physicians. Beginning in the 1970s, some pharmacists in larger hospitals were able to expand their roles in the direction of full utilization of their expertise. They became active participants in the health-delivery system, acting as advisors, consultants, and even teachers of physicians, thus carving out the new role of "clinical pharmacist."

Autonomy

The individual who accepts organizational employment will be expected to submit to organizational authority by surrendering some degree of autonomy. In the interests of coordination and planning, organizations will impose hours, schedules, tasks, and budgets upon its employees. Most professionals will accommodate to such mundane restrictions. It is worth noting, though, that in some circumstances, professionals may be able to challenge even these most fundamental organizational imperatives. Computer programmers during the 1960s were able to enjoy virtually limitless control over the conduct of their work. They were able to name their own hours, define their own schedules, and pursue projects as they saw fit. They were, as one manager put it, "coddled and humored and pampered, . . . immune to control, . . . discipline . . . and challenge" (Sullivan and Cornfield, 1979:186). This rare and brief interlude of independence resulted from the convergence of some special circumstances. Organizations were aware of the enormous potential benefits of electronic data processing and they needed computer specialists, who were in very short supply. But technology was changing rapidly, and competing machine languages and equipment proliferated; it was a field with a bright future but no clear vision of the outline of that future. Organizations were thus willing, albeit reluctantly, to grant unusual freedom to computer experts.

Scientists employed in industry have provided a number of instances that emphasize the saliency of autonomy. Autonomy is an important factor in influencing choices about places of employment. University employment has always been a somewhat more attractive alternative than industry for scientists who place a high value on control over their work (Cotgrove and Box, 1970:73). A British chemist comments, "Universities are, in my opinion, the only places where there is freedom to publish, . . . to decide upon research projects, . . . (and) how much one wishes to do." This observation identifies several of the key potential problems for scientists in industry.

Scientists are socialized into a value system that emphasizes the creation of new knowledge. Those who make meaningful contributions to the fund of knowledge are rewarded with peer recognition and with symbolic awards (like the Nobel Prize) for the most significant breakthroughs. Therefore, scientists value the freedom to pursue scientifically interesting lines of research. In contrast, private-sector organizations must be guided by considerations of marketability. Scientists dedicated to scientific work may thus find their autonomy limited. Projects are initiated and terminated on the basis of profitability rather than scientific value. Commercial secrecy (or military secrecy in some government jobs) may prevent the publication of research results, thus inhibiting visibility in the larger scientific community. Although instances of this form of censorship are uncommon, they can be an irreconcilable source of conflict. Scientists may also face attempts to control their choice of research methodology, the design of their work, or even their use of equipment. These limitations on autonomy make the university a more desirable employer. Personal autonomy is important to most workers, but more than that is at stake here; autonomy takes on special significance in the context of the external professional community.

Most serious threats to professional sovereignty surface when organizational objectives contradict or constrain professional judgment and authority. Physicians employed in corporate medical practice sometimes encounter such problems. One task of corporate physicians is medical adjudication—certifying employee suitability to perform jobs, verifying illness, and planning worker rehabilitation after injury. Administrators and supervisors, whose organizational mandate emphasizes productivity, may look to the company physician to provide a medical rationale to rid themselves of a troublesome employee or to place a disabled worker who appears healthy back on the job (Walsh, 1984). The physician is thus being asked to subordinate professional judgment to other considerations.

Technical Obsolescence

Every professional is confronted with the threat of *technical obsolescence*—a lack of relevant skills and knowledge. Obsolescence can occur in two ways. The first results from the deterioration of expertise. At the completion of technical training, professionals are equipped with broad skills and knowledge in their fields, but they become increasingly vulnerable to the loss of expertise due to disuse of skills or waning intellectual vigor. New knowledge is simultaneously being discovered, sometimes at extraordinary rates. In some fields, whole new technologies emerge and proliferate, displacing old ideas. Laser technology, for example, promises to dramatically alter research and production during the 1980s, just as computers did during the 1970s. Obsolescence can thus also be caused by a failure to keep up-to-date with new knowledge.

Obsolescence renders professionals less valuable to organizations and can jeopardize their careers or even their employment. It can also challenge their self-image as technical experts. Most organizations actively encourage their professionals to update their skills by attending refresher courses. A few larger organizations have their own in-house programs staffed by senior specialists or university faculty, but even the smaller firms provide free time, travel expenses, and tuition. Some states have even mandated that professionals show proof of continuing education in order to have their licenses renewed.

Individual motivation and the availability of refresher courses are not sufficient to prevent the onset of obsolescence. The social organization of work plays an equal role. Studies of technical obsolescence among engineers suggest that the most vulnerable are those whose jobs involve narrow, specialized tasks, heavy administrative responsibilities, and more routine applied engineering work (Rothman and Perrucci, 1970, 1971; Thompson and Dalton, 1976). It is broad and complex technical work that provides a stimulus to maintaining professional expertise and awareness of the latest developments. Other career paths weaken the base of expertise, reducing the potential for advancement and encouraging some engineers to turn to administrative careers as an adaptation to obsolescence.

Blocked Mobility

Professionals are frequently organized into specialized subunits; examples include accounting departments, research and development labs, and urban planning units. This places them in a staff or advisory role within the organization. In some organizations, the highest levels of rewards, in the form of income and symbols of status, are reserved for people in administration. Consequently, knowledge workers face a structurally imposed upper limit on the ability to advance and gain recognition based upon technical performance. Those who hope to continue to advance must abandon their technical careers in favor of administrative positions. Engineers and scientists are among those who must make such a choice, and many are eager to be promoted into management because they believe that it is the only option offering recognition (Thompson and Dalton, 1976). A survey of chemical engineers shows that one-third are no longer practicing basic engineering skills, having instead moved into administration, plant management, marketing, or sales (Boyd, 1979). This often transforms "good engineers into bad managers," according to one corporate president (O'Kelly, 1978). The problem is that the traits that are valued in technical personnel are not necessarily those that contribute to effective management. For example, knowledge workers have been socialized to be independent perfectionists, while supervision requires flexibility, negotiation, and the capacity to delegate.

Since the 1960s, some American firms have developed two-track, or *dual-ladder,* hierarchical systems for their scientists and engineers. Each ladder offers similar and equivalent opportunities for promotions in salary and status. Technical ladders have typically employed distinctive titles, such as "fellow" and "associate," borrowed from the academic world. More recently, this idea has been adopted by some school systems (usually using such titles as "master teacher") in an attempt to retain and reward the most competent teachers. This system allows individuals to continue to work in the knowledge fields for which they were trained, and to be promoted on the basis of technical contributions. It also has the potential to create the anomaly of a technical worker who has higher status and income than the manager who is his or her boss.

"Whistle Blowing"

In 1981, a Minneapolis attorney took the unusual and possibly unprecedented step of hiring a law firm to bring suit against his own law firm (Siegel, 1981). At issue was the size of a contingency fee in a personal injury case. He believed the fee was excessive and insisted that it be reduced. His firm did lower the fee, but not to the level he considered appropriate, and so he turned to the courts. In the aftermath of the case, the lawyer found himself removed from the board of directors and placed on indefinite leave of absence, and had his name purged from the firm's stationery.

This case illustrates a special dilemma that professionals working in organizations may confront. They may feel that their organization's actions are violating the interests of a specific client, or even of a broad class of consumers. In the latter category would be the airline pilot who warned the government of an alleged engineering defect in an aircraft autopilot system after his company had failed to take what he considered appropriate action (Kurtz and Robbins, 1981:17–30). Both the attorney and the airline pilot had first sought to resolve the problem internally but, having failed to do so, felt they had no recourse but to make it a public issue. Both also suffered retaliation for their decisions. The attorney was excluded from practice, and the pilot was grounded without pay.

These people are called *whistle blowers,* employees who have decided that "some actions of their organization are immoral, illegal or inefficient (and) act on that belief by informing legal authorities or others outside the organization" (Walters, 1975:26). The defining characteristic of whistle blowing is that the employees themselves are not the direct victims of the unethical acts. Many workers file lawsuits or grievances when they themselves are harmed, but whistle blowers are invoking some more general concept of harm and some broader level of responsibility. As Ralph Nader and colleagues (1972:vii) put it, whistle blowing is the act of a person who believes "the public interest supercedes the interests of the organization he (or she) serves. . . ." It is, by this definition, an act of social conscience involving a public announcement of alleged wrongdoing.

Documented incidents of whistle blowing have spanned a wide range of issues. Some of the better publicized issues include irregularities in the safety-testing procedures of aircraft (Vandivier, 1972), automobiles (Kurtz and Robbins, 1981), and mass-transit railway cars (Perrucci, et al., 1980); waste and cost overruns in government (Dudar, 1977); fraud on Wall Street (Dirks and Gross, 1976); drug tests with human subjects (Kurtz and Robbins, 1981); and bribes and illegal kickbacks. In some of these situations, the problem was simply bureaucratic inefficiency; in others, it was a case of conflict between corporate profit or production priorities and public welfare considerations. Some involved clearly illegal acts, such as falsifying records, but other disputes hinged upon more ambiguous questions of risk, safety, and ethics—issues which raise ethical questions that have no clear answers.

The very nature of work in modern organizations insulates most people from such dilemmas. They are asked to perform narrow tasks within a broad division of labor, and thus lack knowledge of organizational goals, policies, and strategies that violate the public interest. In contrast, members of the technostructure, by virtue of their positions, have more knowledge of the organization's functioning. Moreover, their expertise enables them to assess the public health, safety, and welfare implications of organizational decisions. Obvious examples are automotive engineers, physicians engaging in drug research, accountants auditing corporate records, and chemists monitoring municipal water supplies.

The potential for conflict between professionals and organizations is apparently widespread. A survey of 800 engineers engaged in all types of work found that most had felt obligated to question some of the activities of their organization (Von Hippel, 1977). Over 20 percent of these engineers had refused to work on a project, and 7 percent had requested a transfer. Another 7 percent claimed that they had once resigned rather than work on a project that was not in the public interest.

For many professionals, such decisions are not merely a matter of personal conscience, but a perspective inculcated during professional socialization and buttressed by ethical codes. The physician who refused to submit a potential carcinogen for clinical testing on human subjects was clearly dedicated to the Hippocratic oath, which requires that she "do no harm" (Kurtz and Robbins, 1981). The code of ethics of the National Society of Professional Engineers confronts the issue directly, pointing out that they have special responsibilities to protect the public. The code explicitly recognizes that this may bring engineers into conflict with the goals of their employers and instructs them to "regard (their) duty to the public welfare as paramount" (Von Hippel, 1977:9). It should also be noted that workers usually are legally protected from dismissal or retaliation for reporting violations of the law.

CASE STUDY: BLOWING THE WHISTLE

Most whistle blowers are apparently neither crusaders nor malcontents at the start of the process (Kurtz and Robbins, 1981:132). In fact, Robert Perrucci and colleagues (1980:156) have argued that whistle blowers are often among the most strongly committed to the organization. They certainly have a strong sense of professional responsibility, which they feel is violated by their employer. They tend to try to resolve their feelings by discussing them with their immediate supervisors. Lea Stewart (1980) has examined a large number of cases and has developed an overview of the process, suggesting a series of steps that emerges after an individual becomes aware of a product or policy perceived as unethical or illegal:

> *First:* Expresses concerns to immediate supervisor; perceives that no action will be taken.
>
> *Second:* Expresses concerns to administrators at a higher level in the organizational hierarchy; perceives that no action will be taken.
>
> *Third:* Takes the concern to the media, the courts, and/or a regulatory agency. (This step of "going public" is, by definition, whistle blowing.)
>
> *Fourth:* Experiences social isolation and/or a reduction in responsibilities.
>
> *Fifth:* Is fired, forced to resign, or made to feel they must resign.

This model suggests that at least part of the problem may be traced to the structure and dynamics of organizations and the perceptions and meanings attributed to the participants.

At the first step, workers are motivated to resolve the issue internally by following the bureaucratic chain of command. They may feel that their information is useful, important, and positive because it reveals an organizational problem in need of remedy. Unfortunately, such information may be stalled at this level because it may be perceived as a criticism of management policies, and it is well documented that unfavorable communications are not likely to be transmitted upward. Supervisors may also feel that such criticism might reflect badly upon their ability to manage their subordinates. Thus, employees are usually advised that the issue is not their concern, or that they should ignore it—"don't rock the boat." Either strategy is intended to defuse the criticism, but they can have just the opposite effect of legitimizing the validity of the claim and encouraging further activity.

Countless instances of perceived problems are resolved at this or the next step. The scheme being developed here focuses upon problems that lead to public disclosure. To take the second step and bring the issue to the attention of higher administration produces a different configuration of responses. The very act of questioning top-level management may be perceived as a challenge to traditional management rights and prerogatives to set policy, goals, and priorities. This helps to account for the fact that whistle blowing is likely to be branded as disloyalty or treason (Vandivier, 1972). Thus, any challenge regardless of its substantive merit may be met with hostility and resistance.

Valid claims of wrongdoing challenge the competence and morality of the decision makers. To identify an unrecognized problem is to suggest incompetence; to identify a disregard for the public welfare is to suggest irresponsibility. One response to an untenable situation like this is to ignore the charge in the hope that it will not be pursued. Another response is to bury the situation in a seemingly endless series of requests for more study and committee reports. Still another is to remind the individual of the complex issues involved.

Again, the situation is one in which the responses can be perceived as confirming both the legitimacy of the criticism and the feeling that no action will be forthcoming.

The third step, which involves the actual "blowing of the whistle," is born out of a feeling of frustration and a sense of principle strengthened by the organization's lack of response. A number of whistle blowers report there is no immediate "official" response from superiors, but social relationships change. The whistle blowers are treated more coldly by their bosses, and colleagues are likely to avoid them. Coworkers may distance themselves because they fear reprisals, but they may also be bothered by a sense of guilt if they had the same information, but failed to act.

It may take weeks or even months for formal sanctions to emerge. Some are demoted, transferred, or stripped of responsibility; others are simply fired. For example, in 1984 a quality control technician at a nuclear plant was dismissed after complaining to the Nuclear Regulatory Commission about lax safety procedures (Franklin, 1985). The company claimed she was fired because she violated company rules. She eventually won reinstatement and was awarded $70,000 for "humiliation and mental suffering" when the government ruled that the alleged infractions were "a pretext for getting rid of an employee who would not stop reporting (safety) violations to the NRC."

The jobs of whistle blowers are protected by law in some situations. Since the 1970s, a number of federal government workers have been sheltered from dismissal for acting in the public interest, and many state courts have reinstated workers who were fired for reporting illegal conduct on the part of their employers. However, reinstatement and financial restitution often involves lengthy and expensive litigation.

Most observers of the process believe that the sanctions brought to bear on the whistle blower have two purposes. Most direct is the need to punish the individual who has challenged the authority system and publicly humiliated the organization. Wilbert Moore (1962:28) has called it the "organizational equivalent of capital punishment." And consistent with the rationale for capital punishment, the second purpose is to make an example of the person as a warning and deterrent to other potential whistle blowers. The sad irony is that apparently most begin with deeply held but naive conceptions of right and wrong, even expecting gratitude for their acts, and become whistle blowers because of the stone wall of indifference and hostility encountered in the process (Dudar, 1977).

Summary

Professionals and technicians trained outside the organization in esoteric areas of expertise may embark upon their careers with perspectives that diverge from the needs and requirements of the organization. Two areas in which this incompatibility is consistently evident are skill utilization and autonomy. Probably the most frequently cited source of dissatisfaction is the perceived failure of employers to fully exploit the expertise of their professionals. More difficult and sensitive problems arise when organizations impinge upon the professionals' sovereignty, asking them to violate the dictates of their expertise.

Other problems emerge from the fact that professionals have dual reference groups and identities. As a result of their staffing policies, organizations may interfere with the professional's opportunities for success in the external community and, at the same time, limit career opportunities within the organization.

FIRST-LINE SUPERVISORS

Changing Work Roles

The role of first-line supervisor occupies the lowest rung of the administrative hierarchy. Whether the position is titled supervisor, foreman, leader, or crew chief, it is invariably dominated by a single task—that of ensuring that production or service schedules are met. As a result, the vast majority of the first-line supervisor's time is spent on the plant floor, in the offices, or in the field at the work site personally supervising the activities of workers who are actually providing the service or producing the goods (Miller and Form, 1980:343–44). Supervisors may have other responsibilities, such as training new workers and maintaining records, but it is evident that meeting production schedules is the overriding concern and the primary criterion for measuring success.

The job of supervisor has narrowed considerably over the last several decades (Miller, 1965). In the early stages of industrialization, supervisors played a larger role in the total production process, often being actively involved with planning, design, and quality control; they were generally master craftspersons elevated to the role of supervisor to coordinate production processes that they knew and understood intimately. As industrial organization evolved under the influence of Scientific Management, such tasks were delegated to technical experts and managers, leaving supervisors with responsibility for merely implementing production and scheduling decisions made by their superiors; they were left out of decision making, but were still held accountable for the results (Feder, 1981).

The authority of supervisors has also narrowed. It was not uncommon for supervisors to be vested with the right to hire new people, reassign them as necessary, impose fines, and even dismiss unsatisfactory workers. Recruitment and promotion decisions have passed to personnel departments in larger companies, and labor unions have circumscribed the arbitrary authority of supervisors. Among nonunion workers and those employed in small plants, however, supervisors may still have a great deal of latitude in controlling jobs.

Supervisory Behavior: Role Conflicts

Supervision and management of the work force was thus always a part of the supervisory role, but it has now become virtually the sole responsibility. This places the first-line supervisor physically and structurally at the intersection between two work systems, the world of workers and the world of administration. Supervisors are usually the only people to interact on a direct, face-to-face basis with both managers and workers. The situation carries the potential for role conflict: The job calls for the supervisor to represent managerial goals and interests, but workers may expect the supervisor to represent their interests upward in the organization. Delbert Miller (1965) has identified several forms of accommodation to a difficult situation. It is a simple typology based on the idea of reference groups.

Identification with workers.   Some supervisors, especially those promoted from the ranks of production workers, use the workers as their reference group. They are willing to adopt their role performance to the needs and activities of the workers (Argyris, 1960). Informal work group norms, even those that restrict production, are respected. Pleasant and unpleasant tasks are distributed fairly. Schedules and work assignments are accommodated to worker preferences. In short, they generally allow workers to function autonomously and attempt to protect them from interference by management, acting as an advocate for their subordinates. Although this philosophy is likely to produce high morale, it may alienate management, which views the supervisor as its representative. The loss of trust and support of higher management may put the supervisors' job at risk, but even if they are retained, they will have less influence and will be less able to protect their workers.

Identification with management.   A second group of supervisors use management as their reference group. A few such supervisors have been elevated from the ranks and have shifted their perspectives accordingly, usually because they have aspirations for further mobility. Also in this category are the young managers hired directly from high school or college and given supervisory positions as a first assignment in a management career. Others simply feel that they owe allegiance to management by virtue of their position in the hierarchy. Because these supervisors' loyalty lies with management, worker productivity takes on a new meaning; it becomes a way of impressing management. Pressure for higher levels of productivity usually takes the form of close supervision or an emphasis upon rules (Gouldner, 1954).

One strategy is to rely on detailed instructions and frequent direct supervision as a means of maintaining production schedules. This style is found among supervisors who continually prowl the work site making sure that workers are busy. It may be a way of keeping people at their tasks, but it also produces resentment and lowers morale (South, et al., 1982). Workers quickly develop devices that convey the impression of activity without productivity. For example, clerical workers use their phones to call people at adjacent desks, thus making both workers look busy (de Kadt, 1979). Interestingly enough, this strategy usually results in lower productivity, not enhanced output (Blau and Meyer, 1971:62).

Another strategy is to strictly enforce work rules as they relate to breaks, work place, and time clocks. Enforcing rules has the function of emphasizing the relative power of supervisors, although Kanter (1977) and others have argued that it is the powerlessness of supervisors that encourages a rule orientation. The point is that work rules are established in the interests of production schedules, and it is logical for the supervisor to enforce them. Punching out at the end of the work shift frequently becomes a controversial issue. Hourly workers prefer finishing production early enough to allow themselves time to organize their work space and wash up before the end of their shift, rather than doing those work-related tasks on their own unpaid time. Overzealous supervisors may insist upon subordinates' working right up to the end of the shift, which will simply encourage workers to stretch out the same tasks to fill the time. Emphasis upon rules generally produces minimal levels of effort, rather than extra effort, and negatively affects workers' morale.

Dual loyalty.   Some supervisors attempt to maintain a balance between the competing loyalties of management and workers. The evidence indicates that this is a difficult stance to maintain, because it subjects the individual to conflicting pressures. Moreover, it may be personally unsatisfying, for the individual will not be fully accepted in either group, which produces a feeling of marginality. This dual orientation is most common among newly appointed supervisors as an attempt to resolve conflicting demands.

The role of supervisor is a complex and difficult one. It has long been noted that workers often have an aversion to promotion to this position (Chinoy, 1955). A number of factors generate such reluctance, but it is clear that many feel the disadvantages outweigh any economic and status gains. It is technically a position in management, but without any real decision-making power, and many supervisors question whether or not they are really members of management. Pressures for improved productivity and quality are channeled through the supervisor without any clear guidelines as to how to achieve such gains. Despite much human relations training, "it seems clear that the influence of supervisory behaviors on productivity is small" (Dubin, 1971:47). Nevertheless, absenteeism and productivity problems focus negative attention upon supervisors. "More and more," concludes one management consultant, "it is not a very good job. As a result, we are seeing less qualified people move in" (Feder, 1981).

CLERICAL WORK

The Proletarianization and Feminization of Office Work

Clerical workers staff the offices of modern organizations. In one way or another, all clerical workers deal with the flow of communications and records generated by modern society—typing, filing, coding, recording. The most commonly encountered job titles are secretary, stenographer, typist, interviewer, receptionist, file clerk, records clerk, mail clerk, time-keeper, bookkeeper, and keypunch operator. Most clerical positions are filled by women, and because the work is often routine, repetitive, and low paying, it is frequently criticized as a "female ghetto" (Benet, 1972).

It was not always so. In fact, for a brief period in the mid-nineteenth century, offices had certain characteristics that made clerical work a desirable occupation, especially for middle-class males. Offices were small, and the division of labor simple. Employers generally shared office space with managing clerks (who were simultaneously bookkeepers, cashiers, and production coordinators) and ordinary clerks (who handled routine office matters). Managing clerks were usually able to maintain a middle-class lifestyle, and it was apparently not unusual for some to be able eventually to earn a partnership in the business. Ordinary clerks earned less, usually about on a par with blue-collar workers, and had less opportunity for upward mobility into the managerial ranks.[1]

Clerical work in the mid-nineteenth century enjoyed a measure of social prestige. The work required special skills—reading, writing, arithmetic—that were not yet common in the population. The pay was good in many cases, and the work offered at least some possibility for mobility into the managerial class. Even those who failed to move upward in the office derived prestige from their personalized contacts with the bankers, merchants, and industrialists. Working conditions were also superior to the hazardous and unpleasant conditions found in the factories and mines. Clerks were often derided for pretentious attempts to emulate the upper classes in dress and demeanor, but it is fair to conclude that clerical work conferred more prestige than blue-collar work.

At the end of the nineteenth century, offices were already beginning to be impacted by a complex of social, economic, and technological changes that were to dramatically alter the nature of clerical work. The sheer in-

[1]This section draws upon Lockwood, 1958:19ff.

crease in the number of organizations and the burgeoning flow of communications and records created an ever-growing demand for clerical workers. In 1870, only a few thousand members of the work force were classified as clerks. The proportion had grown to 4 percent by 1900 and was to undergo even more dramatic expansion during the post–World War I years. By 1980, almost one worker in five was in a clerical job. Accompanying this growth was the influx of women into the work force, as shown in Exhibit 5:4. Clerking was a male domain at the outset, but by the 1920s, the massive recruitment of females was underway, with women eventually holding over 90 percent of such jobs as bank teller, secretary, typist.

Accompanying such demographic shifts were changes in the nature of the tasks, the social organization of office work, the reward structure, and even interpersonal relations. Distinctions between manual and white-collar work were blurred in the process, eroding the socially and economically advantaged position of clerical work. This process is often re-

EXHIBIT 5:4   The "Feminization" of Office Work

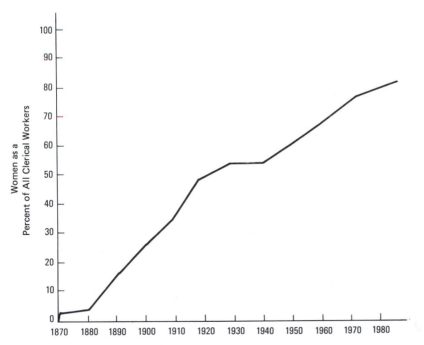

Sources: *1870–1940:* Alba M. Edwards, *Comparative Occupational Statistics for the United States, 1870–1940* (Washington, DC: Government Printing Office, 1943). *1950–1970:* U.S. Bureau of the Census, *Historical Statistics of the United States* (Washington, DC: Government Printing Office, 1975). *1980:* U.S. Bureau of the Census, *Statistical Abstract of the United States* (Washington, DC: Government Printing Office, 1982).

ferred to as the *proletarianization* of clerical work, as it loses its special characteristics and comes to resemble blue-collar work (Glenn and Feldberg, 1977).

C. Wright Mills (1951:249) was among the first to identify the social, economic, and structural changes that have contributed to the narrowing of the gap between clerical work and blue-collar work. Blue-collar workers were able to upgrade certain aspects of their work. The success of trade unions in contract negotiations and as a force in legislative battles brought about some notable advances in wages and working conditions. Over the same period, the educational level of the working class improved, partly in response to the need for a more skilled labor force.

Sociocultural factors also worked to degrade the claims of superior status. By the beginning of this century, men in offices were self-consciously afraid that clerical work was "unmanly." This development was apparently at least partially independent of the influx of women into the office, for it was based not on invidious comparisons with women and "feminine" traits, but rather with manual work. The ideal against which clerical work was judged in this period was the creative, constructive mechanic. The value and meaning of office work was repeatedly questioned, and the question is echoed in the words of a fictional British clerk in 1907:

> Don't we lose our manhood? What do we see of real life? We aren't real men. . . . Pen-drivers—miserable little pen-drivers—fellows in black coats, with inky fingers and shiny seats on their trousers (Lockwood, 1958:123).

Male clerical workers lacked the affluence of the upper middle classes and were cut off from the ideal of "manliness" that could only be validated by physical labor which produced tangible products. The influx of women into the clerical work force strengthened the popular stereotype and encouraged aspiring males to abandon the work. Then too, office work was already in the process of change. The role was evolving in more or less separate directions, and the tasks were being divided among three new categories of workers. Some tasks became fragmented among a new category of workers who performed specialized and highly routinized tasks. Some of these workers performed only a single task, such as operating the telephones. Increasing numbers of workers created the need for continuous supervision, which created the need for an office manager. Finally, responsibility for providing the employer with specific and direct assistance with such tasks as correspondence and scheduling became the responsibility of the personal secretary.

Fragmentation.   The 1870s saw the introduction of two important technological inventions. In 1874, Remington marketed the first efficient typewriter; in 1876, Bell exhibited a workable telephone. These two office machines, and later inventions such as dictaphones, adding machines, key-punches, duplicating machines, and computers, became the basis for specialized occupations organized around the operation of machines or the performance of specialized tasks such as short-hand dictation. Tasks that were once aspects of the clerk's generalist role were delegated to highly specialized workers. Offices were not immune to the lure of Taylorism and Scientific Management, and as the twentieth century progressed, a wide range of specialized new occupational roles was created, including file clerks, typists, stenographers, billing clerks, and data entry (keypunch) operators; each position was highly specialized, routinized, and easily replaceable (Davies, 1982).

Some clerical work was still concerned with processing information rather than operating machines, but such tasks also tended to become fragmented. The task of issuing insurance policies, for example, may be divided along functional lines, so that a single policy may pass through the hands of several clerical workers, each of whom performs a part of the process. One checks the applicant's credit, another determines rates, and another issues the policy, after an auditor has ensured that all steps have been followed (de Kadt, 1979). There may even be two sets of such clerks whose tasks are the same, but who are limited to either commercial or residential insurance.

Clerical jobs were staffed largely by women in the United States after 1880. Clerical occupations drew from a pool of young women who had few other options. Educated daughters of middle-class families were effectively barred from the professions, with the exception of teaching and nursing. For less advantaged women, the office, which was cleaner and less dangerous than the mills and factories, was a somewhat more desirable option. Women tended to fill the more specialized and lower-paying jobs, while men moved into the new office manager positions. By 1930, the majority of working women were employed in offices rather than factories. Research conducted in Minneapolis at that time found that most were young—between 18 and 25 years of age (Benet, 1972:49). There was an expressed preference for young women, and employers generally felt that general education was not of any value for clerical work. This study suggests the solidification of attitudes and patterns of clerical work that have lingered.

The assertion that general education was not a prerequisite for clerical positions tends to confirm that much of the work had already become routinized and was easily learned. The predominance of younger workers reveals the high rate of turnover, with each cohort of young women being replaced by a new group fresh from school. This trend raises an interesting question about the relationship between work and family roles. The usual explanation for departure from the work force is that it reflects voluntary withdrawal in favor of the more desirable alternative—marriage and the assumption of child-rearing and household responsibilities. However, an alternative explanation should also be considered: It may be that marriage was actually the *second* choice, being preferable only because office work was so unrewarding and lacking in opportunities for advancement (Benet, 1972:49).

Some women, albeit a minority, were able to transcend the combination of social and organizational constraints upon occupational attainment. That they were the exception is evidenced by the fact that women who were successfully able to combine paid work and homemaker tasks literally made headlines in newspapers during the 1920s:

> Gertrude Ford proves that it is possible to maintain a house, be a Devoted Mother and conduct a Successful Business[2]

In any occupation, high turnover combined with a large pool of replacements will tend to depress wages, but it also means that there is no incentive to provide career opportunities or invest much effort in training workers for more responsibile positions. As a result, most clerical occupations evolved as dead-end work. Women who remained in office work were able to move into other forms of clerical work—from typist to stenographer to bookkeeper—but seldom into the role of office manager.

In the small-scale office of the nineteenth century, social relationships were direct and personal. The sheer increase in size of modern organizations, combined with the division of labor created the need for other forms of supervision. Office managers, usually male, were made responsible for the supervision and surveillance of female white-collar workers. Over the years, surveillance has become closer and more sophisticated. In countless large and small organizations, the clerical staff labors away at desks aligned in neat rows in spacious, well-lighted rooms. Hundreds of workers may be found in a single work area, unencumbered by any partitions to give even a semblance of privacy. Architecture is used to facilitate the visual surveillance of clerical workers, in the hopes of raising productivity. An executive boasts that, "The mere fact that you are out there, that all eyes are on you, causes you to spend less time lighting cigarettes and visiting" (DeKadt, 1979:244).

Close monitoring of clerical workers appears to be the norm. Telephone companies routinely listen in on conversations to ensure that operators are following minutely prescribed procedures (Langer, 1970). Computers have recently provided an even more continuous and invidious form of checking the work of clerical staffs. It is estimated that two-thirds of the 7 million United States workers using video display terminals are monitored electronically by their employers (U.S. Department of Labor, 1985:5). Computers count keystrokes, record errors, and monitor time

---

[2]Quoted in Kessler-Harris, 1982:235.

away from the keyboard. One airline reservation company gives demerits to clerks who spend more than 109 seconds per telephone call, or allow more than 11 seconds to elapse between calls (El Nasser, 1986).

PRIVATE SECRETARIES

Surveys consistently show that most clerical workers are dissatisfied with opportunities for career advancement (U.S. Department of Labor, 1985:11). Until very recently, the major route to upward mobility for clerical workers required becoming a private secretary to an executive. The term *secretary*, which derives from the Latin *secretum*, was used in medieval times to refer to the people who handled the secret communications of rulers and wealthy merchants (Vinnicombe, 1980:9). The position required skills in writing and computation, of course, but because the job involved highly confidential matters, the employer-employee relationship was built upon mutual trust and loyalty; these remain the most desirable qualities for the private secretary. It is not uncommon for unique personal relationships to develop between bosses and secretaries. Susan Vinnicombe's (1980) research among British women revealed that not one secretary had anything critical to say about his or her boss. Some of the relationships had matured over many years, starting when the bosses had low-level managerial positions and in some cases involving a move from one company to another. The role of private secretary has been one which allows the development of meaningful and rewarding careers that often pay well, carry prestige, allow a good deal of discretion, and make a visible contribution to the functioning of the organization.

The career line for a secretary usually culminates with the position of executive secretary. It typically carries a great deal of responsibility and requires the ability to delegate routine work to other, lower-grade secretaries. A professional secretarial association estimates that the salaries of executive secretaries in business average between $30,000 and $50,000 (Milford, 1984:1C). Tasks involve handling communications, scheduling, coordinating activities, and researching, as well as routine typing, filing, and taking dictation. Because their work is viewed as facilitating the work of their bosses, however, it is not often that they receive credit for such administrative tasks, and it may be the manager who earns credit for the secretary's efforts.

The fragmentation and control which characterize much lower-level clerical work are actually reversed among private secretaries at the executive level. As is shown in Exhibit 5:5, it is the secretary who directs the executive's time, follows up to ensure that tasks are completed, screens visitors and chooses who sees the boss, and effectively determines what kind of information reaches the executive. Moreover, private secretaries

EXHIBIT 5:5   Work Relationships in the Private Secretary Role

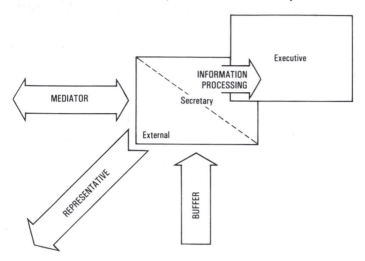

perform a wide variety administrative, staff, and interpersonal functions. Top private secretaries can clearly operate as effective partners for their bosses (Vinnicombe, 1980:55).

Not all secretaries reach this level, and some among those who have reached it have found the relationship unsatisfactory, because the very characteristics that have allowed some managers and secretaries to develop meaningful interrelated careers also have the potential to limit career development and produce unsatisfactory working conditions. Rosabeth Kanter (1977:73ff) has argued that secretarial work is a "patrimonial relic of feudalism." She isolates several elements of patrimony in the social organization of secretarial work, two of which are most relevant.

Principled arbitrariness.   Most jobs in organizations are defined by written job descriptions. The position of secretary, on the other hand, has remained one that rests upon a "personal set of procedures and understandings carved out by secretary and boss." Each secretarial job is a specific, nonbureaucratic relationship negotiated between individuals. It is so specific that managers who are allocated private secretaries for the first time often do not know how to effectively structure their work (Vinnicombe, 1980:27).

Organizational customs, social norms, and the law may set limits, but superiors generally have unusual freedom to demand that private secretaries perform a wide range of tasks—both personal and administrative. Managerial discretion is buttressed by formal authority and control of performance evaluation. When either party departs, a new relationship must be established. The result is wide variability among secretarial positions. Some managers allow their secretaries to exercise initiative and assume administrative responsibility. Thus, some secretaries are able to shape their positions into that of administrative assistant, albeit without the official title or recognition. However, personal secretaries more typically seem to feel that their skills and abilities are underutilized (Kanter, 1977; Vinnicombe, 1980; Kagan and Malveaux, 1986). One of the most common complaints among private secretaries in the aforementioned British study was the amount of time devoted to typing and retyping the same letters and reports (Vinnicombe, 1980:26–28). These secretaries stated that they enjoyed the responsibility that they were able to assume when their bosses were absent and wished that they would be permitted to continue to operate at that level. "A secretary is only as good as her boss will let her be," said one. Many managers were adamant in their refusal to delegate responsibility to their secretaries.

A serious area of contention is that, as the role has evolved in at least some organizations, secretarial responsibilities have expanded from strictly office tasks to encompass a whole range of personal services. In the majority of cases, these services are provided by female secretaries for male employers. In some cases, these tasks involve handling the employer's personal checkbook and private correspondence, sending holiday cards, and keeping the office neat and attractive, as well as making the coffee. It is not surprising that countless observers typify the secretarial role as that of "office wife," for these services are the office equivalent of housework tasks in the home and are divided along the same gender lines. Female managers are less likely than their male counterparts to expect personal services from their secretaries (Kagan and Malveaux, 1986:108).

The office wife analogy may also be extended to the social relationship itself, calling for the secretary to be confidant, adviser, protector. Some secretaries have themselves used the marriage metaphor; one secretary, in recalling how she felt when she was promoted, reveals, "I really felt a marriage was ending when we both talked about my moving. It was almost as sad as getting a divorce" (Kanter, 1977:90). There are many outspoken critics of this perspective, and research indicates that it has at least some impact upon job satisfaction (Grandjean and Taylor, 1980).

Also a controversial issue is the emphasis on physical attractiveness and personality as criteria. This perspective began to emerge early in this century. "I expect from my stenographer the same service I get from the sun, . . . to radiate my office with sunshine and sympathetic interest in the things I am trying to do," noted a businessman in a 1916 *Ladies Home Journal* article (Kessler-Harris, 1982:149). It was at about the same time that the Katharine Gibbs secretarial school was founded; the curriculum heavily emphasized posture, personal grooming, cleanliness, and attractive clothing as well as technical skills such as typing and filing (Kanter, 1977:76). The issue is complex. It may be argued that the Gibbs model is a legitimate expectation for private secretaries who represent the organization to outsiders and who have responsibilities that bring them into contact with upper-level executives, where the importance of appearance and grooming at all levels is part of the conventional wisdom. But there are also non work-related interpretations that focus on secretaries as symbols and degrade them as persons. For the burgeoning middle-managerial class, a personal secretary becomes a status symbol, a symbol of success, an occupational perk to be displayed to others. A more psychoanalytic view suggests that the female secretary of the male manager is typecast as sex symbol, suggesting her potential availability, possibly contributing to the sexual harassment so common in modern offices.

Status contingency.   Just as the feudal ruler's power would define the status of members of the court, secretarial rewards in the form of prestige, privilege, power, and treatment by others is often linked to the rank of the boss, not their own skills or efforts. At the corporation studied by Kanter, there were five secretarial levels, defined almost exclusively by the rank of the managerial superior. In effect, the only way for a secretary to improve salary, office size, and prestige was to remain with a boss who was promoted or to be transferred to an executive who was entitled to pay a higher scale.

Moreover, because secretarial work is often viewed as facilitating the boss' performance, they may fail to receive credit for their efforts. Rather, the manager may win the credit. In other cases, secretaries do not have the opportunity to develop meaningful skills (Grandjean and Taylor, 1980), a process usually called *trained incompetence.* If they do develop these skills, they often are not rewarded for them. As a result, they may not even be aware that they have skills. As a case in point, eight out of ten secretaries in Kanter's study (1977:93) reported having no skill in "interviewing and selecting," when in fact other research shows that secretaries screen virtually all mail, visitors, and telephone calls, and personally and independently handle over 40 percent of all such contacts (Vinnicombe, 1980:105).

About one-third of all women in the paid labor force in the United States are in clerical work of one kind or another. Many perform routine and repetitive tasks under the close scrutiny of supervisors. In Japan, most large companies will not hire women for anything but clerical work, nor promote them into managerial positions (Chira, 1985). Other industrial countries have made more progress in opening channels of upward mobility to women who begin their careers in the clerical occupations. Yet it appears that clerical work continues to be undervalued in terms of rewards, prestige, and recognition of its contribution to the functioning of the organization. Secretaries often facilitate the work of managers in a way that goes unrecognized by the organization and the managers themselves.

CONCLUSION

The context of white-collar work is the organization. The organizational chart is an apt metaphor for the organization. Most people occupy a specific place on an organizational chart, real or symbolic, with standardized *responsibilities*. People move among the positions, but the jobs are institutionalized. The only exception is likely to be the role of secretary, which, along with a few others such as "special assistant," is characteristically not defined structurally, but rather interpersonally with the immediate superior. A few, like data entry operators, have narrowly circumscribed roles offering little opportunity to exercise much discretion in the way they do their work. In general, roles are progressively more abstractly defined at each level, allowing more discretion. For some members of the technostructure, organizational roles prove to be incompatible with membership in larger occupational communities.

Equally salient are the organizational *relationships* mandated by the organizational chart. Authority is implied, but individuals must constantly negotiate their formal right to direct subordinates. This is nowhere more evident than at the executive level, where the overt display of authority is rare, and direction usually takes the form of bargaining and persuasion. By the same token, supervisors who rely solely upon the formal authority of the position generally create the least satisfactory work relationships. Thus, the exercise of formal authority is a delicate and intricate process.

Moreover, the effective performance of both organizations and individuals frequently demands the active cooperation of those outside the formal lines of authority. Organizational charts can only establish direct lines of authority; they ignore the realities of working relationships. Administrative personnel at all levels are concerned with the exercise of different forms of social control—authority, power, and influence. Such activities were long dismissed as merely "office politics," a detriment to the smooth functioning of organizations. Currently, however, they are recognized as inherent in the structure of organizations.

SIX

Blue-Collar Work

INTRODUCTION: MANUAL WORK

The tasks of blue-collar workers are manual: operating or repairing machines, driving trucks, assembling products, building houses, or harvesting fields; in the final analysis, though, it is largely the work setting that identifies blue-collar workers. They labor in the factories and fields, garages and repair shops, and mills and mines, *not* the offices, labs, law courts, and classrooms (except possibly at night to ready them for the white-collar world). Within this group there is great diversity, with some earning high wages and enjoying stable employment, while others face harsh working conditions and an uncertain future. The most useful division that can be made within blue-collar work follows skill lines.

CRAFT OCCUPATIONS: SKILL AND PRIDE

Craft work currently accounts for approximately 10 to 15 percent of the paid labor force in the United States. A wide variety of occupations are counted in this category. Some, such as carpentry, auto mechanics, and construction and electrical work number in the hundreds of thousands, but smaller trades, such as tailoring and shoemaking, employ only a few thousand workers.

All craft occupations require some degree of manual dexterity combined with mastery of a broad knowledge of tools, materials, and processes. All craft work combines *formal* and *experiential* knowledge. These terms distinguish between the more organized knowledge that can best be acquired in the classroom and that knowledge which is acquired, refined, and sharpened by prolonged, first-hand practical experience. This distinction is institutionalized in apprenticeship programs, which currently enroll some 250,000 workers (U.S. Department of Labor, 1984b:18). Most programs specify somehwere between 100 and 800 hours a year of attendance in the classroom, where apprentices learn such skills as trade mathematics, blueprint reading and drafting, characteristics of materials, and fundamentals of subjects such as electricity. Those not apprenticed are exposed to the same kinds of subjects in trade schools, the military, union- or government-sponsored schools, or employer-operated programs.

When not in the classroom, apprentices are involved in on-the-job training under the supervision of senior members of the trade. Most typically, apprentices spend two to four years in this type of training. It is here that the trainee learns to apply classroom knowledge and acquires the skills not easily grasped in the abstract environment of the classroom—how to handle tools, how to judge the quality of materials by mere touch or sight, and how to avoid dangerous situations.

The idea of experiential knowledge is well described by Michael Polanyi's (1962) phrase *tacit knowledge*—"the things we know, but cannot tell" the subtle expertise which emerges from years of work, but which is often difficult for the individual to explain to others. It shows up in the carpenter's knowledge of woods and grains, the mechanic's ability to diagnose the trouble with an engine merely from the sound of it, the steel worker's ability to select the correct cable to lift an iron beam even when he is unaware of the exact weight of the load or the lifting capacity of cable.

Take, for example, the story of "Black Tom" Martin, a seventy-year-old white crane operator at work on a building on Seventh Avenue in New York (related in Cherry, 1974:106–108). One day he was approached by a group of university-trained engineers with a new and theoretically sound technique for hoisting steel beams. His experience alerted him to some flaw in the plan that he was simply not able to verbalize; it reduced him to grumbling, "It will fall down." The engineers, armed with their blueprints and computations, insisted, and the old man agreed to cooperate only after securing the engineers' promise to "run thataway," pointing in a direction away from where he predicted the crane would fall. The crane collapsed, just as he had predicted (and his warning averted any injuries). Black Tom simply picked his way through the rubble and took the subway home. His story has become part of the subcultural mythology of steel workers, demonstrating the triumph of experience over abstract principles.

The craft workers' skill is usually accompanied by a strong sense of pride in their work, and a sense of identification with their occupation. There is no neat sociological or psychological index of this sense of pride, but it is manifested in the way they think about their work, their relationships with their bosses, and even in their hopes for their children. When construction workers gather to share a drink—and they do tend to socialize among themselves—the conversation often turns to their work, and their sense of accomplishment is evident:

> I tell you, Lee, I get a hell of a kick when I see a building I helped put up. You know the Edgewater Hotel down by the lake . . . I worked on that fifteen years ago and she's still beautiful. I did the paneling in that dining room that looks out over the water. Sometimes I drive down there just to see the damn thing—do you think I'm nuts or something? (LeMasters, 1975:23)

Another worker said:

> After building a home I feel a sense of accomplishment, something to last 100 years. I feel I've done something for society. (Mackenzie, 1973:19)

Pride in their craft extends to the point where some will challenge their bosses rather than violate their internal standards. Mike Cherry (1974:209) claims that it is not uncommon to find construction workers walking off a job if their supervisors demand shoddy work to expedite the completion of a job. Construction workers, by the nature of their industry, are one of the few occupations to have this luxury. Finally, it must be noted that skilled craftsmen often harbor hopes that their sons will follow in the same type of work (Sennett and Cobb, 1972). Pride, shared skills, and craft traditions often form the basis of strong occupational subcultures.

THE DESKILLING OF CRAFT WORK

To understand modern craft work, it is useful to evoke an image of work in an earlier era—namely, a preindustrial version of the nature of craft trades: cobblers, printers, blacksmiths, and tailors at work in their homes or small shops, surrounded by other craftspersons producing individualized work; highly skilled artisans, apprenticed as youths, trained in the lore and knowledge of the trade, selecting their own materials, working at their own pace, using their own tools to create beautiful hand-crafted objects (Braverman, 1974:109). This ideal is important for two reasons. First, it describes fairly accurately craft work at an earlier point in time, as well as the conditions of a handful of contemporary crafts. The second, and perhaps more important, reason is that this is the ideal that crafts have long cherished and fought to protect from the encroachment of industrialization. Trade unions, and the medieval guilds before them, have been the vehicles of craft workers' collective attempts to control their work.

The Guild System

Some crafts, such as the ancient trades of stone masonry, pottery, and weaving, are as old as recorded history. However, it was not until the tenth century in Europe that they became a significant force, as people began to congregate in urban areas, creating a demand for processed and manufactured goods. Their work was based upon a broad knowledge of materials and techniques. Weavers, tailors, silversmiths, and shoemakers mastered *all* aspects of the production process, including design, selection of raw materials, pace, and choice of components, as well as the crafting of the finished product. Such skills were acquired during a prolonged (three to seven years) apprenticeship under the supervision of a master craft worker. Artisans were constrained by the demands of employers (many worked for master craftspersons) and the consumers of their products or services, but because of the scarcity of their skill, they were usually able to maintain a significant level of individual autonomy in their work.

Those who practiced these trades formed guilds and were thus able to collectively control many dimensions of their work. At the peak of their power, guilds controlled entry to the trade; regulated prices, materials, and the quality of work; and defended their monopoly against trespassers from other occupations. They maintained a control not unlike that exerted by some contemporary professions (Burrage and Corry, 1981:375). United as they were by the bonds of a skill and by membership in occupational associations, it is not surprising that workers shared a special bond of identity. Some were called "mysteries," symbolizing the subtleness and exclusiveness of their expertise. Many guilds wore insignia and distinctive clothing and marched as groups in parades and other public ceremonies. As Braverman (1974:109) puts it, the craft was the basic unit of production, but the individual worker was "the master of a body of traditional knowledge, and (thus) methods and procedures were left to his or her discretion."

A few contemporary crafts retain these three key characteristics—worker autonomy, occupational control of the conditions of work, and a strong sense of community with other workers—but many observers argue that the history of craft work can be read as a protracted contest against merchants, employers, and the more impersonal social and economic forces of industrialization which have threatened to trivialize their skills and dilute their control. Many previously skilled crafts have been reduced to unskilled work by the introduction of mechanization and the restructuring of industrial production. It has become accepted usage to refer to this process as *deskilling,* although the term blurs some differences in emphasis among authors.

Members of some occupations had apparently formed social and mutual aid associations as early as 1100 (Pirenne, 1962). These evolved into the medieval occupational associations called *craft guilds.* A thirteen-century census in Paris listed some 6,000 artisans organized into 448 craft guilds (Pounds, 1974:294). Most were engaged in the production of food (bakers, butchers, millers, fishers) or clothing (weavers, tailors, mercers, tanners, and skinners), although a significant number of guilds catered exclusively to the specialized needs of the wealthy (goldsmiths and silversmiths, glove makers, and armorers).

Guilds organized on a local basis to protect themselves from competition. They sought and won charters from municipal authorities granting the exclusive right to practice their craft. Only members in good standing were permitted to practice within the town. Municipal authorities at first retained control over the appointment of guild officers and insisted upon guild rules governing the quality of materials and workmanship. Towns also collected an annual fee from the guilds. Thus, early charters may be seen both as revenue generators and as a compromise between artisans seeking to safeguard their own livelihood and town governments attempting to protect the public from unscrupulous and incompetent artisans.

Apprenticeship was the key screening device. Those aspiring to a trade were required to complete an apprenticeship under the tutelage of a master craft worker. Children were apprenticed at ages as young as ten or twelve, and the training could extend for as long as a dozen years. The master provided food, clothing, and lodging in addition to instruction in the intricacies of the trade. Apprentices were legally entitled to decent treatment as long as they were industrious and obedient, although masters often retained the right to beat reluctant novices (Renard, 1918:11). Training culminated with an extensive oral examination or with the production of a flawless example of the craft (hence the word *masterpiece*).

Success earned the status of "journeyman" and the right to employment. Many artisans remained at this level, continuing in the employ of a master, partly because of the practice of limiting the number of openings, as in the town of Limoges (France), which allowed a maximum of six master barbers. Vacancies caused by death were filled by those who scored well on competitive exams. In other guilds, the position of master became hereditary, and only the sons of masters were eligible. Restrictions such as these on internal mobility eventually contributed to the decline of the guilds.

Guilds also strictly regulated the behavior of members. They established hours, wages, prices, and the tools, techniques, and materials to be used. Some of these specifications were minute and precise. They might include statements of the size of the mesh in a fishnet or the number of vats a dyer must use, the prohibition against working by candlelight, limits on the number of apprentices, or a prescribed method for filling a bushel with onions (such as, "Place the arms around it in order to ensure a full measure," [Renard, 1918:33–35]). Violators were punished by fines or even expulsion from the group.

By the fourteenth century in Western Europe, some guilds had gained independence from the supervision of town governments. They won the right to self-government and control over the nomination of senior officials. As they gained political power, guilds were able to accomplish a complete reversal and gain control of municipal government. In Liege in 1384, the administration was headed by a council of representatives of the 32 crafts in the city.

Guilds were more than work associations; they were social groups exhibiting internal solidarity and dedicated to the principle that the welfare of the group should take precedence over individual advantage (Shorter, 1973:11). This philosophy no doubt represented a continuation of their origins as fraternal bodies. The keystone of this philosophy was to be found in the regulations that called for the standardization of materials and methods: Standardization prevented competition. But there were other deterrents to internal dissension. Advertising was prohibited. Work begun by one artisan could not be taken over by another. Limits were imposed on the amount of raw materials which could be purchased and on the number of apprentices any master could employ.

Guilds were also oriented toward the mutual aid of members and their families. Artisans could turn to the guild for financial help in time of need or for medical care in case of illness. Money was dispensed to widows and orphans of guild members. Members provided hospitality for traveling journeymen in search of work. A death in the guild called for closing shops, attending the funeral, and coming to the aid of the family. Many guilds held regular banquets. It was thus a group held together by social as well as economic ties (Renard, 1918).

Guilds flourished between the thirteenth and fifteenth centuries, but were already declining in importance in the sixteenth century. They were formally abolished in France during the Revolution, and soon after in most other countries. The guilds were destroyed by internal problems coupled with changing social and economic conditions. Internal problems centered on the breakdown of the old economic and social solidarity. Achieving master status became increasingly difficult because many positions were hereditary; even when they were not, the number of vacancies was limited. This situation blocked mobility for a large cadre of journeymen and served to accentuate the differences in income and working conditions between the two levels. There were many instances of journeymen attempting to seize control of guilds, organizing strikes, or forming independent associations.

Another internal problem was that some craft guilds began to be infiltrated by merchants who did not work at the trade and may not even have served an apprenticeship (Burrage and Corry, 1981). In London, the guilds of clockmakers, masons, blacksmiths, and chandlers remained predominantly handicraft associations for most of their histories, but the guilds of vintners, drapers, and others were dominated by merchants whose interest was in buying and selling rather than in the manufacturing process.

Internal divisions were further compounded by the guilds' inability to cope with changing social and economic conditions in the larger society. Centralized national governments were growing in power and influence at the expense of guilds, towns, parishes, and other locally organized groups. A widening of the market for manufactured goods rendered guilds more and more dependent upon merchants who purchased and marketed their products (Schneider, 1969:39). Emerging capitalism and industrialization created the need for large numbers of workers and freedom of movement, and placed a premium on innovation and minimization of costs. The guild system was, in short, well adapted to protecting the individual craft worker and the occupation in the decentralized conditions of the early medieval world, but it was not able to survive in the face of industrialization and capitalism.

Craft Workers in America

Some craft workers such as shoemakers, coopers, and tailors attempted to establish guilds in America as early as the mid-1600s, but none survived much longer than a year (Rayback, 1966:16). Any successes achieved by craft workers were accomplished by trade unions. Employed craft workers sporadically formed *combinations* (as the early unions were called) to protest declining wages all during the eighteenth century. Tailors in New York City called the first authenticated strike in 1768, followed by carpenters in New Jersey six years later. Combinations formed during this period were generally short-lived.

The first deliberate and enduring attempts at forming permanent unions for mutual protection and worker control appeared at the end of the eighteenth century. Between 1790 and 1820, shoemakers, tailors, printers, carpenters, masons, coopers, cabinet makers, and others organized locals in major metropolitan areas such as New York and Philadelphia. Progress was sporadic over the next several decades, with union activity often interrupted by cycles of depression and unemployment caused by overcrowding, which weakened the workers' bargaining position. In addition, employers successfully persuaded the courts that unions were "conspiracies in restraint of trade." Those that were able to organize were also able to maintain a high level of control over the work process.

Most printers in the composing rooms of newspapers, for example, had qualified for their trade by apprenticeship to a master printer, for a period lasting until the age of 21 for males and 16 for females. During this training, an apprentice was expected to master all phases of the printing process—layout, hand composition, and presswork. In each phase the printer utilized many skills and exercised high levels of discretion and judgment. Composition was more than merely setting the type by hand—although that was a complex task requiring a great deal of manual dexterity, spacing judgment, and knowledge of spelling, punctuation, and hyphenation rules. The compositor reviewed the manuscript, selected the typefaces, laid out the pages, pulled proofs of the completed page, and proofread the work (Baron, 1982).

Printers considered themselves "companions" and equals, linked by the bonds of tradition and common occupational culture. Workers were paid as a team, and the team decided on the internal division of tasks and rotation of assignments. The work process was supervised by printers, not employers (Baron, 1982:34). Other craft workers enjoyed some of the same advantages. For example, as late as 1889, the skilled steelworkers' union had authority over every aspect of the steel-making process at Carnegie's Homestead mill (Stone, 1974:118). Hiring, apportioning work, and regulating machinery all required the consent and approval of the Amalgamated Association of Iron, Steel, and Tin Workers.

However, technological innovations and new forms of industrial organization had already begun to reshape craft work. The most visible events were the new forms of mechanization. Sophisticated machinery had the potential to simplify previously complex tasks and enable replacement of skilled workers with unskilled machine operators. In some dramatic cases, craft workers were reduced to factory operatives within their own lifetimes. Shoemakers are but one example. As late as 1840, shoe shops were small cottage industries employing a few journeymen who made shoes by hand using methods learned during an apprenticeship lasting several years. Within two decades, the entire process was mechanized, beginning with a sewing machine capable of stitching soles to uppers, followed by buffing, dying, and leather-splitting machines. By the 1860s, most shoemakers found themselves machine operators in shoe factories with jobs such as beating, binding, cutting, dressing, or edge setting (Rodgers, 1978:23; Rayback, 1966:50). Likewise, glovers, blacksmiths, glassblowers, coopers, cigar makers, hatters, and other craft workers who had once mastered the making of an entire product or a total process now found the need for such skills to be all but eliminated.

These processes spawned new skilled trades. Machinists, electricians, and railroad engineers are all products of this era, just as auto mechanics and television technicians are more recent trades. In some cases, the work process became more complex, leading to internal divisions within previously homogeneous crafts. Printing presses became larger, faster, more complex, and capable of printing several colors simultaneously. Press operators began to evolve as a separate specialty. Coinciding with this were innovations in the making of plates (reproductions of the typeset pages) for the presses. Metal plates, followed by rubber and plastic, evolved as did new methods of reproducing photographs, with the result that platemaking became a second specialty requiring new and complex skills. Eventually, new craft unions splintered off from the original International Typographical Union, which initially represented all printing crafts (Zimbalist, 1979).

Employers apparently implemented mechanization for a variety of reasons. Machines produce a more standardized product and the opportunity to reduce costs and increase output. Braverman (1974) and Clawson (1980) argue that machine-paced work also reduces the autonomy and decision-making capacity of the worker, and places control over the pace of the work in the hands of the employer. Deskilling is thus a means of asserting employer control over the work place.

Even where no new machinery existed, employers sought to weaken the position of craft workers by subdividing the process into simpler components. The more routine work could thus be assigned to lower-priced workers. Newspaper publishers, for example, tried to teach simple typesetting (straight text without headlines) to nonunion workers as a means of weakening their reliance upon union printers. Publishers also attempted to circumvent the apprenticeship system by hiring and training their own workers. These workers, trained for narrow and specific jobs, lacked the broad skills which afforded apprentice-trained workers the freedom to leave for other employment. In other cases, trades became overcrowded, creating a pool of skilled workers willing to work for lower wages and willing to submit to the authority of employers.

Some trade unions were successful in forestalling the encroachments of mechanization and subdivision. The printers' union—the International Typographical Union (ITU)—is a notable case (see Lipset, Trow, and Coleman, 1956:22ff; Zimbalist, 1979; Wallace and Kalleberg, 1982). The perfection of the Linotype machine in the 1890s had the potential to displace countless hand typesetters and enable them to be replaced with relatively unskilled machine operators. The union responded by creating its own Linotype training schools and insisting that operators also serve conventional apprenticeships which qualified them in all the printers' skills. The battle was joined in a series of strikes until the ITU prevailed. Increases in productivity occasioned by the Linotype machine were translated into shorter hours, a situation that prevailed at least until World War II.

Printers as a group enjoyed some special advantages in their struggle. For one thing, printers everywhere during this period exhibited a strong sense of pride in their craft and an accompanying sense of solidarity. This facilitated organization and collective action. Strikes by printers in France were recorded as early as 1539, and printers from Russia to Argentina were among the first crafts to organize in response to industrialization (Lipset, Trow, and Coleman, 1956:28). Then, too, their skills were not easily replaceable. Compositors needed manual dexterity plus a working knowledge of grammar, punctuation, syllabification, and spelling in order to read copy, correct errors, and set type; they also needed some artistic and aesthetic flair to design pages (Baron, 1982:32). Finally, the nature of schedules and deadlines in newspaper printing meant that even short strikes or slowdowns could cost publishers a good deal of money.

At the peak of its power in the 1950s, the craft union dictated "manning rules" (in which the union determined the number of persons required to operate machinery), "priority" systems (lists of hiring preferences compiled by the union), and rules forbidding employers from transferring printers from one task (say typesetting) to another (such as proofreading). In some cases, they even enforced closed-shop requirements despite their illegality.

More recently, technological advances and shifts in the structure of the industry have produced changes that are overwhelming the craft aspects of printing. Photocomposing and computer-operated typesetters have the potential to bypass the composing room entirely. Persons with average secretarial skills can type copy onto a tape, which is fed into a computer, which produces a finished tape—correctly justified, hyphenated, and ready for an automatic typesetting machine. At the offices of large newspapers, reporters can compose their copy at video display terminals, where it is edited and transferred directly into the computer for typesetting at 150 lines a minute, compared to 3 lines a minute for a Linotype operator (*Time*, 1974).

During this period, changes were also occurring in the newspaper industry itself that facilitated and encouraged the implementation of new technology. Declining profit margins encouraged larger employers to attempt to reduce high labor costs by mechanizing the labor process. There was a concurrent trend toward a concentrating and centralizing capital in the hands of a smaller number of publishing firms. The result has been an erosion of workers' skills and craft control in composing rooms (Wallace and Kalleberg, 1982). It is reflected in a decline in their relative wages when compared to other printing occupations, and especially to the skilled construction trades.

The construction trades have also been able to maintain a good deal of control, especially in large urban areas. The selection and training of new apprentices is in the hands of a joint union-contractor committee. Construction is carried out under work agreements between contractors and associations of building trades which carefully allocate specific tasks to specific groups. These jurisdictional boundaries are seen in the use of the "Chicago boom," a crane-like device for lifting equipment and materials such as glass between floors of buildings under construction. The ironworkers' union erects the boom, oilers fuel and maintain it, operating engineers operate it, and glaziers handle the glass (Cherry, 1974). Hiring and firing of workers is in the hands of the union, and work at the site is distributed either by the union supervisor or informally by the workers themselves. For example, it is a common practice to give the least strenuous work to the older workers. Although each craft jealously guards its own jurisdiction, the crafts respect each other and will accommodate their own work to the needs and concerns of others. Workers may slow their pace or change the sequence of their work in deference to others (Riemer, 1979:22).

As was the case with printing compositors, there are special circumstances that help to account for construction workers' advantaged position (Riemer, 1981). One of the most important is the very nature of the construction process. The work necessarily takes place at the site, making it difficult to introduce the close supervision which characterizes factory work. Each building or job has unique characteristics (with the exception of some residential tract housing), so it is difficult to standardize the tasks. Finally, the work tends to be seasonal and unpredictable, and the need for particular trades varies over the course of a job. Therefore, contractors cannot usually afford to employ a regular work force, but must employ craftspersons as needed. The result is that over half of all construction workers are independent entrepreneurs who are hired where and when needed (Eccles, 1981:450). Many more are organized into small firms of two to five workers in the same trade who subcontract for a specific part of the building (such as the electrical or plumbing components). With many potential contractors, and with hiring in the hands of the union, workers are not dependent upon a single employer. It is within this context that craft unions became powerful enough to retain occupational control over the work process.

The ideal model of the skilled craft worker also prevails in other situations, usually among those who work in small shops dealing directly with consumers. Some blacksmiths, tailors, jewelers, watchmakers, auto mechanics, and television repairers are the most common examples. They learn their trades on the job or in trade schools, become expert at all aspects of jobs, and enjoy a good deal of autonomy. However, most craft workers are employees of government or industry. As a consequence, responsibility for training, employment, allocation of work, selection of materials, quality control, and determination of work pace—all of which once resided with either the individual or the association—has shifted to the employer.

RACIAL AND GENDER SEGREGATION IN THE CRAFTS

Craft work in America in the century between the Civil War and the 1960s has generally been a white male domain. Up until as late as 1970, the proportion of women in the crafts hovered around 2 or 3 percent except during World War II, when men called into military service were temporarily replaced by women. Black male participation in the skilled crafts was also restricted during this period, usually representing no more than 6 percent after 1900. The origin of these patterns is intimately linked to the search for maintaining control over the work process and the struggle against deskilling.

In some cases the barriers were formalized, as when machinists excluded blacks from union membership in 1888 (Marshall, 1967), or as when barbers excluded women (Foner, 1964:226). Most craft occupations came to be identified as white male work. Consequently, even after restrictive practices were eroded by legislative and judicial action and changing social values, the excluded groups continued to confront discriminatory practices. Also important is the fact that crafts frequently came to be organized around white male values and traditions; others became "outsiders," and it was difficult for them to break into the occupational subcultures.

The overall levels of participation of women and blacks obscures differences among specific jobs. Within the building trades, for example, blacks have always been able to claim a greater share of work as cement and concrete finishers than as electricians or plumbers. This is because occupational segregation evolved at different points in different industries, and the process was influenced by the unique history and circumstances of each craft.

Gender segregation of the crafts. Focusing upon the struggle between craft workers and employers over the control of the work process illuminates the origins of gender-based segregation in the printing trades.[3] Women frequently worked beside men in the early print shops and newspapers of eighteenth and nineteenth century America. It must be remembered that shops were often small, rural, and family-run, and that women made up a significant proportion of the hand compositors—nearly one-half according to an estimate during the Civil War period.

Between the 1850s and 1870s, the owners attempted to exert control over the work process and reduce their dependence upon skilled printers. Women became embroiled in this struggle. Publishers began to have some of their more routine typesetting done outside the newspaper composing room, thus circumventing the control of skilled printers. Skilled women printers from rural areas were recruited to work in these "job shops," as they were called, and were paid lower wages. Publishers also drew upon a pool of unskilled women workers as "rats" (cheaper labor) and "scabs" (strikebreakers). They attempted to recruit women from the clothing and textile industries and to train them for semiskilled printing work and as

---

[3]This section draws extensively upon the analysis of Ava Baron, 1982.

lower-paid typesetters. These workers were attracted to the opportunities in the newspapers because of the notoriously poor pay and conditions in the textile industry. Unfortunately, some middle-class reformers bolstered this movement, hoping to raise the wages of women in the sewing trades, but stopping short of arguing that women should receive the same wages as their male counterparts. During the 1860s, women were employed as strikebreakers at newspapers in Boston, Philadelphia, St. Louis, and Rochester. Not all women took this route, however. Many women joined typographical unions and called (and won) strikes for wages equal to those paid to men.

Still another strategy was to establish publisher-sponsored schools to recruit and train a "female corps of compositors" to circumvent the apprenticeship system. Printers in Chicago accused publishers of secretly teaching female typesetters "in remote rooms of the city" so that they could displace male union printers. Male printers referred to the influx of women as the "petticoat invasion." It was opposed at the outset, not exclusively on the grounds of gender, but also on the grounds that it was an attempt by proprietors to deskill newspaper work. This is evident in the fact that men and women printers cooperated in the fight for equal pay, the inclusion of apprenticeship-trained women in unions (Augusta Lewis, the president of the first women's local, was a member of the executive council of the predominantly male national union), financial support for women's locals, and the refusal of women to act as strikebreakers. This solidarity broke down, however, and by the early 1870s, newspaper composition was headed toward becoming an exclusively male domain.

The sources of the exclusionary trend have been located in a number of different factors (Baron, 1982). Publishers continued to employ unskilled women at lower pay, and the previous history of women strikebreakers lingered on. Male workers were also concerned that an influx of women would create overcrowding and serve to depress wages. Thus, the exclusion of women would prevent the devaluation of men's labor. This issue of wages articulated contemporary cultural conceptions of male and female roles. It was not uncommon for men to argue that earning a "family wage" was their right, as part of their responsibility to maintain their position as providers and protectors of the family unit. In 1905, Samuel Gompers argued, "In our time, . . . there is no necessity for the wife contributing to the support of the family by working" (Foner, 1964:224). Gompers and others ignored the fact that the majority of women in the labor force depended upon the income for the necessities of life.

Other issues also surfaced, occupational health and protective legislation for women being one of the most controversial. In 1908, the Supreme Court in *Muller versus Oregon* endorsed special legislation for women on the grounds that they were not as strong as men, were dependent upon men, and were the mothers of future generations (Hill, 1979). Women were excluded from night work, for example, which was a disadvantage in baking and newspaper printing. This too reflects the cultural conceptions of gender. Moreover, some manufacturers supported protective legislation to exclude women for health reasons, as an alternative to improving conditions for all workers (Stellman, 1977). Craft unions were known to lobby for women's health legislation as a means of restricting membership.

Thus, a variety of factors combined to undermine the position of women in the crafts. A few unions expressly forbade the admission of women—barbers and railroad switchers among them. The molders' union resolved in 1907 to seek "the restriction of the further employment of women labor in union core rooms and foundries, and eventually the elimination of such labor in all foundries" (Foner, 1964:226). Women had apparently come to be viewed as competitors for skilled jobs. This conception prevailed well into the 1950s in some craft occupations.

Since 1960, female participation in the skilled crafts has, on the whole, expanded, as shown earlier in Exhibit 1:7; the changes have been uneven, however. Lower levels of employment in a particular craft cannot necessarily be completely explained by discrimination and active resistance to women, although these factors are not to be discounted. The number of women employed in the crafts also reflects the choices and decisions of women, as well as the more subtle socialization and allocation processes that channel people into particular places in the labor force.

Racial segregation.   The skilled crafts historically systematically excluded black workers (Foner, 1964:238). The Civil War and its aftermath is probably among the most decisive of events. Although the exclusion of blacks predated the Civil War, the economic dislocation and racial turmoil that accompanied the period certainly exacerbated the situation. Once the process was set in motion, it fed upon itself.

Emancipation freed southern blacks to compete in the labor market. Many of these workers were skilled craftspersons, having been trained while they were slaves as carpenters, blacksmiths, and tailors. Thomas Brooks (1971:243) estimates that 100,000 of the 120,000 artisans in the South in 1865 were black. In the decades that followed, blacks were steadily eliminated from skilled jobs. Employers refused to hire them; unions refused to allow them into the unions. Machinists, among others, formally excluded blacks between 1888 and 1948 (Marshall, 1967). Unions prevented their members from working with people who were not union members. At the same time, other tactics inhibited the training of the next generation of black workers, with educational opportunities limited, and apprenticeship programs generally closed off.

Many factors were at work in the process of exclusion. For one thing, introduction of any large pool of new workers was certainly perceived by the crafts as having the potential to drastically reduce wages and weaken their bargaining power. This is evident in the fact that the unions later (around 1900) also resisted the immigration of central and eastern workers, about 20 percent of whom were skilled workers (Foner, 1964:257). "Racial purity" was a common term during the period, but the word *racial* encompassed Italians, Poles, Jews, and Asians. Blacks were, of course, victims of the racial prejudice that simmered throughout American society long before this period. Overt racial conflicts occurred in many northern cities, notably in Philadelphia, between 1828 and 1842 (Guerin, 1976:144). Craft union segregation of black workers can best be viewed as the interaction between prejudice and resistance to the threat of deskilling.

Employers in some industries were more than willing to exploit this situation in their battle against unionization. One turn-of-the-century factory owner admits,

> it is one good result of racial prejudice that the negro [*sic*] will enable us in the long run to weaken the trade union so that it cannot harm us. We can keep wages down with the negro, and we can prevent too much organization (quoted in Foner, 1964:241).

Using blacks as strikebreakers was a key element in this strategy. William Tuttle (1970) has illuminated the process by focusing on the meatpacking industry centered in Chicago at the turn of the century. This was a very crucial time for the skilled butcher trades. The industry had come to be dominated by a handful of large packing houses that were seeking to replace skilled butchers by dividing the process of carving the carcasses into many simple operations and hiring unskilled workers to do specific tasks. During a violent ten-week strike in 1904, thousands of black workers served as strikebreakers. One contemporary observer claimed that 1,400 strikebreakers streamed into town on a single train. The response was repeated during a teamsters strike the following year.

This kind of event helped to foster an image in the minds of white workers that all blacks were "scabs." A few opportunistic southern politicians exploited this, as evidenced by this speech to white meat packers, "It was the niggers that whipped you in line. They were the club with which your brains were beaten out" (Tuttle, 1970:93). This image was also advantageous to employers, for it helped to pit black workers against white workers, rather than uniting them against capitalists as a class. Even American Federation of Labor leaders singled out blacks for special abuse; Samuel Gompers wrote of "hordes of ignorant blacks . . . possessing but few of the attributes we have learned to revere and love . . . huge strapping fellows ignorant and vicious whose predominant trait was animalism" (quoted in Foner, 1964:242).

The image of blacks as perpetual scabs appears to have gained wide currency despite countless cases of black-white labor unity in Chicago and elsewhere. During the 1905 teamsters strike, for example, 5,800 strike-breakers were used, but 5,000 of them were white. Most of the black teamsters apparently sided with the union (Foner, 1964:244). It must also be remembered that some unions organized across racial lines—the Knights of Labor had 60,000 black members in the 1880s. The union of cigar makers—a skilled handcraft—had 5,000 black members among a total of approximately 50,000 in around 1910 (Foner, 1964:187;254).

In order to understand both the vulnerability of blacks to strikebreaking activity and their general alienation from the labor movement, it is important to consider their general situation. As aforementioned, they were often excluded from the higher-paying craft unions. Therefore, strikebreaking presented an opportunity to gain access to jobs otherwise closed to them. In addition, many who had migrated north were from rural backgrounds and did not understand their role in the labor struggle. Some black leaders also argued that employers were the natural allies of black workers. Booker T. Washington advised blacks to seek, "the friendship and confidence of a good white man [in other words, an employer] who stands well in the community" (Tuttle, 1970:105).

Black participation in the skilled crafts as a whole dropped to less than 5 percent by 1910 and remained low for some decades. Access was more severely restricted in trades with apprenticeships (such as plumbing and carpentry) than in the trowel trades (bricklaying, masonry, concrete finishing), in which it was easier to obtain employment as an unskilled helper and learn enough to qualify for the trade. Formal racial exclusionary policies began to crumble in the 1940's; since the 1980's, most craft unions have expanded opportunities for black workers. As a consequence, employment in the skilled trades has increased by over 30 percent between 1970 and 1980 (Westcott, 1982). Moreover, in the building trades in 1978, about 19 percent of all registered apprentices were minorities (U.S. Dept. of Labor, 1980:6).

Skilled craft work is frequently referred to as the "aristocracy of labor," an allusion to its advantaged position in terms of economic and social position. Skilled craft work commands higher wages (on the average) than other blue-collar jobs, and it ranks higher on scales of occupational prestige. Craft workers tend to think of themselves in this way, identifying with the skill that sets them apart from the bulk of blue-collar work.

Craft workers have long fought to protect their heritage of skill, first in the guilds and later in trade unions. There can be little question that they sought to inflate wages by restricting membership and limiting apprenticeships. In the process, women and racial and ethnic minorities were long denied access. But there is more to their history and dynamics than economic gain. Craft workers were also striving to protect the integrity of their skill and their autonomy from the encroachment by both technological innovation and employers who sought to deskill their trades. Skill and pride still characterize some craft work; for most crafts, however, control over employment, training, and the work process resides with employers. The crafts continue to exhibit some vestiges of the racial and gender segregation that originated in an earlier period.

Operatives: Machine Work

The second major block of blue-collar workers have traditionally been called *operatives,* reflecting some connection to the machinery of modern manufacturing. Their work involves operating, adjusting, feeding, tending, or maintaining machines of one sort or another. The operative category only makes sense if it is recognized to include a range of machines, from the simplest hand-operated power tools to drill presses and sewing machines to steel furnaces. Moreover, it also includes tasks, such as assembly-line work, in which the worker does not actually control the machinery but rather attends a mechanized process. Many operative occupations are new, having emerged from the industrialization process; others are deskilled versions of earlier craft work.

CASE STUDY: FEEDING THE MACHINES

Much of the blue-collar work in this category is highly specialized, short-cycle, and repetitive. The epitome of such jobs are found on the assembly lines of auto plants and other mass-production industries. A "wet sander," for example, sprays water over the seam where two panels are welded together and sands the joint smooth while moving approximately 30 feet along the conveyor following the chassis. Seventy strokes are required, and the sandpaper is replaced after every other car (Meissner, 1969:101). Other jobs, even those that are not machine-paced, have the same characteristics, as in the case of "bottoming," a subprocess in the manufacture of shoes (Horsfall and Arensberg, 1949). Racks of partially completed shoes are wheeled to a work station, where "trimmers" pick them up, trim the excess material from sole and heel, and pass them to "pounders," whose machines smooth the edges. "Roughers" press the shoes against a revolving wire brush to roughen the surface. At the "shanker's" machine, a small reinforcing strip is stapled in place. "Cementers" spread glue and place the shoes on a rack to be moved to another work station. The duration of each operation can be measured in seconds.

It does not require much time to master such jobs—usually a few days. After that, hand movements become habituated, requiring workers to focus visually on their hands, but not demanding active mental involvement. Many workers report that they are free to think about other things, such as the potential breakdown of the line or the slow passage of the minutes until lunch or quitting time. It was among sewing-machine operators that Donald Roy (1960) uncovered the subcultural ritual of "banana time" (described in Chap. 3), an attempt by workers to relieve the monotony and cope with the endless repetitiveness of their work.

To free themselves from the unremitting pace, workers like to "get ahead" by working as fast as they possibly can to build up a small reserve of parts, thus allowing themselves a few moments respite to chat with coworkers, have a smoke, or just relax. Another strategy is "doubling up"—one worker takes on two jobs for short periods while the other takes a short break. Doubling up has, on occasion, been the source of worker–management conflict (Kreman, 1979). At the Lordstown Chevrolet plant, management outlawed the practice on the grounds that it would lead to lower quality. The auto workers claimed that it produced fewer errors and better quality. At the normal pace, boredom prevailed, causing poor concentration and mistakes, whereas at a maximum pace, workers were forced to concentrate and believed that they actually made fewer errors.

Focusing on the technical tasks involved in these forms of blue-collar mechanical work emphasizes the essential nature of the work—it is monotonous and unremitting. It is monotonous in the sense that it requires constant repetition of the same operations and lacks any real opportunity to vary the process; it is unremitting in the sense that it confronts the worker with what must seem like an endless and constant flow, without any chance to vary the pace. Small wonder that such workers devise ways to interrupt the regime, or that they may burst into applause when the conveyor breaks down. The design of these jobs must also be conceptualized in a broader context, however, for they represent the outcome of certain ways of thinking about workers and the nature of work.

Taylorism and the Specialization of Work

To understand the social organization of this form of operative work, one must understand the ideology that dominated the thinking of administrators and owners in America, Britain, Germany, and France beginning in the late nineteenth century. This approach to administration is usually attributed to the work of Fredrick W. Taylor, who claimed the title *Scientific Management* for his approach to the organization of industrial work. The label itself lost favor in the 1930s, but the basic principles were in vogue in American management circles until at least the 1970s. The term *Taylorism* is frequently used generically to refer to a general set of principles for organizing work; it is used in that context here.

At the end the last century, owners and administrators were confronted with a complex array of problems. Mechanization was changing the scale and nature of the industrial process, and they sought to reorganize industry to take advantage of the potential of the new industrial era. An obvious goal was to increase productivity and, in turn, profits. Maximum output was inhibited, in their view, by several factors.

Probably the most obvious was the unsystematic manner in which these workers approached their work. Many of them came from rural areas, so they lacked familiarity with even the simplest machinery. Workers usually learned to operate their equipment by observation and by trial and error. The result was often inefficient. In addition, Taylor himself was fond of estimating that workers were producing only one-third of what could be expected, because of what he called loafing, or *soldiering*. In part it was "the natural instinct and tendency of men to take it easy," but there was also systematic soldiering, those informal agreements among workers to set limits on output that are today understood as part of worker subcultures (see Braverman, 1974:98). Taylor was convinced that workers set these group norms deliberately to prevent employers from knowing how fast any job could actually be done.

Beyond efficiency, however, there was also the goal of wresting control of the work process from the worker, both individually and collectively. It must be remembered that jobs that are today highly mechanized were once the domain of versatile skilled workers who controlled the entire manufacturing process. The first Ford automobiles were assembled in 1903 by a crew of highly skilled mechanics who, starting with the bare frame and moving around to pick up tools and select parts, built each car in one place (Braverman, 1974:146 ff). By the standards of productivity and profits, this was a slow and inefficient process, and by the time the Model T was introduced in 1908, stock runners were employed and assemblers were required to specialize in certain assembly operations. Decomposing a complex process and assigning the routine elements to the unskilled had already been effective in shoemaking and meat packing, giving employers control over the work process.

Although it is more difficult to document, the potential for the emergence of working-class solidarity among blue-collar workers was another consideration for employers. Solidarity could be the impetus for demands for higher wages, better working conditions, and control over the work process, as had occurred among printers, skilled construction workers, and others. The union movement, which had generally been confined to the activities of the skilled trades, was gaining momentum among less skilled workers. The ill-fated Knights of Labor sought to encompass all workers—white and black, women and men, native and immigrant, skilled and unskilled—in a single union. In addition, a number of experiments in worker control had sprung up, including worker councils, elected managerial staffs, and employee-owned firms (Guzda: 1984); each could be viewed as a threat to profits or control.

Stimulated by these motives, administrators and owners adopted a set of organizing principles for blue-collar work. Specialization was probably the key attribute. Jobs were minutely subdivided into separate operations which could be assigned to unskilled or semiskilled operatives. Assembly of

cars was eventually divided among several hundred workers, each performing a few simple operations. One study (Walker and Guest, 1952)
found that 45 percent of the assemblers performed only one or two operations, taking an average of 90 to 120 seconds. The combination of specialized workers and the conveyor belt produced great leaps in output, on a
magnitude of 1,000 percent by 1914. As Braverman (1974:170) aptly puts
it, this was the process of disassembling a craft and returning it to the
workers piecemeal, "so that the process as a whole is no longer the province
of any individual worker."

The next step was to dictate the precise manner in which these jobs
were to be performed. Rather than simply identifying the tasks and allowing workers to perform them as they chose, scientific management assumed responsibility for the design and execution of virtually every movement. Taylor set out to scientifically study jobs in order to determine the
most efficient and rapid methods. Workers were observed, filmed, and
timed while at work. Experiments were undertaken to uncover the best
method for doing a job, whether operating machines, laying bricks, or
assembling products. Taylor himself conducted over 30,000 tests on a lathe
in an attempt to find the fastest, most economical methods of making
machine tools (Braverman, 1974:111). Later research done by Taylor's
followers, Frank and Lillian Gilbreth, focused on elementary operations—
reaching, grasping, bending—which were considered the basic building
blocks of all work activity. These were called "therbligs" (Gilbreth spelled
almost backwards). The idea was to create ideal jobs that are independent
of the skills and abilities of workers.

A consequence of this was that workers were sometimes reduced to
factors in mathematical equations. A journal article of the period describes
a machine operator as "a man who may be regarded as a chain consisting of
the following items (1) sensory devices, (2) a computing system . . . (3) an
amplifying system—the motor-nerve endings and muscles . . . (4) mechanical linkages . . . whereby muscular work produces externally observable
effects" (Braverman, 1974:179). Advocates of this perspective gave little
attention to the human element in their research, causing Braverman
(1974:180) to conclude that Taylorism viewed the worker as "a general
purpose machine to be operated by management."

Convincing workers to accept this new role and pace proved to be a
problem. Turnover was high, especially in the auto industry, where Ford
was forced, by one estimate, to hire 52,000 people to fill 13,000 positions
due to attrition produced by distaste for the new forms of work (May,
1982:410). Henry Ford, who was not convinced by all of Taylor's ideas,
chose to raise wages well above prevailing rates, with the introduction of
"the five-dollar day" in 1914. While historians continue to debate whether
Henry Ford's motives were humanitarian or a crass capitalistic response to
attrition and labor unrest, it is clear that high wages came to be adopted as

one way of asserting employer's control over the work process. The five-dollar-a-day wage was double the previous wage and proved to be an effective incentive in convincing workers to accept the new industrial regime.

Other industries turned to piecework and incentive pay to exert employer dominance. Taylor himself was able to produce significant increases in output by minimizing the idea of hourly or daily rates and linking pay directly to specific units produced. Minimum levels had to be met for fear of discharge, and bonuses were offered for higher output. This strategy was followed by the electrical manufacturing industry, among others. There the method for compelling worker productivity was simple, "We keep the piece rate so low that they have to keep right at it to make a living" (an electrical plant superintendent in 1945, quoted in Milkman, 1983:176).

The two industries—automobile and electrical manufacturing—developed different patterns of gender-based occupational segregation. Auto manufacturing became a male domain. By 1925, 88 of the 110 auto-factory job categories were exclusively male (Milkman, 1982:344). This pattern prevailed until World War II, when large numbers of women were drawn into the plants; as soon as the war began to wind down, though, women were systematically excluded and replaced by men. In contrast, electrical manufacturing generally was the work of young women. Eighty percent of light-bulb assembly work was female by 1910, when it was still a hand operation (Milkman, 1983:166). This pattern has generally prevailed and is also found in other countries. Once such patterns emerge they are highly resistant to change.

At the time that this pattern of segregation developed, gender stereotypes were used as justification. It was argued that women lacked the physical strength to do the hard manual labor of auto work. Moreover, it was claimed that women excelled in the tasks of electrical component assembly—dexterity, speed, endurance, and attention to detail (Milkman, 1983:170). This division of labor is based at least in part on cultural misconceptions of differences in "men's skills" and "women's skills."

Operative-type work often has one other important attribute, which Braverman (1974:114) calls "the separation of conception from execution." In the process of deskilling and fragmenting tasks, workers were effectively excluded from any significant role in decision making about tasks, pace, or quality. These items became part of what are usually called "management prerogatives," which include broader organizational practices such as wages and profits, hiring and firing, and organizational goals. In short, it became management's right to design jobs without input or participation from the people actually doing the work. This mentality was dramatically evident when the Lordstown auto workers tried to redesign their own jobs by doubling up; management argued that they knew how best to design jobs and, when challenged, fell back on a simple assertion of their rights—"It's our plant" (Kreman, 1979:222).

Thus, operative tasks in many American plants became narrowly specialized and repetitive, with workers denied any discretion in the design of work. This pattern was dominant until the 1970s, when it became evident that Taylorism contributed to the alienation of workers. The lure of wages and job security, which had effectively placated workers for several generations, were not of themselves sufficient to overcome the boring, repetitive, unchallenging work; worker dissatisfaction and sporadic strikes protesting work speed-ups resulted. Worker dissatisfaction manifested itself in turnover, absenteeism, and declining quality. At some auto plants, for example, 70 percent of the cars coming off the line were defective because workers became careless or could not keep up with the line (Holusha, 1984). These problems, combined with an unimpressive record of quality, have stimulated a movement to "humanize" the work place.

UNSKILLED WORK

In this decade, somewhere between eight and ten million people are employed in unskilled work in the United States. One broad group of four million is labeled "helpers, handlers, equipment cleaners, and laborers." This classification system includes some readily identifiable occupations such as garbage collecting and parking lot attending, but more often the label is attached to a technical task—cleaning, sorting, packing, or helping. To this must be added probably one million persons classified as paid agricultural workers, who do the routine physical labor on farms—cleaning, clearing, harvesting fruits and vegetables, and field work. In addition, many occupations in the service sector are unskilled—dishwashing, cleaning in offices, factories, and hotels, and some food service jobs. Over two million workers perform such tasks.

Almost none of this work requires any unusual training or capabilities. People can, in effect, be hired "off the street" and learn whatever is necessary in the course of doing the job. This does not mean that some workers do not become quite adept and productive at certain tasks. There is certainly some skill involved in packing boxes or picking fruit. The point is, of course, that unskilled workers can be replaced by others who will be able almost immediately to perform at a minimum level.

The early phases of industrialization generated the need for a large force of unskilled workers to dig the canals, lay the railroad tracks, work the factories, and mine the coal. Unskilled factory labor expanded until the turn of the century, when one urban worker in eight was unskilled. Since the peak years around 1900, the unskilled segment has declined steadily, with large numbers of people replaced by mechanization, a process that continues today.

Several key attributes characterize virtually all unskilled jobs—physical strength, routine tasks, uncomfortable working conditions, close supervision, and strict production quotas. Physical strength is at a premium in construction labor, a category employing nearly one million workers. These are the men and women who perform the rough physical labor at construction sites—hauling bricks, stone, tar, lumber, and nails; maneuvering wheelbarrows of cement and mortar; digging trenches; laying sewer pipe; shifting equipment; erecting scaffolding; cleaning tools; and clearing debris and rubble. In manufacturing plants, packers are also physical laborers, lifting boxes onto and off conveyor belts, or loading and unloading trucks.

The narrow repetitiveness of unskilled work is evident at a cosmetic packaging plant, among a work group of nineteen women handling spray perfume (Garson, 1975:57). The "lead lady" places the bottles on a conveyor belt. Next, two women attach little silver tags as the bottles move past them. Further along are nine workers who, in turn, pick a bottle and slide it, along with a leaflet and protective packaging, into boxes. At the end of the line are seven wrappers who enfold the boxes in colored tissue paper and place them in cartons. Other workers remove the cartons. The conveyor moves about fifty bottles a minute past these workers.

Uncomfortable working conditions are an inherent part of many unskilled jobs. Seasonal farm labor may be an extreme example, for it combines a number of unpleasant attributes. The work is long, often from dawn to dusk, and arduous, involving stooping to pick tomatoes, stretching to reach apples, or digging to uncover carrots. Migrant laborers work in the hot sun and are exposed to the chemicals used in pest control. Occupational injuries such as cuts, bruises, and strained muscles are common.

Unskilled factory workers tend to have the most undesirable working conditions, in addition to the unpleasant attributes of the work itself. These workers rarely have such comforts as air conditioning, and often lack such simple amenities as uncluttered work places, proper heating, separate eating facilities, and clean rest rooms. In some cases, unskilled workers toil in conditions reminiscent of the "sweat shops" associated with nineteenth-century industrialization.

Thus, the very nature of unskilled work is physically demanding, either because it is strenuous or because of the unremitting pace of it. In addition, unskilled workers are frequently subjected to close supervision and strong pressure to maintain a rapid pace. Production quotas are common, and supervisors who oversee the work often use verbal exhortations and harassment to elicit greater effort. "Let's go, girls; let's keep at it" are phrases commonly heard on the line at a tuna-packing plant visited by Barbara Garson. Resistance to this verbal barrage is not tolerated. Supervisors are empowered to immediately dismiss workers who dare to reply with a remark as mild as, "Mind your own business," or "Get off my back" (Garson, 1975:51).

The pressure for productivity at this plant also takes the form of cancelling rest breaks and lunch periods to accommodate the incoming supply of fish. Workers' time cards are attached to their backs, and supervisors follow them around to punch on and off different jobs so that time is not wasted in moving between the time clock and the work location (Garson, 1975:52). In other plants, workers are forbidden to talk or chew gum, and in one case, a worker was fired for playing his guitar during his lunch hour. Garson suggests that employers impose these rigid standards because they assume it is the only way to ensure that workers will do these unpalatable tasks. Whatever the motivation, these policies make the jobs even more unpleasant.

Most unskilled work is dead-end. It is difficult for most workers to get promoted beyond some other unskilled grade, or to machine operator. This has as much to do with the nature of the work as with the people who do the work. The jobs do not require any actual skill, so it is difficult to demonstrate any ability except speed. Lacking in real responsibility or in the opportunity to demonstrate initiative or creativity, workers are left without a chance to develop those capabilities that merit consideration for better jobs.

UNSKILLED WORK: RACIAL AND ETHNIC PATTERNS

Unskilled labor, by its very nature, is one of the least desirable forms of contemporary work. As a result, it has always drawn a large proportion of its workers from among those with the fewest options—those without educational credentials or with poor employment records. In addition, unskilled work has traditionally been the province of two broad groups—racial and ethnic minorities and displaced agricultural workers. These two groups are not mutually exclusive; the internal migration of rural workers to the industrial Northeast included a disproportionate number of blacks, and many of the Southern and Eastern European immigrants who flooded into America had rural origins. The point of identifying these two groups is to illustrate that somewhat different processes are operative. Displaced agricultural workers usually had less formal education and lacked skills for the urban market. Minority group members—whether rural or urban—bring with them language, cultural, or religious differences which handicap them in the labor market. Some brought a heritage of discrimination (blacks, for example, and Irish Catholics seeking employment from English and Welsh Protestants). Even those lacking such a heritage may become the object of discrimination. Donald Noel (1968) and others have argued that minority groups perceived as competitors for scarce resources such as jobs set the stage for the emergence of discriminatory attitudes. This process has previously been described in the discussion of exclusionary practices in the skilled trades.

Using this perspective, a consistent pattern of disproportionate rural and minority employment can be traced in the unskilled occupations. In the process, minority status has often been exploited; this is most evident in dual wage systems. The exploitation of minorities is only an extreme manifestation of the potential for exploitation of all unskilled workers. People in this category have the fewest employment options, are readily replaceable, and have the least power to improve their conditions (Buroway, 1976).

It is possible to trace the flow of various groups in unskilled work throughout American history. The best-documented cases start with the Irish around the Civil War period. Irish immigrants formed the second largest white nationality group in America during the Revolution, but it was not until the 1840s and 1850s that they entered the country in massive numbers (Feagin, 1984:80ff). Many were of rural origins, forced to flee their native land by the potato famine (1845–1847). Their arrival here revived smoldering English–Irish religious conflicts dating to the seventeenth century. By 1850, there had been anti-Irish violence, including the burning of churches, in every major city.

Overt discrimination and lack of skills left the Irish with few options in the labor market. The men were forced to become laborers in the mines or factories or on the docks, and Irish women were channeled into domestic work. By 1876, 50 percent of all non-native Irish in America were concentrated in unskilled occupations, and this pattern continued throughout the nineteenth century. Subsequent generations of native-born Irish-Americans were more successful in breaking out of the unskilled trap of their parents. A study of Boston in 1890 suggests that some 40 percent of American-born Irish had moved into white-collar work.

Irish immigrants benefited from the influx of Italian immigrants, who came in large numbers after 1880 (Feagin, 1984:122ff). Members of these early waves of Italians were largely the unskilled, the urban poor, and small farmers. In one group who immigrated around 1900, over two-thirds of the men were farmers or farm workers, and most of the rest were industrial workers. This lack of urban skills combined with the language barrier meant that most Italian immigrants had very few choices. Despite their agricultural backgrounds, very few became farmers. High proportions found work as unskilled laborers, miners, and fishers, in many cases replacing the Irish in railroad building and as helpers in the construction trades. Some were used as scabs during this period, thus further hindering their acceptance by native white workers. At the end of World War I, about one-half of all Italian immigrants were unskilled laborers. During the period of the worst discrimination, there was a blatant dual wage system. Advertisements for laborers on a New York City reservoir offered $1.30 to $1.50 a day to "whites" and $1.15 to $1.25 a day to "Italians" (Feagin, 1984:123).

By about 1930, only about one in ten people of Italian background was engaged in unskilled work. They were replaced by rural blacks. A massive migration of workers to northern urban areas began around

World War I (Feagin, 1984:228ff). Overt racial discrimination, the decline of cotton farming, and the increasing marginality of small, black-owned farms combined to act as "push" factors. These blacks were "pulled" northward by the lure of industrial employment. At the same time, immigration was severely curtailed by restrictive legislation (beginning in 1921). As was the case with the groups that preceded them, this generation, and those that followed, many lacked urban skills and all carried the burden of racial prejudice.

Occupational data for 1940 provide a clear picture of concentration in unskilled work (U.S. Bureau of the Census, 1979:73). The majority of black women were channeled into domestic work (60 percent), with most of the rest working as farm laborers or in service jobs such as restaurant work. At least 40 percent of black men were classified as laborers—either farm or industrial—and large numbers worked in service jobs, which are essentially unskilled labor. Slowly but steadily, the proportion of blacks concentrated in unskilled work declined; in 1980, the proportion of men who were laborers and women who were domestics was less than 8 percent. (Westcott, 1982:30). Evidence of the persistence of a dual wage system here is suggested by the fact that black male laborers earned 14 percent less than their white counterparts.

CASE STUDY: THE MEXICAN WORKERS OF THE SOUTHWEST

While blacks came to dominate the unskilled occupations in the northeast, it was the Mexicans who provided the pool from which unskilled labor was drawn in the southwest. The first large wave of Mexicans flowed across the border between 1910 and 1930, with over one-half million entering during the 1920s alone (Barrera, 1979:62ff). As was the case with other immigrant groups, a disproportionate share were rural agricultural workers driven north by poverty, overpopulation, and the political upheavals of the Mexican Revolution. The Mexican experience differs from that of some other immigrant groups in that employers—the mines, large farms, sugar refineries, and railroads—were actively recruiting an unskilled labor force. The Mexican immigration was beneficial to southwestern employers, and it was not until 1929 that the government acted to impose the same immigration restrictions that applied to other non-native groups.

Census data for 1930 show that over half of all Mexicans in the southwest were in unskilled work. The men did most of the common labor in the copper mines, picked cotton, sugar beets and vegetables, and made up more than 85 percent of the track-laying crews on the railroads. The women found their way into hired farm labor, common laundry work, and cleaning jobs. Pay differentials were also widespread. Unskilled labor was paid at about 40 cents an hour, except for Mexicans, who earned 25 cents; white teamsters earned $4.50 a day, while nonwhites earned $2.50 (Barrera, 1979:89).

The pool of unskilled workers now includes more recently displaced agricultural workers and/or racial-ethnic minorities. Since the 1960s, Puerto Ricans have done much of the "dirty work" in metropolitan areas—cleaning the factories and hotels, working the restaurants and modern sweat shops. Vietnamese have drifted into the low-paying fishing industry along the Gulf coast. Haitians and Jamaicans are picking fruits and vegetables along the East coast.

Unskilled work is sometimes called the "dirty work" of an industrial society. It is certainly not agreeable, often requiring strenuous effort under unpleasant conditions, or cleaning up after the more affluent segments of society. The work is often made less desirable because of the manner in which it is organized and carried out. It is not surprising to find that unskilled work tends to rank at the bottom of prestige scales, or that there is low job satisfaction and high turnover.

The very nature of the work and of the pool of people who provide the bulk of the workers creates the potential for exploitation by unscrupulous employers. Any worker is quite easily replaced by another, at least as long as there is a reserve of unemployed workers to draw upon. Various employers would therefore benefit from loose immigration laws allowing the unrestricted influx of cheap labor. For example, it is well documented that business support was instrumental in preventing exclusion of Mexicans during the 1930s (Feagin, 1984:263). In the 1940s, employers agitated for the *bracero* program, which imported hundreds of thousands of temporary seasonal workers. More recently, East coast apple growers favored the importation of Jamaican pickers even when there was a supply of resident and foreign workers (Rosenthal, 1978). Any large reserve of workers will serve to depress wages even further.

The workers themselves, especially racial and ethnic minorities, are extremely vulnerable. Discrimination and a lack of marketable skills severely limit their options. Most vulnerable at present is the illegal alien population. Their illicit residence deters them from fighting exploitation. Abuses include cases of outright extortion, in which aliens had to pay for the right to work, physical abuse, wages as low as 50 percent below the minimum wage, and substandard conditions (Crewdson, 1979; 1980). It is sometimes argued that the plight of unskilled workers originates in the nature of the work, but it must also be noted that some employers, either on their own initiative or prodded by unions or government, have tried to upgrade conditions. In the 1970s, for example, the Minute Maid division of the Coca-Cola Company significantly improved the working conditions of its seasonal fruit pickers in Florida (Blank, 1975). They instituted health-care plans, day-care centers, subsidized loan programs, and social services, and created a pleasant environment in which to work. The labor may continue to be difficult, but at least it is not degrading.

CONCLUSION

Matters of skill form a dominant theme in the history of blue-collar work since the Industrial Revolution first began to reshape society. Industrialization has generally raised the skill levels required of members of the labor force (see, for example, Form, 1981). This is evident in such broad trends as the steady decline in the proportion of workers in unskilled occupations over the course of the twentieth century, and the accompanying expansion of professional, technical, and craft occupations. There may also be a general elevation in the skills needed to do the work of an industrial society. An obvious example would be the infinitely more complex skills and abilities required to repair today's sophisticated automobile engines compared to the much simpler earlier models.

However, as Stone (1974), Braverman (1974), Clawson (1980), and others point out, skill is required not only in the form of expertise and dexterity, but also in the organization and control of the entire work process. The printing and construction crafts exemplify attempts to protect their autonomy and monopoly and the integrity of their skill from fragmentation into a series of operations performed by machines or workers who are less skilled. (Those who failed, such as cigar makers or cobblers, have either disappeared or become machine operators.) Many would argue that Taylorism and the trend toward specialization and repetitive tasks characteristic of most blue-collar work was motivated less by a concern for efficiency than by a concern with attempts to reduce their potential power. These issues will be encountered again in the discussion of job satisfaction and work reform.

SEVEN

Direct-Service Work and Housework

INTRODUCTION: THE SERVICE RELATIONSHIP

Service work has been growing at an unprecedented rate since the mid-1970s. Ninety-five percent of the 25 million new jobs created in the United States between 1969 and 1984 were in the service sector (Kirkland, 1985:38).[1] Many of these were in the area of providing some direct personal service to customers—preparing and serving drinks on planes and in bars, dispensing hamburgers, selling shoes or houses or hardware, and cleaning homes. *Customers* is the word that defines this type of work and separates it from other social relationships organized around the provision of a service. For example, medical personnel and lawyers provide services, but to "clients" rather than "customers." Educators do not have customers, nor do librarians. More than semantics, tradition and customary usage are at work here, as is evident from the tenacity with which members of these occupations hold to this distinction. *Customer* involves an expectation of being served and the right to control and direct the relationship. It has different manifestations in different work situations, but it is this common

[1]The Bureau of Labor Statistics divides the economy into a *goods-producing sector*—manufacturing, mining, farming, and construction—and a *service-producing sector*, which includes all other jobs. "Service" thus includes most professional, managerial, and administrative support workers, as well as the service workers included here.

theme which links the work of most salespersons, personal-service workers (barbers and beauticians), domestics (maids and servants), and some protective workers (police).

Police officers constantly experience the effects of "customer" expectations. Police departments are inundated with calls from citizens wanting services that clearly evidence that they view the police in (and have been able to impose upon them) the role of domestic mediator, chauffeur, and repair person. Police records in Atlanta reveal the following list of tasks performed in response to calls: settling domestic disputes, quieting a barking dog, escorting a woman from a building to her car, removing an abandoned car from the street, and driving the downtown streets for over an hour with a tourist couple who had forgotten where they parked their car (Remmington, 1981). Apparently, more than a few citizens take the phrase "public servant" quite seriously and literally.

SALES WORK

Approximately 6.5 million people are engaged in some form of direct-sales work. A majority are retail salespersons dispensing shoes, clothing, furniture, cars, televisions, and cosmetics. The remainder are classified as sales representatives, a category which includes realtors, insurance agents, and stockbrokers, as well as wholesale, industrial, and commercial salespersons. It is, by any standard, a diverse occupational group. The products and services being sold are diverse, ranging from computers to carpets. Transactions range from a few dollars for items of personal clothing to hundreds of thousands of dollars in property transfers. Work settings may vary from retail stores and used-car lots to corporate offices and customers' homes. In each transaction, direct personal interaction takes place between worker and customer.

It is this attribute of sales work that is central to understanding the nature of the role, the way it is enacted, and the attitudes and responses of sales workers. A cursory view of the distribution of men and women among different types of sales work suggests that employer perceptions of the worker-customer relationship influence the allocation of people to jobs. Men and women are selectively employed on the basis of the type of customer most likely to be encountered and in consideration of which gender is assumed to confer greater knowledge and expertise in which area. Consequently, in 1983, men tended to dominate sales work in motor vehicles (93 percent), hardware and building supplies (77 percent), and repair parts (89 percent), while women dominated door-to-door (81 percent) and apparel (83 percent) sales. Certainly other factors are also relevant, but the gender-based dynamics of the worker-customer relationship does play a role.

The Sales Relationship: Uncertainty and Vulnerability

The interaction between sales worker and customer is often a transaction between strangers, but it is structured by social conventions that define appropriate behavior, and is influenced by the resources, meanings, and values that are brought to the relationship by both parties. It is a relationship which leaves the sales worker extremely vulnerable.

Subordination.   Salesperson and customer enter into the transaction as incumbents of specific roles which impose some constraints upon the form of the relationship. In most forms of retail sales, the salesperson occupies a position of implied subordination, or even subservience. It is the salesperson's job and obligation to "serve" or to "wait on" the customer. Therefore, the whims of an ill-tempered or rude person, which would be inappropriate in communication among equals, must sometimes be endured by salespersons. Most stores respond most unfavorably to complaints that a salesperson has refused a customer's request or was uncooperative, however unreasonable the customer might be. The old cliché of sales work, "the customer is always right," neatly symbolizes this unequal role relationship.

Caveat emptor.   "Let the buyer beware" is another cliché which colors the transaction. American consumers have generally learned to be cautious when entering into a purchase. Warranties and return policies protect some transactions, but the buyer is legally and socially expected to exercise caution, which often leads to a generalized distrust of the verbal claims of salespersons. This distrust borders on institutionalized disbelief in approaching those who sell used cars and encyclopedias. "Every guy who comes in here is sure he's getting cheated," insists a car salesman (Browne, 1973:45). In these areas, distrust is sometimes mutual. Customers are viewed as attempting to misrepresent or overvalue their trade-ins (Browne, 1973; Miller, 1964).

Control of the sales decision.   The ultimate decision to purchase resides with the customer, thus giving him or her control over the outcome of the transaction. Financial considerations cannot be ignored, because to some extent every sales worker is judged on volume, and for those on quota or commission arrangements, sales will have a direct impact on salary. C. Wright Mills (1951:174–175) has noted that the economic incentive may dominate the behavior of some sales workers. He invented the image of the "wolf," prowling departments in search of potential customers, ready to pounce upon them. "Every well-dressed customer, cranky or not, looks like a five-dollar bill to me," admitted one. This behavior may generate greater sales, but at the cost of alienating those coworkers who are outmaneuvered and forcing them into make-work kinds of tasks, such as dusting and rotating stock, to avoid the appearance of idleness (Dalton, 1974). Wolves thus usually encounter social pressure to modify their aggressive behavior.

Self-concepts. More than money is at stake in the sales transaction. Inherent in every transaction is the potential for damage to the sales worker's self-concept (Howton and Rosenberg, 1965). Making a sale is "psychic income," a demonstration of ability and persuasiveness. If a successful sale is interpreted as a validation of ability, then a rebuff is a failure, a personal humiliation. Thus, a part of learning the work is learning how to accept an unsuccessful sale as a hazard of the job and not a personal failing.

The retail sales transaction is characterized by uncertainty and vulnerability on the part of the worker. Potential customers enjoy great freedom to enact the inherently superior role as they choose, because they control the single most important resource—the sale. Intentionally or not, consciously or not, they have the power to influence income, to humiliate, to rebuff, and to terminate the transaction at their pleasure. The sales workers' vulnerability is most pronounced when they are selling standardized products at predetermined prices, a condition which describes the vast majority of sales at the retail level. In such situations, the seller is left with virtually no room to bargain or influence the transaction if the customer is disinclined to buy.

THE RETAIL SALES TRANSACTION

By focusing on the unequal distribution of power in retail sales, a number of authors have suggested that the transaction may be viewed as an unfolding drama in which sales workers attempt to reduce uncertainty and vulnerability by channeling and controlling the direction of the interaction. Observations, supplemented by the analysis of materials contained in prepackaged manuals for sales trainees, suggest a four-stage process. This process is obviously not operative in every transaction. It is most likely to emerge when there is strong pressure for sales volume and/or when the customer is reluctant or resistant. These admittedly pronounced cases are chosen to illustrate the process.

The contact: Categorizing customers. Sales workers learn to categorize customers as a means of anticipating how to proceed with the transaction. The most fundamental categorization is a simple dichotomy between "buyers," who represent at least a potential sale, and "nonbuyers," who are presumed to have no intention of making a purchase. Conventional labels for nonbuyers often become part of the argot of the occupational subculture. Travel agents call them "brochure collectors"; in auto sales, they are "suspects" (Miller, 1964), and in department stores, "lookers." There apparently are no firm rules for making this distinction, but more experienced sales personnel pride themselves on their ability to identify nonbuyers on the basis of clues derived from the customer's posture and demeanor.

This categorization is a presumption and, of course, may be an inaccurate appraisal of the situation, but the decision does dictate the future of the interaction. To define a customer as a nonbuyer is likely to lead to behavior that will discourage a sale—polite but cursory inquiries, inattention, or even failure to establish personal contact. If "making a sale" were the *only* consideration, this would be incomprehensible, for every contact *might* eventuate in a sale and should logically be pursued. But it makes good sense if it is understood that, from the salesperson's perspective, the pursuit of a reluctant nonbuyer would require a greater investment of time, effort, and personal involvement and thus increase the risk of humiliation if rebuffed. Stephen Miller (1964) argues that salespersons prefer to avoid transactions that are unlikely to afford them control of the negotiations.

Many products, including cosmetics, magazines, and insurance, are sold door-to-door. The largest cosmetics firm alone had a sales force of 430,000 in 1982, and the total volume of all "direct sales" (as it is called in the trade) is 8.5 billion dollars annually (Purdum, 1985). Direct sales workers confront a different situation than that confronted by those in stores, where the customer initiates the interaction by their presence. They must often initiate a contact with people who have no expressed interest in the product and may very well be distrustful. In this situation, trainees must be taught to assume that the contact is a "buyer," and to accomplish this are encouraged to work from a preprogrammed training manual designed to counter any form of resistance that might be encountered (Bogdan, 1972). Forcefulness is a key element in overcoming resistance. An insurance company manual instructs trainees:

> One reason many underwriters sell only a small volume of insurance is that they are too nice [and] nice guys are easily put off and turned down . . . there comes a time in almost every sales interview when downright force and steady pressure must be used. (Pothier, 1974)

This approach perpetuates the image of the "high-pressure" salesperson.

Gaining access is unquestionably decisive for the rest of the transaction. The home owner's doorway is a physical and symbolic barrier. Unscrupulous firms have been known to condone the use of misrepresentations by their door-to-door sales force (Bogdan, 1972). Encyclopedia salespeople may claim to be educators or advertising executives. Dependence upon such "false fronts" has an interesting rationale; because the public imputes foul play to salespersons, misrepresentation is adopted as an acceptable strategy to overcome distrust.

The pitch. Assuming that the customers are, or have allowed themselves to be defined as, potential buyers, the interaction will proceed to the stage commonly called "the pitch." Crucial here is to get customers to talk about themselves and reveal information that will allow the seller to anticipate their needs or overcome resistance. Apparently innocuous small talk about the customer's job and family may be designed to reveal information about the potential buyer's financial status or level of sophistication. One training manual calls this the "smoke out" technique, designed to isolate the sources of potential resistance (Pothier, 1974).

CASE STUDY: THE LANGUAGE OF SELLING

During the "pitch" phase of the transaction, language takes on a special meaning. Experienced salespersons frequently compose lists of words to be avoided in dealing with customers. A realtor provided the following rules for the use of colorful, descriptive, glamourous language in an issue of a real estate trade journal (reported in Eskey, 1985):

Never say "I'm calling to confirm our appointment," for it offers customers an opportunity to change their minds.

Never say "deal"; say "transaction."

Never say "afford" or "qualify," which raises the question of cost and may make potential buyers apprehensive.

Never say "You won't be sorry," or people might begin to think they will be.

Never say "Would you like to buy this home?" Rather, ask "Would you like an opportunity to invest in this home?"

Never say "down payment"; say "initial investment."

Never say "Let's go out and look," or that is what customers will be doing. Invite them to "select."

Armed with this information, the salesperson may attempt to play upon the buyer's pride, or fear. Sellers of children's books can, for example, try to convince parents that a purchase reveals their intelligence and ability to provide for the future, or is even a measure of their love for their children (Bogdan, 1972). Browne (1973), in her study of the "used car game," argues that salesworkers develop a set of stereotypical categories of buyers. Each, she notes, is negative and serves the important function of providing justification and rationalization for the pitch.

Customers may be stereotyped as dishonest, thus permitting dishonest activity on the part of the seller. Or, customers may be innocent and childlike, which justifies their manipulation. Or, if the customer is out to cheat the salesperson by misrepresenting a trade-in, then the seller is entitled to reciprocate. These stereotypes emerge out of the very nature of the interaction; the salesperson selectively perceives or misinterprets the customer's behavior and then uses the stereotype as a mechanism by which to reconcile his or her own patently manipulative behavior.

The close.   If the pitch is successful, the customer will reach a point of willingness to buy. Sales workers may attempt to facilitate this process by creating opportunities for the purchase rather than depending upon the consumer to make the decision. The training manual advises the seller to move in with pen and application, saying, "Let's cover you today while you have the health to protect . . . How do you want to handle this, by check or cash?" (Pothier, 1974). A book on successful sales even offers rules on the proper technique for offering the contract and pen (Molloy, 1983).

In automobile transactions in which the price is not firmly fixed in advance, the close can only be accomplished if the buyer believes that the best possible deal has been negotiated. One strategy for convincing the customer of this is "changing sides" (Bogdan, 1972). The salesperson implies that the deal is very generous—so generous, in fact, that the sales manager may not approve it. "I know the sales manager is going to jump all over me . . . (but) let me see if I can get that car at your price." The salesperson has now apparently joined with the buyer against the manager. In reality, the agency usually has already set a bottom-level price, but the salesperson will disappear for a while to give the appearance of bargaining before returning with the approved contract and some comment like "You really got me in a lot of trouble."

Cooling the buyer.   The decision to buy does not terminate the transaction. Buyers may have second thoughts, especially when presented with a bill. At the least, they could be dissatisfied with the purchase; at the worst, they might consider rescinding the deal. To forestall any such problems, the customer is quickly elevated from the status of "buyer" to that of "owner." Salespersons disengage themselves by handing the new owner over to other workers such as cashiers and packagers or, in the case of automobiles, to service managers.

The retail sales transaction may be characterized by exploitation and manipulation on the part of the sales worker, but this is not always true, or even typical, of sales work. When it does prevail, however, it must be understood as a patterned response to a situation in which the income, self-respect, and autonomy of the salesperson are at stake in an interaction which clearly favors the customer.

PERSONAL-SERVICE WORKERS

Personal-service workers serve customers in direct, face-to-face relationships. There are between 12 and 13 million personal-service workers, depending upon the classification scheme used. Some occupations employ extremely large numbers of people. There are 1.3 million waiters/waitresses, 700,000 hairdressers/cosmetologists, and 90,000 barbers.

In the transaction between the personal-service worker and the customer, there is unusual potential for conflict. What appears on the surface to be a simple and straightforward exchange of a service for a fee is often a very complex and difficult relationship for the worker. Overt conflict is frequently suppressed because the customer controls all salient resources: income, repeat business, tips, and complaints. Conflict, whether latent or manifest, originates in the contrasting perceptions and expectations brought to the transaction by worker and customer, and centers on control of the content and pace of the work tasks.

THE SERVICE RELATIONSHIP

Customers "contract" for a service, either by paying a fee directly (to barbers or cab drivers) or as part of a relationship with an organization providing a product (restaurants) or a service (airlines, government agencies). It is an unequivocally unequal superior-subordinate relationship. The *raison d'être* for employment is to serve the customer. Moreover, clear expectations originating from both employers and customers emphasize and reinforce subordinate status (Shamir, 1980). Workers are compelled to address customers by honorific titles like "Sir" or "Madam," while the customer is frequently encouraged (by the use of name tags) to use first names or nicknames, or even the name of the job as a form of address ("Janitor," "Waiter," "Driver"). The latter practice is especially annoying, as revealed in this retort, "Don't call me Waitress. I don't call you Customer or Eater" (Howe, 1977:104).

Training for the role usually emphasizes subordination. Not infrequently it involves adopting a standard uniform which is a public announcement of subservience, such as restaurant costumes that mirror the clothing of butlers and maids. Further, service workers are exhorted not to offend customers, even if they engage in rude or inappropriate behavior. The following statement by an airline attendant no longer applies, but it reveals the subservient mentality that organizations once sought to instill in their employees: ". . . like he's rubbing your body somewhere, you're supposed to just put his hand down, not say anything and smile at him" (Terkel, 1972:79).

CASE STUDY: THE STATUS DILEMMA

Service work of all kinds has historically been low-status work, largely because of the connotations of servitude and inferiority. It has consequently been the province of people occupying second-class citizenship. The low-social-status implications of service work produce a unique problem, a status dilemma (Gold, 1952; Shamir, 1980). A *status dilemma* exists when people of higher social status must in their occupation perform services for persons of lower social status. Persons in low-status occupations may be better able to accommodate to the role if their customers are of a higher social status. In such situations, subordinate status in the occupational role is consistent with lower status on other criteria. A washroom attendant complains, "I don't enjoy waiting on my peers. I feel that if I occupy a position that's menial, let it be to someone perhaps a cut above me" (Terkel, 1972:154). A variety of factors have usually combined to produce this situation. For simple economic reasons, the people who could afford the luxury of services—restaurant meals, maids, cosmetic services, and transportation—were more affluent than poorly paid service workers. They tended also to be "superior" in terms of social class, age, race, and ethnicity.

Gold (1952; 1964) reports on the experiences of building custodians whose income was better than that of some low-income residents. They reported feeling uncomfortable in contacts with these people, and a bit resentful of having to do their dirty work. Moreover, the low-income tenants were also apparently sensitive to, and threatened by, this status discrepancy, for they were the most likely to attempt to downgrade his financial situation and remind him of his lowly occupational role. "The people who don't have anything put up the biggest front and squawk a lot," observed one (Gold, 1964:45). As a general rule, such people were the recipients of the worst service, the janitor's response to the status dilemma.

Theodore Kemper (1979) has used the same concept to explain why our city streets are so dirty. He argues that sanitation jobs have traditionally been allocated to those who occupy the lowest social status, meaning that they were expected to serve people of higher or, at worst, equal social status. Unionization, though, has raised these workers' pay, security, and working conditions at the same time that cities are being abandoned to an "underclass of poor whites, blacks, and Hispanics." Thus, higher-status persons are being called upon to perform dirty work for lower-status persons, making them reluctant to do a good job of cleaning the streets.

The notion of subservience is generally unpalatable to Americans, for it runs counter to cultural values of democracy and equality. Service workers in Western European countries with deep historical traditions of social class distinctions appear to be more comfortable with such roles (Shamir, 1983). Nevertheless, in response to concerns about job security and as a result of occupational socialization, most are apparently willing to concede that the customer has the authority to expect competent, prompt, courteous treatment. Such rights are not without limits and must be balanced against the workers' need to develop schedules and routines to meet the demands of multiple customers, get along with coworkers, and satisfy employers whose concerns frequently exceed their rights as perceived and defined by workers.

Customers violate, with disturbing regularity, the expectations of service workers, for a number of reasons. They may act out of ignorance, being unaware or insensitive to the problems of workers. Many transactions are fleeting and impersonal (hiring a cab is a good example) and thus lack the consistency which would allow customers to understand the nature of the relationship. "Repeat customers," in the sense of frequent users of cabs or restaurants or airlines, or "regular customers," who are regular patrons of a particular bar, tend to develop shared understandings with the people who serve them and are usually seen as the best customers (Spradley and Mann, 1975).

In other situations, customers may hold inappropriate perceptions of the service relationship. A frequently voiced complaint is that customers treat workers as their personal servants (Gold, 1964:12). In fact, older waitresses recall a time not so long ago when customers expected to be regularly served by the same person, who would cater to their specific whims (Howe, 1977:109). Each new generation of airline attendants hears the (mythical) story about a passenger who ignores offers of a drink; her husband explains, "I'm sorry, she's not used to talking with the help" (Terkel, 1972:78). It may not be a coincidence that waitresses in countless restaurants are still required to wear black and white uniforms (often with aprons) reminiscent of the costumes of Victorian housemaids. This personal-servant expectation can place great strain on the relationship by causing the customer to feel justified in making a variety of unreasonable demands.

CLIENT TYPOLOGIES: DEFINING "BAD" CUSTOMERS

Experienced service workers often develop a vision of an ideal client (Mennerick, 1974). Some workers are able to verbalize the characteristics of the ideal client. A waitress defines them simply as customers who understand. "They see what you're up against and don't ask for the impossible. . . They're the best" (Howe, 1977:103). More often than not, however, the image is vague and is revealed by customer behavior that deviates from the norm. Those who vary from the ideal are classified as "*bad customers*." Lewis Mennerick (1974) suggests that customers may be labeled "bad" on the basis of five criteria.

Interruption of the work process.   Customers, by their actions and attitudes, can either facilitate or hinder workers in their attempts to render service. All waiters, bartenders, janitors, and airline attendants are under great pressure to serve large numbers of customers within fixed periods of time, and the surest way of being labeled a bad customer is to squander their time. Building custodians are infuriated by inconsiderate residents who insist that they ignore other duties to repair a leaky faucet or remove trash (Gold, 1964). The least-favorite diners in restaurants are those with an "I-want-service-now-or-else" attitude, who insist upon constant attention to their every whim with no regard for the other customers. Whether such customers are motivated by ignorance or by malice is often difficult to determine, but the service worker is apt to attribute it to malice. This is an understandable interpretation, for the workers find it difficult to comprehend how reasonable people could be so insensitive and blind. It is, they assert, impossible for a customer to fail to see the work they have to do.

Other customers seek special treatment for other reasons. Waitresses and airline attendants are alert for one person sitting alone; he or she is likely to attempt to monopolize their time. Solitary men are often away from home on business and seeking female companionship. Some will make unwanted advances. Single passengers or diners, especially those who are older, may seek to engage in conversation simply because they are lonely and want someone to sit and talk with them. While service workers may feel sympathy for such a person, the issue violates their ideal of the cooperative customer.

It is interesting to note that waitresses everywhere in the United States seem to concur that groups of older women are the most likely to *unintentionally* interfere with their work (Spradley and Mann, 1975:129 ff; see also Howe, 1977:103). Anthropologists Spradley and Mann found striking contrasts in the way men and women were oriented to, and behaved in, bars and concluded that social drinking is a symbolic communal activity for men but not for women, and that bars are structured around this male subculture. As a result, men behave in ways that subtly facilitate the work tasks of waitresses.

Men are likely to order rounds of drinks, while women order separately. For a female, a bar is a place to purchase drinks, but for males, it is a place to be part of the social life of the bar. To order a round of drinks for all members of the group is thus an expression of group and male solidarity. In the process, the waitress' work is made much easier because she need make only one trip, place one order, and collect one bill.

Women are also likely to pay separately, but one man will pay collectively for the group. The small but salient inconvenience of separate bills and numerous cash exchanges is consistent with the female idea of the purchase of a drink as an individual business transaction. Men are just as likely to pay separately at lunch, but in the evening, drinking becomes imbedded in the subculture of the male social group. Paying for drinks for everyone reinforces group solidarity, but also involves the norm of reciprocity. All other members of the group are subtly obligated to repay in kind. Reciprocity symbolizes friendship and equality among males in American society.

Women are willing to ask questions about drinks, but men almost never will. To question a waitress about the contents of a mixed drink slows her work, but it is not consideration that motivates men; rather, it is reluctance to display their ignorance. Expertise in drinks and drinking are intimately related to perceptions of masculinity and adulthood and membership in the social group of the bar. Drinks are not likely to be viewed as symbols of identity by women, though. Rather, they are menu items to be tasted, drunk, explored.

Men tend to stay with the same drink, unlike women, who are likely to change orders frequently. Again, this has to do with the symbolism of drinks. To become identified with a specific drink validates one's position as a regular, a continuing member of the social community in a bar. Waitresses thus can memorize the drink orders and expedite service. Women, freed of the fetters of symbolism, enjoy the opportunity to switch drinks for the sake of variety or taste or to vary the alcohol content.

These situations suggest the many ways in which customers can hinder the work process by impinging upon the scarce time of service workers. Whether intentional or inadvertent, their behavior can cause them to be perceived as "bad" customers. The most common response is to minimize contact and to attempt to direct the interaction into an impersonal and businesslike transaction.

Control. An ideal customer will grant the worker the right to define the appropriate way of performing the service. Bad customers impinge upon the workers' autonomy by instructing them about how to do their jobs. Among the most irritating examples are passengers who give cab drivers unsolicited street directions, diners attempting to instruct waiters and bartenders on drink preparation, and tenants who conspicuously inspect the cleaning activities of janitors. These service workers are the most likely to be subject to attempts at customer control; because it is assumed that no special skills are required, customers feel entitled to believe that they can do the job as well as the worker.

Tipping. Because many service workers depend upon tips, this factor becomes another criterion for differentiating between ideal and bad customers. Consequently, stereotypes of classes of customers emerge, based on their anticipated tipping behavior. Among cab drivers, fares are placed in four categories (Stannard, 1971). "Tourists" and "working stiffs" (blue-collar workers) are good fares because they are likely to overtip. Tourists are not particularly good customers by any other criteria because they ask too many questions and are often uncertain about their destination, but they are tolerated because their tips are good. Working stiffs, possibly because they share working-class orientation, are also generous tippers. "Businesspersons" are the most reliable fares in tipping and by all other criteria. They represent no danger, allow the driver to be efficient, and can be depended upon to reward the driver with a fair tip. The "shopper," armed with packages, has the reputation as the worst tipper.

CASE STUDY: THE SOCIOLOGY OF TIPPING

Social historians have frequently sought to discover the origins of the practice of tipping. It apparently originated with a London coffeehouse practice of attaching coins to notes marked "To Insure Promptness" (TIP) (Crespi, 1968). Others trace the origins to the wealthy householders' practice of dispensing bonuses to loyal domestic servants. Both interpretations imply a direct link between the gratuity and the quality of service performed. As the practice has evolved, it has taken on additional symbolic meanings and forms.

The most evident shift has been the tendency to institutionalize the tip as an obligatory addition to the basic costs of a service, regardless of its quality. Newspapers, tour books, travel agents, cruise lines, and hotel associations all publish lists outlining the size of an appropriate tip for cab drivers, baggage handlers, wine stewards, and barbers. All sources warn us to anticipate rudeness if we fail to tip, even for poor service. Tips in the form of "service charges" are routinely added to bills at hotels and restaurants in Western Europe. A few luxury restaurants and resorts in America have experimented with the practice, and it is almost standard for special parties everywhere. Tipping has clearly become an accepted custom, although people may quibble over the exact percentage.

Employers have a vested interest in the practice of obligatory tipping, for it allows them to maintain wages at lower levels than would otherwise be possible. Women service workers are among the lowest-paid occupational groups. The low pay is supplemented by tips, which are, of course, paid by the customer. Moreover, until recently, it was relatively easy to avoid taxes on income derived from tips by simply not reporting them.

The idea of a tip as a fixed obligatory percentage of a bill has interesting consequences for the relationship between server and customer. The provision of better-quality service does not generally produce higher tips (Karen, 1962), thus removing the economic incentive to service. Rather it encourages servers to attempt to entice customers to run up higher bills, which will generate bigger tips. Servers in training are taught many little devices to accomplish this. "May I serve you a cocktail?" is claimed to be more effective than "How about a drink?" Experimental research has shown that such tactics can increase the size of restaurant bills by an average of 10 percent (Butler and Snizek, 1976).

Economics aside, it must be remembered that tipping serves as a symbolic reaffirmation of the subordinate status of the service worker. Tips are never given to equals, or by subordinates to superiors. It is revealing to note that some Eastern European countries with officially socialist ideologies have formally banned the practice. A waitress complains, "Tipping should be done away with. It's like throwing a dog a bone. It makes you feel small" (Terkel, 1972:xv).

The tip also has important symbolic meaning to both customer and service worker. It is well known in the subculture of service work that a young couple on a date will usually produce a sizeable tip because of the symbolic meaning it conveys (Howe, 1977:103). Men often leave a large tip to create an impression of success and affluence. The tip might also be used as a symbol of sophistication and experience. One would not want to run the risk of any display of disapproval generated by undertipping.

From the worker's perspective, the tip also has several implications. It is, at the most basic level, tangible recognition of the effort devoted to the transaction. Even minimal (not substandard) service is assumed to merit a minimum tip; a minuscule tip thus signifies a failure to recognize the worker's efforts. It violates the implicit exchange of the impersonal role relationship between customer and worker. However, the strong emotional reactions (such as anger and hostility) produced by small tips (or no tips at all) suggest that something more is involved. It suggests a high degree of personal ego involvement in the transaction—individual effort, pride, a demonstration of skill, and risking one's self-concept as a service worker. Undertipping is thus a personal affront and a personal humiliation. Worse yet, if tips are pooled or compared at the end of the shift, it may become a public humiliation.

Danger. It is not always readily evident, but customers can and do pose a physical threat to service workers. Cab drivers, who are especially vulnerable to holdups, are constantly on the alert for clues to reduce the potential for an encounter with a dangerous fare (Stannard, 1971). In the cabbie subculture of San Francisco, the dangerous customer is referred to as a "no go"; the category encompasses drunks and "nuts" as well as holdup men. The "no go" is a prime topic of conversation when cabbies congregate at cab stands and airports. Certain rules or taboos have emerged out of this interaction. Neighborhood, race, and class are the criteria usually employed to anticipate bad (dangerous) fares (Henslin, 1968). Drivers assume that there is less danger in middle-class residential areas and feel safer picking up passengers who are white, middle-class, female, and have luggage (taken to characterize a real fare rather than potential mischief).

Women service workers must constantly be alert to physical harassment from male customers. Female prostitutes have to cope with "dumpers," who take pleasure in inflicting pain (Murtagh and Harris, 1958:183). Waitresses and airline attendants have too-frequent contacts with men, aptly labeled "hands," who engage in offensive touching. There can be little doubt that employers who outfit their waitresses in skimpy costumes help to invite the continuation of this behavior. It is certainly degrading for waitresses to have to watch their every move to avoid unwanted physical contact.

Over the last few years, there has been a puzzling increase in the incidence of verbal abuse and physical assaults against airline flight attendants, both male and female. "It used to be that passengers were demanding; now they're getting mean," is how one described it (Pontell, Salinger, and Geis, 1983:298). The physical conditions of the situation certainly contribute to the problem by raising the level of passengers' irritability; anxiety about flying, lengthy waits in airports, alcohol consumption, and long periods of time in confined places are all contributing factors. Added to these, though, are the contradictory elements in the social relationship. Flight attendants are employees, perceived as service workers, but also expected to act as authority figures by enforcing smoking, drinking, and luggage rules and curtailing the physical movement of passengers. Some passengers apparently resent being ordered about by subordinates, and these passengers are likely to find it even more unsettling if the subordinates also happen to be young or female or black.

Moral acceptability. Some customers are "bad" because they offend the workers' moral sensibilities in the areas of cleanliness, sex, or decorum. Among the most annoying are those who violate common standards of behavior, such as the diners who leave their tables in a shambles or parents who fail to discipline their children. Cab drivers are constantly asked for drugs. Female prostitutes encounter customers who demand aberrant acts—groups of male teenagers are apparently the worst offenders (Murtagh and Harris, 1958). Perhaps the acts are more offensive because of the underlying attitudes they reveal. They imply a moral judgment about the worker as a person; all waitresses (possibly all women) invite sexual overtures, or all drivers are dealers. In short, bad customers violate workers' moral standards by imputing immorality to them by virtue of their role.

Such typologies are important because they influence the manner in which service workers approach transactions with customers. They wisely attempt to avoid bad customers, who represent potential problems. Thus, when confronted with a choice, a cab driver will bypass a "shopper" in favor of a "tourist." Waitresses who fail to "see" certain tables are attempting to avoid the eye contact which would commit them to service.

Service workers who frequently encounter threats to their autonomy respond by attempting to upgrade the quality of their expertise either verbally, by exaggerating their skills, or actually, by efforts to master special skills. The verbal strategy may be more appearance than substance, as a beautician admits, "I tell her, . . . you are going to get the best haircut you have ever gotten in your life. I bullshit her because you see it's all a game. If I can get her mind in the right attitude . . . she'll really believe what I do is good" (Howe, 1977:41). A more direct response would be to actually develop esoteric skills, such as hair coloring or frosting. Developing these skills sometimes requires courses at hair-styling schools, and the certificates awarded by these schools are framed and conspicuously displayed. At a collective level, occupational groups have attempted to "professionalize"— witness the shift in job title from beautician or hairdresser to cosmetologist, accompanied by attempts to develop licensing laws and codes of ethics.

DOMESTIC WORK

The Domestic Worker: A Profile

In the nineteenth century, domestic work was *the* occupation of women in the labor force. In 1870, over half of all female wage earners were employed in some sort of domestic work (Grossman, 1980:17). The work tended to be specialized in that era. The wealthy and powerful might well employ a dozen different servants, including butlers, valets, coachmen, footmen, housekeepers, lady's maids, cooks, waitresses, scullery maids, parlor maids, chambermaids, and laundresses (Katzman, 1978:118). Among less affluent families, the most common servants were cooks, servants, and washerwomen, and when there was only one domestic worker (and that was the most frequent situation), she was called "maid-of-all-work." Most domestic work today is of such a generalized nature and is still performed by women.

The Bureau of Labor Statistics uses the categories of cleaners and servants, and maids and housemen to describe people employed in private homes. The latter category is usually reserved for "live-ins," who are hired on a long-term basis to cook, clean, and care for children, and who reside with their employers. The former are the "day workers," hired on a daily basis to do the most physically demanding and unpleasant household tasks—scrubbing, cleaning, washing. Over one million workers were counted in both forms of domestic work in 1985, but it is generally agreed that census figures underestimate the actual number of day workers.

The Workers

The numbers of persons employed in household work have been declining, largely as a result of expanding opportunities in other forms of paid employment; these opportunities have allowed women to avoid domestic work, which has never been popular among those with choices. Because there is a constant shortage of workers and because the skills required in the work, especially day work, are familiar to most women, it does provide employment opportunities for those with few other options. Whatever advantage there is, however, must be weighed against the lack of opportunity to develop any skills that might allow women to escape domestic work. Domestic workers have very little chance of moving into higher-status, better-paying jobs. Follow-up studies show that after five years, over 81 percent remain domestics, and another 11 percent are in other forms of service work (Katzman, 1978:380). Only 4 percent are operatives, and 1.7 percent are able to find clerical work. Approximately 98 percent of those in domestic work are women, but the characteristics of white and black women are quite different (Grossman, 1980).

Black women.   Most black female domestic workers have age and educational liabilities. They are both older and less educated than other black female workers. In statistical terms, the typical domestic worker is most likely to be a black woman, 54.2 years old, with 8.8 years of schooling. Some 20 percent are over age 65! Their family situations are also very revealing. About one-quarter maintain their own families, and another 35 percent are married to men who are either unemployed or are not in the labor force. Of husbands with jobs, *all* are blue-collar, service, or farm workers; none are white-collar workers. In short, black domestic workers are a group of older women with few occupational options, but with significant financial responsibilities for themselves and their families.

White women.   A number of white women in domestic work bear exactly the same demographic and financial burdens as their black counterparts, but on the average, they are better off. Only one in ten maintain single-parent homes; all but 15 percent have employed husbands. Most of these husbands have lower-paying blue-collar jobs, but at least some have white-collar jobs. Although the women have low educational attainments, they still average 11.9 years, which to some extent increases the opportunities for mobility.

Wages.   Domestic workers have consistently earned the lowest wages of any paid occupational group. In 1979, 45 percent of all black household workers earned less than the minimum wage. They earn an average of one-third less than other women who work full-time, according to official statistics.

Vulnerability and Powerlessness

All service workers are vulnerable to the demands of their employers, who can control the terms and conditions of the work. However, the way in which domestic work is organized makes this a much more complex situation for it has several characteristics unlike any other form of paid work.

Isolation and supervision.   Domestics are isolated in the homes of their employers during the work day. In some cases they are left alone in the house and thus enjoy certain advantages, such as the freedom to set their own pace. When the employer is present in the house during the day, domestics may find themselves subject to the constant presence or threat of supervision, without the social support of coworkers. Many report being constantly watched by the homemaker, or even being followed around to ensure that they are earning their pay. It creates an atmosphere in which many are reluctant to take a break or even to take time for lunch. The live-in worker, despite formal hours, can find herself on call at any hour of the day or night.

The social isolation of domestic workers has two important consequences (Katzman, 1978). One is that it produces a certain degree of loneliness, cutting workers off from the companionship of coworkers. Over the
years, domestics may develop friendships with other domestics who ride
the same buses, but while at work they are isolated. The other consequence
of this social isolation is that it contributes to the powerlessness of domestics
in the marketplace by making it difficult for them to organize.

Individualized work.   In most jobs, workers can anticipate performing
a specific set of technical tasks. As is the case for secretaries, the domestic
worker's job description must be negotiated with a specific person. Because
they have multiple employers, day workers may need to negotiate each job
differently. Apparently, this is often a source of conflict, with home owners
insisting on tasks and/or standards that violate the worker's tolerance. The
most frequently expressed complaint seems to center on floor care (Terkel,
1972; Curry, 1983). Homemakers are prone to insist that floors be
scrubbed by hand, a most arduous and demeaning task, and one that
homemakers themselves avoid.

Domestic workers do not have the sources of countervailing power
available to other groups of workers. Few are unionized. Domestic work
has never enjoyed the legal protection possessed by most other workers.
They were not covered by the Social Security Act until 1951, nor by the
Fair Labor Standards Act (which set minimum wages) until 1974. Fewer
than six states have insurance laws to protect house workers against either
work-related accidents or nonwork injuries that prevent them from working (Curry, 1983:1A). Some are not in position to utilize legal remedies
against exploitative employers because they choose not to report their
earnings in order to avoid taxation on their meager incomes.

Domestic workers are also at a disadvantage because interpersonal
networks are often the only means by which to obtain employment. Homemakers recommend day workers to friends and neighbors. A dissatisfied
homemaker thus threatens both immediate employment and referrals for
other jobs.

Women employing women.   Work routines for domestics emerge in a
most uncommon context: Both employer and employee are women, and
this can lead to problems in the relationship (Katzman, 1978). Homes have
important personal and symbolic meanings for home-owning women (and
men, but to a lesser extent). Homes have histories and futures, reflect social
and financial status, and express personality traits, personal preferences,
and creativity. Home owners' feelings about their homes can lead them
both to view domestic workers as extensions of themselves and to attempt
to minutely direct the care of the home. In contrast, domestic workers
usually have a fund of experience and have developed their own styles.

Therein lies the potential for conflict. Apparently a few homemakers view domestic women as their personal servants, with the right to treat them accordingly.

More likely is the possibility of discomfort in the role of employer. Part of the reason for the discomfort is that women are less likely to have accumulated work experience supervising others. Another problem arises when the employer finds herself supervising an older woman, which is a position accorded some deference in the larger society. Employers may also feel ambivalent because they are paying low wages and demanding heavy physical labor; at a deeper level, it is often the dilemma of liberating middle-class white women at the expense of lower-class black women, who are left with the tasks the middle-class women reject.

Domestic work is generally held in low esteem in American society, because of its low pay, poor hours, and association with dirty work. Formal studies of occupational prestige consistently rank it at or near the bottom, but its rank is more expressly manifested in the treatment that many domestics must endure. There is no better indication of the low status of the work than the history of the people allocated to it. Indentured servants and slaves provided the majority of the early domestic help. Later, waves of ethnic and racial minorities were recruited. For example, one study found that during the peak flow of Irish immigration to the United States in the mid-nineteenth century, three out of four New York City servants and maids were Irish (Feagin, 1984:93). The Irish were displaced by subsequent waves of immigrants and later by the black migration from the South. David Katzman (1977:78) has traced the influx of black women into domestic work in Philadelphia; in 1900, 28.6 percent of domestics were black women, 38.6 percent in 1910, and 53.9 percent in 1920. Domestic work is generally left to those socially defined as second-class citizens.

HOUSEWORK

Defining the Role

Since work is a place to which one went and the thing one did in exchange for money, the home production that is a woman's primary responsibility is obviously not work. Since no money is paid for the services, it is not only not work, it is valueless (U.S. Justice Department report published in 1979, quoted in Minton and Block, 1983:22).

It is still no easy task for most people to conceptualize twentieth-century housework as an occupation, because a combination of features render it unique. The most obvious is that it is deeply embedded in sociocultural systems that identify it as women's work and as an intrinsic aspect of the social role of women. Consequently, "housework" has frequently been a battleground of competing ideologies, with skirmishes among family members over the nature and division of household tasks. Looking at it from an occupational standpoint also reveals certain uncommon attributes. It is a form of work carried out among people whose relationship to each other is familial rather than contractual. The structural features are also unusual. Unlike most other forms of work, housework is not performed in direct exchange for pay, although some homemakers receive a household and/or personal "allowance." Except for domestic work and farm work, it is one of the few forms of decentralized work left in industrial systems, in the sense that its members do not travel to some central location, whether factory or store or office. Decentralization has the potential to isolate individual houseworkers from each other for a large proportion of the time they work. In some instances it is a multiperson career, with the work shared, albeit usually unequally, among more than one person.

Although not usually conceptualized as such, *housework* can be analyzed as an occupation, broadly defined as the activities necessary to maintain a home and its occupants. With this perspective, the following technical tasks are included: budgeting household finances, physically maintaining the dwelling, house cleaning, washing clothing, interior decorating, grocery shopping, preparing food, dish washing, and, in many cases, child care. The allocation of these tasks among women and men, questions of the relative priorities of the various tasks, and questions of the standards, pace, and quality of household activities are the key issues involved in understanding the evolution of the role of homemaker. The role cannot, of course, be understood independent of larger social and technological events.

THE EVOLUTION OF HOUSEHOLD WORK

Time Studies

Time clocks do not record the number of hours spent doing housework, and it is thus difficult to develop an accurate picture of the amount of time consumed by household tasks. The first systematic studies (conducted in the late 1920s) showed urban American women who were not in the labor force spending an average of 51 hours a week doing housework (Vanek, 1974). Subsequent research revealed that the absolute number of hours rose during the following decades to an average of over 55 in the 1960s and 1970s, despite the evolution of household technology. Some new studies suggest the possibility of a rapid decline to about 40 hours for full-time female homemakers in the 1980s (Hickey, 1985). Such figures are averages, and as would be expected, the amount of time married women (and single female and male parents) spend at household tasks increases with the number of young children in the household. The number of hours devoted to household tasks is lower for women who work outside the home. In the most recent study, women with full-time paid employment outside the home cut the time devoted to housework in half, to about 5 hours a day, for a combined total of 60 hours per week on the two jobs.

As Hartmann (1981) has noted, during most of this period, husbands' time devoted to housework has tended to be to be fixed at somewhere between 7 and 11 hours, regardless of the employment status of the woman or the presence of children. The allocation of time among various household tasks appears to be generally divided as follows (Walker, 1973):

Meal preparation	30%
Cleaning	30%
Family care	15%–25% (depending upon family size)
Clothing care	15%–25% (depending upon family size)

The "Domestic Void": from production to service

Underlying these dry statistics are shifting conceptions of the role of women and housework, technological and manufacturing innovations, and dramatic demographic shifts in the composition of the work force. Contemporary definitions of housework apply only to urban and advanced industrial households, which are generally not units of production.

In vastly simplified outline, it can be observed that as an economy industrializes, households move from subsistence, through simple commodity production by the entire family, to a transitional phase during which men enter the paid labor force while women tend to remain in the home producing things for the family and perhaps products for the market, and finally to a point at which the household becomes primarily a social entity and a unit of consumption (Jensen, 1980). This last transition occurred at different points in time depending upon the social class location of families. Upper-class households were always able to afford domestic servants. Middle-class women abandoned market production late in the nineteenth century, and some were able to allocate domestic work to servants; working-class women never enjoyed this luxury, however, and were apparently still taking in boarders as a means of supplementing family wages well into the 1920s and 1930s.

As late as the nineteenth century, married women produced domestic crafts: cloth, butter, candles, and soap for the family. The aspects of family life directed toward household activities were apparently guided by very different standards in the preindustrial world. Cleaning was an annual spring event rather than a daily or weekly chore; food preparation required cooking and baking, but meals were simple and standard; dirty clothing could accumulate for as long a month between washings (Ehrenreich and English, 1979:143).

The deskilling process which transformed skilled craftspersons into factory laborers also had an impact upon the household. Home-produced textiles were all but supplanted by machine-made cloth by the middle of the nineteenth century, soon followed by mass-produced candles, butter, and other items, leaving what Ehrenreich and English have called a "domestic void." Like men, women were stripped of access to skilled creative crafts that could give meaning and dignity to their lives. Many working-class women were compelled to join men in the factories, but the middle classes, who were more affluent, better educated, and more concerned with status distinctions between themselves and the working classes, were caught up in the emerging "domestic science," or "home economics," movement which transformed housework into an occupation by World War I.

The movement represented the convergence of a number of social trends; among them were a renewed concern with the breakdown of the family, medical science's discovery of the germ theory of disease (and by some strange twist of logic the housewife became accountable for sanitation), wider availability of home ownership, and scientific child rearing. The hallmarks of the role were becoming apparent—an emphasis upon decoration of the home and scrupulous cleanliness, and a concern with nutrition and complex food preparation. By 1916, 20 percent of all high schools were offering home economics courses for young women.

Taylorism was explicitly extended to housework in about 1912, when Christine Frederick, an advocate of Frank and Lillian Gilbreth, began to urge the application of Scientific Management principles to the home. Housewives were encouraged to analyze (and time) how they performed chores (Frederick clocked bathing a baby at 15 minutes), keep records, plan tasks in advance, find the best way to peel potatoes, and inventory household possessions. A long list of new technical components was thus added to the role, including complex meal planning and strict scheduling which usually allocated Monday to washing, Tuesday to ironing, and Wednesday to cleaning.

Technological innovations began to invade American homes in earnest in the 1930s and 1940s. The introduction of "labor-saving" devices—electric irons, vacuum cleaners, automatic washing machines—actually increased the number of hours required for housework. One reason was that new appliances often created more time-consuming activities than they eliminated. Washing machines reduced the time factor on each load, but encouraged more frequent washings and, in turn, more ironing. More time was also required for shopping in the pre–shopping center era. In general, technology and mass-market advertising apparently led to ever higher standards of housework, as producers of vacuum cleaners exhorted home-makers to seek out and destroy the slightest hint of dirt (Cowan, 1985).

Thus, while technology was creating the potential to streamline the work, the hours devoted to it were actually increasing, in part because advice magazines and mass-market advertisers were imposing ever higher standards of effort and cleanliness; in some cases, these ideals evolved into subcultural standards within neighborhoods and social groups, with home-makers competing with each other for the cleanest houses, or for being the first to hang out the wash. Vanek (1974) also suggests another reason. Because the tasks were repetitive and their value unclear compared to paid labor, women felt pressured to devote long hours to housework, emphasizing the effort, not the output.

CASE STUDY: WHAT IS A HOMEMAKER WORTH?

One technique for placing a price tag on work within the home is the *replacement cost approach*. The reasoning is that since a homemaker does housework, she or he could be replaced by a paid employee at prevailing wage rates. Economists and others have been exploring this issue at an abstract, academic level since at least the 1920s, but it took on new meaning when, in 1978, an attorney introduced the matter into a contested divorce case (Minton and Block, 1983). His goal was to place a value on "the contribution of a spouse as a homemaker" for purposes of a financial settlement.

His computations suggested that his client's work in the home should be valued at $40,288.04 a year. The court admitted that the services of a home-maker do have economic value but declined to place a specific price tag on them, although the client was awarded $40,000 a year. The technique used for determining the economic value of household services is reproduced in Exhibit 7:1, with wages adjusted to 1983 wage levels. The most salient feature of this list may be the range of services included in the role.

Beginning in the 1960s, a new configuration of social, demographic, and technological forces began to reshape housework once again. Families became smaller. A new generation of time-saving technological advances emerged—wash-and-wear fabrics, self-cleaning appliances, supermarkets, and convenience foods. But rather than causing an expansion of work and greater dedication to household tasks, as was evident earlier in the century, these advances were apparently accompanied by a decline in the number of hours devoted to housework.

The reduction in the length of the work day reflects a shift in the fundamental approach to household tasks. The increasing educational attainments of middle- and working-class women rendered the routine and repetitive round of cleaning and cooking less and less satisfying. In a 1984 poll, 68 percent of women surveyed agreed that their standards for a clean

EXHIBIT 7:1   The Replacement Value of a Homemaker

JOB PERFORMED	HOURS/WEEK	RATE/HOUR	VALUE/WEEK
Buyer, food & household	————	$ 6.44	————
Nurse	————	7.99	————
Tutor	————	7.20	————
Waitress	————	3.81	————
Seamstress	————	4.20	————
Laundress	————	3.47	————
Chauffeur	————	6.16	————
Gardener	————	5.60	————
Family counselor	————	28.00	————
Maintenance worker	————	5.48	————
General child care	————	3.50	————
Cleaning woman	————	3.59	————
Housekeeper	————	5.32	————
Cook	————	5.32	————
Errand runner	————	4.24	————
Bookkeeper/budget manager	————	7.20	————
Interior decorator	————	35.84	————
Caterer	————	8.63	————
Child psychologist	————	40.00	————
Dishwasher	————	3.47	————
Dietitian	————	7.61	————
Secretary	————	5.60	————
Public relations/hostess	————	22.50	————

Weekly value	$ ————
Yearly value (×52)	$ ————

Source: "Appendix," p. 178, *What is a Wife Worth?* by Michael H. Minton with Jean Libman Block. Copyright © 1983 by Michael Minton and Jean Libman Block. By permission of William Morrow & Co.

house had declined "a great deal" (Hickey, 1985). Increasing participation in the paid labor force left less time for household activities, and the level of affluence brought paid domestic work within the reach of more families. The individual private-household worker has been supplemented by innovations in the provision of domestic work. Corporate house-cleaning or food-catering services can supply teams of men and women to descend upon homes and complete all the tasks within a few hours.

GENDER DIVISIONS OF HOUSEHOLD WORK

Probably the most perplexing issue intertwined with the changing perceptions of the nature of housework is the question of the allocation of tasks between husbands and wives. The same poll of women that revealed changing standards of cleanliness also uncovered a widespread feeling (81 percent) that men should be doing more mopping, scrubbing, and bed making. The division of household labor that was institutionalized during the "white glove" era is apparently in the process of renegotiation. As in all cases in which stable patterns are disrupted, change is uneven and there is the potential for conflict as well as smooth accommodation.

Mention of an important methodological caveat is appropriate at this point. Because housework is decentralized, research almost universally depends upon self-reports, whether through daily logs, retrospective recall, or judgments of relative effort. Unfortunately, such techniques are not subject to verification.

As housework emerged earlier in the twentieth century, there was a socially sanctioned division of housework within the broader division of labor among husbands and wives. Husbands' responsibilities centered on provision of a "family wage" by paid labor and on household tasks consistent with the gender role expectations (largely home maintenance). Strictly household tasks (cooking, shopping, cleaning, everyday child care) became "women's work." Despite the value of such tasks, housework never achieved much social prestige. But the power of the cultural ideal cannot be underestimated, however exploitative and restrictive it may appear in retrospect. It became the social standard by which many men and women who were socialized in that era judged themselves and others. Research among the unemployed showed it to be a devastating experience for men, for it undermined their roles in the family as well as in the larger society (see, for example, Komarovsky, 1962). A study of college-educated wives of college-educated men in the 1960s found one-quarter adhering to social roles that centered on unshared home and child care and that held males responsible for the financial support of the family (Lipman-Blumen, 1972).

By the 1980s, the ideal of shared household tasks had gained wider currency in the United States, yet men generally do not participate extensively in all activities usually thought of as household tasks (see, for example, Condran and Bode, 1982). Laundering, cooking, and grocery shopping are most likely to be the sole responsibility of wives (Maret and Findlay, 1984). Dishwashing, child care, and house cleaning are, in that order, most likely to be shared among husbands and wives.

United Nations studies indicate that housework is typically women's work the world over (Sciolino, 1985). It is estimated that African women do virtually all the domestic chores, plus 75 percent of the agricultural work. A report from Italy reveals that 85 percent of married women with children, who work full time, get no help at all from their husbands with domestic tasks.

By the 1980s, the ideal of shared household tasks had gained wider currency in the United States. A survey of high school seniors shows that an equal distribution of child care between husband and wife is clearly the preferred arrangement (Herzog, et al., 1983). Both men and women agree on this, but there is less agreement on the division of other household tasks, where women are more favorably disposed to shared responsibilities than men. Despite the expressed preference for shared household work, men do not generally participate extensively in all forms of housework (Condran and Bode, 1982; Huber and Spritze, 1983). Laundering, cooking, and grocery shopping are most likely to be the sole responsibility of wives, with dish washing, child care, and house cleaning most likely to be shared between husbands and wives (Maret and Findlay, 1984).

CONCLUSION

Direct service occupations may be the most demanding of all forms of work in the United States. Members occupy low social status by virtue of the fact that their job calls for providing personal services to others. Moreover, most service jobs are structured to emphasize subordination to the demands of customers.

Their subordination is verified by their name tags and uniforms, and by social conventions such as tipping. Subordination is further reinforced by the fact that service workers everywhere are constantly reminded not to offend customers. Programmed smiles and uncomplaining acceptance of customer demands are the most evident aspects of subordination to the customer, but it also extends to more personal matters. Possibly the most dramatic aspect of this is the pressure to submerge their own identity and personality in favor of what Hochschild (1983) calls "outgoing, middle class sociability." Over the years, airlines have been known to establish standards for their flight attendants' height and weight, the length of their hair, and the color of their underwear.

Most customers are polite and cooperative, but the very nature of the situation creates the potential for rude, malicious, and even abusive behavior. It is due in large part to the fact that the service worker occupies a position that renders them more vulnerable to degrading treatment than members of other occupations. Those who provide personal services are highly sensitive to the potential for conflict, and attempt to manage social relationships to their own advantage.

EIGHT

Work, Earnings, and Unemployment

INTRODUCTION: WHAT DO PEOPLE WANT FROM THEIR WORK?

People enter the world of work with a complex set of expectations. They hope to realize a number of different goals, earn a variety of rewards. In some ways the best time for people to begin an examination of what they want from their jobs is some time before they actually embark upon full-time careers, prior to the point at which expectations are modified by concrete realities.

High school seniors in 1976 and 1985 are the source of the data in Exhibit 8:1. They were asked to rate various attributes of jobs. Their answers reveal their aspirations as they prepare to enter the job market or continue their education. There emphasis has changed somewhat over the last decade, but the relative importance of these features has been quite stable.

Jobs offering advancement opportunities are consistently favored over all others by both men and women, and career considerations have tended to become more important. Financial rewards are ranked second and have also become more salient, with a more pronounced emphasis occurring among women. Women continue to be more likely to show concern with the broader societal implications of their work than men, but the importance of helping society has declined slightly for both groups. Pres-

EXHIBIT 8:1 Attributes of Jobs Rated as "Very Important"

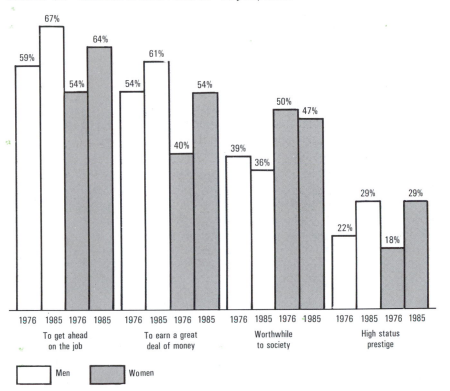

| 1976 | 1985 | 1976 | 1985 | 1976 | 1985 | 1976 | 1985 | 1976 | 1985 | 1976 | 1985 | 1976 | 1985 | 1976 | 1985 |

To get ahead on the job   To earn a great deal of money   Worthwhile to society   High status prestige

☐ Men   ▨ Women

Source: Developed from data reported in Marilyn Elias, "Today's Women Value High Pay" *USA Today* (June 18, 1985), p. 1D.

tige and status considerations rank last among these four considerations, but they have tended to become more important.

Even this brief survey reveals that people have complex expectations about their work. Compensation in exchange for work is the major source of income for most individuals and families in industrial societies. Because earnings set upper limits on consumption patterns, mold life-styles, and determine accessibility to leisure, it is not unexpected to find "pay" ranking high on the list of important job characteristics. It is apparent, however, that work has meanings that transcend the strictly financial. Jobs must offer an opportunity for progress, advancement, and personal growth (as well as more money). Employment is one of the most important sources of social status in industrial societies. And it is through work that individuals hope to make some meaningful contribution to society. Unemployment would thus be an important consideration if for no other reason than that it disrupts established patterns of consumption. Because the implications of jobs extend far beyond the issue of access to goods and services in the marketplace, however, the threat of joblessness is one of the more meaningful aspects of the study of work.

OCCUPATIONAL DIFFERENCES IN EARNINGS

Many social, economic, demographic, and political factors influence the general range of compensation for occupational groups. The *scarcity of qualified personnel* is one factor. All other things being equal, income will respond to the dynamics of supply and demand in market economies. When the availability of potential workers exceeds the number of jobs, incomes tend to be depressed. People with rare skills are often able to command a premium, at least until more workers enter the field. This was dramatically evident during the construction of the oil pipeline through Alaska during the 1970s, when construction workers and even unskilled workers were able to command a premium for their labor. In fact, Alaskan workers continue to have the highest per capita income among all the states.

Collective organizations (trade unions and professional associations) have long been able to improve the earnings of their members in two basic ways. They can improve earnings *directly*, through the advantages of collective bargaining, and ultimately by strikes and threats of withholding services. For example, the average income for unionized workers in the United States was $404 a week in 1984, compared to $303 for the nonunion employee (Blaine, 1985). Unionized workers' advantages may be declining, for their earnings have recently been growing at a slower rate than that for other workers. This may reflect a long-term erosion of the power of labor unions. Membership has been declining for over a decade as the traditional blue-collar strongholds in manufacturing (steel and autos) have succumbed to foreign competition and encroachments from nonunionized workers willing to work for lower wages. Union activity has recently shifted toward the protection of existing jobs. Contracts negotiated in the 1980s frequently incorporated concessions such as wage freezes, even wage cuts, and a newer system called *dual wage scales* or *two-tier systems*. They allow new workers to be hired at lower rates and to be given smaller raises than existing employees. About 800,000 workers accepted such agreements in 1984 (Brophy, 1985a). This was one of the concessions made by airline pilots in a 1985 strike against United Airlines, with pilots agreeing to a contract with a top rate of $52,008 (after 20 years) for new pilots, compared to the then-current scale of $76,404. Such trends may reflect a weakening of the traditional power of unions to ensure higher wages for their membership.

Organized groups may also be able to *indirectly* improve wages by restricting the number of workers. American trade unions were influential in limiting the flow of foreign workers into the United States by helping to enact restrictive immigration laws in the 1920s. The self-regulating professions have also been accused of this practice through the control of admissions and licensing (see, for example, Larson, 1977).

The *skill levels* required of workers is apparently a prime factor, with occupations requiring higher levels of skill, training, or education generally being better rewarded. This is not always an easy relationship to document, for "skill" is difficult to measure, especially among jobs with similar educational requirements.

Finally, *tradition and cultural values* may influence earnings. It is argued that the members of prestigious occupations sometimes earn more simply because it is socially appropriate for them to be paid more than lower-level workers. The fact is that people do tend to believe that more prestigious occupations merit higher pay (Alves and Rossi, 1978; Jasso and Rossi, 1977).

These processes, singly and in combination, help to explain the relative earnings of different occupational and social groups, but they do so only in part, for the wage determination process is far from clearly perceived at this point.

WOMEN'S WAGES: THE "EARNINGS GAP"

The relative income for women workers in the United States has apparently always lagged behind that of men. To cite one example, an analysis of early nineteenth-century wages suggests that prior to industrialization, females employed in manufacturing earned thirty cents for every dollar earned by males (Goldin and Sokoloff, 1982). The relative earnings of women in blue-collar work rose rapidly during the period from 1820 to 1850, and then at a somewhat slower pace until about 1930, when they reached approximately 58 percent of men's wages; women's relative wages hovered at or near that figure into the 1980s. The ratios vary among occupations, as shown in Exhibit 8:2, but contemporary data show that, on the average, women earn somewhere between 65 percent and 68 percent of what men earn, and that this differential has persisted at approximately the same level for several decades. Some observers detect an improvement in the relative economic position of female workers, but even assuming that this trend does continue, women in the paid labor force will remain at a disadvantage for the foreseeable future. Such an economic discrepancy is apparently a common feature of industrial societies, whether capitalist or socialist, although the differential may be less in European nations (Swafford, 1978).

EXHIBIT 8:2   Earnings of Men and Women, Selected Occupations, United States, 1983

OCCUPATION	MEN	WOMEN	WOMEN'S EARNINGS AS A PERCENT OF MEN'S
Weekly earnings, Full-time workers	$379	$252	66.5%
Executive, managerial	530	340	64.2
Public administration	510	361	70.8
Marketing, advertising	614	367	59.8
Professional	505	363	71.9
Engineers	604	500	82.8
Registered nurses	403	402	99.8
Elementary school teachers	404	351	86.9
Designers	501	257	51.3
Technicians	395	248	62.8
Sales	400	204	51.0
Realtors	458	307	67.0
Cashiers	201	164	81.6
Retail	259	166	64.1
Administrative support/clerical	362	249	68.8
Secretaries	340	250	73.5
Bookkeepers	307	249	81.1
Investigators, adjusters	452	256	56.6
Precision	399	251	62.9
Craft			
Repair			
Butchers/bakers	337	192	57.0
Mechanics/repairers	368	326	88.6
Operators	307	205	66.8
Fabricators			
Inspectors	398	220	55.3
Assemblers	304	226	74.3
Laborers	249	208	83.5
Service	255	172	67.5
Police	392	298	76.0
Waiters/waitresses	210	152	72.4

Source: Earl F. Mellor, "Weekly Earnings in 1983," *Monthly Labor Review* 108 (Jan. 1985), table 1, pp. 55–59.

The *earnings gap* measures the overall difference between the "average" man and woman working *full-time* in the paid labor force. Therefore, a number of factors combine to produce the observed differences. In part, they may be traced to differences in experiences in the labor market, such as hours worked, union membership, and job tenure. The earnings gap is also perpetuated by the fact that men and women hold different kinds of jobs.

Age and education. At one time, the educational attainments of males exceeded that of females, giving males an advantage in competition for white-collar and skilled blue-collar work, both of which tended to pay more. Since World War II, this difference has generally disappeared, and it currently accounts for less than 1 percent of the earnings gap (Mellor, 1985:18). Despite the disappearance of differences in schooling, more formal education simply does not translate into better pay for women; female college graduates' salaries are about 67 percent those of male graduates.

It is frequently noted that the earnings gap is narrower for younger women, with females under the age of twenty earning 88 cents for every dollar of male income. This may mean that compensation patterns are beginning to change for new workers entering the labor market. However, half these jobs are concentrated in the service occupations, and others are at or near the minimum-wage level.

Hours. It has long been noted that women on hourly rates generally work fewer hours a week than men, thus reducing their take-home pay (Fuchs, 1971). The fact that fewer hours are worked certainly reduces weekly and annual incomes, but does not eliminate the discrepancies in pay; if earnings are computed on an hourly basis, women's hourly rates are still only 64.3 percent of men's (Smith and Ward, 1984:23).

Unionization. Male workers are more likely to be members of trade unions and thus enjoy the advantages of collective bargaining for wages. Overall, about 23 percent of men in the labor force are unionized, compared to 14 percent of women (Adams, 1985:29). Current union membership patterns reflect the legacy of the period of deliberate exclusion of women from blue-collar occupations. More importantly, white-collar work, which has long employed a disproportionate number of women, was never really a stronghold of union activism. White-collar workers (both women and men) have been encouraged (and have tended) to identify themselves with management and have perceived unions as a blue-collar movement, creating at best a reluctant involvement. Union organizers shared this perception, discouraging active recruitment practices. White-collar women in earlier periods were also less likely to be responsive to recruitment because of a weaker commitment to long-term work.

Over the last decades there have been a number of successful collective-bargaining breakthroughs. Teachers and nurses have organized, and the Service Employees International Union claims 650,000 members and is devoted to organizing female clerical workers who earn, on the average, $5,000 less than males (Shabecoff, 1981).

Occupational patterns.   The most direct and obvious source of the income gap may be traced to the differences in employment patterns between men and women. Women are underrepresented in the more highly paid professional and managerial jobs, and overrepresented in the lower-paying clerical, retail sales, and service occupations. About one-third of all women in the paid labor force have been concentrated in clerical work since at least the 1950s. Statistics have shown that as little as 5 percent or as much as 15 percent of the difference in incomes can be accounted for by this pattern (Mellor, 1985).

The occupational distribution is even more invidious than it appears, because workers in these occupations (regardless of sex) earn low entry-level salaries *and* are less able to improve their earnings over time by the personal strategies that American ideology proclaims as the means to upward mobility—education and work experience. Economists are fond of referring to this as "returns on human capital," measuring the income increments associated with more education or longer work experience. Clerical, service, and sales work do not produce significant returns on human capital (Bibb and Form, 1977). This is largely due to the fact that most of these are low-ceiling careers, lacking in meaningful promotion opportunities into more highly paid ranks.

Intermittent work patterns.   Also to be considered is the fact that women who marry (and over 90 percent of all American women and men do marry) are likely to have more discontinuous or intermittent work careers than those who do not. A study of employed women shows that those who had *never* married worked 92 percent of the time since completing school, compared to 56 percent of the time among women who had married (Treiman and Terrell, 1975:187). Thus, men accumulate more seniority and job-specific experience. Men average nearly a two-year advantage in seniority in their current jobs (Mellor, 1985:24). Disruption of careers can be costly. Government research shows that women with a two- to four-year break in employment average salaries that are 13 percent lower than those earned by women with a continuous work record; if the interruption lasts for five years, the loss is 19 percent (U.S. Bureau of the Census, 1979b).

Intermittent careers (and also the unequal hours and the occupational patterns) originate in large part from the competing demands of work roles and family roles facing women in American society. Women generally place higher priority upon family roles and responsibilities than do men; in some cases socialization is imposed upon them. A 1985 Gallup poll reports that about three-quarters of American women feel that marriage and children are the "most satisfying" way of life for them (Gallup Organization, 1985). Over one-half would prefer to combine a full-time career with a family, and, of course, many women are forced to work outside the home by economic necessity. The point is that family roles depress female earnings by disrupting their careers, causing women to work fewer hours and encouraging them to remain in traditionally female sales and service occupations which offer the advantage of flexible hours.

Several factors interact to produce the negative effects of intermittent careers. First, seniority is lost, and earnings are frequently based on tenure. Loss of seniority also renders workers more vulnerable to layoffs under the rule of "last hired, first fired." Second, job skills may atrophy during absence from the workplace. Many white-collar occupations, such as banking, which employs large numbers of women have undergone dramatic changes as a result of the introduction of electronic data processing; returning workers are thus placed at a competitive disadvantage. Finally, it is often overlooked that absence from a job can penalize workers because of the simple fact that they are not physically present to be considered for salary increments or, more importantly, promotions to better positions. Kanter (1977) has noted that the peak age for child-rearing responsibilities (25 to 35) coincides exactly with the years in which employers are making fateful decisions about the futures of its younger employees.

Summary.   Statistical analysis should make it possible to estimate what women would earn if they worked similar hours, had equal proportions of union membership, and had employment patterns comparable to those of men. Unfortunately, such studies offer widely varying results; Some explain only a small proportion of the earnings gap, while others claim to account for most of the difference. That the difference remains "unexplained" may be interpreted as a measure of the unintentional and overt discrimination that occurs in the workplace.

BLACK-WHITE EARNING DIFFERENTIALS

When median earnings for blacks and whites are compared over time, it appears that some measurable improvements have taken place since the 1940s. This was a decisive period, for it signaled the reversal of a pattern stretching back to the days of slavery. The relative economic position of blacks seems to have deteriorated between the Civil War and World War II, in response to the exclusionary and discriminatory practices of the period; these practices not only tended to exclude black males from both white-collar work and the more highly paid craft occupations, but also produced unequal pay scales within similar jobs (Becker, 1975).

Black women were concentrated in domestic work. In 1939, the first year for which there are reliable statistics, black men earned an average of 45 percent of what white men earned, and black women approximately 38 percent of what white women earned (U.S. Bureau of the Census, 1979a:136). The earnings gap slowly began to narrow, achieving about 66 percent for both men and women by the beginning of the 1960s. The earnings gap for black men has continued to narrow, but slowly, and stood at about 70 percent in 1982 (U.S. Bureau of the Census, 1983:184). In contrast, black female earnings have continued to rise, and, by 1982, black women earned about 92 percent of what white women earned, but their earnings are still burdened by the gender gap. A combination of factors serve to effectively hold black male earnings below those of white males.

As is the case for gender, the concentration of black males in jobs at the lower-paying end of the scale accounted for a sizable part of the cost of being black. Part of the income differential can be traced to underrepresentation in professional, managerial, and craft work, and their overrepresentation in the operative, service, and unskilled work. There are two other factors which are also important.

Educational credentials.   Differential educational attainments also handicap black workers. Blacks generally have a lower level of formal education, and are thus more likely to be channeled toward lower-paid work, or toward using the dual-labor-market model into the secondary sector. However, it must be emphasized that blacks simply do not earn the economic rewards for education that whites do! It has long been observed that blacks are destined to earn less than whites at every educational level (Siegel, 1965). Thus, blacks who have attained the educational credentials to qualify for managerial positions are still at an income disadvantage, and it is proportionately greater than that suffered by blue-collar workers. Some attribute this to an inferior quality of preparation in the schools attended by blacks, but it has also been argued that it may have less to do with the *actual* value of the education credentials than with the *assumption* of inferiority on the part of employers. This may be a disguised form of racial discrimination used as a rationale for limiting promotion opportunities or not paying wages similar to those earned by whites in comparable positions.

Demographic factors.   Some of the earnings differential may have its origin in the demographic characteristics of the black male population. Age is one consideration: Black workers are, on the average, younger, and young workers, regardless of race or gender, earn relatively low pay, if they are even able to locate work. The geography of residence also seems to work against blacks. A large percentage reside in the South, where earnings are generally lower than in other regions. In fact, some of the overall income gains reflect the patterns of migration out of the South that began in the 1960s, so there may be reason for some degree of optimism for the future. Urban residence also puts blacks at a disadvantage as job opportunities in the better-paying manufacturing sector are lost and are replaced by poorer-paying service work.

Earnings for black women have been approaching parity with those

EXHIBIT 8:3 Occupational Earnings, Black and Hispanic Workers: United States, 1982

	MEAN EARNINGS, FULL-TIME WORKERS			
	MEN		WOMEN	
	Black	Hispanic	Black	Hispanic
Full-time workers (As a percent of white workers of same sex)	$16,963 (70%)	$17,900 (74%)	$13,250 (92%)	$12,236 (85%)
Managerial	23,468 (73)	24,339 (75)	19,338 (103)	17,196 (92)
Professional	25,160 (78)	36,666 (113)	17,780 (92)	16,578 (86)
Technical	n/a	n/a	14,643 (92)	n/a
Sales	16,405 (65)	19,567 (77)	11,600 (91)	10,413 (82)
Administrative support	17,915 (85)	16,193 (77)	13,422 (99)	13,135 (97)
Service	13,392 (81)	13,889 (84)	9,800 (106)	8,716 (94)
Precision crafts	17,406 (79)	18,242 (83)	n/a	n/a
Operators, fabricators	15,469 (83)	15,429 (83)	12,457 (107)	9,641 (83)
Farming, etc.	8,824 (85)	10,955 (105)	n/a	n/a

Source: U.S. Bureau of the Census, *Money Income of Families and Persons in the United States, 1982*, Series P-60, no. 142, table 52, p. 184.

of white women much more rapidly than among men. In fact, in some occupational categories, median income is actually balanced in their favor, something almost never found among their male counterparts. As more and more black women have been able to break the barriers that held them in the traditional domain of domestic work in favor of blue-collar and lower-level white-collar jobs, the overall position has improved.

It is possible that, by a sad and ironic twist, the improved position of black women may have its origins in the sociocultural heritage of American racism and discrimination. Young black women tend to value work as a part of their adult roles and anticipate a lengthy working career, probably because they anticipate low earnings for themselves and their future husbands (Hurdis, 1977). In the face of anticipated discrimination, women develop greater commitment to work, and the income-producing aspects of activity, thus expending greater effort on the job, which could be translated into greater rewards.

Summary: Work and Earnings

Income derived from working must be viewed as being determined and limited by the interaction of three sets of forces. Social, political, and economic forces shape the economic value of occupations, and thus set upper and lower limits upon the earnings of members of those occupations. Access to occupations, and in turn the associated range of potential income, is limited or enhanced by the acquisition of educational credentials, work experience, or other prerequisites (human capital). Human capital attainments are shaped and influenced by socialization experiences and allocative processes which channel and direct men, women, whites, and minorities in different directions. Finally, the same ascribed social characteristics that influence the attainment of human capital may be differently evaluated and rewarded in the workplace, resulting in a situation in which people with otherwise similar qualifications receive unequal pay.

"COMPARABLE WORTH"

Long-standing patterns of wage discrimination based on gender, age, race, religion, and national origin were prohibited by the Equal Pay Act of 1963 and by Title VII of the Civil Rights Acts in 1964, although the issue was not finally settled by the Supreme Court until 1981 in *County of Washington v. Gunther*. These legislative initiatives and case law guarantee nondiscriminatory treatment in all aspects of employment, including compensation. Thus, women and minorities cannot be

> denied equal pay for equal work;
> intentionally paid differently than male or white workers;
> discriminated against in initial job placements;
> intentionally segregated into certain jobs;
> denied the right to apply for any jobs, particularly higher-paying jobs or jobs with greater career advancement potential;
> denied training, transfers, promotions, or any other job opportunities; or
> subjected to intentional job evaluation manipulations that downgrade their pay. (from Williams, 1984:149)

Victims may be entitled to back pay and wage adjustments, although there are charges that the government has been lax in the enforcement of the law.

A major issue for the 1980s and beyond will be the more complex and emotionally tinged matter of *comparable worth*, or *pay equity*. The debate evolves out of the persisting gender and racial gaps in earnings, and their disproportionate concentration in some occupational categories. The most commonly used language in the states that have adopted this doctrine of *comparable worth* calls for "equal pay for males and females doing work requiring comparable skill, effort, and responsibility under similar working conditions" (Bellak, 1984:75). Originally almost exclusively a women's issue, the doctrine has, in New York, for example, been expanded to focus on jobs predominately held by blacks, such as cooking, janitorial work, elevator operating, and window washing (Steinberg, 1984:101).

Wage discrimination laws are designed to eliminate any barriers that might inhibit movement into more responsible, better-paying jobs. However, adherents of pay equity argue that wage differentials also exist because the jobs held by women and minorities tend to pay lower wages even though they require levels of responsibility and effort equivalent to other jobs. Comparable worth articulates two separate ideas: (1) jobs, although dissimilar in content, may be compared on "objective" criteria to determine their relative worth or value to an employer, and (2) jobs of approximately similar value should be equally compensated (Chi, 1984:34). Recognizing that objective job evaluations are not all that simple, research in several states does indicate that "comparable" jobs filled largely by women are paid between about 5 percent and 20 percent less than those that tend to be filled by men (Treiman and Hartmann, 1981:Chap. 4). The following are some examples of pairs of jobs that received the same point values on standardized job evaluations:

In the state of Minnesota:
    Registered Nurse (female) $1,723 a month
    Vocational Education Teacher (male) $2,260
In San Jose, California:
    Senior Legal Secretary (female) $ 665
    Senior Carpenter (male) $1,040
In the state of Washington:
    Dental Assistant (female) $ 608
    Stockroom Attendant (male)   816
(data from Steinberg, 1984:108)

The central tenet articulated by advocates of comparable worth is that of *undervaluation*—the idea that the value of technical work tasks has traditionally been lowered by virtue of their association with women or minorities. The tenet is clearly tautological: Work performed by women is less valuable because it is performed by women. Undervaluation may be deliberately discriminatory, but it can just as likely be embedded in tacit cultural assumptions and stereotypes. In one celebrated U.S. Labor Department case, the male job of zoo keeper was rated higher than the female job of nursery school teacher because the evaluators regard caring for a child not as a job-related skill, but rather as a quality intrinsic to being a woman. In other cases, women's work tasks may be depreciated because it is assumed that the requisite skills are gained during the "normal" process of growing up and not through specialized training. Thus, one state assumed that all women must certainly have learned to type, and thus downgraded that aspect of training and preparation. In other cases, the job evaluations themselves are flawed, for they fail to encompass all the skills demanded in a particular position. Female and minority workers in correctional facilities have failed to receive credit for their record-keeping activities because it was assumed that only office personnel did such tasks.

Demands for pay equity based on comparable worth introduce some complex and sensitive issues. Job evaluation itself does not always precisely calculate the skills required of specific jobs, much less the value of dissimilar tasks. Then too, it must be remembered that the historical origins of unequal pay reflect the operation of market forces as well as discrimination. The U.S. Supreme Court noted that it was understandable, and a matter of sound economics, for employers to take advantage of the opportunity to pay lower wages for work of equal value to any group willing to accept (or unable to prevent) them (Bellace, 1984:695). The threat of government-imposed wage scales worries still other observers, independent of the merits of specific cases.

Despite the problems inherent in comparing dissimilar work and concerns over the disruption of wage scales set in the marketplace, comparable worth has been implemented in some places. State and local governments have been the leaders, with at least twenty-five states and one hundred municipalities involved in studies of pay equity. Nineteen states had comparable worth laws in 1984, although most are ambiguously worded and of limited scope. (Bellak, 1984:75). There have been some important improvements, however. In May 1985, for example, the city of Los Angeles agreed to increase the wages of 3,900 female employees to bring them in line with comparable male jobs. The salary paid to typists was raised from $16,932 to $19,620 (Brazil, 1985). In the United States, the federal government has been slow to take action on the issue of comparable worth. In contrast, the ten members of the European Economic Community have enacted legislation guaranteeing women equal pay with men for work of equal value (Bellace, 1984:702). Each country must have a court or other agency empowered to handle equal-pay disputes.

UNEMPLOYMENT AND THE MEANING OF WORK

The overwhelming majority of Americans claim that they would continue to work even if guaranteed sufficient money on which to live. Studies, beginning in the 1950s and replicated since, find that over 70 percent of workers at every occupational level admit that they would stay on the job even without the economic imperative (Morse and Weiss, 1955; Renwick and Lawler, 1978). Working women are less likely to concur, especially blue-collar women who are both working mothers and heads of households (Dowd, 1983). The winners of lottery jackpots who could actually enjoy the luxury of limitless leisure confirm this, for most do return to some form of paid labor after a vacation period.

Thus, work must offer some benefits and have some meaning beyond the simple material rewards. Workers themselves provide some insight into this when asked to react to the possibility of not being forced to work by economic necessity. A summary of their answers is reported in Exhibit 8:4.

People have many reasons for working, but this study asked workers to identify the single "most important" factor influencing their desire to continue at work. Their replies can be organized into several major groups.

Performance. The most frequently cited reason was simple and straightforward; the inner satisfaction derived from the performance of the work. C. Wright Mills once described this as the *ideal of craftsmanship,* where "There is no ulterior motive in work other than the product being made and the process of its creation" (Mills, 1951:216). A feeling of pride in craft may be most evident in the skilled work of craftspeople or professionals, but it may be experienced at any level in the occupational structure. Even tasks that might seem menial to an outsider can be approached with the desire to perform to the best of one's ability. For example, a woman relegated to the unpleasant chore of cleaning tuna on an assembly line reports feeling great pleasure in being thorough and competent, in seeing the neat piles of tuna accumulate under her guidance (Garson, 1975).

EXHIBIT 8:4   Reasons for Continuing to Work, Even with Enough Money to Live Comfortably

REASON GIVEN	MEN	WOMEN
I enjoy what I do on my job.	29.0%	28.6%
I derive the major part of my identity from my job.	25.8	27.5
Work keeps me from being bored.	17.4	18.2
My work is important and valuable to others.	13.9	10.8
I enjoy the company of my coworkers.	5.3	8.1
I would feel guilty if I did not contribute to society through gainful employment.	4.4	3.4
I would continue to work out of habit.	4.2	3.4

Source: Patricia A. Renwick and Edward E. Lawler, "What You Really Want from Your Job," *Psychology Today,* 11 (May 1978), p. 57. Reprinted with permission of *Psychology Today* magazine. Copyright © 1978 American Psychological Association.

The deskilling of work associated with industrialization may have steadily reduced the opportunity for satisfying work, but such responses suggest that work need not be satisfying to be meaningful.

Self-identity. Almost equally important is personal identity. In part, this reflects the importance of occupation to the self-image. *Self-image* is that complex of qualities people attribute to themselves. Simultaneously perceived responses of the image are presented to others and are thus a source of approval, rejection, or indifference. Many personal qualities and social roles interact to create this definition of self, but none is more important than work. When asked to complete the statement, "I am . . . ," occupation is typically the most frequently mentioned role, ranking before family, religion, gender, or ethnicity (Mulford and Salisbury, 1964).

Activity. A fairly large number of people feel that their jobs are enacted out of habit, or to forestall boredom. Underlying this kind of answer is an awareness that work tasks and routines structure people's lives in a number of subtle ways (Warr, 1984a). Paid work offers variety, taking the individual out of unchanging domestic environments and exposing them to new people, places, and ideas not otherwise available.

Work imposes structure upon the daily and weekly passage of time, dividing it into work time versus personal time, work week versus weekend, work year versus vacation. The unemployed often find it difficult to remember and locate events in the past because of the lack of structure. Jobless Austrian factory workers observed during the depression of the 1930s lost their sense of time; were unable to recall what had been accomplished during the day, and activities that could not have taken more than a few minutes were recorded as though they had filled a morning (Jahoda, et al., 1971). Perhaps the key here is that work gives people something (as opposed to nothing) to do, an outlet for physical and mental energy.

Social value. One group emphasizes the importance of their work to others. They would thus continue because people depend upon them or are served by them. The service may be direct, in the form of contact with customers, or indirect, in the production of a socially useful product. A mail carrier expresses this feeling when he discusses how his work contributes to society:

> This is a profession that everyone has looked up to and respected. They always say, "Here comes the mailman"—pony express or something. . . . Everyone likes to receive mail. I feel it is one of the most respected professions that is throughout the nation. You're doing a job for the public and a job for the country (Terkel, 1972:361).

Social contacts. Only a few expressly focus on valued social relationships, probably underestimating the importance of this dimension of work. Whether or not fully recognized, work locates people in subcultures and in a complex web of relationships with coworkers who provide friendships and social support in dealing with supervisors. Work-based relationships may mature into friendships and shared leisure activities that extend beyond the workplace. A local bar may actually become an extension of the job. This situation has frequently been noted among construction workers, for whom pubs become the center of a shared social life, making it difficult to distinguish between social and work roles (see, for example, LeMasters, 1975). For teachers, the bar may be a "backstage" setting where they can unwind and commiserate about work-related issues (Pajak, 1983).

Summary. Work has many meanings and meets many needs, money being merely one. Unemployment thus takes on special significance. The financial burden imposed by the lack of a job is only the most obvious and direct consequence. Unemployment disrupts social relationships and threatens the basis of one's identity and role in the larger society. Because it touches families and others who are not directly affected, it is a social problem, not just an individual one.

UNEMPLOYMENT: THE SCOPE OF THE PROBLEM

Unemployment rates vary widely over time. During the worst years of the Great Depression of the 1930s, one-quarter of the population was involuntarily idled. In contrast, the peak demand for workers during World War II reduced unemployment to about 1 percent. Since mobilization for the war, official unemployment rates have fluctuated between 5 percent and 10 percent. Such abstract percentages must be translated into human terms: 10 percent in a year such as 1982 means that approximately eleven million people were looking for work at some time during the year.

It must also be noted that the widely circulated "official" government data on unemployment rates underestimate the extent of joblessness because they include only those who were "available for work" and had made specific attempts to locate a job within the past *four weeks*. The job-search activity requirement excludes many others who are not working and would like paid employment. A more comprehensive picture of the scope of joblessness is offered in Exhibit 8:5, which includes people not counted in the computation of official rates.

During 1983, the official annual average unemployment rate of 9.6 percent represented 10,717,000 individuals, but a closer examination of

EXHIBIT 8:5 Employment and Unemployment in the United States, 1983

EMPLOYMENT STATUS	NUMBER OF PEOPLE
Population 16 years of age and over	174,215,000
Employed	100,834,000
Not in labor force	62,665,000
Looking for work (officially unemployed)	10,717,000
Not in labor force:	
Want a job, not looking	6,503,000
Discouraged (think they cannot get a job)	1,641,000
Unemployable (illness, disability)	765,000
Excluded due to school, household, or other respon- sibilities	4,097,000
Underemployed: In labor force, but involuntarily on part-time schedule	6,266,000

Sources: *Underemployed: Monthly Labor Review,* 108 (Nov. 1985) table 4, p. 62. All other data from U.S. Bureau of Labor Statistics, *Handbook of Labor Statistics,* Washington, D.C.: Government Printing Office, June 1985, table 14, p. 38.

the situation suggests that more than twice that number could also be considered involuntarily unemployed or underemployed. This larger figure is calculated by including several categories of people beyond those currently looking for work. There were over 1.6 million *discouraged workers,* a category comprising those who would like to work, but were not actively searching because of personal reasons, because they believed that there were no jobs or that they were not qualified for those that might exist. About one-third had looked within the past year, but not within the four-week period preceding the survey, which is the cut-off point (Flaim, 1984). Another group that includes some people wanting to work are the *unemployable,* those prohibited from working by ill health or some physical disability. A third group is made up of those 4 million people *excluded* from employment because of school attendance, or home or child-care responsibilities. Finally, there are the *underemployed,* those 6 million men and women involuntarily working a part-time schedule due to material shortages, slack periods, seasonal variations, or the inability to find full-time employment.

VULNERABILITY TO UNEMPLOYMENT

The threat of joblessness is not equally distributed in a society. Several clear and enduring differences persist in unemployment rates among occupational categories, racial and ethnic groups, and for gender and age cohorts. Exhibit 8:6 focuses upon the reasons for joblessness. Economists point out several forms of unemployment having different causes and consequences and unevenly impacting these categories of people. *Frictional unemployment* is a general term, here applying to the "job leavers" (7 percent) who depart one position in search of a more desirable job and those 11 percent entering (and 21 percent reentering) the job market. These groups are considered part of the "normal" circulation of people between jobs and between school (and family responsibilities) and jobs, but not all of these are people voluntarily unemployed.

Certain groups are heavily overrepresented. Many are youths seeking first jobs but lacking marketable skills. This helps to explain why teenagers are consistently unemployed at a rate two to five times greater than that for adults in virtually every industrialized nation. In China they are called *daiye gingnian*, literally meaning "youth waiting for work" (Wang, 1979). Regardless of the terminology, these people represent a world-wide problem—young people completing their education but unable to find jobs. This is an especially severe problem for those with limited skills, but its effects are not limited to that group. "We study for jobs that don't exist," worries a university student in the Netherlands (Nordheimer, 1983).

EXHIBIT 8:6   Unemployed Persons by Reason for Joblessness, United States, 1982

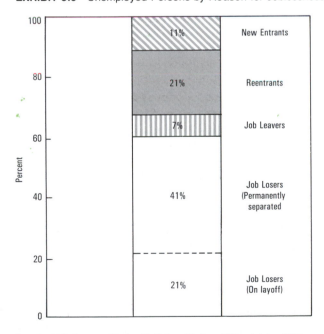

Source: U.S. Bureau of Labor Statistics, *Workers Without Jobs, 1983.*
Washington, DC: Government Printing Office, chart 26, p. 57.

Also overrepresented are adult women attempting to reenter the work force after time out of the paid labor force because of family responsibilities. They frequently find that their skills have become outdated, putting them at a competitive disadvantage. A large number of mature women in this situation are concealed among the "discouraged workers" because they believe they cannot find work (Flaim, 1984). Women with continuing child-care responsibilities have more trouble locating a suitable job because their household activities limit their hours or geographic mobility.

Seasonal unemployment is caused by periodic variations in the demand for certain skills and tasks; *cyclical unemployment* is caused by fluctuation in business activity. Some 21 percent of the jobless are on "layoff." Both argicultural work and the construction trades are impacted by the weather, while retail sales work responds to peak holiday periods. Countless blue-collar workers face this form of unemployment in response to either shifting sales or periods of retooling for new products.

Structural unemployment refers to the combination of social, demographic, economic, and technological forces which render whole categories of workers unemployable even during periods of prosperity. The British have long used the word *redundant* to identify such people, and Americans are beginning to adopt the term *displaced worker*. Automation and robotics are displacing large numbers of unskilled workers and even skilled workers. A report on computerization in France warned that 30 percent of all jobs in banking and insurance could be eliminated (Anderson, et al., 1982:78). The geographic movement of industries within counties and across international boundaries creates jobs in one area at the cost of jobs in another. The American auto industry has probably permanently lost 200,000 jobs over the last decade (Devens, et al., 1985). In short, these multiple forms of structural unemployment mean either that people cannot find work unless they retrain, relocate, or accept a demotion or that in some cases there will be no work under any circumstances.

Blue-collar operative and unskilled workers are especially vulnerable to structural unemployment, and these groups always suffer the highest joblessness rates, regardless of the state of the economy. Jobs lost to computers and laser technology are now beginning to impact the skilled trades on a large scale. The General Electric Company recently automated one plant at a cost of $300 million. The plant has the capability to produce a locomotive frame in one day, untouched by human hands (Holusha, 1983). Prior to the computerization of the process, it took 70 skilled machinists 16 days to produce the same product.

THE CONSEQUENCES OF JOBLESSNESS

The personal and social costs of unemployment can be harsh, touching many aspects of life.

Financial effects.   Financial problems are the most immediate and direct consequence of job loss. Income is typically interrupted or reduced, although the impact may be cushioned by severance pay, insurance, or social welfare payments. Eligibility for unemployment benefits has many restrictions. One study revealed that almost three-fourths of jobless workers (nearly 6 million people) got no unemployment benefits during October 1985 (Guy, 1985). The first casualty is expenditures on entertainment, such as films and vacations, and "luxuries," such as clothing. (Warr and Payne, 1983). These unemployed people tend to go to stores without buying anything. In the event of prolonged joblessness, families are called upon to use savings, cash in insurance policies, and even sell personal effects such as televisions and cars; some will be forced into cheaper housing (Wilcock and Franke, 1963).

Social relationships.   The combination of the loss of work and the loss of income disrupts some social relationships and places a strain on others. The most immediate consequence is that the link to the work subculture is severed, although some contacts may be maintained and can be the source of important job leads. However, the situation also carries the potential to interrupt nonwork friendships. Friends may be reluctant to include unemployed persons in social plans requiring the expenditure of money for fear of embarrassing them if they can no longer afford such activities (Powell and Driscoll, 1973). Other friends may avoid them because they anticipate being asked for a loan (Wilcock and Franke, 1963:86).

Family relationships also may be altered. Free time among men is largely directed toward domestic activities, with most undertaking household chores, shopping, child care, and meal preparation (Warr, 1984). Nonworking spouses may be pressed into seeking some form of paid work. These new activities demand the readjustment and renegotiation of well-established family roles. In the most extreme cases, it may call for at least a temporary role reversal, with husband and wife exchanging "homemaker" and "breadwinner" roles. This can be an extremely stressful compromise, for both partners suffer some loss of their traditional roles. A study of low-income families showed that the probability of separation increased by 16 percent following a period of unemployment (Sawhill, et al., 1975).

Self-esteem.   A major casualty of unemployment may be self-esteem (Kasl, 1973; Perfetti and Bingham, 1983). Even in cases in which the job loss may be traced to structural or cyclical causes, there is the possibility of turning the blame inward upon oneself (see, for example, Rainwater, 1970). Countless victims feel that if they had only worked harder or been better, they would have been retained and others displaced. The frustrations and humiliations of unsuccessful job hunting can also deal a blow to personal pride. Those who do find work later do not have the same level of self-esteem as those who were never unemployed (Perfetti and Bingham, 1983).

Physical and mental health.   The economic, social, and personal dislocations caused by joblessness may also have health implications. The unemployed are likely to suffer nervousness, tension, fear, boredom, headaches, stomach upsets, and sleep problems. A few people, about 10 percent, begin to drink more (Warr and Payne, 1983). The stress produced by joblessness seems to be a factor in physiological changes such as elevated serum cholesterol and blood pressure levels, which in turn increase the risk of illness such as heart disease (Kasl et al., 1975). A link to psychiatric disorders has even been suggested (Warr, 1984b).

RESPONSES TO JOB LOSS

Several studies have followed people through the process of coping with unemployment (Powell and Driscoll, 1973; Hill, 1978; Schlossberg and Leibowitz, 1980). Emerging out of this research is a fairly consistent pattern of response, with individuals progressing through clearly differentiated phases. Following displaced workers through the ordeal provides real insights into the stresses and accommodations of forced joblessness.

Shock and disbelief.   The most immediate response is generally one of disbelief, even among those who suspected impending layoffs. A few may even refuse to accept it, harboring the futile hope that "maybe it's not true" (Schlossberg and Leibowitz, 1980:212). "Why me?" is the most frequently asked question. Anger, fear, confusion, bitterness, and a sense of betrayal are experienced. Anxiety is common (Slote, 1969). Sleeplessness and increased illness are reported (Kasl, et al., 1975).

Search.   The initial shock is usually followed by a period of intense optimism. Some workers start looking for work immediately upon learning of their impending termination, and at least some companies establish relocation programs to aid in finding jobs. Younger and more skilled workers may delay initiating the job search longer than their older, less skilled counterparts because they are more optimistic about their job prospects. Those with this luxury, or those protected by insurance programs, may even treat termination as a form of "forced vacation." Older men may "retire" at this point rather than cope with the problems of joblessness. A brief holiday may be taken, domestic projects completed, hobbies pursued.

The unemployed typically approach the prospect of finding a new job with enthusiasm, viewing themselves as "between jobs." In fact, employment counselors encourage people during this period to think of themselves having a full-time job of "finding a job," or as "hiring themselves" to find employment. The search tends to be systematic and persistent, and utilizes many techniques, including calling upon friends, responding to newspaper ads, contacting employers directly, and hiring employment services. "I literally memorized the want ads," said one; another kept a notebook of leads on jobs. Social relationships with family and friends are especially helpful in preventing stress during this period, offering job leads and providing emotional support and encouragement. Optimism, the effort of the search, and the support of spouses, family, and friends are critical in sustaining and motivating the unemployed during this period. It is actually a period of low stress.

Doubt.   Some are able to maintain this pace for weeks. Those who fail to find work spend progressively less time and effort looking, and begin to slip into a mood of self-doubt and pessimism. Failure erodes their confidence and weakens their resolve. Feelings that they are obsolete or too old, surface, and they begin to question whether they are in the right career. Job hunting becomes sporadic, as frustration replaces enthusiasm, and depression displaces optimism. It is at this point that they themselves and others begin to think of them as "unemployed," although most would fit the official category of "discouraged worker."

Family relationships deteriorate as despair peaks. Violent rage turned inward becomes depression. Frustration turned outward precipitates interpersonal conflicts within families and contributes to the incidence of domestic violence. At best, they feel themselves to be a burden on their families. It is now that men contemplate suicide (Powell and Driscoll, 1973).

Social relationships outside the family also deteriorate. Behavior that was once offered and perceived as support and encouragement may now be experienced as condescension. People who once were friends begin avoiding each other. Friends may feel guilty about having a job, and the victims feel twinges of envy. Failure to find work makes them even more flexible about the kinds of work they will accept, with most adopting the idea that they must accept a pay cut, change occupations, or move to another city.

Apathy.   After weeks of disappointment, they are likely to drift into malaise and cynicism. They rarely look for work. Mood swings from hope to hopelessness are prevalent. Relationships with spouses can actually improve as both accommodate to their new roles (with many spouses providing the economic support), but most are permanently isolated from former friends. The phasing out of old friends is a common feature of major role transitions, for it is very embarrassing to interact with people whom one has known on a different basis prior to job loss. New sets of friends—post-post job-loss friends—are found.

CASE STUDY: STARTING OVER IN CHICAGO

In September 1977, the Zenith Corporation cut back operations in Chicago, laying off some 1,500 workers. Three years later, *Forbes* magazine was able to trace 150 of those former workers. One person's story gives meaning to the raw statistics and shows that job loss can leave permanent scars, even if better-paying work is found.

Consider, for example, the case of Fred Wilkoszewski, a stocky 200-pounder with burly shoulders who used to think that he was afraid of very little in this world. He began to know fear in the spring of 1977, when serious rumors started to crop up that Zenith was moving its color TV production to Mexico and Taiwan. He began to hate getting up in the morning. He downed milk by the quart to quiet the rumblings in his stomach. He bit the nails of his calloused hands to the cuticles. The layoffs came. Neither the unions nor the sacred seniority system could save jobs.

Wilkoszewski, then a 31-year-old maintenance chief, was asked whether he wanted to stay on as a janitor. It meant a loss of seniority and, far worse, a cut in pay from $1,200 a month to $500. It wasn't much of a choice for a man with a wife and three small kids: either a huge pay cut or no job at all. Wilkoszewski, who years earlier had quit the construction business for Zenith "because it was regular work, not seasonal," became a janitor. A couple of weeks later, he took sick leave with an ulcer, and never returned to Zenith. The more than $7,000 in profit sharing he took with him somewhat eased the pain of his departure. Today he works as a scaler at United Packing Co., earning about $20,000, nearly twice what he made at Zenith. And no more ulcer. But Wilkoszewski is still bitter. . . . He still rankles at the suddenness of it all. "Pow! They come up to me after 13 years and say, 'Tomorrow, you're a janitor or you're out.' No questions. No ifs. No buts. From a salaried foreman to a janitor in eight hours. Just like that." He still shakes his head in disbelief over how "people were bumping their best friends" in the layoff scramble to hang on to their jobs. The fact that he is better off now than he was appears to be no comfort when he looks back on what the layoffs did to people he thought he knew well.

Reprinted with permission from Bob Tamarkin with Lisa Gross, "Starting Over in Chicago," *Forbes* (Apr. 28, 1980), 74–75.

CONCLUSION: THE IMPLICATIONS OF UNEMPLOYMENT

The specter of joblessness confronts virtually all workers in market economies. Some workers may be protected by long-term contracts and tenure arrangements, but even they cannot be absolutely free from the threat of displacement. The widely publicized Japanese practice of "lifetime employment" probably most closely approximates an exception to this situation. Only about one-third of all workers enjoy this arrangement, however, and it seldom includes female workers. The problems of instability are handled by classifying some workers as "temporary workers." Moreover, the arrangement does not shelter workers from the possibility of unemployment as a result of forced retirement or other forms of pressure to resign during periods of economic recession. One large industrial firm encouraged the departure of 10,000 workers during the oil crisis of the 1970s by offering large severance payments (Koshiro, 1984). It is reported that unneeded workers are sometimes exposed to a more subtle social practice called "window siding"—having their desks relocated near a window and being given unimportant tasks, as a means of encouraging them to resign voluntarily (Chapman, 1979).

The short-term financial implications of joblessness can be buffered by unemployment insurance, and various relocation and retraining programs assist workers in finding new employment. However, most people who are displaced end up in a worse situation than they were in before displacement. The consequences of involuntary unemployment were evident in the United States during the period from 1979 to 1984, a time of dramatic structural dislocation. In this five-year period 11.5 million people lost a job for structural reasons (Flaim and Sehgal, 1985). Many were the highly vulnerable young workers with few skills and limited experience, but 5 million had at least three years' experience. Of these experienced workers, 1.3 million (25 percent) were still looking for work at the end of the period, meaning that for some, joblessness had dragged on for four or five years. About 733,000 dropped out of the labor force, joining the ranks of the "discouraged." Many older workers "retired" in the face of displacement, also disappearing from the labor force. Among those who were able

EXHIBIT 8:7 Unemployment and Social Stress: Cumulative Impact of a 1.4 Percent Increase in Unemployment on Selected Health Indicators, United States, 1970–1975

HEALTH INDICATORS	PERCENT INCREASE IN INCIDENCE	NUMERICAL INCREASE IN INCIDENCE	ECONOMIC COSTS
Suicide	5.7%	1,540	$63 million
Admissions: State psychiatric hospitals	4.7	5,520	82 million
Admissions: State prisons	5.6	7,660	210 million
Homicides	8.0	1,740	434 million
Mortality: Cirrhosis of the liver	2.7	870	n/a
Mortality: Cardiovascular disease	2.7	26,440	1,372 million
Total Mortality	2.7	51,570	6,615 million

Source: M. Harvey Brenner, *Estimating the Social Costs of National Economic Policy.* Washington, DC: Joint Economic Committee of the Congress, 1976, pp. vii–viii.

to locate work, approximately one-half were in an entirely different kind of job, and although many improved their economic position, one-quarter were forced to accept pay cuts amounting to 20 percent of their previous wages.

M. Harvey Brenner (1973; 1976; 1980) has been in the forefront of social scientists attempting to translate the cumulative personal consequences of joblessness into a broader societal context. His analysis, reproduced in Exhibit 8:7, explored the implications of each 1.4 percent increase in the level of unemployment. The cost, over the subsequent years, is 28,000 human lives, in the form of suicides and mortality from cirrhosis of the liver and cardiovascular disease, caused in part by stress. Less dramatic, but still serious, are the increases in admissions to the psychiatric hospitals. Finally, the incidence of some forms of violent crime noticeably increases, suggesting that some may turn their anger and frustration outward. Such analysis and interpretation is not without its critics (Spruit, 1982), but it does graphically capture the potential implications of unemployment both for the job losers and for those who must live with them and share their pain.

NINE
Occupational Prestige

INTRODUCTION: THE MEANING OF OCCUPATIONAL PRESTIGE

Occupations tend to be arranged in hierarchies of *prestige,* reflecting their esteem, honor, or "social standing." Occupational prestige represents a general social evaluation of the relative worth or desirability of various forms of work. Prestige is the outcome of a complex interaction between socialization experiences, fundamental societal value and belief systems, and the prestige-enhancing activities of occupational groups. Occupational prestige would be important even if it involved nothing more than the admiration and respect that it confers on people as a result of having a particular job. People are sensitive to the evaluations of others, and work roles are a major component of the total prestige a person can claim.

However, the implications of occupational prestige extend beyond questions of social approval and ego gratification. Workers are treated differently at various hierarchical levels; people tend to show deference toward those ranked above them and expect deference from those inferior to them. Members of occupations, both collectively and individually, sensitive to their public status, devote themselves to improving (or protecting) the prestige of their work. These efforts are evident in group attempts to "professionalize" by developing new titles for their work, as well as in everyday social interaction as workers seek to improve, defend, or protect the social standing of their positions.

Moreover, specific behavioral and personality traits are attributed to individuals based on occupational prestige (Borgatta and Evans, 1967; Crowther and More, 1972; More and Suchner, 1976). For example, there is a direct (positive) relationship between an occupation's prestige and the perceived traits of intelligence, competence, responsibility, and assertiveness. Thus, in responding to the prestige of occupations, people impute desirable traits to those in high-status work and often attribute demeaning attributes to those at or near the bottom of the hierarchy.

OCCUPATIONAL PRESTIGE RANKINGS: CONSENSUS AND STABILITY

Research examining the social prestige of occupations originated in the 1920s among vocational counselors (see, for example, Counts, 1925), and sociologists have been systematically studying the concept since the 1940s. The resulting body of research confirms that occupations form hierarchies of prestige.

In all societies, roles such as physician and lawyer consistently rank above garbage collector and butcher. There is a great deal of consensus among members of a society about the relative position of jobs, and the rankings have been found to remain remarkably stable over time. Unlike income, which forms neat, objective scales, prestige rankings are subjective judgments, created by combining and averaging individual evaluations of the standing of occupations. Despite some isolated variation, relative placement of occupations is generally agreed upon. It is true that people tend to inflate the social standing of their own occupations (and similar ones) to a slight degree, and that some groups of people (for example, the more educated, males, younger people) generally assign lower absolute scores to jobs, and that economic rewards are a more salient criterion for people at the lower end of the stratification system, while educational attainment is given more weight by those at the upper end. Overall, however, no significant differences are noted in ranking along class, racial, ethnic, or gender lines, leading one researcher to suggest that the deviations from perfect consensus that do exist are the product of a large number of small and random differences (Treiman, 1977:62).

One measure of consensus and stability is provided by an examination of specific roles, such as that of justice of the Supreme Court. The title has been included in many studies and has consistently achieved the highest possible score (Smith, 1943; NORC, 1947; Brown, 1955; Hodge, Siegel, and Rossi, 1964). Such consistency was remarkable considering that the role was occupied by many men with divergent political orientations over the course of those decades. The Court was also the focus of intense controversy during this period, having rendered the Brown school desegregation decision in 1959. Through it all, the role of justice maintained a high level of prestige.

The United States

Exhibit 9:1 provides a sampling of occupational scores from a study conducted in Baltimore during the 1970s. The range of values is from 0 to 100. It is representative of many other studies and reveals some broad, general patterns.

The top of these hierarchies is consistently dominated by members of just two occupational categories. Clearly the most prestigious are the self-regulating professions that have achieved the highest levels of monopoly and autonomy (physician, lawyer, college professor). Executive positions, represented by the titles of mayor, school superintendent, and factory owner, tend to appear just below them. (Governmental office holders [state governors, cabinet officers, and members of Congress] have been found to be in the same range, although they were not included in this study.) Almost no other occupations had scores of 80 or above, confirming that these represent the most prestigious work roles in American society.

A second level of occupations is formed by the remaining professionals—usually organizationally based managers and technicians—generally with scores in the 60s and 70s. Prestige rankings typically reflect organizational authority patterns, with superiors ranking above subordinates, as in the case of superintendent and teacher; however, there is also within this mix of occupations the potential for inconsistent social relationships. Comparison of the roles of office manager and accountant is an instance of a person who occupies an administrative position requiring the supervision of a worker who has greater prestige, creating another manifestation of the idea of *status dilemma*.

Clerical workers and craftspersons tend to form a third level, with scores clustering in the 40s and 50s. Private secretary occupies the top of this level (8 points above office secretary), probably indicating an awareness of the administrative responsibilities required of the role. Electrician ranks well above the other crafts, although the reasons are not so clear. Homemaker also ranks on this level, along with police officer. The third level is the most heterogeneous of all prestige strata, with white- and blue-collar jobs coexisting with service jobs.

Direct-service work occupies an unusually wide range of positions, varying from a score of 42 for beauticians down to 11 for domestic workers such as maids (female) and household workers (male). Notably, the label applied to a form of work can have some influence on evaluations. The titles of beautician and hairdresser may both refer to the same set of technical tasks, but the former commands somewhat greater prestige.

Almost all jobs in the operative category have scores in the mid-20s.

EXHIBIT 9:1   Occupational Prestige Ranking: United States

CLASSIFICATION	OCCUPATION	SCORE
Professional	Physician	95.8
	Lawyer	90.1
	College professor	90.1
	Electrical engineer	79.5
	Registered nurse	75.0
	High school teacher	70.2
	Elementary school teacher	65.4
	Social worker	63.2
Administrative	Mayor	92.2
	Superintendent of schools	87.8
	Factory owner; 2,000 employees	81.7
	Office manager	68.3
	Hotel manager	64.1
	Circulation director; newspaper	63.5
	Supervisor; warehouse	56.4
	Supervisor; assembly line	53.8
Technicians	Accountant	71.2
	Hospital lab technician	63.1
	Dental assistant	54.8
Clerical	Private secretary	60.9
	Stenographer	52.6
	Office secretary	51.3
	Bookkeeper	50.0
	Telephone operator	46.2
	Typist	44.9
	Post office clerk	42.3
	File clerk	34.0
Direct Service	Stock broker	81.7
	Police officer	58.3
	Homemaker (f)	51.0
	Salesperson; wholesale	46.2
	Beautician	42.1
	Hairdresser	39.4
	Shoe store salesperson	35.9
	Waitress (f)/Waiter (m)	22.1
	Janitor	12.5
	Maid (f)/Household worker (m)	11.5
Crafts	Electrician	62.5
	Plumber	58.7
	Carpenter	53.5
	Welder	46.8
	Auto mechanic	44.9
	Butcher	38.8
Operatives	Assembly line worker	28.3
	Textile machine operator	27.9
	Delivery truck driver	26.9
	Stock clerk	24.4
	Coal miner	24.0
	Garbage collector	16.3

EXHIBIT 9:1   *Continued*

CLASSIFICATION	OCCUPATION	SCORE
Unskilled	Box Packer	15.1
	Laundry worker	14.7
	Salad maker in a hotel	13.8
	Yarn washer	11.8
	Parking lot attendant	8.0
Farm Work	Cotton farmer	32.4
	Fruit harvester; for own family	26.0

Source: Christine E. Bose and Peter H. Rossi, "Gender and Jobs," *American Sociological Review* 48 (June 1983), pp. 327–28.

The lower end of the prestige hierarchy is anchored by unskilled and service workers. Occupations such as box packer, laundry worker, and parking lot attendant imply heavy manual labor, unpleasant working conditions, or low pay. None earn a score higher than 15.

COMPARISONS AMONG COUNTRIES

Similar studies of occupational prestige have also been conducted in at least sixty other countries (Inkeles and Rossi, 1956; Hodge, Treiman, and Rossi, 1966; Treiman, 1977). Such rankings tend to correspond closely to American rankings. (In statistical terms, the rank-order correlations are usually between .80 and .95.) Occupations tend to be rated similarly in almost all societies.[1]

It is interesting to see how occupations are ranked elsewhere, focusing on both consistencies and variations. Examples from Africa, South America, and Eastern Europe are reported in Exhibit 9:2. The first is from the Hausa, who live in a partially industrialized area of Northern Nigeria where British colonial policy sought to minimize intervention in native cultural patterns (Armer, 1968). There are some clear similarities between the United States and the Hausa. Government officials rank at the top, followed by the medical, legal, and religious professions. Office workers, store clerks, and school teachers rate somewhat lower than professionals, but clearly above manual occupations. This ranking may reflect the stage of industrial development, not unlike earlier periods in the histories of countries such as the United States and England, where educated and literate white-collar workers enjoyed higher levels of prestige.

[1]Certain conceptual and methodological considerations caution against uncritically accepting this assertion. The question of comparability of occupations in different societies is important; for example, are the tasks of "priest" similar in all societies? Another potential source of bias in these studies is the tendency toward overrepresentation of urban and educated populations.

EXHIBIT 9:2 Prestige Rankings for Nigeria, Brazil, Czechoslovakia

HAUSA (NIGERIA)	BEZERROS (BRAZIL)	CZECHOSLOVAKIA
Government official	Cabinet member	Doctor
Lawyer	Priest	Collective farmer
Mallam (priest)	Doctor	Miner
Teacher (elementary school)	Lawyer	Teacher (High school)
Factory worker	Farm owner	Mason
Police officer	Teacher	Cabinet minister
Tailor	Auto repairer	Priest
Farm owner	Police officer	Judge
Leather worker	Carpenter	Police officer
Praise singer (beggar)	Garbage collector	Sewage worker

Sources: J. Michael Armer, "Intersociety and Intrasociety Correlations of Occupational Prestige," *American Journal of Sociology* 74 (July 1968), p. 32; Archibald O. Haller, et al., "Variations in Occupational Prestige: Brazilian Data," *American Journal of Sociology,* 77 (March 1972), pp. 952–55; Roger Penn, "Occupational Prestige Hierarchies," *Social Forces* 54 (Dec. 1975), p. 355.

The occupation of farm owner is accorded less prestige than might be expected using an economic-development analogy. In the United States, farm owners were apparently held in high esteem during the early stages of industrialization, and even into the twentieth century—a link to the time when land ownership was a prime source of social standing. Butchers and leather workers receive low rankings because they are engaged in work considered to be "unclean" by local cultural standards. At the bottom are "praise singers," who are considered beggars, and hence not gainfully employed.

The second prestige hierarchy depicted in Exhibit 9-2 is from an isolated rural area of Brazil (Haller, Holsinger, and Saraiva, 1972). A majority of people (74 percent) are engaged in agriculture. The upper levels of the hierarchy are similar to those previously described, with central government officials and professionals sharing high prestige. The role of priest rates higher than in either Nigeria or the United States, possibly reflecting the more central role of religion in less industrialized societies. Agriculture is the major livelihood, and the farm owner ranks above the white-collar worker (bookkeeper), the "lower" professional (teacher, artist), and the skilled manual worker (auto repair). Even the sharecropper, a low-status form of work in the United States, in Brazil is placed above the carpenter, merchant, and police officer. Urban occupations—clerk, merchant, store manager, and bartender—are also near the bottom of the hierarchy. And garbage collector is, as in all societies, viewed as among the very least desirable occupations.

Czechoslovakia, one of the socialist East European countries, exhibits some sharp differences in occupational ranking (Penn, 1975). Governmental positions do not generally enjoy high prestige; the posts of cabinet minister and judge are well down on the scale. In contrast, blue-collar work tends to fare better than it does in America. The occupations of miner and mason receive high ranking, which seems to confirm the dominant sociopolitical philosophy that has sought to enhance the value of manual labor. The difference in the ranking of the collective farmer—second only to the physician—epitomizes the distinctions between capitalist and socialist ideologies. The related deemphasis of religion may help to account for the relatively modest position of the priest in the overall ranking.

The differences that do exist should not obscure the fact that there is some similarity to other ranking systems. Highly educated professionals are generally accorded high prestige. The physician ranks at the top of the hierarchy, with scientist third, and engineer sixth. "Dirty" work (sewer cleaner), unskilled labor (construction worker), and domestic service (housekeeper) are without much respect, as is true for both the Western and less industrialized nations.

These examples suggest both the diversity and the commonalities found in occupational prestige around the world. Diversity may be rooted in the unique values, beliefs, or history of a society; this is manifest in the proletarian ideology of Czech society that serves to elevate manual labor, the cultural concept of "unclean" that degrades the Hausan butcher, or the political history of Brazil that places a military role at the pinnacle of prestige. Then, too, the level of industrial development is a factor. But underlying this diversity is some consistency. Professions tend to receive high ratings, while unskilled work is depreciated. The role of physician always has very high prestige. Crafts are seldom rated below factory work. Finally, there are in every society some marginal or deviant occupations which form a kind of underclass lacking in public respectability.

THE COMPONENTS OF PRESTIGE: ASCRIPTION AND ACHIEVEMENT

The relative prestige accorded an occupation by members of a society appears to be influenced by two analytically distinct processes. One is rooted in socialization experiences; the learning process originates in early childhood and carries on through the life cycle, as various pieces of information converge to reinforce the idea that occupations are arranged in a hierarchy of public esteem, and that specific jobs occupy certain relative positions in the hierarchy. This may be labeled *ascribed prestige*. In contrast, occupations also earn prestige on the basis of a cognitive evaluation process in which the perceived characteristics of the work or its rewards are compared against some standards of desirability. For example, as a general rule, prestige is highly correlated with income and stringency of training requirements. This suggests some general criteria that are used to judge specific occupations. Prestige conferred on this basis may be called *achieved prestige.*

ASCRIBED PRESTIGE

Socialization into the general values, beliefs, and norms of a culture exposes one to some subtle but clear clues that not all occupations are of equal worth. One observes that occupations are rated relative to one another. Some jobs, such as mayor or physician, are singled out as worthy of respect, while others, such as garbage collector or prostitute, may be depreciated. The same kind of evaluation may apply to entire classes of occupations— professionals have higher social standing than auto mechanics, although both perform a service. In short, one learns that those around them ascribe certain increments of prestige to certain occupations. The prestige hierarchy is part of a society's culture and is transmitted both formally and informally.

The idea that prestige hierarchies are at least partially the result of cultural transmission, rather than objective evaluation, is supported by the observation that people, when asked to rank occupations with which they are unfamiliar, can and will assign scores consistent with general rankings. Very young children are able to reproduce the adult prestige scores, despite very little actual knowledge of the nature and rewards of the work being ranked (Simmons and Rosenberg, 1971). The occupation of nuclear physicist has been a prestigious one since the 1940s, despite the fact that many raters do not have even a vague idea of the work; they are responding in terms of the prestige assigned by others.

As is the case with other forms of social learning, the ascription of occupational prestige is a combination of both deliberate attempts to convey a particular point of view and the unintentional learning that evolves from exposure to the values and preferences shared among members of the group or society. Three less-than-obvious sources of conceptions of occupational prestige deserve mention.

Interpersonal contacts.   Children begin to meet representatives of many occupations early in their lives. Police officers, mail carriers, clergy members, supermarket clerks, teachers and principals, garbage collectors, physicians, and janitors are a very real part of their social environment. As they are introduced to such workers, children observe how such people are treated, at the same time that they themselves are encouraged in direct and subtle ways to show more respect to some than to others. People tend to exhibit deference toward members of some occupations by exaggerating politeness, using of courtesy titles ("Doctor," "Ms.," "Sir," "Your Honor"), providing favors, repressing disagreement, or acquiescing. In contrast, members of other occupations are treated less well, conveying their relative social standing. One may, for example, quibble with a waiter about a bill, but pay a lawyer's fee without question. The sum of these interpersonal interactions will tend to reproduce the existing hierarchy of prestige.

Career aspirations. Children like to speculate about jobs they might want to hold when they are old enough to enter the work force. Parents and grandparents, teachers and peers confirm the importance of such speculation with the eternal question, "What are you going to be when you grow up?" Adult reactions to choices such as prison guard, or garbage collector, or bank robber are not likely to be very enthusiastic and are likely to be accompanied by a lecture listing the endless disadvantages and handicaps of such work. Working parents sometimes unintentionally disparage their own occupations when they encourage their sons and daughters to seek to better themselves. A butcher explains, "If my son wanted to be a meat cutter, I'd cut off his hands" (Meara, 1974:262). The prestige of other occupations is enhanced by their definition as good career choices. This is expressed in the proud mother's cliché, "My son, the doctor."

Television. Children are exposed to many hours of television, and what they see can mold their view of the world. Research indicates that television is a major source of occupational perceptions. This is evident when it is considered that television portrayals are sometimes the only contact children have with certain occupations. Most children have no direct personal contact with judges, lawyers, reporters, professional athletes, military personnel, or corporation executives, yet these are among the roles most frequently found in television programming (DeFleur, 1964). In fact, some research suggests that most knowledge of occupational roles originates with television (Jeffries-Fox and Signorielli, 1978).

Television tends to confirm the patterns of deference and derogation observed in the "real" world at the same time that it misrepresents the occupational world and, in the process, conveys a message about social standing. Although much of the work force is in blue-collar or service work, such occupations are rarely seen, and their invisibility suggests a lack of importance and value.

The characterization of people in occupations may be a most subtle and salient message. Melvin DeFleur (1964:71) reports that lawyers are almost always portrayed as intelligent and clever, police are frequently depicted as impersonal (and usually less resourceful and intelligent than the glamorous private investigators), and salespersons as glib and superficial. The media thus teaches that the people in some jobs have more desirable traits than those in other jobs. An awareness of the prestige ascribed by others seems to significantly influence subsequent personal judgments about prestige (Haug and Widdison, 1975).

ACHIEVED PRESTIGE

The term *achieved prestige* focuses on a more deliberate judgmental process in which jobs are measured against various criteria of desirability, such as income or education. Since people are not always able to conceptualize and verbalize the criteria they utilize, sociologists have come to depend upon a more indirect measurement method. Respondents are asked to rate occupations on selected criteria which are then compared to prestige ratings. The result is a statistical correlation, but it assumes that perceptions of the attributes of occupations combine to produce a composite evaluation of that job for the rater (Haug and Widdison, 1975:6). Using this technique, four broad categories of criteria can be identified, as summarized in Exhibit 9:3.

Prerequisites.　Several of the qualifications for admission to a particular kind of work are considered in determining prestige. The level of intelligence, the complexity and difficulty of training, and the amount of education required all directly correlate with prestige. This helps to account for the high ranking of the professions, which involve lengthy formal education. Moreover, as a general rule, professions that require graduate education or training (college professor, physician, scientist, and lawyer) are placed above those requiring a bachelor's degree (teacher, architect, accountant). The fact that the crafts involve apprenticeships may contribute to their standing above those blue-collar jobs viewed as not requiring extensive occupational training. Jobs that do not require any particular qualifications—unskilled and service positions—have the lowest prestige.

EXHIBIT 9:3　Criteria of Achieved Prestige

Prerequisites for membership	Intelligence
	Training
	Scarcity of qualified personnel
Rewards	Income
	Opportunity for advancement
	Responsibility
Characteristics of the work	Cleanliness
	Safety
	Creativity
	Power/Influence
	Importance to Society
Characteristics of the workers	High status

Scarcity of qualified personnel may also be a factor. Although it is difficult to assess scarcity objectively, it may help to account for the generally high prestige of occupations perceived as demanding rare and special attributes, such as the physical dexterity of the athlete, the analytic ability of the scientist, or the creative impulse of the artist.

Rewards.   One consistent finding in both the United States and other countries is a high correlation between income and occupational prestige (Treiman, 1977). Income itself confers prestige in the United States, for it has symbolic value when used as a rough measure of success. Income also has indirect value since it can be translated into a particular style of life. There are, of course, notable exceptions. Teachers and clergymembers have higher levels of prestige than could be predicted using income as the sole criterion, while butchers are accorded less prestige than would be expected.

Characteristics of the work.   Occupations earn prestige on the basis of the tasks involved, the social organization of the work, and working conditions. Cleanliness and safety are factors (Gusfield and Schwartz, 1962). Physically dirty or unsafe work tends to be devalued. Routine, repetitive work is accorded less prestige than interesting, creative work. Level of responsibility and autonomy are also considerations (Marsh, 1971). Jobs requiring the supervision, evaluation, and direction of subordinates rank higher than those that are under the control of superiors and allow little individual discretion. Many authors would claim that power is a decisive factor in understanding prestige hierarchies, arguing that power is universally valued in all human societies (see, for example, Lenski, 1966; Treiman, 1977:21). This might explain the high ranking of governmental roles in the United States, since all exercise unusual power.

The concept of the functional importance of jobs is widely debated. It has been hypothesized that certain types of occupations are essential to the welfare and functioning of all societies (Davis and Moore, 1945). As those who subscribe to this hypothesis see it, religion occupies a central role because it serves to integrate members of a society through a common value system; the importance of government derives from its role in the organization and defense of society; and scientific and technical occupations develop the technique and hardware to achieve national goals such as the exploration of space or the eradication of disease. It is imperative that these roles be filled and that people be motivated to perform these essential services. Prestige and income are among the major rewards that can be used to motivate people, and thus prestige becomes one of the rewards attached to the more important positions in society. Prestige is thus an "unconsciously evolved device by which societies insure that the most important positions are conscientiously filled by the most qualified persons" (Davis and Moore, 1945). It is not at all clear that people utilize this abstract concept of functional importance in considering the prestige of occupations. They are, however, able to rate occupations along a continuum of "importance to society," and this is another prestige-predicting factor. (NORC, 1947; Haug and Widdison, 1975).

Characteristics of the workers.   The kind of people who tend to fill particular jobs can in some cases influence occupational prestige. Jobs perceived as employing low-status people (on some other societal criteria) can degrade work, creating a self-perpetuating process. Work that is undesirable will recruit racial and ethnic minorities or the uneducated who have no other choices, thus further depressing the prestige accorded such occupations.

There is debate over the issue of whether jobs typically identified as "women's work" have lower prestige because they are filled by females. Some recent research has shown that identification of a male or female incumbent of an occupation does affect the prestige scores of specific jobs, but there is no clear pattern. In the study used in Exhibit 9:1, a female advertising executive rated about five points higher than a male, and female washer repairers had an eleven-point advantage. There was, however, no overall evidence that women incumbents depress the scores of all jobs; for example, male welders rated six points above female welders (see also England, 1979). Other research does suggest that the presence of men or women in a job negatively affects scores if the work is sex-typed as being typical of the other sex, or if it is assumed to require gender-related traits (Powell and Jacobs, 1984).

Many criteria contribute to subjective ratings of occupational prestige. Education, income, working conditions, and the usual incumbents appear to be the most salient. The relative placement of any occupation seems to reflect a combination of many factors. A huge income in and of itself does not guarantee prestige any more than a modest income prohibits an occupation from earning esteem. Raters may focus on a single demeaning aspect of work to the exclusion of all positive attributes, or may employ different criteria with different occupations. Throughout, however, a high degree of consensus prevails.

DEVIANT WORK: ILLICIT, MARGINAL, AND MORALLY AMBIVALENT WORK

The lowest levels of prestige hierarchies tend to be reserved for a class of specific occupations. They form a kind of "underclass" or "outcast" group. Prostitutes and pool hustlers, carnival workers and strippers, armed robbers and pickpockets are members of the American version of this group. The bond linking such types of work is a lack of broad public acceptance and respectability, because the work in some way violates the social, moral, or legal standards of a segment of the population. All may be called *deviant occupations*.

Legal and social deviance must be distinguished at the outset because they do not always converge. Not all forms of work that violate societal (or community) standards are prohibited by law, and conversely, some illegal activity is condoned (Becker, 1963). The simple diagram in Exhibit 9:4, which combines legal and social standards, illustrates this. Most forms of work are both legal and socially approved, resulting in what might be called conventional work. In other instances a society's laws and value systems are in agreement, labeling the work illegal *and* socially deviant. Illicit activities, which offer livelihoods and careers for some, are outside the law and violate sociocultural standards for acceptable work.

There are two areas in which social and legal standards diverge. In complex, heterogeneous societies, not all illegal activities will necessarily violate the social standards of all segments of society: laws may be imposed by numerical minorities; cultural standards evolve and change; laws can be at variance with actual behavior patterns; and subgroups may hold different values. Occupations such as prostitution are in this category. This tends to create an attitude of moral ambivalence toward the work among large segments of the society. Finally, not all cultural notions of inappropriate behavior are codified in the law. Some work roles, such as carnival work, violate community standards, or what is usually called "the spirit, if not the letter of the law." Easto and Truzzi (1974) call this "marginal" work.

EXHIBIT 9:4   A Typology of Deviant Work Roles

		SOCIAL NORMS AND VALUES	
		Disapproval	Approval
	Illegal	**Illicit Work** Burglary Robbery Safecracking	**Morally Ambivalent Work** Prostitution Gambling Drug sales
Legal Norms			
	Legal	**Marginal Work** Pool hustling Carnival work Stripping	**Conventional Work**

Suggested by a typology developed by Patrick C. Easto and Marcello Truzzi, "The Carnival as a Marginally Legal Work System," in Clifton D. Bryant, *Deviant Behavior*. Chicago: Rand McNally, 1974, p. 347. Reprinted with permission of copyright holder, Clifton D. Bryant.

ILLICIT WORK

This category is limited to illegal occupations, not the illegal activities of people in the conduct of conventional work. A number of careers involve illicit work. Some would seem to threaten the fundamental mores of a society (the paid killer, for example), but most others violate concepts of private property or privacy (burglary). Societal reactions vary, if a small-scale study of college students (Exhibit 9:5) is at all representative (Cullen and Link, 1980). On a scale of 1 (no prestige) to 7 (highest), over a dozen deviant occupations were ranked.

Illicit work is, by definition, in violation of criminal codes, but the public apparently makes some distinctions among criminal careers. The responders in this sample were willing to assign at least some prestige to all the criminal occupations. All the processes underlying this hierarchy are not clear, but it does suggest that even criminal careers are differently evaluated within American society. It may be that the same criteria used in ranking legal occupations are evoked in judging illegal ones. The investigators found that prestige correlated with expertise and scarcity of qualified personnel, which accounts for the relatively high score of safecrackers. It is possible that organized crime figures and drug traffickers are assumed, on

EXHIBIT 9:5   Prestige Ranking of Deviant Occupations

Organized crime "boss"	5.08
Safecracker	4.13
"Call girl"	3.42
Bookie	3.03
Drug smuggler	3.02
"Hit man" (paid killer)	2.85
Check forger	2.80
Average prestige score	2.74
Pickpocket	2.54
Pimp	2.48
Bank Robber	2.43
Fence	2.43
Burglar	2.38
Drug pusher	2.18
Shoplifter	2.06
"Street walker"	2.03
Mugger/robber	1.39

Source: Computed from Francis T. Cullen and Bruce G. Link, "Crime as an Occupation," *Criminology* 18 (Nov. 1980), p. 404.

the basis of media presentations, to be wealthy and powerful. The paid killer is somewhat of an anomaly considering the value of human life in American society, unless it was assumed that their potential victims would be limited to other criminals.

The lower-ranking illicit occupations do not have the advantages of wealth, or power, or expertise. The very nature of the activities and public perceptions of the life-style would seem to degrade them. They are unlikely to be viewed as heroic, for they prey upon the innocent and vulnerable. The threat of arrest, questioning, prison terms, and harsh treatment in the criminal justice system is ever present. In addition, these careers do not offer great financial reward. One study of habitual offenders estimated an average of $312 of income for each offense, which translates into a few thousand dollars a year (Petersilia, et al., 1978:71).

MORALLY AMBIVALENT WORK

A few occupations operate in an area of moral ambivalence in a society. Such work is illegal and tends to have low status, but it must have value or acceptability to some segments of the society, as indicated by the unremitting demand for such services, combined with the frequent attempts to "decriminalize" such activities. The roles of drug smuggler, pusher, bookie, "call girl," and "street walker" from Exhibit 9-5 would be in this category. The strength of the condemnation may be a reflection of the ambivalence of those who employ them; responses to illegality and societal condemnation do color the relationship between these workers and their clients.

MARGINAL WORK: THE "OUTSIDERS"

Criminal careers involve a violation of a society's laws, but not all sociocultural notions of inappropriate activity are codified in the law. Many forms of behavior violate either the "spirit of the law" or widely held values, beliefs, or norms—what might be called *moral standards*. The work of the pool hustler (Polsky, 1969) and the card shark (Mahigel and Stone, 1971) illustrate this. All are exceptionally skilled players earning a living by betting against those with whom they compete. Polsky (1969:32) argues that the hustler's first offense is that work associated with gambling is not generally considered a respectable and legitimate occupation for an adult, at least by most segments of the population. This can probably be traced to religious prohibitions against card playing and gambling, combined with the folk belief that gamblers are compulsive and irresponsible, squandering money which ought to be spent supporting their families. A second and more serious offense is that the hustler violates the American concept of "fair play." Hustlers typically conceal their true level of skill in order to lure good amateur players into one-sided contests which they have no chance of winning. This is inconsistent with the basic rules of competition that prevail in America. Other occupations that seem to be in this general category are masseuse and nightclub stripper because they are associated with commercialized sex; circus and carnival workers because they mutilate their own bodies or seek to profit from a physical deformity (Easto and Truzzi, 1974).

The term *outsider* was coined by Becker (1963) to describe people whose work is labeled as deviant by the larger community. It is an appropriate term because those failing to meet community standards of propriety are outsiders both symbolically and socially. They are social outsiders in the sense that their occupations are considered to be outside the realm of conventional work and hence of marginal prestige. Nightclub stripping is viewed as "degrading," "useless," "immoral," and "dirty" (Boles and Garbin, 1974). It is an easy step from maligning the occupation to attributing negative characteristics to those who hold the job. Female strippers are thought of as "exhibitionists," "oversexed," "prostitutes," or "hard women." In part this is a logical extension of the view that the job is marginal; therefore, so are the people doing the work. Moreover, this view tends to be reinforced by beliefs about the life-styles of people in outsider work. The stripper or the masseuse is believed to be a prostitute or a lesbian; the pool hustler is assumed to be a cheat and a drifter.

Deviant work and the public perceptions of the character of those who hold such jobs make them social outsiders, which contributes to their isolation. Some, by the nature of their work, are transients—hustlers and fraudulent medical practitioners must be geographically mobile. For most others, the stigma of their work discourages contacts with the larger public. Members of the community deliberately avoid them, and the outsiders themselves tend to turn inward, forming closed groups which limit contacts with nonmembers. This is a form of protection, but it is also a form of rejection of those who fail to accord them respect.

DIRTY WORK

Other forms of work have low prestige simply because they involve the undesirable work of a society—what Everett Hughes (1958) calls the *dirty work*. The fact that garbage collector is a universally low-ranking occupation suggests that cleaning up human trash and residue is depreciated everywhere. Dirty work differs from illegal and immoral work in the sense that there is a grudging awareness that the work is necessary and useful, even vital. It is work that must be done, but doing it does not earn social rewards because it is unpleasant, physically disgusting, or associated with things that are symbolically "unclean."

The role of public executioner must certainly stand as prime example of dirty work (Robin, 1964; Hornum, 1968). In those countries endorsing capital punishment, the hangman, guillotiner, or electrocutioner is placed in a paradoxical situation: Although they enforce the law and perform a relatively skilled task involving a convicted criminal, the job is without public esteem. Other forms of dirty work in the United States would be jailing (contacts with criminals), garbage collecting (human refuse), and undertaking (preparing the dead). Handling the dead is considered dirty work even in hospitals; whenever possible, attendants will leave a body to be prepared by the next work shift (Sudnow, 1967). American society assigns much of its dirty work to the police—controlling criminals, clearing the carnage of auto accidents, monitoring the drunk and disorderly, and settling domestic problems.

Because of their low prestige, these jobs are difficult to fill. In the Middle Ages, convicted criminals were sometimes given the unenviable choice of being executed or taking the job of town executioner (Hornum, 1968). Recruitment is a problem for contemporary occupations such as jailer, with the result that states have been forced to eliminate virtually all qualifications in order to attract sufficient numbers of people to monitor the prisons (Jacobs and Retsky, 1975).

Dirty work wounds people's dignity. Those doing dirty work are often treated as social inferiors. This kind of treatment is resented, and is countered by feelings that the work is good, useful, and meaningful. A grave digger comments:

> Not anybody can be a grave digger. . . . You have to make a neat job. . . . A human body is goin' into this grave. That's why you need skill when you're gonna dig a grave. . . . It's like a trade. It's the same as a mechanic or a doctor. . . . A grave digger is a very important person (Terkel, 1972:658–60).

CONCLUSION

Workers doing the dirty work of society respond by seeking to give it meaning and stature, to make it "honorable." Deprived of social status by the very nature of the tasks, they will organize the work and its relationships to outsiders in a way that allows them to develop pride and dignity. A sense of honor is evident in the behavior of butchers, for example (Meara, 1974).

CASE STUDY: HONOR IN DIRTY WORK

"The trade of butcher is a brutal and odious business," wrote Adam Smith in 1814, commenting on the work in the slaughter houses and meat packing plants of an earlier era. The conditions of work have improved, but it remains "dirty work." In terms of prestige, the job of butcher scores 38.8 (Exhibit 9:1), at the bottom of the skilled crafts. This score cannot be explained by reference to objective criteria of prestige. For example, the average weekly wage for butchers is $324, some $24 more than the wage earned by auto mechanics, who score 6 points higher, and $2 more than carpenters, who rank 15 points higher. Nor is it accounted for by training requirements. Rather, it is explained by the perceptions of the work. Exposure to cold temperatures, associations with blood, working with animal carcasses, and the high risk of injury combine to create the image of "butcher." It is no accident that today, the role is more likely to be that of "meat cutter."

In search of honor, meat cutters redefine their work—the tools, the environment, and the product—in relations with customers and among themselves, creating a subculture which allows them to confer honor upon themselves. They *endure the cold* and take great pride in being able to withstand it. They almost never give any outward sign of discomfort and are rarely heard to complain. They *confront and ignore danger*. Meat cutting is quite hazardous, involving as it does saws, knives, and other cutting implements. Butchers emphasize their injuries (rather than concealing them) and seem to have a subcultural hierarchy of valued injuries, with lost or deformed fingers at the top of the scale. They derive honor from the danger and risk inherent in their work, and from their ability not to be deterred by danger. The occupation *excludes women*, and, as in other predominately male occupations, this exclusion serves as a means of bringing dignity to the work by raising it above the level of common labor that could be performed by anyone. Toughness confers honor. Finally, butchers *avoid customers* and much prefer working in the back room to dealing with customers, for having to interact with outsiders reaffirms the dishonor of their work.

Most work at the bottom of the prestige hierarchy offers few advantages. The work itself tends to be unpleasant or hard or unclean or dangerous. It is defined as deviant or degrading. Although some find the work exciting or challenging, most are recruited from the ranks of those with few qualifications or those experiencing discrimination in the labor market. Occasionally the income is good, but it is generally low. Incomes seem to rise only when some incentive is needed to lure people into an otherwise unrewarding job. Further, members of the larger community tend to engage in a number of exclusionary practices designed to maintain social distance. Carnivals, jails, and migrant-worker camps are relegated to the fringes of towns. Zoning restrictions and community pressure combine to restrict the spread of red-light districts. At the interpersonal level there is outright ostracism or subtle reminders of social inferiority.

TEN

Job Dissatisfaction
and Work Reform

INTRODUCTION: DISCOVERING JOB DISSATISFACTION

The 1970s witnessed the "discovery" that, for large segments of the American population, work was not a particularly satisfying experience. Occupations organized around the principles of Taylorism were singled out: "Dull, repetitive, seemingly meaningless tasks . . . are causing discontent among workers at all occupational levels," warned the widely publicized report *Work in America* (O'Toole, 1973). Some research suggested that more than half the working population were unhappy in their work (see, for example, Sheppard and Herrick, 1972).

The most obvious and immediate consequence of job dissatisfaction is that it makes the hours spent on the job very unpleasant. In addition to being psychologically unrewarding, workers with lower morale appear more susceptible to accidents, illness (Herzberg, et al., 1959:108), and heart disease (Sales and House, 1971). Job satisfaction may also be the single best predictor of general health and longevity, according to some observers. Work-related dissatisfaction can also interfere with personal life beyond the work place. One study of American workers found that although people made a conscious effort to separate work from home life, three-fourths conceded that they brought their work problems home with them (Renwick and Lawler, 1978:60). Studies of industrial workers have identified an association between job satisfaction and satisfaction with certain aspects of family and community life.

Employers had long wrestled with the problem of job satisfaction, for it evidently influenced the way workers approached their jobs, showing up in reduced productivity, decreased quality, absenteeism, turnover, and even deliberate misconduct in the form of theft, damage, or inferior work. During the 1930s and 1940s, producing "happy workers" became the keystone of the *Human Relations* school of management. The emphasis was upon communication, training supervisors in interpersonal skills, and leadership.

The negative implications of worker dissatisfaction had been evident for some time, but they captured national attention and came to be symbolized by a 21-day wildcat strike at the Lordstown (Ohio) Chevrolet plant (Aronowitz, 1973). The strike itself in March of 1972 was preceded by an explosion of worker grievances (5,000 in 6 months) and informal sabotage (keys broken off in ignitions and washers dropped into carburetors). The official issue was the speed of the assembly line (100 cars an hour), but deeper issues centered on the nature of work in a plant that epitomized Taylorism—simplified, standardized, segmentalized, and specialized. Workers found their jobs monotonous, boring, unrewarding, and tiring.

Proponents of a number of theories of human motivation had long argued for the central importance of individual discretion, participation in decision making, and interesting, challenging work as an alternative to the restrictive specialization that characterized much industrial and clerical work in the United States, but there was a general reluctance to accept such ideas. Taylorism was assumed to offer economic advantages and, as critics claimed, a means of controlling workers, but there was also a general lack of concern for job satisfaction, and so a manager of the period could argue: "Yes, I made the job more boring in order to get higher productivity, but after all isn't productivity what business is all about?" (Lawler and Hackman, 1971:47). Moreover, many employers seemed to share the ideas of Henry Ford II, "The average worker . . . wants a job in which he does not have to think," and a union staff member, "This concept of deadly monotony on the job is an intellectual middle-class concept—we wouldn't stand it—but for the worker it is acceptable because he doesn't have to think about what he's doing" (Sherrill, 1973:2).

The explosion of overt worker dissatisfaction and the challenge of imported products which competed successfully in terms of price and quality, which occurred during a period of worldwide economic reorganization partially created by the oil crisis, caused American industry to reexamine its basic approach to organizational structure and the shape of work roles among both blue- and white-collar personnel. As a result, management's long-term commitment to the norms of Taylorism appear in decline in some organizations. Experiments with new forms of work that grant employees greater discretion and a new role in the decision-making process are common. At a more fundamental level, the basic principles of Taylorism are being questioned, and in some instances are being discredited. Companies like People Express are being extolled by both the mass media and the Harvard Business School. These events may well signal a revolution in the social organization of work roles.

JOB SATISFACTION: EXTRINSIC VERSUS INTRINSIC REWARDS

Systematic research on job satisfaction dates back to the 1930s and has often produced results that are difficult to interpret. A common approach has been to confront workers with a straightforward and direct query, "All in all, how satisfied would you say you are with your present job?" The consistent finding, reaffirmed over several decades, has been that the overwhelming majority of American workers (80 to 85 percent in most studies) appear "generally satisfied" with their present jobs (Quinn, et al., 1974:54).

It is now recognized that such research was flawed by some complex methodological and conceptual problems that still exist. Measuring job satisfaction is no easy task because it is has so many subtle dimensions. Moreover, verbal expressions may mask deep worker discontent; in addition, expressing satisfaction can be a way of *coping* with dissatisfaction. The very nature of the question may elicit a defensive response from workers. People may feel that admitting to dissatisfaction will reflect badly on them; work is so central to modern life that to reveal that a job is unsatisfactory is to accept a degree of personal failure in the choice of such a career and/or in the inability to find a more rewarding position. Thus, surveys may overestimate the level of satisfaction. Levels of satisfaction may also be inflated by the responder's use of the psychological defense mechanisms of rationalization or compensation; a worker caught in an unrewarding position might attempt to minimize the problem by exaggerating the position's positive aspects, at least to the interviewer.

PATTERNS OF JOB SATISFACTION

Despite the shortcomings of this research approach, it is a useful means of uncovering relative levels of satisfaction among various groups of workers. Virtually every study confirms the same general patterns. Job satisfaction is clearly influenced by the type of job, by age, and by race, as shown in Exhibit 10:1.

Type of occupation.   A clear association has been noted between type of occupation and level of job satisfaction. Individuals in managerial and professional occupations consistently report relatively high levels of job satisfaction, while members of unskilled and operative occupations have the lowest levels. This pattern holds for women, men, whites, and blacks.

Employment status.   If workers are separated on the basis of employment status—salaried and wage workers versus the self-employed—it is clear that self-employment produces significantly higher levels of job satisfaction (Stains and Quinn, 1979).

Age.   Age is one of the major factors influencing the level of job satisfaction. Younger workers are clearly among the most dissatisfied. The highly dissatisfied young worker is a product of the 1960s. Younger work-

EXHIBIT 10:1   Patterns of Job Satisfaction, United States, 1978*

VARIABLE	MEAN
Occupational Group	
Managerial	2.55
Professional	2.55
Craft	2.50
Sales	2.48
Service	2.31
Clerical	2.28
Operative	2.18
Unskilled	1.89
Race	
White	2.43
Black	2.01
Gender	
Male	2.38
Female	2.39
Age	
Less than 20	2.14
20–29	2.67
30–39	2.35
40–49	2.43
50 and older	2.55

***Note:** Question—"On the whole, how satisfied are you with the work you do?" Scores range from 0 (very dissatisfied) to 3 (very satisfied).
Source: Charles N. Weaver, "Job Satisfaction in the United States in the 1970s," *Journal of Applied Psychology* 65 (Nov. 1980), table 2, p. 366.

ers studied between the 1930s and the 1950s were very positive about their work. Youth, during this earlier period seem to have entered the work place with great enthusiasm and interest, but their level of satisfaction declined over time. This might be accounted for by disillusionment with pay, slower-than-anticipated promotions, or dull and routine jobs. In contrast, social and demographic developments since World War II appear to have altered the situation to the point where youth enter the work force with a different set of expectations. They are better educated than their parents, have grown up with affluence, and have experienced less restrictive socialization, which seem to have combined to create much higher expectations for that first job; frustration of these expectations manifests itself in dissatisfaction early in the career, followed by increasing levels of satisfaction.

Contemporary research indicates that workers report higher levels of satisfaction as they grow older. This tendency begins somewhere in the late twenties or early thirties. A number of processes are apparently at work, each contributing to a full understanding of the observed pattern. One factor is that the early years are a sorting-out period, with dissatisfied workers shifting between jobs and careers, within the limits imposed by their education and experience, until they find one that is more rewarding. Another factor is that those workers who remain in a job for any length of time begin to accumulate benefits (in the form of seniority, pay increments, promotions, and work-based friendships) which can serve to neutralize the initial sources of discontent. Still a third factor has less to do with actual changes in job conditions and focuses instead upon individual adaptations. People may have to readjust their goals, dreams, and expectations downward, or substitute hopes for the success of their children for hopes for their own success (Chinoy, 1955). Declining expectations might then lead to a lessening of discontent.

Race. Expressed job satisfaction among blacks rates well below that of whites, and this appears to have been the case for several decades. Some of the reasons are straightforward. Blacks continue to be overrepresented in lower-level occupations, and black males earn less than white males in every occupational category. In addition, perceived discrimination has been shown to have an impact on satisfaction. Sixteen percent of the blacks in one survey reported on-the-job discrimination (Stains and Quinn, 1979). Each of these factors could contribute to dissatisfaction with work among blacks and other minorities.

Gender. The uneven distribution of women and men within the occupational structure would tend to predict lower levels of satisfaction among females. When compared to men, women tend to earn proportionately less, are concentrated in less rewarding clerical and service occupations, and continue to be confronted with the problems of concurrently managing a home, a family, and a job. No consistent pattern of lower job satisfaction among women emerges, however. The relatively disadvantaged position of women in the work force is not translated into overall job dissatisfaction, but the reasons are unclear at this point (Varca, et al., 1983).

EXTRINSIC VERSUS INTRINSIC FACTORS

Overall measures of job satisfaction assume that every job has both advantages and drawbacks, and that responses to global questions allow workers to balance various elements against one another to arrive at a generalized feeling of satisfaction. Such an approach ignores the specific features of work roles that prove satisfying or dissatisfying. Current research tends to divide the characteristics of jobs into two broad categories—"extrinsic" variables and "intrinsic" variables. Unfortunately, there is no consensus on the conceptualization and operationalization of such terms.

Extrinsic Factors

Work characteristics classified as *extrinsic* focus on tangible rewards (earnings, fringe benefits, job security), working conditions (hours, physical surroundings, safety, and health), adequacy of resources, relationships with coworkers, quality of supervision, and role conflicts. The emphasis is on the work environment and the reward system. Exhibit 10:2 reports the frequency of work-related problems that are extrinsic in nature.

Earnings. Inadequacy of income is a problem for one person in five. Twenty percent of workers, then, feel that they do not earn enough to cover their expenses. The severity of the problem is not easily gauged, however, because expectations about what constitutes an appropriate lifestyle tend to be highly variable. The question of equity is also a frequently mentioned problem. Many workers claim that they earn less than others who do similar work. Fringe benefits were a source of discontent among at least half the workers. They expressed the need for either additional benefits or improvement of existing benefits. The four most frequently requested benefits are medical/hospital insurance, a retirement program, dental insurance, and paid vacations.

Income and economic benefits clearly are important, especially for blue-collar workers, who usually rate it most important (Quinn, et al., 1974). Economic benefits are one of the major reasons for staying in a particular job, even in the face of an otherwise unrewarding situation. Among British blue-collar workers, income is often mentioned as the only reason people remain in routine, repetitive jobs (Goldthorpe, et al.,

EXHIBIT 10:2   Frequency of Work-Related Problems

Problem Area	Percent Reporting Problems

Earnings, Income

Inadequate Income	21%
Earn Less Than Deserved	39%
Need Additional Fringe Benefits	55%
Likely to Lose Job This Year	15%

Safety, Health

| Unpleasant Environment | 37% |
| Exposed to Hazards | 78% |

Work Content

Inconvenient Hours	34%
Skills Underutilized	37%
Conscience Violated	28%

Source: Graham L. Stains and Robert P. Quinn, "American Workers Evaluate the Quality of Their Jobs," *Monthly Labor Review*, 102 (Jan. 1979), p. 6.

1968:29). However, it appears that increasing numbers of American workers are expressing a preference for "trading away" some additional income in return for more leisure time. Surveys show that one worker in five would be willing to work less and earn less (Best, 1978:32). The most favored choice is more vacation time, with substantial numbers saying they would be willing to surrender a 2 percent pay increase for five additional days of paid vacation.

Work content. Several problems with job structure are frequently mentioned. Many workers complain that they are called upon to put in excessive or inconvenient hours. Such workers might be receptive to variable work schedules or to the opportunity to set their own schedules. Some one-quarter of the workers surveyed report having had their consciences compromised by the demands of their work. Such compromises may involve workers' having to produce inferior products, mistreat customers, or do things they consider wrong—problems that have already been noted among members of the technostructure. Others are in positions that are unstable or have an unpromising future.

Safety and health hazards.   Occupational health, which emerged as a major issue among American workers in the 1970s, was a frequently mentioned problem in this survey. Over one-third report that they must work in an unpleasant environment. Seventy-eight percent are exposed to some hazard or unhealthy condition, making this the most frequently mentioned problem. This unusually high figure is partly the result of a change in the wording of the questionnaire which made it more likely that people would identify health as a problem. It also reflects changes occurring in the occupational sphere, however. Safety and health are receiving more attention in the media and from unions and the government, which makes workers more sensitive to the potential of work-place danger. Then, too, recognition of an ever-expanding list of hazards means that more categories of workers are exposed today than in the 1960s. The most frequently cited hazards are air pollution (40 percent), threat of electrical shock or burns (30 percent), excessive noise (30 percent), and dangerous chemicals (29 percent). Fifteen percent of the group actually suffered a work-related illness or injury within the last three years. Thus it is clear that workers view their jobs as dangerous to their health and well-being.

Intrinsic Factors

Work characteristics classified as *intrinsic* focus on the actual content of jobs and the extent to which they offer opportunities for self-direction (or autonomy), intellectual and physical challenge, utilization of skills, and self-expression. Attention to intrinsic factors has its intellectual origins in the work of a number of social theorists over a long period of time. Several of the most influential deserve special mention. One of the earliest and most enduring conceptualizations was developed by Abraham Maslow, who popularized the concept of *self-actualization*—the need for self-fulfillment and realization of individual potential (Maslow, 1954). According to Maslow, self-actualization occupies the pinnacle of a hierarchy of human needs ordered as follows:

self-actualization (fulfillment of human potential)
esteem (approval of others, self-respect)
belongingness and love (affection, social relationships)
safety and security (security, protection, freedom from fear)
physiological (hunger, thirst, rest)

All needs demand satisfaction, but the most basic physiological needs must be met first. Once a need has been satisfied, the next need in the hierarchy emerges and dominates the individual's consciousness and activities.

Chris Argyris (1960) emphasized the idea of personality development in his work. He argues that individual maturity should occur along seven dimensions:

passivity to activity
dependence to independence (autonomy)
inflexibility to flexibility
shallow interests to deep interests
short-term to long-term perspective
acceptance of subordination to desire for equality
lack of control to self-control

Bureaucratic organizations stifle the emergence of mature personalities and thus encourage immature behavior and dissatisfaction.

Robert Blauner (1964) used a conflict perspective in exploring the impact of work structure on alienation. Alienation is a multidimensional concept characterized by

powerlessness (lack of control over events)
meaninglessness (incomprehensibility, unpredictability)
self-estrangement (lack of identification with activities)
social isolation (loneliness, exclusion)

Research has confirmed that alienation is most likely to be found among workers involved with mass production technology in the United States (Shepard, 1971) and Britain (Cotgrove, 1972), and Italy, India, and Argentina (Form, 1973). The source of alienation seems to lie in the structure and context of assembly-line work. Machine pacing contributes to a feeling of powerlessness. Narrow specialization means that workers perform only minor and sometimes trivial parts of the total procedure, and hence leads to feelings of meaninglessness. Estrangement results from the repetitious performance of standardized, routine tasks. The physical separation of workers arrayed along the line combined with the noise and the pressures of time effectively hinder the development of social relationships with coworkers.

Finally, there is the important work of Frederick Herzberg, who was largely responsible for coining the terms *extrinsic* and *intrinsic,* but who is best known for an alternative explanation of the dynamics of job satisfaction called the *two-factor* theory. He has contended that satisfaction and dissatisfaction are not opposite ends of a single continuum, but rather are separate configurations (Herzberg, et al., 1959; Herzberg, 1966). The absence of dissatisfaction does not usually create satisfaction, except in the short run. Dissatisfaction tends to be caused by working conditions, pay, supervision, and general company policies—the extrinsic factors. Removing problems reduces dissatisfaction but does not produce satisfaction. Satisfaction is produced by the content and tasks of the job and by opportunities for the fulfillment of needs for recognition, achievement, personal growth, and responsibility. Some independent research has confirmed that intrinsic factors have a greater impact on job satisfaction than extrinsic factors (Saleh and Hyde, 1969; Waters and Roach, 1971), but other research has proved inconclusive (Ewen, et al., 1966).

The importance of intrinsic factors is not rated equally by members of all occupational groups. As a general rule, professional, technical, and managerial workers are likely to emphasize extrinsic factors more than blue-collar workers will (see, for example, Walker, Tausky and Oliver, 1982). Differential expectations are a result of the interaction of prework experiences and work experiences. The social background, education, and socialization of professional, technical, and managerial workers produce higher expectations for personally rewarding work. Blue-collar workers, as a result of their experiences in more structured jobs, are less likely to anticipate intrinsic rewards.

REVITALIZING THE WORK PLACE

The discovery of job dissatisfaction, converging with a number of social, economic, and demographic forces, has generated interest in the reorganization of work and work roles. All proponents of the work reorganization movement seem to share a concern about the demeaning and dehumanizing aspects of dull, repetitive, standardized work, but there are different approaches to the perceived problems. One trend has focused on the restructuring of existing jobs to make them more meaningful and rewarding. A second trend has been the movement toward worker participation in decisions about the work place. Both have tended to look beyond the borders of the United States for models. Finally, some broader, more searching examinations of the work process have culminated in attempts to completely rethink and reorganize the work process. Many of the models for these efforts are American firms that have abandoned the conventional wisdom and have produced unusual successes.

A number of motives have stimulated this searching reexamination of work roles, which some have alluded to as "the third American Revolution." As is the case with all attempts to understand human motives, it is difficult, if not impossible, to impute a single cause in specific instances. Rather, a number of goals may coexist in bringing about change. It must be assumed that one factor is a sincere concern with the welfare of employees and a desire to make their work meaningful and challenging. Consequently, there is much talk of "infusing organizations with humanistic values." Another consideration is that some changes are merely minor adjustments that can be made to adapt to the needs of employees without completely disrupting the organization. Flexible work schedules are a case in point. Some employers have been lured into making adjustments because they have become convinced that there will be a significant payoff in terms of efficiency and productivity. Management consultants (and academics) are often guilty of making grandiose claims about the potential profit gains to be realized by reorganizing the work place. Organized labor has also been instrumental in effecting change by bringing pressure to bear upon employers. Finally, some critics argue that this change is merely the latest in a long history of managerial attempts to control and manipulate workers. This approach looks to the history of American labor relations, which has evolved into an adversarial relationship characterized by a mutual distrust that can generate resistance to sincere attempts to revitalize the work place.

ALTERNATIVE WORK SCHEDULES

One direct strategy has been to abandon the traditional, fixed 9-to-5 work day and five-day week, either by replacing it with a shorter work week or by allowing flexible scheduling.

Four-day weeks. In the 1970s, a number of firms began to experiment with the idea of replacing the conventional work week of five, 8-hour days with a four-day week of 10-hour days each. (This is also referred to as a "compressed work week" [CWW].) It evolved in response to both expressed worker preference for longer periods of free time and some practical considerations, such as the potential fuel savings associated with fewer commutes to work. The idea has not been widely accepted, but a recent study does indicate that about 2 percent of American companies use a four-day week (Brophy, 1985b).

The results are, at best, mixed (Ronen and Primps, 1981). Not all workers are attracted to the idea of shorter work weeks at the cost of longer work days, so worker participation is sometimes involuntary. Levels of perceived fatigue are consistently increased, which may enhance accident risk. Most studies show generally positive attitudes toward the 4/40 program, however, and in some instances it has significantly improved job satisfaction and productivity (see, for example, Millard, et al., 1980). Improvements in job satisfaction derive largely from the additional discretionary time, but no studies have followed workers for a long enough time to account for the potential of the Hawthorne effect.

Flexitime. The idea of flexitime is simple; Workers are allowed to choose their own hours, within some limits. "Core" hours are established (usually 10 AM to 3 PM), during which all employees must be at work, surrounded at either end of the day by two "bands" (7 AM to 10 AM, and 3 PM to 6 PM), during which workers are free to schedule their own time to complete a full eight-hour day. By the beginning of the 1980s, a number of major firms (including Northwestern National Life and Control Data Corporation) and government agencies had adopted flexible scheduling. A recent study indicated that over 15 percent of companies used it in one form or another (Brophy, 1985b).

One definite but largely unanticipated consequence of flexible scheduling is that it has reduced a prevalent source of conflict between supervisors and managers—tardiness. Delinquent employees can simply make up lost time at the end of the day. An informal shift to the earlier part of the day has created a new standard work day that extends from 7 AM until 3 PM. Workers who choose the later hours complain of the absence of co-workers in the late afternoon.

A number of advantages have been claimed for this plan, but the most direct and obvious is that it frees workers to schedule their hours around leisure pursuits, child-care demands, and personal preferences. Flexitime seems to produce generalized feelings of satisfaction with life (although not with the job), because it provides more control over nonwork time. A study of British men indicated that time devoted to housework increased modestly among those with a predisposition toward shared domestic tasks; most of the newly acquired free time was spent with the children (Lee, 1983).

Some observers predict that a general decline in job satisfaction will accompany the introduction of flexitime (see, for example, Rainy and Wolf, 1981). It may be that the amount of additional time that can be effectively used is limited. Or it may be that the additional free time will serve to emphasize the unpleasant aspects of the work, because flexitime does not enrich unrewarding roles or shorten the time spent doing unfulfilling work; it only modifies the specific times during which such work must be done. But alternative work schedules do not address a more fundamental issue—that of authority and decision making. Flexitime continues to be based on the idea that management retains the right to design jobs. In contrast, many more complex and far-reaching attempts are being made to restructure the work setting and focus on active worker participation in the work process.

Job sharing.   In a small number of cases, probably less than 1 percent of the paid work force (Brophy, 1985b), two workers share one full-time job and divide the salary and benefits. It is an attractive practice in theory, for it allows two people with external constraints upon their time to maintain careers, while allowing an employer to devote a fixed amount of space and support facilities to two workers. In practice it has presented complex scheduling problems and causes difficulties in maintaining continuity of work flow. It is not the splitting of technical tasks that poses the major problem; it is the social aspect. Coworkers and supervisors must coordinate their activities with more than a single person, communications to one job-sharer may not be transmitted to the other, and teamwork may be disrupted.

JOB REDESIGN: RESHAPING WORK ROLES

Job redesign is a general term referring to reorganization of work tasks so as to reduce specialization, standardization, and repetitiveness. The job redesign movement has tended to focus on the demeaning and dehumanizing aspects of work roles, especially those on the assembly line. In the 1920s and 1930s, the assembly line was a proud symbol of the burgeoning productive capacity of industrialization. More recently it has come to epitomize the dull, narrow, repetitive, standardized work that has become so widespread. The central thrust of job redesign has been to reduce the negative aspects by increasing the scope of responsibility, providing interesting and challenging activities, and improving communication by instituting formal feedback on worker effort. The practical applications are likely to take one of three forms, involving different degrees of actual change in technical tasks and worker control of the process.

Job rotation.   Variety can be introduced by having workers rotate among different jobs rather than limiting them to a single job, a pattern common in some European auto firms. For example, auto workers at the Swedish Volvo plant have long been on a four-day rotation system. One group assembles fuel tanks on Monday, fits windows on Tuesday, does interiors on Wednesday, does rear axle work on Thursday, and then shifts back to fuel tanks on Friday (Mire, 1974:6). Rotation does not necessarily involve any change in the nature and scope of the activities; it merely frees workers from the monotony of a single job. It should be noted that workers have been observed doing this on an informal and unauthorized basis since the early Hawthorne research.

Job enlargement.   This approach is aimed at reducing dissatisfaction by expanding the number and variety of activities in a single work role. An example would be having a typist file and operate duplicating equipment. Herzberg (1968) and others have rejected this strategy as useless in the long run since it merely adds more meaningless tasks to an already meaningless job.

Job enrichment.   The term *job enrichment* encompasses a variety of ways of reorganizing jobs to provide people with more responsibility and greater autonomy. An innovative program for keypunch operators in a large American insurance company illustrates a successful case of enrichment (Glaser, 1976:102–10). Prior to initiation of the program, keypunch operators were given data to be punched on to computer cards and were told to reproduce it exactly as provided and then ship the cards directly to the data-processing center, where they were checked for accuracy. Job enrichment gave the operators much greater latitude and control. They assumed responsibility for establishing and meeting their own schedules. They were encouraged to look for coding errors and given the authority to make corrections. Operators were put in contact with the people who originated the work and were freed to discuss problems directly rather than having to communicate through a supervisor.

Each of the forty workers involved in the experiment was thus given more discretion and more responsibility; in addition, the very scope of their jobs was expanded to include a more meaningful segment of the total flow of work. After a year, there were dramatic changes in behavior and attitudes.[1] Absenteeism fell by 24 percent. Productivity (cards punched per hour) increased by over 30 percent. The number of errors declined. The average level of job satisfaction improved by 16 percent. Salary complaints dropped. The company estimates that it actually saved $64,305 from these improvements in productivity. Admittedly, this program was unusually successful, and there is always the possibility that the passage of time may erode the positive outcomes.

Job redesign takes many forms, all involving some rearrangement of technical tasks among specific jobs. As such, it is directed at the boredom and repetitiveness of industrial and clerical work. Some go no further, but enrichment programs extend to an expansion of responsibilities, addressing the issue of the opportunity for challenging work which allows workers to exercise some discretion. This raises the more fundamental question of worker participation in meaningful decisions about the work process.

Machine-paced work, especially on the assembly line, epitomizes lack of worker control over the conditions and pace of work. Auto workers report daydreaming about the breakdown of the line, applauding when it does falter, even sabotaging it. It was appropriate that it was the assembly line at Lordstown that brought national attention to worker alienation. The concept now called "ownership" locates some control over the process in the worker.

Academic research has long shown that people perform better when

---

[1]Several general points should be kept in mind when evaluating virtually all research in this area. First, organizations that innovate may not be representative of all organizations. In fact, some would argue that by the very act of innovating they demonstrate that they are not typical. Second, the quality of research varies widely. Some is based on anecdotal evidence; some is impressionistic; and some is motivated by a vested interest in demonstrating success. Third, the *Hawthorne effect* must be considered: The very act of singling out a group of workers for special treatment may produce positive results.

they have some control over the tasks at hand, leading the Ford Motor Company to institute worker control over the line at some plants (Peters and Austin, 1985). Every worker was given access to a button which could stop the line. And they did stop it, thirty times the first day. But after that first day the number of shutdowns leveled off at about ten, each with an average duration of about 10 seconds—just enough time to allow workers to do some tiny task, like tightening a bolt or adjusting a part, prevented by the regular pace.

The experiment challenges the widely held notion that workers will not work as well or as hard as they should unless they are tightly controlled and supervised. Productivity remained unchanged, but the number of defects in the cars coming off the line declined dramatically, from an average of 17.1 per car to 0.8. As a long-time employee described it, "It's like someone opened the window and we can breathe." Experiments like this are going on in countless plants and offices in the United States. Even more dramatic programs are being tried to give workers a direct voice in the decision-making process.

INDUSTRIAL DEMOCRACY/WORKER PARTICIPATION: DEMOCRACY IN THE WORK PLACE

The inclusion of workers in the decision-making process is a significant departure from dominant patterns of authority prevailing in the United States. Historians like to pinpoint the decades between 1840 and 1860 as the period of the demise of employer-employee cooperation and the beginning of a relationship in which employers assumed the authority to run their firms without worker participation. For example, up until 1980, the nature of the relationship was written into contracts with the auto industry, with the unions granting the company, ". . . the exclusive right to manage its plants and offices and direct its affairs and working forces" (Simmons and Mares, 1983:251). The comment noted earlier by a manager at the Lordstown plant, "It's our plant," exemplifies a more adamant position. Workers' ability to gain some degree of control has generally been reactive, through strikes and collective bargaining, but also through the informal subcultural arrangements which allow them some control over the way work is to be organized.

In current usage, *worker participation,* or *industrial democracy,* refers to institutionalized, active involvement in the design of the work process by the people who create the goods or provide the services. Most of this involvement takes place at the work-role level, with participation in decisions relating to the design of technical tasks, setting of work schedules, establishment of quality control, allocation of work among people, and work rules. But worker participation may range all the way to self-manage-

EXHIBIT 10:3   Levels of Industrial Democracy

LEVEL	TYPE	EXAMPLES
Maximum	**Self-Management:** worker authority	Plywood cooperatives
	Codetermination: joint decision making	Sweden
	Coinfluence: worker-management cooperation	Quality circles (Japan)
	Advisory: workers advise; management retains final authority	Quality circles (Unites States) Scanlon plan
	Collective Bargaining: management initiates; workers approve/veto	
Minimum	**Suggestion:** workers encouraged to make suggestions	Suggestion boxes
Absence	No formal mechanisms	

ment, or, in a practice called *codetermination*, extend to the organizational level and include participation (directly or through elected representatives) in the formulation of policy. Exhibit 10:3 orders the various possible levels of participation.

SELF-MANAGEMENT: THE PLYWOOD COOPERATIVES

There were about twelve worker-owned, worker-operated plywood factories in 1983 in the Pacific Northwest, descendants of the first cooperative mill founded in 1921 by a group of 125 craftspersons (Zwerdling, 1980; Simmons and Mares, 1983). There are a few other scattered co-ops, such as the Vermont Asbestos Group, a mining company bought by the workers in 1975. Organization varies among the different firms, but there are certain basic principles found in each. Each worker owns one share in the company, and votes that share in matters relating to policy and operations— electing the board of trustees (who are workers), who hire a nonmember general manager, retaining the right to vote to remove the managers, and approving large capital investments and company policy on issues such as sick leave. Every worker (owner), from janitor to board member, earns equal pay and shares equally in annual profits.

In some co-ops, the workers have surrendered their authority to hired managers who are free to run the company as they see fit; in others, workers closely control their company. At Puget Sound Plywood, board meetings are held bimonthly and the managers' actions are carefully scrutinized. Worker-initiated actions have included negotiations of contracts with suppliers and the dismissal of a worker found guilty of smoking marijuana. Formal control is supported by informal gatherings of workers to discuss issues and by subtle pressure on the board members, who are, of course, working in the plant. Unresponsive board members are frequently turned out of office at the end of their one-year terms.

Co-ops are not without problems. Management turnover is high, because managers must be responsive to hundreds of active owners. The more dedicated members complain of a segment of apathetic workers who lack the co-op spirit. More recently, co-ops have encountered recruitment problems. When co-ops first started, membership shares could be bought for as little as $1,000, but the very success of the firms has inflated the costs to upwards of $100,000, making it very difficult for young workers to afford membership. Many have turned to hiring nonmember workers at lower pay rates and excluding them from profit sharing and participation in decision making. In the process, they have created internal divisions and eliminated the democratic impetus to worker involvement.

Cooperatives in the United States have emerged, not as ideological socialistic enterprises, but rather in response to a need for jobs or as buyouts of faltering firms. They have instilled a strong sense of pride among some members, and those plywood companies that have survived have records of higher productivity than those found in conventional arrangements.

CODETERMINATION: THE CASE OF SWEDEN

In 1972, Sweden joined West Germany and a number of other European nations in moving toward a policy of *codetermination*—legally mandated inclusion of labor representatives on corporate boards and other policy-making groups within an organization (Albrecht, 1980; Haas, 1983). In response to widespread labor unrest surfacing during the late 1960s, the Swedish Parliament enacted a number of laws enhancing workers' influence over the management of the work place. In 1972, employees (in firms with one hundred workers) gained the right to elect two voting members to boards of directors. Two years later, union safety stewards (in firms with as few as five people) were granted the power to halt any production process they considered hazardous and seek a ruling by a government inspector. In the same year, corporations earning $25,000 were required to divert 20 percent of their pretax profits to employee approved projects designed to improve working conditions. And finally, in 1976, a codetermination law explicitly limited employers' authority to formulate company policy unilaterally. Any action affecting employees became a matter for collective bargaining—work assignments, scheduling, production methods, supervisory appointments, marketing policies, and even corporate mergers!

The Swedish version of codetermination was designed to bring all these matters into a process of negotiation between labor and management, finally to be adjudicated by a national Labor Court. The mechanism is still in its early stages, and it apparently suffers from procedural problems and continued opposition from segments of both labor and management. One study suggests that sizable numbers of workers feel that the law has fostered improved relations between employers and employees and has increased their influence on decisions, but a majority perceive no change.

Codetermination represents a form of industrial democracy rarely found in the United States. It is true that the Chrysler Corporation voted United Auto Workers' president Douglas Fraser a seat on the board of directors in 1980, but that was a first for a major American corporation, and it has not been repeated. Rather, this form of industrial democracy has more frequently been found in smaller firms through some form of advisory system. Lincoln Electric in Ohio, for example, has elected two members to an advisory board since 1914 (Serrin, 1984).

COINFLUENCE: QUALITY CIRCLES IN JAPAN

Quality circles (QCs) are small groups of workers (perhaps three to fifteen) who meet regularly, in addition to their regular work tasks, to identify and solve quality, safety, and production problems. Quality circles are always voluntary, and they involve some training in problem solving and quality control (statistical) analysis. The fundamental premise is to tap the expertise of the worker and use it as input into the design of the work. It is estimated that 4 million Japanese workers (about 12.5 percent of all employees) are in quality circles (Cole, 1979). They are much more common in larger firms.

Quality circles originated in the 1950s as a synthesis of three separate strands of thought (Bradley and Hill, 1983). Ironically, all were American ideas. The work of Edward Deming introduced statistical quality control and the premise that quality should be "built into" products, rather than "inspected for" at the end of the process. J. M. Juran argued that quality assurance should be decentralized throughout an organization, rather than being the responsibility of a specific group of engineers and professionals. Finally, Japanese industry noted American social science research demonstrating that employee participation in decision-making processes fostered job satisfaction. These ideas took root, producing a national commitment to quality articulated through quality circles, which were probably invented by Dr. Kaoru Ishikawa at the University of Tokyo (Wood, Hull, and

Azumi, 1982). Quality circles originated and fluorished in large Japanese industrial firms because they were consistent with a broader employment system. Dore (1973) describes it as a system in which all permanent members of an organization (remembering that many practice lifetime employment) actively participate in administration and production. Administrators and employees share a common interest in the survival of the firm, trusting each other and depending upon each worker to perform to the best of his or her ability. Thus, quality circles are merely one structural manifestation of worker participation in the functioning of the organization. There seems to be no evidence that QCs alone make a major contribution to the high levels of productivity achieved by Japanese industry. Rather, they are merely one of a number of factors.

The process of decision making in organizations influences the way in which QCs function. An emphasis on consensus, rather than on the idea of one "right" solution, eliminates the need for selling decisions to higher levels of management. The fact that consensus has been reached in a QC validates its merit.

ADVISORY SYSTEMS: QUALITY CIRCLES IN THE UNITED STATES

Impressed by the productivity and quality of Japanese industry in the postwar period, American managers sought to identify and adopt those techniques which seemed to offer some promise of arresting the widespread alienation of workers. Probably the most widely emulated Japanese device has been the quality circle, first tried in the United States in 1974. There are no definitive data for the United States, but a management consulting association has claimed that as many as 2,000 firms had instituted them in 1982 (Shannon, 1982).

Some structural modifications have been made to the QC to adapt it to the American situation. Quality circles are generally grafted on to the existing line structure, often creating a separate administrative system with the existing hierarchical structure. QCs can only suggest alternative plans; management approval is required prior to adoption. Because the process of worker participation is not institutionalized as it is in Japanese organizations, the role of "facilitator" has been created. The facilitator acts as liaison with other units in the organization and as advocate for the implementation of group suggestions.

QCs are part of standard Japanese managerial practice, and they are continued independent of any financial contribution they may make. Less than an estimated one-third produce any notable improvement in productivity. American organizations have usually taken an instrumental view of QCs, instituting them to solve production problems, not quality problems.

Supermarkets, for example, have instituted them to cope with absenteeism and employee theft. As a result, they are judged by the usual "bottom line" criterion of cost-effectiveness. Probably the key difference is that management in the United States retains the right to adopt or reject any suggestion; they do not consider QCs part of the usual internal decision-making process.

There have been some problems with implementing QCs caused by unfamiliarity and uncertainty both within and outside the organizations. Some workers have no interest in QCs because they offer no immediate financial rewards. Interestingly, middle-level managers have often failed to cooperate and have helped to render QCs ineffective. They feel threatened, worrying that authority and responsibility are being usurped by the downward delegation of activity. They fear that problems raised by QCs will reflect negatively on their ability to do their jobs, and in at least one case they complained that they were passed over for promotion because they had less responsibility.

Not all American labor unions have been convinced of the desirability of QCs. At one level, they express concern that this may be merely another way of manipulating and controlling workers without actually granting them any real role in the decision-making process. At a more pragmatic level, there is concern that worker-management cooperation will undermine the trade union's traditional role in the work process.

American adoption of QCs has frequently proceeded on the assumption that they will be able to improve job satisfaction, reduce industrial conflict, generate identification with corporate goals, and foster cooperation between workers and management. In fact, by 1982 no reliable evidence had yet shown that QCs have a positive long-term effect upon any of these factors. Such global expectations are clearly unrealistic, are unwarranted on the basis of the Japanese experience, and demand too much from a minor organizational innovation if unaccompanied by major structural changes. QCs may even be nothing more than a managerial fad, prompted by the legendary accomplishments of postwar Japan.

COINFLUENCE: QUALITY OF WORK LIFE PROJECTS

Quality of work life projects are another team approach to problem solving. They take such a wide variety of forms that they defy description, and they go by a number of names (including employee involvement groups, participation groups, and others). In those cases in which they have the authority to implement their ideas without management approval, they qualify as a form of coinfluence. The usual format brings together small groups of workers, first-line supervisors, and representatives of management to deal with both production issues and working conditions, as well as broader issues such as health, safety, and new process implementation. Some are formalized in union contracts; others are informal.

CONCLUSION: RETHINKING TAYLOR

Most of the work reform innovations attempted in the United States, regardless of scale, have been structural modifications—adjustments to the more blatant excesses of Taylorism. But there have also been advocates of a massive rethinking of the most fundamental premises. New theories are emerging, and companies that were once treated as anomalies are awarded new respect. An indication of the current popularity of this more revolutionary idea is manifest in the sales of *In Search of Excellence* (1982), Thomas J. Peters and Robert H. Waterman's analysis of some of America's most productive companies—five million copies in fifteen languages! It is impossible to predict the shape of work in the decades ahead, but the 1980s will be remembered as the decade in which Taylor's premises seem to have been discredited. It remains to be seen whether the flourishing of work reforms will result in lasting changes in work roles, participation in the decision-making process, and erosion of the adversarial relationships between employers and employees.

CASE STUDY: PEOPLE EXPRESS—PORTENT OF THE FUTURE?

Mention of People Express airlines usually conjures up images of cheap tickets, waiting lines, crowded terminals, no-frills service, and carry-on meals. However, People Express may be most important as an example of fresh ideas about the organization of work. It is a company lacking in the organizational charts, hierarchical patterns of authority, and neat job descriptions that are associated with Taylorism in American organizations. Founder Don Burr is one of a number of people who have recently built firms using innovative ideas about what motivates workers and how work roles should be structured. The model has several key elements (Rimer, 1984; Walton, 1985).

Worker financial involvement.   New employees are required to purchase at least one hundred shares of stock, at discounted prices. They collectively own one-third of all outstanding shares, the idea being that workers have a financial stake in the profitability of the firm, not just a fixed salary or wage.

Multiple work roles.   According to the *cross-utilization* approach, workers are encouraged and expected to learn and do any number of specific jobs. Flight attendants are expected to register passengers and meet incoming flights, as well as to learn some entirely different area of airline operations, such as accounting. And the rule does not apply just to lower-level employees;

pilots are expected to master scheduling, and managers sell tickets and serve drinks. The threat of boredom is reduced, workers understand the tasks and problems of others, and a cooperative spirit prevails.

Communications. The very fact that people move among jobs fosters knowledge about the functioning of the various parts of the organization. This knowledge is supplemented by daily closed circuit television programs focusing on company news, and by monthly meetings at which the officers respond to questions on subjects ranging from corporate finances to long-term strategy.

Small work units. Employees are organized into units of three or four persons, directed by "team managers." They are granted broad decision-making freedom, much more than even the Japanese version of Quality Circles. Groups enjoy a great deal of responsibility.

ELEVEN
Occupational Choices and Attainments

INTRODUCTION: SOCIALIZATION AND ALLOCATION

A basic issue in the study of work is the question of why and how people first enter specific occupations, or types of work. It is clear that it is a developmental and cumulative process; choices change over time, and are influenced by previous experiences. At an early age (under age five), children are able to express quite specific occupational choices, with media figures (astronauts, athletes, and political figures), parents, and people in their immediate environment being important role models. Ginzberg (1972) refers to this as the *fantasy phase*, pointing out that choices are uninformed by any realistic appraisal of their own abilities or the requirements of the work, and uninhibited by the social constraints which will later effectively limit occupational attainments. As individuals mature and enter school their perspectives change, likes and dislikes develop, and they begin to develop some conception of their own capabilities and limits. They meet with academic success and failure, and are channeled in certain directions. By the time they reach high school, most formulate concrete objectives and take action (select educational programs) to prepare for future work, sometimes in a specific curriculum, or merely some general level of educational attainment. Finally, armed with educational and other credentials, they actually seek work and confront the employment interview.

The terminology "occupational choice" as used to describe the process leading up to entry into the labor force is imperfect, but it continues to be used for lack of a better term. "Choice" implies a conscious, logical, rational, decision-making approach to careers. People do make some choices, but it must be remembered that choices that are made can be shaped and limited by events and forces that the individual has little, if any, ability to control. It is important to recognize that choices occur in a social context, commencing at birth and continuing through childhood and into early adulthood as individuals are introduced to cultural stereotypes and work values and as they are subjected to an array of social and family experiences. In the educational system peers and teachers and other school personnel influence educational and vocational development. Finally, even at the point of actually searching and applying for work, these social factors can help to explain why people end up in particular types of work.

It is important to distinguish between two separate aspects of the occupational attainment process: socialization and allocation (Kerckhoff, 1976).

Socialization.   *Differential socialization* focuses upon the formation of beliefs and perceptions and aspirations. As used here socialization includes both deliberate attempts to inculcate values and perspectives as well as the unintentional but systematic differences in experiences associated with structural position and group membership—parental occupation and social class, gender, and race and ethnicity. The impact of gender socialization can, for example, be noted as early as age 6 (or before) in America when gender-linked occupational stereotypes begin to emerge. The consequences of differential socialization can follow individuals through the later maturation process and the school system right up to the point of applying for a job. Gender socialization, for example, produces perceptions and values that contribute to the perpetuation of segregated occupational patterns.

Allocation.   As we have noted, occupational attainment is seldom solely a matter of personal choice and effort. Countless relevant decisions and options are only partially subject to control by the individual. Grades in school, curriculum placements, college admissions, acceptance into apprentice programs, and hiring decisions are in the hands of others, and we often find that people are channeled in certain directions on the basis of externally imposed criteria such as gender, race, and social class. For convenience, the term *gatekeepers* can be used to refer to those persons who by virtue of their roles (structural location) are in a position to direct career choices. The major categories of gatekeepers are: parents, teachers, vocational counselors, school administrators, and personnel directors. The most important gatekeepers may very well be the people who screen job applicants and conduct employment interviews. Overt discrimination may operate, but perhaps more prevalent are the generally unintentional and often unrecognized subtle stereotypes and socially conditioned beliefs and perceptions. Thus, membership in certain social groups can be the basis for allocation into certain types of jobs and exclusion from others.

Thus, occupational choice can be understood as the outcome of two analytically distinct processes. At the sociopsychological level it is possible to trace the impact of differential socialization upon aspirations, attitudes, and accomplishments. At the same time socially imposed criteria are the basis of actions that allocate people into particular careers.

OCCUPATIONAL ATTAINMENTS: GENDER, CLASS, AND RACE

The early years of life are a decisive period in understanding the overall process of career development because it is during these years that children begin to acquire some general perceptions and beliefs about the nature of work as a social activity; they may also form some specific impressions about specific types of jobs. By the time they reach school most children have developed some fundamental knowledge of the world of work (Goldstein and Oldham, 1979). Apparently about 80 percent understand that work is the source of money, and about one-third define working as the primary responsibility of being an "adult." The vast majority are aware that some jobs pay more than others and have greater or lesser prestige; however, children generally lack a clear understanding of the source of such inequities. Most are able to articulate some specific occupational choice or preference. Background factors such as community, parental occupation, socioeconomic status, family structure, and experiences as well as broader cultural influences have already begun to impact career choices.

Community

Although it may seem trivial and unimportant, the type and size of community in which an individual matures can influence subsequent occupational choices. Children growing up in urban areas tend to have both a wider range of choices and higher educational and occupational aspirations than those reared in rural areas, and levels of aspiration tend to be further elevated by the size of the city (Otto and Haller, 1979; Dawkins, 1980). This pattern apparently reflects unequal exposure to the occupational world. Ever larger cities offer the visibility of a greater range of workers, especially in the white-collar managerial and professional categories which tend to concentrate in urban areas. More heterogeneous urban areas will also bring children into contact with peers from divergent origins and expressing more diverse occupational goals. In addition, the diversity of educational opportunities is likely to be related to the size of the community. These conditions would seem to combine to produce a narrower range of occupational information for youths growing up in rural areas and smaller communities. Finally, those who do develop higher aspirations must confront the problems required by migration to metropolitan areas, not the least of which is having to sever long-standing social ties with family and friends.

Gender at Home, in the Media, and in the Schools

Boys and girls first form ideas about men's work and women's work at home and from exposure to the media. Frequently, household chores are (intentionally or not) assigned on the basis of gender (White and Brinker-hoff, 1981). Girls are overwhelmingly expected to do cleaning, cooking, dishwashing, and babysitting—skills, which, if they lead anywhere occupationally, it is into food service and personal services. Trash removal and yard work are boys' tasks conveying the impression that physical work and outdoor work are the purview of men. Such ideas unfortunately are later reinforced in the schools where boys are more likely to be called upon to do physical tasks (moving furniture) or mechanical ones (running film projectors) while girls are given responsibility for social tasks such as serving refreshments (Chafetz, 1974:89).

By the time children enter school they have already formed some important ideas about the labor force and their place in it. Some kinds of work are *gender-typed*, viewed as appropriate for men or women, but not for both, while other jobs have no such connotation. The data in Exhibit 11:1 suggests the persistence of such typing among rural school children into the 1980s. Although perceptions of some occupations as the exclusive domain of men or women have begun to weaken, there is still a tendency to question the appropriateness of some lines of work. Gender typing articulates both self-selection (limiting perceptions of choices) and allocative processes that channel boys and girls in different directions.

The media and occupations.   The media in its various forms and manifestations—television programming, children's books, advertising, and commercials—are of more than trivial interest because the images and ideas portrayed there are a major source of early childhood perceptions and misperceptions about occupational roles. Ideas about the nature of jobs (especially those which children have no direct contact with) are largely drawn from television (DeFleur, 1964). The media also, at a more general level, reinforce existing gender roles, as shown by the observation that traditional gender role development increases directly with the number of hours devoted to TV.

Dozens of studies have confirmed the presence of stereotyped images of women and men on television and in children's books. A key finding

EXHIBIT 11:1   Gender-typing of Occupations among High School Students in the United States

	Female Students		Male Students	
	Percent Naming Job as Inappropriate for:			
Occupation	Men	Women	Men	Women
Gender-typed as male				
Logger	1%	64%	4%	75%
Plumber	1	43	3	61
Construction worker	2	42	3	64
Truck driver	2	37	3	51
Mechanic	1	33	3	56
Gas station attendant	1	23	2	43
Gender-neutral				
Postal worker	1	3	4	6
Store manager	1	2	3	9
Bank teller	4	2	8	5
Accountant	3	1	5	3
Physical therapist	2	3	4	5
News reporter	1	3	3	6
Gender-typed as female				
Homemaker	52	2	55	5
Licensed practical nurse	25	1	41	3
Secretary	32	1	38	4
Hair stylist	12	1	32	4
Model	32	1	44	3
Home economics teacher	31	1	37	3

Source: Faith Dunne, "Occupational Sex-Stereotyping Among Rural Young Women and Men," *Rural Sociology* 45 (Fall 1980), pp. 404–5.

reveals that women tend to be portrayed functioning in a narrow range of occupations. A 1972 study of reading textbooks found males holding 147 different jobs compared to only 26 for women (Women on Words and Images, 1975). Since children exhibit greater interest in occupations portrayed by members of the same sex the media offer women fewer successful role models (Fox and Hesse-Biber, 1984).

An interesting and subtle sidelight of the textbook study cited in the preceding paragraph was the fact that males tended to be shown as job holders and fathers, but women were job holders or mothers. Here, the media portray the idea that work and motherhood are mutually exclusive roles despite the fact that currently a majority of women work outside the home. The proportion of young women who hold the view that "a woman should not work if she has children" is, by all indications declining, but those women who subscribe to this view tend to behave in ways that can inhibit later occupational attainment. Teenagers adhering to exclusive roles tend not to engage in extensive planning for paid employment, anticipate discontinuing their education earlier, and do not perform as well in school as young women who disagree with this view (Ireson, 1978:189). Thus, the young women who are unprepared for employment will be at some disadvantage when they subsequently enter the job market.

Family experience among women in nontraditional occupations.   Some few people—both men and women—have always been able to circumvent social barriers and enter nontraditional occupations. Men have become nurses and secretaries, women have entered construction and the military and the proportions seem to be increasing. Considering that profound socialization and allocative pressures usually combine to discourage such behavior, it is logical to assume that there must be something unusual (nontypical) in their biographies that helped them to overcome the constraints of conventional gender roles. It appears that early family experiences are a decisive factor. Admittedly, it is an extremely complex process, and one that is not yet completely understood.

For women, one factor is simply the presence of a mother employed outside the home (Hansson, et al., 1977). Maternal employment presents a less traditional gender-role model for daughters and sons, perhaps contradicting and weakening conventional stereotyping and freeing youth to pursue independent careers. Mothers' educational/occupational attainments also have some influence on the aspirations of daughters with high-level occupational aspirations more likely to be found among the daughters of college-educated mothers.

The biographies of women in blue-collar jobs reveals a consistent pattern of what Walshok (1981) calls "independence—building experiences." Their family experiences during youth and adolescence presented them with the opportunity (or forced them) to develop independence, responsibility, and autonomy. In some cases, it was the outcome of a conscious philosophy of childrearing designed to foster the assumption of personal responsibility. These women remember being trusted with valuable possessions, being given responsibilities, and being offered freedom in dress and play and choice of friends, or being expected to hold down some sort of a job. In other cases, independence-building experiences were imposed by family conditions. Having to assume responsibility for siblings while parents worked was common, as was working because the family needed additional income. Or, it may have been that personal tragedy— families broken by divorce, death, or alcoholism—imposed the need to develop independence early in life. Circumstances varied, but the common element was an early childhood or adolescent environment stimulating personal growth and a feeling of self-confidence.

The interaction of forces that shape occupational attainment are nowhere more evident than in recruitment of women into scientific and technical occupations.

CASE STUDY: WOMEN AND MATHEMATICS AND CAREERS

In 1973 Lucy Sells called the study of mathematics the critical filter in occupational selection of women in America. Research at that time indicated that women were significantly less likely to enroll in advanced mathematics courses. In 1973 only 40 percent of twelfth-grade females had completed calculus, compared to 68 percent of the male students (Fox, 1981:13). The absence of a math background effectively eliminates a person from access to many professional and technical careers. During the ensuing decade this gap has narrowed and may even have been reversed in some schools. Despite many changes, subtle differences in experiences based on gender remain and combine to act as a barrier to many young women.

The traditional exclusion of women from advanced math represents a convergence of socialization and allocation with perceptions and expectations at the core of the problem. Mathematics has been inextricably linked with males in the minds of both boys and girls during maturation. It has been a subject defined as appropriate for boys, no doubt in large part because it is consistent with conventional sex-typed masculine traits such as analytic ability (Brush, 1980). This pattern is not limited to the United States, but is also found in Europe (Runge, et al., 1981). In addition, there is a widespread belief in the larger society sometimes "confirmed" by social science research that males benefit from a gender-linked aptitude for mathematics (for recent evidence on this issue see Benbow and Stanley, 1980).

The internalization of these perceptions would be enough to induce some degree of self-selection toward math for boys and an avoidance of math by girls, even in the absence of external pressures. But these external pressures exist and are reinforcing. Parents, obviously sharing general perceptions, subtly contribute to the formation of gender roles in their daughters by tending to be less overtly supportive of math-based careers; this, in turn, is a major factor in selecting courses. Some math teachers may unintentionally direct females away from math by exhorting boys to make an extra effort after mistakes while simply praising girls for trying or by merely paying more attention to boys than girls (Sternglanz and Lyberger-Ficek, 1977). It should also be noted that math teachers are more likely to be men, adding the advantage of a male role model. Further, women often report that they generally have not received encouragement from counselors.

Even the emerging "computer revolution" may place females at a subtle disadvantage. Early access to computers can facilitate entrance into a variety of scientific and technical careers. Parents are more likely to purchase home computers for sons than daughters, and enrollments at computer camps favor boys by a margin of three to one (Kiesler et al., 1983). The social organization of video game arcades—the place where many children first confront electronics—is still another arena where male involvement is fostered. The games themselves are oriented toward male interests—race car driving, military action, and so forth. The locale itself has become a place where young men are likely to congregate and interact, in some ways replacing the pool halls of an earlier era. It is claimed to be rare to find a solitary girl in a video arcade—though it is a common gathering place for boys.

PARENTAL OCCUPATION: ALLOCATION AND SPONSORSHIP

A proportion, sometimes a large proportion, of sons and daughters eventually embark upon the same careers as their parents. Inheritance may be a direct response to parental pressure and intervention. At one time it was a "taken-for-granted" assumption that the sons of farmers would follow their fathers on the family farm, leaving children little real "choice." Residuals of this phenomena still prevail, as in the case of the fishing industry in the North Atlantic where father and sons or all brother crews have been a constant feature for decades (Jorion, 1982). It is not uncommon for parents to directly encourage their children to follow in their occupational footsteps. This is especially relevant in professional and craft work where parents have developed a strong sense of involvement and pride in their work and want their children to continue in the same work. A recent study of Chicago-area lawyers reveals that family influence was remembered as a decisive factor in career choice in about half the cases of children with a lawyer parent (Zemans and Rosenblum, 1981:37).

Even in the absence of direct pressure, there is differential socialization in that children are exposed to work values and preferences that favor some kinds of work and depreciate others. Such preferences may very well be internalized, thus becoming the basis of children's goals, aspirations, and choices. Longshorers (dock workers) in Portland, Oregon illustrate the impact of fathers' work on sons' occupational decisions (Pilcher, 1972). Male members of this occupation have traditionally placed great emphasis on work that permits them to demonstrate masculine traits of courage and physical strength. Longshoring, along with other occupations such as logging and firefighting, are seen as a means of validating one's virility. The work also has other desirable attributes. It is outdoor work; work schedules are flexible; and workers have a good deal of autonomy despite the arduousness of the tasks. Longshorers are open and outspoken in their disdain for any job lacking these advantages.

There can be little doubt that their preferences are reproduced in their sons, both in the work they choose and especially in what they avoid. Many follow their fathers into longshoring, while others opt for the armed forces or skilled construction trades. Equally interesting is that almost none become farmers, which although it is outdoor work with flexible hours, puts the individual at the mercy of the uncontrollable forces of nature. Pilcher found that not one son became a clerical or a factory worker—the classic 9 to 5, indoor jobs that offer little in the way of demonstrating courage, self-reliance, or masculinity.

Once similar vocational goals are formed, parents are often in a position to facilitate entry into an occupation. Simply by being a member of an occupation provides parents with "insider" information about job requirements and prerequisites that will aid their children in career planning. In some specific instances parents may be able to directly sponsor their children. At one time some medical schools gave preferential treatment to the children of alumni, a practice now officially discontinued. Some craft occupations depend upon parental sponsorship in accepting people into apprenticeship programs. Many organizations offer children of employees preferential access to summer work and part-time jobs. This enables children to accumulate valuable experiences that give them an advantage over others in the competition for access to jobs.

Parental sponsorship must be understood in a broad social context, not merely as a self-serving device for passing jobs from generation to generation. In the process of screening applicants, members of an occupation will prefer (all other things being equal) candidates who possess two attributes—a realistic perception of the demands of the work and the character traits necessary to perform in the job. Both are subtle, difficult traits to assess in advance, but passing jobs through the generations has advantages. Children who have grown up in intimate contact with people actually doing the work would be more likely to have a realistic appraisal of the conditions of work. Thus, the child of a police officer could be expected to be better equipped to confront the realities of police work than someone whose perceptions were formed by the media where the glamor and glory are emphasized.

Jobs in which patterns of sponsorship are found usually require some unusual abilities, such as courage, self-restraint, reliability, or trust. Parents are obviously in a position to judge their children's potential, and it must be recognized that parents will be subjected to social pressures to be selective in their sponsorship. Personal feelings and familial obligations might be expected to push parents toward unqualified support of all offspring, but it will be tempered by considerations of status within the work community. Not every son or daughter will have the required abilities, and the parent who insists upon sponsoring a less-able child risks loss of prestige and censure from coworkers, for it casts doubt on their dependability and judgment. Moreover, in occupations depending upon teamwork, an inept worker can reduce the efficiency of the entire group. Where hazards are present (mining, police work), competence is even more essential. Thus, parents face cross-pressures that can deter them from sponsoring children lacking the skills and attitudes required for the work.

SOCIOECONOMIC ORIGINS

Parental socioeconomic origins are one of the most powerful and pervasive factors in occupational choice. The influence of socioeconomic status is evident that every point in the process, and the impact is cumulative. Thus, for example, we find a direct relationship between social origins and educational aspirations. However, even controlling for levels of ability and aspirations, children of higher status parents tend to achieve higher levels of education (Blau and Duncan, 1967). Further, higher status children tend to attain better jobs than lower status children with equivalent levels of education. The continuing impact of socioeconomic status reflects the interaction of a combination of factors including the advantage of economic resources, and differential values and orientations, and subsequent experiences in the schools.

The financial dimension.   Access to jobs depends upon educational credentials, and despite the presence of systems of free public education and a superstructure of scholarships and financial aid, inequalities in economic resources cannot be neutralized. As an example, the organization of educational preparation for an occupation such as law effectively excludes many children of the financially less advantaged blue- and lower white-collar classes. Law school applicants must first earn a bachelor's degree, followed by the financial burden of an additional 3 years of full-time schooling. Scholarships are rare, and law schools do not encourage outside employment, which is difficult anyway simply because of the workload. Herbert Jacob (1978:38) concludes that "the sons and daughters of those Americans who earn less than the median family income cannot usually afford law school."

The consequences of parental capacity to bear the burdens of tuition (and other costs) are most evident in professional and managerial occupations requiring extensive educational preparation—but there are also more subtle differences. At lower economic levels, children tend to be exposed to more pressure to discontinue formal education in favor of the more immediate income of a job. In a more indirect way, it means that fewer economic resources can be devoted to providing newspapers, magazines, books, and other materials facilitating the development of abilities. Home computers are a prime example—a costly investment beyond the reach of many lower-class families, placing their children at a long-term disadvantage in the competition for jobs. Moreover, children growing up in poorer school districts tend to be provided with fewer facilities in the schools (Shiller, 1976:141). Thus, economic inequality can create a general environment that will encourage or discourage the accumulation of human capital.

Further, all measures of ability, such as IQ tests, must be treated with caution for it is generally impossible to parcel out the relative contributions of heredity and environment to such scores. With this caveat in mind, it should be noted that there is a modest statistical relationship between parental income and measured intelligence for white students. This suggests that economically advantaged social position can contribute to elevating test scores, which will, in turn, have implications for subsequent educational experiences.

The attitudinal dimension.   Economic inequalities do not exhaust the impact of socioeconomic status upon occupational attainments. The evidence suggests that some fundamental occupational attitudes are forged within the context of the stratification system. Parents develop attitudes and perceptions about the occupational system and how it functions, and they transmit these both directly and unintentionally to their children. Parental attitudes are in turn shaped by the parents' own position in the stratification system. In a number of subtle ways the experiences and structural position of each class conspire to produce attitudes in one generation that influence aspirations in their children. As one author describes the process: "Whether consciously or not, parents tend to impart to their children lessons derived from the conditions of life of their own social class—and thus, help prepare their children for a similar class (and occupational) position" (Kohn, 1969:200).

Melvin Kohn (1969), among others, has explored variations in child-rearing practices between the middle classes and the working classes. In general, middle-class families place greater emphasis on autonomy and self-improvement and are taught that jobs that provide opportunities for challenge and the exercise of initiative are the most desirable. Members of the working class certainly do not discourage occupational ambitions, but they are more likely to emphasize economic security than the nature of the work tasks. At a more general level, there is a link between socioeconomic status and aspirations, which is in part due to differential socialization. These attitudes can, in turn, mediate the direct link between ability and human capital. People with higher aspirations tend to progress farther in school than those of similar measured ability but more modest aspirations (Portes and Wilson, 1976).

Parental perceptions about the distribution of opportunities in society is a case in point. Upper-level parents almost universally visualize American society as a land of open opportunity where people can realistically hope to succeed in school and the world of work and are limited only by their own ability (Rytina, et al., 1970). In many cases, their own biographies validate this view, with many having experienced upward mobility from blue-collar or lower white-collar origins. Moreover, their occupations—professional, managerial, technical—do in fact offer career advancement opportunities. A view of the world characterized by unlimited opportunities is in and of itself likely to allow strong aspirations to flourish.

In contrast, parents at the lower end of the socioeconomic scale are much less likely to perceive an open opportunity structure unrestrained by their social origins. It is logical to expect that this perspective would be enough to cause parents to disparage high aspirations—either unintentionally or in a deliberate manner—in an attempt to forestall the frustration and disappointment they have been led to anticipate. The outcome shows up in the differences between aspirations and expectations. As you descend the class hierarchy, adolescents are more likely to anticipate a discrepancy between the kinds of jobs—and the amount of education— they would prefer in an ideal sense, and the levels they actually expect to attain (Della Fave, 1974).

The continuing impact of socioeconomic status.   Some part of the class-related differences in educational and occupational attainment may also be traced to the manner in which children progress through school systems on the basis of their origins. Among students in the lowest quartile of ability, those from higher-class origins are nine times as likely to graduate from college as those from lower status origins (Heyns, 1974). The effect of stratification is less pronounced among the more able students, but even here higher status children experience a two-to-one advantage. This suggests that human capital in the form of grades, type of curriculum, and years of education are an outcome of both academic competence and desirable behavioral and attitudinal characteristics (such as, perseverance, self-discipline, drive, and so forth). Those focusing upon allocation processes argue that school systems tend to be dominated by "middle-class" persons who unintentionally discriminate against working- and lower-class children by assuming they lack the appropriate character traits. There is some scattered evidence to support this, but research is far from conclusive (Persell, 1977).

Others (for example, Porter, 1974), argue that socialization experiences intervene between social origins and academic outcomes, with differential socialization producing what he calls "personalities" that are advantageous to middle-class children. They are more likely to be sociable and internally motivated—traits that will, along with perceived competence, affect success in school. Because the ultimate issue is one of whether or not teachers perceive such traits, research has focused on this point. Some data does indicate that teachers see blue-collar children (when compared to managerial and professional children) as having poorer study habits, being less sociable, and less cooperative in the classroom (Wrong, 1980). Thus, whether it is allocation or differential socialization, children of lower socioeconomic parents are at a disadvantage in the schools, thus helping to explain the disproportionally fewer number of such children ending up in college preparatory curricula.

The college preparatory track in high school clearly bestows some advantages upon students. Two consequences are fairly well established. One is that tracking tends to elevate the test scores of students in a college-bound curriculum and depress test performance among children in other tracks (Rosenbaum, 1976:129–31). Self-concept is also affected in a similar manner, having negative consequences for lower track students but inflating those on higher pathways (Percell, 1977:94). This is, in turn, linked to an apparent unequal distribution of quality teachers, school resources, and in some cases different grading systems (Heyns, 1974). There are also subtle differences in patterns of interaction. Lower track students report disparaging remarks about their ability and discouragement from participation in school activities. More objective observation of classroom behavior shows higher track students enjoy more praise, more frequent use of their ideas, and experience less criticism and direction (Percell, 1977:90).

The college preparatory track can also offer some advantages beyond the obvious ones of enhancing the chances of higher education. Even if they fail to attend college, curriculum experiences may provide students with a more positive attitude toward higher level occupations, and some skills and knowledge (such as math, creative writing, language) needed in higher status jobs. Following a college preparatory curriculum will thus aid them in the competition for jobs in both direct and subtle ways.

ETHNIC SUBCULTURES

Ethnicity and religion can be salient in occupational choice if groups have subcultural traditions or socialization practices that influence orientations toward education or work. Native American Caughnawaga Mohawks provide a prime example of how a subcultural tradition has been translated into concentration in a particular occupation—erecting the steel girder framework for buildings (Mitchell, 1960; Blumenfeld, 1965). The men of this tribe, originally located near Montreal, have been found in high-steel construction work since the 1880s. Excluded from conventional occupations by overt racial discrimination they were forced into farming, unskilled laboring jobs in lumbering, risky work avoided by those with a choice (mercenaries, as well as construction work), or exploitative jobs such as Wild West circus performers. Most of these occupations deprived the Mohawks of the opportunity to demonstrate traditional Indian virtues of bravery and courage. High-steel work always involved some danger because of the heights and materials, but in a perverse kind of way a major bridge-building disaster in 1907 was a decisive event. Ninety-six men were killed, and it was after this tragedy that high-steel work became a more desirable type of work to Mohawks because the element of personal risk enabled them to validate their bravery and courage. High-steel work thus replaced the traditional tests requiring combat with other tribes or white men. Mohawk boys hear tales of herosim and bravery in high-steel work from adults. Some jobs are so dangerous, they are told, that only a Mohawk can undertake them. Here then is a case where subcultural values and beliefs channel members into a specific occupation.

EMPLOYMENT PRACTICES AND DISCRIMINATION

Law and custom have long combined to restrict employment opportunities. Statutory exclusion of women from some types of work was common in all industrial countries during the early part of this century. Legislation apparently designed to protect the health and safety of women prohibited activities such as night work, strenuous effort, and jobs that involved physical danger. In some cases pregnancy was a legitimate basis for termination or an involuntary leave of absence. However, modern medical research has challenged the validity of the risks of illness and injury, and this, combined with the efforts of women's movements, have caused a relaxation of these laws, although there are, for example, still some restrictions on night work for women in Italy, England, and Israel (Wolkinson, et al., 1982).

People have also been allocated in certain directions by culturally based perceptions of the psychology and sociology of gender. Women seeking employment have been limited to occupations perceived as extensions of traditional home and childrearing roles (teaching, midwifery, cooking) or jobs that require attributes assumed to be female (typing, keypunch operators, and assembly work, which require manual dexterity and patience).

Overt and intentional bias may be reduced by laws prohibiting discrimination; however, bias may prevail at an unrecognized level because it is grounded in deep-seated social perceptions. Israel in the 1980s, for example, although ideologically committed to social equality, manifests a residue of such patterns (Wolkinson, et al., 1982). Advertisements for typists, telephone operators, and lab technicians frequently specify female candidates. The military will employ only women in the manufacture of detonators because, "only women have the necessary delicacy of touch and patience for the job." Women expressing interest in police work are informed the program is open only to men. Other jobs advertising for "men only" include chief accountant, mechanical engineer, and farm supervisor.

The survival of outright discrimination cannot be ignored either. People in search of work frequently turn to employment agencies for leads on jobs. In New York City alone there are a thousand such enterprises. During 1980 an investigative reporter in that city found frequent discrimination against blacks and women (Pifer, 1980–81). Some agencies accepted job vacancy listings accompanied by explicit instructions that they should not refer black or female applicants. Half the agencies refused to participate in such a flagrant violation of the law, but the other half agreed. One agency representative offered an insight into the process, "If you don't want blacks, don't admit it outright. Just say you want no 'numbers' . . . ," a veiled reference to the device of assigning the number 6 to minority applicants, which is itself a residue of an earlier overt practice of coding candidates on a scale from 1 (WASP) through 5 (Jews) and 6 (blacks) to 9 (gays). Within agencies that did engage in discrimination, the discrimination took the form of the referral of blacks to fewer jobs, less desirable jobs, and lower paying work.

Those who discriminated offered the explanation that they were merely responding to demands of employers who were "farming-out" this messy task and would send their business and their commissions elsewhere if an agency failed to cooperate. Whatever the source of the discriminatory impulse, it clearly works to the disadvantage of blacks, both male and female.

Applying for work is influenced by perceptions of opportunity. Beliefs about discrimination in hiring can discourage people from pursuing certain careers. As a general rule blacks perceive more discrimination than whites, regardless of sex and social class (Turner and Turner, 1975). More important, blacks perceive greater discrimination in some occupations than others. College students view positions as business executive, advertising/marketing executive, government executive, personnel manager, and lawyer as the most closed to members of their race (Turner and Turner, 1981). The military, social work, and postal work positions are the most open. It is logical to expect that such perceptions would help to deter applications for such work. And we have no way of measuring how such perceived discrimination had discouraged aspiration and preparation for such jobs much earlier in the educational process.

THE APPLICATION PROCESS

At the point when people "choose" an occupation, or are compelled by circumstances to seek some form of work, they must confront the final hurdle—the application for a position. The actual event can be an application for a job or for admission to a required training program such as medical school, a police academy, or an apprenticeship program. The application process is a social drama in which the participants play out social roles, engage in social rituals, and follow socially prescribed patterns. The preparation of resumes, searching out letters of recommendation, and filling out forms are all elements of the process. The idea of drama is nowhere more evident than in the employment interview, that fleeting encounter in which the person plays the role of "applicant" interacting with some representative of the occupation or organization. Countless manuals and seminars offered by college placement offices are designed to aid the applicant at every stage in the process—from the preparation of resumes to offering rules for dress and presentation of self in interviews. The proliferation of such devices confirm that more than credentials and objective measures of competence have a bearing on the outcome of the application process.

The fundamental issue in the application process, as posed by social science research, is this: Are otherwise equally qualified candidates placed at a disadvantage because of social characteristics, ascribed statuses, or group membership? In certain circumstances there is strong evidence to support this contention. It may take the form of overt discrimination in law or practice, but it may also be traced to the structure and dynamics of the process.

Differential Evaluation of Qualifications

The first step in the application process is the presentation of credentials to a prospective employer. Generally it is an "impersonal" contact in the form of filing a written application in response to an advertisement or some other indication of an opening. In theory it is a strictly objective evaluation based upon the qualifications of a candidate, and applicants are advised to emphasize their grades and work records and to be careful in the selection of references. These are certainly important, but applicants may not be aware that the completion of the application itself, independent of substance, is the first of many hurdles they must pass. And it is important to note that each step is enacted at two levels, the overt (where objective qualifications count) and the covert (where perceptions, stereotypes, and attributed meanings operate).

It is frequently noted that misspellings, errors in punctuation, and simple sloppiness are almost certain to disqualify even the best candidate. Leaving a space blank, or an inconsistency between two facts on a form is another common source of disqualification. The importance of such minor and apparently irrelevant considerations must be understood from the perspective of those doing the evaluation. Faced as they usually are, with large numbers of qualified applicants, they must find some criteria for screening them, and most choose to look for *negative* clues that will allow them to eliminate people. Sloppiness is such a readily observable criteria, as is an inconsistency or a lack of information. These criteria take on importance because of their obviousness, and because they are assumed to reflect undesirable personal traits: sloppiness, inattention, or even an intent to deceive.

Among those applications that pass the initial screening there is then the question of evaluating those who are qualified. Earlier research conducted in both actual employment situations and in experimental conditions has produced one general and consistent observation, that women with credentials equal to men tend to be evaluated less positively (see Arvey, 1979 for a systematic review of this literature). This generalized devaluation of female candidates in work-related situations has taken a number of forms, ranging from women being less likely to be recommended for hiring, lower suggested starting salaries, and a depressed level of predicted success. There have even been some studies showing that products (written work, musical compositions, art) believed to be produced by men were rated higher than if the same pieces are assumed to be by a woman (see Etaugh and Rose, 1975). More recent research has shown that the devaluation of female candidates is likely to be more pronounced in certain situations, and in certain jobs (Etaugh and Foresman, 1983).

Central to an understanding of the unequal evaluation of females is the concept of gender stereotypes that apparently persist among some segments of the population. *Stereotype* here refers to tacit, often unrecognized, beliefs and assumptions about categories of people. Part of the stereotyping process involves attributing typical traits to members of these categories. It is necessary to refer to older studies, uncontaminated by the current social and legal constraints that often limit the validity of current responses, to identify these stereotypes. Traits such as intelligence, bravery, responsibility, leadership, independence, dominance, and ambition have generally been attributed to males, with tact, gullibility, submissiveness, dependence, and gentleness more likely associated with females (McKee and Sherriffs, 1957; Rosenkrantz, et al., 1968). Another aspect of stereotypes is evaluative: the relative rating of traits and whole categories. The research cited here also showed that male traits were more likely to be rated as "socially desirable"; studies also revealed a general acceptance by both men and women (although to a lesser extent) of the statement, "Men are superior to women" (McKee and Sherriffs, 1957).

Such stereotypes are part of the cultural heritage of a society, are transmitted during the socialization process, and are slow to change. They subtly affect perceptions of people in these categories and influence responses to them, especially in ambiguous situations. Stereotypes are most likely to come into play in the absence of other information, hence they can unintentionally impinge upon the evaluation of job applicants because men will be assumed to be more qualified. When women candidates are clearly portrayed as equally competent in specific work-related qualifications for a specific job they are more fairly evaluated (Gerdes and Garber, 1983). Demonstrated competence apparently invalidates the stereotype.

The role of stereotypical categories is clearly evident in the evaluation of candidates for jobs typed by race or gender. One study of hypothetical applicants, identical except for race, showed raters more willing to hire black men for custodial work (a job dominated by blacks), but favored white men for lathe operator (Terpstra and Larsen, 1980). When the job was neutral, "warehouseman," neither group was rated higher. A number of studies have shown men receiving higher ratings than women for jobs that have usually been filled by males—automotive salesperson, hardware clerk, and personnel technician (Arvey and Campion, 1982). In contrast, women candidates enjoyed an advantage in competition for grocery clerk, telephone operator, and receptionist jobs. The disadvantage for women in competition for management careers seems to be based on the assumption that they are less likely to have the traits assumed to be necessary for success (Schein, 1975). The traits associated with feminity (modesty, creativity, tact) are not perceived as those leading to success (aggressiveness, self-reliance, ambition). Women are also at a disadvantage because evaluators question their long-term commitment to careers or willingness to stay with the organization (Gerdes and Garber, 1983).

The evaluation of credentials is a situation in which evaluators actually have very little information. As members of personnel departments, they seldom know much about the requirements of the job beyond the stated prerequisites, and they are limited to the standardized data provided on an application form. The obviously unqualified can be eliminated, but in sorting among the remainder, personnel evaluators can be influenced by stereotypes.

The Interview

The vast majority of people must successfully complete a personal interview at some point in their careers. The employment interview is the most commonly used method of selecting employees. (Upper level white-collar positions typically require several interviews.) Apprenticeship programs usually require an interview, and many professional schools rely on interviews for admission. A few years ago New York University School of Medicine received over 4,000 applicants and eventually interviewed 1,500 people to fill 170 places (Kleiman, 1979). Some prestigious East Coast colleges employ alumni to interview prospective students. The interview is widely used despite the fact that it is not a particularly successful way of predicting future performance (Schmitt, 1976).

An interview is unlike any other interpersonal relationship. It is:

brief (seldom lasting more than 30 minutes);

impersonal (between persons who have no prior social contact and can anticipate none in the future);

competitive (applicants are usually competing against others for a limited number of openings);

dichotomous (interviewers are limited to a simple "hire" versus "not hire" decision);

contrived (the applicant participates with the intent to convey the best possible image, [to engage in "impression management"]; interviewers can anticipate

that candidates will attempt to convey an inflated, misleading, or even dishonest image); and
ambiguous (interviewers seldom have clear knowledge of the nature and requirements of the position.

It is a situation in which the interviewer must make judgments, and in the absence of complete information, can be influenced by many factors. Several consistent patterns of behavior in interviews have been identified by Neal Schmitt (1976).

Quick judgments.   It is clear that firm judgments are reached quite early in the interview and seldom change after that point (McGovern and Howard, 1978). Four minutes seems to be the average time required to form an opinion, confirming the importance of "first impressions."

Negative factors.   Interviewers tend to emphasize negative factors in arriving at decisions. Research shows it easier for them to explain their reasons for disqualifying candidates than to identify the basis of positive recommendations. Confronted with the need to make a dichotomous decision in an ambiguous and contrived situation, it is logical for interviewers to look for reasons to eliminate candidates; it is preferable to err on the side of disqualifying good candidates rather than accepting unqualified candidates, a mistake that would reflect badly on the interviewers' performance.

Visual clues: physical appearance.   It is certainly not unexpected, but it is important to note that physical appearance does influence judgments about candidates. Physical appearance encompasses things such as facial features, clothing, weight, and the wearing of eyeglasses. All other things being equal, physically attractive people are apparently at a distinct advantage in the interview process, especially in competition for jobs requiring face-to-face contacts with others (Dipboyle, et al., 1975). At a superficial level it suggests that in a society such as the United States which places such a premium on external appearances people will simply prefer attractive people over the less attractive. In one case, an obese woman was denied a position on the grounds that her physical appearance would be unpleasant for coworkers (Brophy, 1985c). She was, after protracted litigation, able to win employment, but the case does illustrate the very direct way in which physical appearance can work to an individual's advantage.

But the role of appearance is more complex than that for it also articulates stereotypes. The fact is that people tend to categorize others and attribute behavioral traits to them on the basis of visual clues. It is, for example, well documented that obese people are likely to be viewed as being less likable than people of average weight, and that taller people have an advantage over short persons. Thus, at the outset of an interview, tall, thin attractive candidates are at a subtle advantage over their less attractive counterparts because they convey the impression of having more desirable traits.

CASE STUDY: EYES RIGHT FOR SUCCESS

"Four eyes" is the term used by young children to taunt their peers who wear eyeglasses. Such juvenile antics apparently carry over into adulthood, for the presence of glasses, and their style, influence perceptions of people. A women wearing glasses is likely to be rated as less attractive, less sophisticated, more conventional and shy, and even more religious than the same person seen without glasses. In a recent study, undergraduate students were asked their impressions of a photograph of a woman (the same person in all cases) with different types of glasses (Ryon and Rosenblum, 1983). Rectangular plastic frames created an impression of independence and sophistication. Wire frames produced an even more pronounced impact on those characteristics and elevated perceptions of trustworthiness. Wearing outdated plastic frames influenced judgements of her warmth and friendliness. Perceptions of many specific traits are unaffected by eyeglasses, but those that are are might very well influence beliefs about the ability to perform some types of work.

In an ironic twist, gender and beauty may interact to produce negative consequences for women in competition for some kinds of work. In a still controversial study Heilman and Saruwatari (1979) found that attractiveness was an asset for males (compared to those equally qualified) in competition for any kind of job, and for females competing for secretarial work. However, when the job in question was managerial, attractive women were rated as less qualified and were less frequently recommended for the position. The authors suggest it is because beauty is equated with "femininity," which in stereotypical perceptions is linked to traits of indecisiveness, passivity, and other behaviors that would render a person a less successful manager.

There is thus a great deal of evidence to suggest that stereotypes operate to the disadvantage of women and minorities, especially in cases of ambiguity about the candidates and the requirements of the job. The clear message for recruiters and interviewers and employers is the need to specify job requirements and expand the work-relevant data on applicants.

Visual Clues: Nonverbal Behavior

Some interviewers see the interview process as a game—a dirty game—in which it is their job to catch candidates lying and misrepresenting themselves (Molloy, 1981:67). Not all interviewers have such a dismal perspective, but they certainly must be aware that it is a contrived situation, and that there is some deceit involved. Experienced recruiters claim that fully one-quarter of all resumes contain false—not just exaggerated—information (Brophy, 1985d). At the least, interviewers can anticipate that applicants will be presenting the best possible image by attempting to dress and speak well, maintain a good posture, and say the right things. Interviewers, especially experienced ones, will thus intentionally focus on nonverbal behavior for clues to such difficult-to-measure traits as maturity, motivation, and ability to work with others. To some extent, interviewers might also unknowingly be influenced by nonverbal behavior.

There is no doubt that persons coached in presenting a favorable nonverbal image (verbal presentation, eye contact, posture, smiling) have an advantage in interview settings. The issue is not whether some individuals perform better than others in interviews, for they certainly will, but rather whether gender and race and social class can place people at a nonverbal disadvantage in the interview process. The research in this area is suggestive rather than definitive, but it does imply that the differential socialization experiences of members of these groups can produce subtle disadvantages which handicap them.

People present a set of nonverbal clues, some of which have their origins in subcultural behavioral styles. If interviewer and applicant do not share the same subclutural origins there is the potential for misunderstanding and misinterpreting subtle behavioral clues. There is, by way of illustration, some indication that this is the case among black and white Americans. One area in which differences in subcultural styles are evident is *interpersonal space,* the physical distance separating people in normal conversation. White Americans tend to stand further apart than blacks, Mexican-Americans, and other ethnic groups (Shade, 1982). By unintentionally and unknowingly moving closer during an interview they can make a person uncomfortable and suggest an aggressive or threatening posture. Another visual clue of some importance is eye contact, or "interpersonal gaze" as it is called in the literature. Regular eye contact is interpreted positively among white middle-class persons, suggesting warmth and honesty. Again, the typical black style is at variance with the typical white style, with blacks making less eye contact. Even the casual conversation that some interviewers use at the outset of an interview can be interpreted differently and can inhibit communication. Blacks are likely to view inquisitiveness as an improper intrusion into a private area (Kochman, 1981:97ff.). These subcultural differences are especially invidious because they have the potential to affect the outcome of interviews at a level unrecognized by the participants.

CONCLUSION

Dramatic social changes occurring in the United States during the last several decades have eroded most of the legal barriers that deprived people of access to occupations on the basis of ascribed status such as race, class, and gender. The explicit exclusion of women from military combat roles is probably the last remaining vestige of such earlier practices in the United States. A popular media exercise is the celebration of "firsts"—that is, the first woman or the first black to enter previously closed careers such as astronaut, Supreme Court justice, vice-presidential candidate, or coal miner. The symbolic value of such milestones is inestimable, but the fact remains that large segments of the labor force continue to be segregated.

As people's lives unfold they are exposed to different experiences grounded in socioeconomic status, gender, race, and ethnic background. Such experiences shape their perceptions of the world of work and their place in it, and influence the actions they take. Occupational choice is simultaneously enacted in direct relationships with teachers and parents and others, with choices constrained by the deliberate and unwitting actions of gatekeepers that channel people toward certain careers and away from others. The idea of how the direction of careers are shaped in the dynamics of social interaction is nowhere more evident than in the interview process.

The application process attempts to screen candidates on several criteria, the most obvious being technical abilities. Does the candidate have the prerequisite education, skills, and abilities to fill the position? This can largely be assessed by the review of credentials. Less easily measured are the subtle attitudes and traits that are also considered important; judgment, loyalty, reliability, responsibility, and the ability to get along with coworkers. Many employers have, in recent years, turned to lie detector tests and drug screening programs to augment conventional methods. The legal and ethical issues are as yet unresolved. After having successfully negotiated the application process, individuals confront the task of learning to work.

TWELVE
Learning to Work: Patterns of Socialization and Learning

INTRODUCTION: TYPES OF SOCIALIZATION EXPERIENCES

Learning to work can involve an infinitely rich variety of different experiences. Police work, for example, combines: formal classes on subjects such as law and departmental regulations; fire arms practice on the pistol range; casual observation of informal police routine while on patrol with senior officers; indoctrination and subtle tests of the ability to perform under pressure; and learning to cope with the temptations of "graft." Experiences such as these combine to produce the technical and cognitive abilities and the values and attitudes required of the role of police officer, as well as the social skills necessary to function within the subculture of policing.

These disparate socialization experiences can be divided into three broad categories. First there is the *formal training*, which takes place at the police academy and on the pistol range as instructors convey specific occupational knowledge and enforce official rules and norms. Second is the less formalized *on-the-job training*, which takes place between the recruit and senior patrol officers in the patrol cars and on the streets. This differs from the first in that it occurs in the real work setting and it is here that newcomers are made aware of the unofficial norms that characterize any occupation. The term *directed socialization* may be applied to both these types since some specific individuals are responsible for transmitting and evaluating occupational skills. A third type of learning experience occurs in both these settings and in others. It will be called *experiential learning* in the sense that even in the absence of directed training, recruits learn a great deal by observation, trial and error, and through interaction with criminals, the public, and the courts. Each of the three types brings the new member of an occupation into contact with different kinds of instructors, involves different kinds of relationships, and rewards different kinds of abilities.

Formal Training

The term *formal training* can be used to identify work-related socialization, which has two specific characteristics. One is that it occurs under the direction and guidance of a specific individual (or group of individuals). These persons are representatives of the occupation and have the responsibility for passing on some fairly well-defined body of knowledge and/or skills and evaluating the progress and performance of people in the program. They occupy the role of "teacher." Examples are the faculty of university-based professional schools (law, medicine, engineering, management), commercial schools (secretarial, funeral directing) training academies (police, military), and company-sponsored training schools (pilots, managers, salespersons).

Those in the programs are expected to play the role of "student." The overriding requirement of this role is the mastery of subject matter demonstrated by passing tests or by accumulating a specified number of experiences. Pilots must thus acquire specific hours of flight time and barbers must complete some specific number of haircuts, shaves, and shampoos (Woods, 1972). A second, and sometimes equally crucial aspect of the student role calls for learning appropriate attitudes and demeanors. This varies among occupations but usually requires manifesting a commitment to the career and a positive attitude toward learning. It may be a question of impression management as much as actual learning, as suggested by the process in a nursing school:

> It was the business of the (nursing) students, given the aspiration to be professional persons, not only to become, but also to convince the faculty they were becoming professionalized. (Olesen and Whittaker, 1968:150)

It is evident that teachers are the single most decisive agents of control. They control resources that determine success both during the socialization stage (that is, grades, financial aid, knowledge) and later in access to the membership stage (references, sponsorship, postgraduate appointments). Hence, faculty individually and collectively define the technical and intellectual operations as well as the social and attitudinal aspects of the career. The faculty also define the sequencing of the educational process since they are required to certify success at each succeeding point in the education.

This is not to imply that it is only teachers who are important during the process of formal training. Other students—usually the more senior ones—comprise another potential agent of control. Senior students possess information that is important for both the learning process and for adopting the student role. Their experience is a resource that can be negotiated in return for deference or may be more freely given in a spirit of camaraderie. In some cases, such as in military academies, upperclasspersons are delegated a formal and central role in socializing recruits.

The second key aspect of formal training programs is that they take place at a physical location removed from the actual work site. Such places are often traditional classrooms with books and lectures and films. In rare cases they are simulations of real-work conditions such as flight simulators for pilots or combat-training courses for soldiers. However, it is not the site *per se* that is important, rather it is the fact that socialization is physically separated from the context in which the work will eventually be practiced. Thus, students do not have the opportunity to observe and experience the actual intricacies of the job and to anticipate routine problems and acquire the necessary experience. Academy-trained police officers may be surprised to discover they have not been prepared to:

> communicate effectively with the public, make complicated investigations, write lengthy technical reports, be subjected to real verbal and physical altercations, mediate disputes . . . make unsavory arrests . . . and testify in court. (Drummond, 1976:17)

There are instances where formal training is intentionally segregated in order to provide intensive socialization free from the contaminating influence of the social environment. It is a pattern found in the military and in preparation for careers in religious orders. In other instances a discrepancy may evolve because formal training is in the hands of a full-time cadre of faculty operating in an organizational environment that articulates a different set of tasks and objectives and that employs criteria of performance that do not apply among regular practitioners. University or hospital—based medical faculty may, for example, be oriented toward and rewarded for the creation of new knowledge (research and publication) rather than the application of existing knowledge. As a result physicians trained in research-oriented urban hospitals may find their schooling emphasizes the study of esoteric acute illness to the neglect of a concern with the case of ambulatory patients who will comprise the overwhelming majority of their work if they enter private practice (White, 1973:9).

Formal training can lead directly to a job in the occupation, as is the case with engineering, accounting, or law. There will be a period of additional socialization within the specific employing organization, but completion of the training program formally certifies the individual as a member of the occupation. Formal training can also lead directly into a period of on-the-job training. This is the case with physicians, pilots, and police officers. In addition, training for a wide range of occupations commences on the job.

On-the-Job Training

In on-the-job programs the individual occupies a role that may be labeled "trainee." Trainee experiences can be anywhere from lengthy, formalized and well-institutionalized apprenticeships (such as in the case of printers, plumbers, plasterers) and management training programs, to the brief, informal and spontaneous socialization that takes place in much secretarial, clerical, and production work. Unlike the student role, the trainee works with senior members of the occupation directly in the actual work setting; there is no physical discontinuity between the trainee and the setting in which the occupation is performed. This does not, of course, mean that no physical, social, or psychological distance intervenes between the individuals and their environment. Physically, neophytes may be assigned to an out-of-the-way space. For example, brand new high-steel workers are limited to the ground (Haas, 1974), apprentice butchers are relegated to meat wrapping machines (Marshall, 1972), and beginning salespersons may be located in the most inaccessible departments. It is common for trainees to be socially isolated from more senior colleagues. They are seldom accepted as fully fledged members.

As Howard Becker (1972) has noted, informal on-the-job training programs are more likely to place the initiative for learning upon the trainee. In contrast to the student role where the individual must navigate a predetermined program with content and sequence elaborated by teachers, the trainee role is relatively more unstructured and open-ended. A myriad of potential learning opportunities exist, and it is the responsibility of the trainee to take advantage of these situations by observing, questioning, and practicing. In a real sense trainees are expected to define their own "curriculum," and have the opportunity to choose the people who will do the teaching. The instructor plays a role that is best described as "tutor."

On-the-job training is a socialization experience rewarding assertiveness. More assertive trainees are likely to learn more simply because they take advantage of a greater number of learning opportunities. Moreover, it is apparently common for senior members of the occupation to believe that it is only the very best trainees who will press them; if the trainee does not push, "he probably does not have what it takes" (Becker, 1972:100). This ideology stands in stark contrast to the situation with respect to the role of student where it is acquiescence rather than aggressiveness that is most likely to be rewarded.

Responsibility for socialization and for the important task of certification of the acceptability of new members is widely dispersed. Any or all senior people may function as tutors. Responsibility is collective, residing with the group. This is evident in occupations where any given individual's rewards or success is partially contingent upon the performance of coworkers. Such interdependence is salient in team sports (hockey, football), collaborative performance occupations (musicians), and those where there is danger and risk (police work, mining, the military, high-steel iron workers). In these occupations group members assume an unusual role in the socialization process.

"Students" usually depart from schools armed with formal knowledge, but lacking an understanding of the subtleties of the real work. Thus, part of on-the-job training involves unlearning some of the things learned in school. The police recruit typically departs from the academy with formal training in the legal code, emergency medical services, self-defense, care and use of firearms patrol procedures, report writing, and techniques of criminal investigation. These do not fully prepare the rookie police officer for the field. An academy instructor admits, "There are tricks of the trade we can't teach you in the academy, but you'll learn them." (Harris, 1973:87). This is confirmed by contact with more experienced officers who tell them that in order to become "real police officers" they will need to forget everything learned at the academy (Niederhoffer, 1967:44). To facilitate this transition many police departments assign rookies to veteran (and in some cases specially trained) officers for additional on-the-job training.

One of the main things the police recruit learns is the group norm of "complacency" (Van Maanen, 1973). It is not aggressive performance that is encouraged, rather it is to develop a low profile. As one veteran puts it,

> The only way to survive on this job is to keep from breaking your ass . . . if you try too hard you're sure to get in trouble. Either some civic-minded creep is going to get outraged and you'll wind up with a complaint in your file, or the high and mighty in the department will come down on you for breaking some rule or something and you'll get your pay docked. (Van Maanen, 1973:415)

Aggressive law enforcement—whether strict adherence of traffic laws or assertive investigative procedures—merely escalate the visibility of the police and increase the possibility of complaints, and is therefore discouraged.

The discrepancy between formal training and the demands of actual practice may reflect a conscious division of the subject matter between academic knowledge and practical knowledge. This is most typical in the science-based professions. It is assumed (and is probably true) that cognitive skills can best be learned in an educational institution. This training provides the student with the foundations of basic knowledge and skills that are necessary for the job, and the actual application skills are subsequently developed in the work setting.

Experiential Learning

The third type of learning may be called experiential in the sense that it involves the acquisition of work-related skills and abilities without anyone providing direct instruction. People may learn merely by observing the work of others around them, or by a process of trial and error. This is the major form of learning in some occupations. Railroad workers are, for example, specifically channeled in this direction. They ride the trains and are admonished to read the manual, to watch, and to learn; questions are actively discouraged (Kemnitzer, 1973). This pattern is also common in unskilled occupations that are perceived as not requiring any special skills, and among household workers who are expected to have acquired their skills prior to taking a position.

Casual, experiential learning is not, however, limited to occupations at the bottom of the skill hierarchy. It is an integral part of the work role of all occupational groups. Practicing attorneys report that most of the major competencies necessary for the effective practice of law were acquired on their own after completing law school (Zemans and Rosenblum, 1980). Included on this list are such basic interpersonal skills as interviewing, oral expression, and negotiation, and research skills such as fact gathering and the capacity to marshal and organize facts. This may, in part, be attributed to institutional flaws in contemporary legal education, but it also serves to highlight the fact that no directed socialization program can possibly offer experiences in all the capabilities necessary to perform in the world of work. Casual learning provides the opportunity to learn by experience, and some things are best learned by that method. Casual learning also provides individuals with the opportunity to construct and negotiate their work role in a manner consistent with their own needs and capabilities.

PATTERNS OF SOCIALIZATION

The process of learning to work is typically a combination of more than one of the three types. Different occupational categories exhibit some fairly clear patterns as suggested by Exhibit 12:1, although the definition of learning experiences does not exactly coincide with the terms used here. In addition, because the research is somewhat dated, the proportion requiring formal training has probably increased. Overall, 30 percent of the workers report having had some formal training for their present job. Over one-half went through some on-the-job program, and over 40 percent de-

EXHIBIT 12:1   Types of Socialization among Occupational Groups

Occupational Group	Percentage Reporting the Job Learned by . . .*			
	Formal Training	On-the Job Training	Experiential Learning	No Training Required
Professional	65%	67%	33%	2%
Managerial	36	57	56	4
Sales	23	60	47	8
Clerical	54	71	30	2
Crafts	41	65	48	2
Operatives	13	62	43	9
Service	25	46	43	14
Unskilled	7	40	51	18
Farm work	20	18	80	8
All workers	30	56	45	8

Source: *Formal Occupational Training of Workers.* U.S. Department of Labor, Formal Occupational Training of Workers. Washington, DC: Government Printing Office, 1964, p. 18.
*Percentages exceed 100 percent because people could select more than one form of socialization.

pended upon experiential learning. Only 8 percent claim that their jobs required no training whatsoever.

Socialization for the professions and clerical occupations is most likely to require formal training, either as part of the curriculum of secondary or university education or within professional schools. Both require abilities that are presumably best developed in a context of the classroom. In the case of clericals, skills presented best in a formal setting include office management, typing, dictation, and shorthand; in the professions, it is the body of specialized technical knowledge that is best taught in the classroom. Such training is typically supplemented by on-the-job training where abstract theory or technical skills are applied in concrete situations and where trainees can develop abilities that cannot be taught in a formal setting. The careers of physicians progressing through medical schools, internships, and residencies illustrate the process. Even after this burden of directed socialization in the medical profession there remains some learning that must be left to the individual—but it does comprise a smaller part of the total learning process than in any of the other occupational categories.

In contrast, on-the-job training and experiential learning is the primary source of job skills in managerial, sales, service, and semi-skilled work where careers typically begin with field training under the tutelage of a senior worker followed by a period in which recruits are expected to develop their own skills. Salespersons, for example, are often assigned to train with experienced people who can explain and demonstrate the elements of an effective "sales pitch." Armed with the knowledge of the senior salesperson, new workers are then expected to refine their personalized skills by working on their own.

In unskilled and agricultural work individuals acquire the most significant skills without direct socialization. A major factor is that the basic required traits are common manual abilities. It can be noted that these workers frequently report that no training is required. The learning that does take place is largely individual adaptation to the job in the form of learning the most comfortable and efficient method of performing routine physical tasks.

Socialization involves more than the acquisition of the techniques required to perform mental or manual tasks. Jobs are embedded in a subculture of work that may be viewed as a customary and traditional way of thinking about and doing things that is generally accepted by members of the work group and the organization. Thus, it is equally important that recruits learn the meanings, attitudes, norms, and beliefs shared by fully fledged members of the occupation. This subculture is transmitted both passively by simple exposure to the language, myths, and symbols, and more actively by training, encouragement, social pressure, and sanctioning. The goal of socialization is to integrate newcomers into the group without disrupting established work procedures.

Socialization into work subcultures is a complex, multifaceted process directed at introducing changes in orientation, attitudes, and behavior. The content of socialization varies with the nature of the work, but it is possible to isolate several fundamental patterns that show up consistently. All occupations require some *resocialization,* a reorientation of basic values and perspectives, ranging from the dramatic as seen in the military to more modest changes found in most other occupations. A second process may be called *neutralization,* that is, reconciling self-images with social images of the work. Testing for *trustworthiness* is found in some form in virtually every occupation. Finally, there are problems of assuring *compliance* with occupational norms, and learning when to *evade* them.

RESOCIALIZATION IN TOTAL INSTITUTIONS

Resocialization in the Military

The most intense directed socialization is found among occupations that require the assimilation of entirely new perspectives and the development of new attitudes. The transition in the military is, for example, summarized as a transition from "civilian" to "soldier," suggesting the need for a radical commitment to unique ways of thinking and acting. The term *resocialization* is often used in such cases to emphasize the military recruits' need to unlearn a whole set of civilian perspectives; the resocialization process is also readily evident in religious occupations where the "secular" life must be abandoned. Socialization for such occupations typically takes place in what Goffman (1961) has called *total institutions*—military training camps, convents and seminaries, as well as prisons and mental hospitals. They are "total" in the sociological sense that virtually all aspects of the recruits' lives can be defined, controlled, and programmed. An examination of the process in the military is instructive, but the same process, differing only in scope and intensity, can be observed in occupations such as police work, law, medicine, science, and others which demand a dramatic restructuring of attitudes and behavior.

Social and physical isolation.   Successful adoption of a radically new or different social role is facilitated by socially separating people from competing roles. To the extent that old roles are rendered obsolete the new role becomes more salient. Consequently the military career typically begins in the physical isolation of a "boot camp" behind a chain link fence or within the walls of a military academy. The nonmilitary world is excluded, usually to the extent that even phone calls and visits from civilian friends and relatives are prohibited or severely reduced. Social contacts are limited to the impersonality of the mails, which helps to explain why letters generally take on an added significance. Severing personal linkages weaken the salience of old roles such as son or daughter, husband or wife, as well as that of private citizen.

Suppression of previous roles.   For the military, it is also routine procedure to suppress all outward signs of previous identities. Standard uniforms replace civilian clothing that carries implications of social class, education, regional origin, wealth, and personal style. Economic inequalities are leveled by the prohibition of displays of personal wealth. Haircuts of a single type eliminate the expression of style or individuality. Even the postures and gestures we use to signify individuality are stripped away and replaced by standardized positions and measured paces. Finally, the most personal of possessions, *names*, are eliminated in favor of terms such as "swab" or "boot" or "recruit." The individuals, and those who interact with them, are left with few clues to their identity in the nonmilitary world.

A substitute privilege system.   As recruits' ties to a civilian identity are being challenged a new framework of rules and rewards—a new system for earning privilege—is instituted (Goffman, 1961:48). At first it may be rigid and punitive, as expressed by a drill sergeant:

> Recruits must stand at attention at all times. Recruits will not eyeball. Recruits will double time everywhere. Recruits will do nothing without permission; they will not speak or swat bugs or wipe sweat or faint without permission. Recruits will call everyone, except other recruits, "Sir." Recruits will never use the word "you" because "you" is a female sheep and there are no ewes on Parris Island. Recruits will never use the word "I" because "I" is what a recruit sees with, not what he calls himself. (Warner, 1972:46)

Such systems serve to confirm to the newcomer that the institution has control over the most trivial dimensions of behavior; the system begins to offer guidelines for the construction of a new identity acceptable to those controlling resocialization. The destruction of old identities renders recruits more receptive to acceptance of new roles. Conformity brings rewards; deviance elicits punishment. Obedience is central to a military model of organization aimed at developing a chain of command capable of efficiently executing orders.

Solidarity.   Learning obedience and the formal rules of behavior is only one aspect of socialization. Equally vital is the need to develop a sense of solidarity—to form a cohesiveness among people in the military who will be called upon to live, work, and possibly fight and die together. Solidarity is fostered by a number of means. In part, it emerges from the very sharing of the degrading experiences of training camp. Military uniforms and endless drill in the lore and history of the unit also contribute to a sense of unity. Symbolism is also employed, especially those surrounding important events. For example, sailors who are promoted can expect an elaborate and boisterous chase and ritual capture ending with a dunking in a barrel of cold sea water. In exchange, the sailor must offer cigars to the captors (Zurcher, 1965). On the surface it is a trivial event, but it symbolizes participation in a distinctive subculture.

Another device emphasizing a shared destiny is the American Army tradition requiring that officers and drill instructors share some of the same rigors as the recruits. They share meals, suffer the same obstacle course, and later endure the same combat risks. A sense of solidarity is imperative in work demanding cooperation during periods of severe stress. It begins to emerge during training camp when recruits spontaneously come to the aid of stragglers on long marches by carrying their weapons, equipment, or even physically carrying them (Warner, 1972). This feeling fits well with the reality of combat situations where the most prized virtues are reliability and dependability.

Modern military organizations are based on the premise that they can function effectively only if members are willing to sublimate personal interests and personal safety to broader tactical objectives by fostering a sense of dedication to the organization and its objectives; this is done by first weakening old loyalties and then replacing them with a new identity and set of values centering on the military.

Elements of Total Institutions in Other Occupations

Radical transformations in orientations are not limited to the military. Countless occupations depend upon some radical transformation and a sense of commitment to the work and other members of the occupation. Resocialization attempts to produce an active affective involvement with the job including internalization of the group's goals and values, identification with the interests of the group, and a feeling of loyalty or attachment to the occupation. Committed individuals are expected to sacrifice personal motives and priorities to the requirements of the work role. Elements of resocialization are found in occupations dedicated to serving vulnerable clients (nurses, clergy, social workers), occupations directed toward broad societal functions rather than narrow economic interests (the military, teachers, scientists, government officials) or those responsible for the lives and welfare of others (law, medicine), and finally in occupations organized around collective rewards (musicians, athletes in team sports).

The law student must, for example, learn to "think like a lawyer," which involves taking an analytic, dispassionate, impersonal stance toward human relations. There may be no fences around law schools (or medical colleges or police academies) but students are effectively segregated from competing influences. The physical location of buildings, classrooms, and libraries isolates them from other students. All classmates are other people preparing for the same occupation. The demands of time needed to study slowly constrains their interaction, cuts them off from friends and relatives. Law students come to think of themselves as "One Ls," a separate and distinct group.

Faculty control the usual academic resources of grades—which are powerful because they are the only route to successful completion of the program. Faculty are also the source of references for jobs later. Study groups are formed, later supplemented by participation in on-the-job experiences (mock trials among lawyers; ward rounds among medical personnel), and faculty share lunches with students, all contributing to building a sense of solidarity with the profession.

The transition is a slow, subtle process. Law students undergo a definite change in orientation toward social relationships. For example, one student, while buying a hamburger, found himself wondering if he had entered into a legal "contract" with the clerk (Turow, 1977). Later he reported having domestic problems with his wife centering on the problem that he could no longer even engage in an argument like a regular person; he realized he chided her for being too emotional—a human trait, but one that has no place in "thinking like a lawyer."

FACILITATING ACCEPTANCE OF UNDESIRABLE ROLES

Techniques of Neutralization

As a general rule, the probability of successfully socializing new members of any group is enhanced if recruits perceive the group as having desirable characteristics or if membership is consistent with their own self-image. People tend to be reluctant to adopt the standards of groups with which they do not identify.

Occupations can be viewed as undesirable for two main reasons. One is simply that people are recruited into jobs for reasons other than voluntary choice. It may be a matter of chance, or opportunity, or failure to achieve preferred careers that causes an occupation to be defined in an unfavorable light. The undesirability of an occupation may be a question of discrepancies between aspirations and attainment. Occupations are also rated as undesirable because of discrepancies between the nature of the work and dominant societal standards and values.

Low status can be ascribed to occupations for a number of reasons. Illicit occupations such as prostitute, bookie, drug dealer, fence, or burglar are in this category (Cullen and Link, 1980). Other occupations, although not in violation of the law, violate community standards of propriety. Carnival workers (Easto and Truzzi, 1974), dance musicians (Becker, 1963), and pool hustlers are examples. Dirty work is, almost by definition, undesirable; these jobs include garbage collectors, prison guards, janitors, and some aspects of police work. Finally, many occupations have low status for no reason other than they are viewed as requiring no skills or offering no substantial rewards.

It is not uncommon for low status occupations to develop an ideology that repudiates the conventional standards and judgments that stigmatize the work, or an ideology that discriminates against members (Becker, 1963:38). This ideology becomes part of the occupational subculture and is transmitted during the socialization process. The term *techniques of neutralization* (Sykes and Matza, 1957) has been used to describe the varied strategies employed by a group to rationalize and justify its particular form of work and minimize and explain departures from conventional standards. These techniques provide legitimation and meaning for the group's work and can also serve the useful function of allowing people in the occupation to reconcile discrepancies between their own self-images and public definitions of "deviance."

Prostitution, whether male or female, is generally illegal and, even where it has been decriminalized, remains a disreputable form of work. The words of a woman in a commercial sex massage parlor convey the dilemma:

> At first I couldn't look at myself as a prostitute, everyone knows a prostitute is the lowest form of human life. But then I just couldn't deny the facts, it was me out there, the real me out there, taking money for sex. I guess that's prostitution. (Rasmussen and Kuhn, 1975:274)

It is not uncommon for men and women in America to have internalized the dominant standards of morality, and to have confronted the problem of being in a deviant career. The transition is facilitated by exposure to an ideology of prostitution during their socialization. Prostitutes are conventionally divided into several groups. "Streetwalkers" operate, as the label suggests, in public to make arrangements with potential customers. Socialization is usually provided by pimps and seldom extends beyond learning methods of controlling customers during preparation for the sexual encounter (Gray, 1973). Virtually all other aspects of the work are acquired by experiential methods.

House prostitutes work on an appointment basis either in their own residence or in those of their customers. Contacts are made by phone and they may have a regular clientele. Socialization is carried out usually by other prostitutes who either tacitly assume responsibility for the training or more formally accept it at the instigation of a pimp. Occasionally, the pimp himself supervises the training. It appears that the process takes women approximately 2 or 3 months to complete (Bryant, 1965). During this time the recruit is taught specific technical skills such as handling telephone arrangements, physical and sexual hygiene, techniques of assuring payment, and developing a clientele.

"Massage parlor" prostitutes work within specific establishments and hence are integrated into relatively stable work groups which include more experienced women (Velarde, 1975). The managers, who have a vested interest in developing commitment among their employees, also take an active role in socialization. As a consequence of the structure of the work situation, these prostitutes are in frequent and intense interaction with senior representatives of the occupation.

Neutralization is a complex process that facilitates acceptance of a marginal occupational role by providing a conceptual and attitudinal structure that explains, legitimizes, justifies, and rationalizes the work and the motives and goals of those in the occupation.

Denial of responsibility.   Recruits into low status occupations must confront the dilemma of disreputable work. One way of doing this is to deflect responsibility away from the individual by emphasizing forces and incidents over which they had no control, but which were decisive in directing them into these careers. This can thus relieve them of some responsibility for having to engage in degrading work. Studies of female prostitutes reveal this tendency. Large numbers claim to have been the product of broken homes, and rejected by parents (Greenwald, 1969). A street prostitute who ran away from home at age twelve neatly fixes blame upon a parent:

> All the kids used to think that my mother loved me more because she never hit me and let me do what I wanted, but if she had been stricter I wouldn't be in the predicament I'm in now. (Schenker, 1979:1H)

Denial of injury.   Members of illegal or deviant occupations may claim that their behavior does no harm and in fact may be therapeutic. Within the subculture of prostitution this technique takes the form of emphasis upon the important psychological and social functions of their work (Hirshi, 1962; Bryant, 1966). The women stress that they give emotional and physical satisfaction to men who would otherwise be denied because of isolation, interpersonal ineptness, physical deformity, or the failures of their regular partners. This idea can then be carried a step beyond, suggesting that prostitution deters rapes and other crimes having their origins in frustrated sexual drives, or can, in fact, help to salvage marriages that might otherwise fail.

Condemnation of condemners.   Subcultures of deviant or illegal occupations frequently confront the members of society that condemn them by turning criticism back upon their critics. This takes the forms of charges of hypocrisy or inconsistency or challenges to the validity of such judgments. A prostitute expresses this view when she challenges the right of other women to judge her:

> . . . actually all women are whores in my opinion whether they get married for it or whatever it is. There are just different ways of being a whore. (Bryant, 1966:444)

In the early 1970s prostitutes organized into lobbying groups for the express purpose of challenging the legitimacy of the morality that condemns prostitution. One such organization is called COYOTE (Come Off Your Old Tired Ethics).

Denial of the victim.   The subculture of prostitution involves certain forms of exploitation of customers—relationships are cultivated in order to assure regular business, nothing is given, except for a price, sexual pleasures are simulated, and prices can be inflated. The customer is a victim in this sense, although he is a consenting adult and a party to his own victimization. But another dimension of neutralization involves transforming the client from victim to a wrong-doer and deserving of exploitation. Men in general tend to be degraded in the socialization process and are labeled with negative characteristics (Bryant, 1965). Prostitutes are taught that men are corrupt, stupid, and exploitative. It is pointed out that their customers include husbands cheating on their wives and moralists betraying their publicly stated values. And prostitutes are frequently warned of the men who will cheat them out of their fees. It is only appropriate that men be exploited as they exploit women.

Appeal to different loyalties. In addition to rejecting the standards of the larger society the subculture can seek to provide a substitute reference group. That group is typically the occupational community itself. The result is emphasis upon internal loyalty and solidarity within the group. To quote a pimp who stresses the isolation from the larger society and the importance of prostitutes,

> So when you ask me if I teach a kind of basic philosophy, I would say that. Because you try to teach them in an amoral way that there is a right and wrong way as pertains to this game . . . you teach them that when working with other girls to try and treat the other girl fairly because a woman's worst enemy in the street (used in both a literal sense of where they work and a figurative sense of the whole society) is the other woman and only by treating them decently can she expect to get along. . . . Therefore the basic philosophy I guess would consist of a form of honesty, sincerity and complete fidelity to her pimp. (Bryant, 1965:92)

Each of these techniques is evident during the training of prostitutes. Not enough is known at this point to be able to determine whether it is a conscious or an unintentional strategy. It does however make sense as a logical response by a group defined as deviant by some segments of American society—a group that generally lacks the power to alter deep-seated values and beliefs. The ideology helps to bring legitimacy to an illegal occupation, and for individual women entering the trade probably facilitates the transition from the straight world into the occupational world of prostitution.

Negative Aspects of High-Status Occupations: Dentistry

Even high status occupations may have negative aspects, or be perceived as having a negative image. For example, dental college students have generally felt that the public believes that they are merely oral technicians who cause pain and charge excessive fees. One student summarizes this view in a single sentence: "The average guy thinks you are an overcharging, sadistic mouth plumber" (Quarantelli, 1961:168). In the process of socialization students are exposed to a subculture and an ideology that allows them to accommodate this image.

Denial.   The image of a dentist as a mere technician is directly confronted and rejected by students and practitioners in the field. Education stresses the position that dentistry is a medical specialty concerned with a part of the total health of clients. The dominant theme is, therefore: Dentistry is a separate and independent health service whose services are essential to total health. At the occupational level this has taken the form of attempts to enlarge the role of dentistry to include the diagnosis of oral cancer as well as a focus on preventative care rather than simple restorative work.

Displacement.   The pain and discomfort associated with dental work has always been a problem for the profession. At various times the profession has emphasized "painless dentistry" as a means of neutralizing this undesirable feature. In dental schools pain is accepted as a natural part of the process, but responsibility is shifted to the patient. It is they who must accept the blame for allowing their teeth to deteriorate to a point where pain becomes an inevitable side effect of treatment.

Acceptance.   Another aspect of neutralization takes the form of accepting the undesirable features of the work as necessary to achieve larger broader goals. Discomfort and high costs are something that patients must accommodate in the short run if they desire long-term oral health. Pain is necessary to restore teeth to good condition; fees are most reasonable considering the expertise, training, and experience of skilled dental practitioners. Thus, some unflattering parts of the work are merely accepted as inherent in the nature of the service being provided.

MEASURING TRUSTWORTHINESS: FEAR AND TRUST ON THE HIGH STEEL

Cooperative endeavors are part of work routines everywhere. People need to rely upon the performance of coworkers in order to accomplish their own goals. It is nowhere more evident than in high-risk occupations such as mining, lumbering, and police work; consequently, it is not uncommon to find new workers being called upon to demonstrate their trustworthiness as a prerequisite to acceptance into the work group. Trust has a special meaning in hazardous occupations where a worker's error or failure can cause physical harm to others; but measuring trustworthiness is not limited to them—it is a matter of concern in all forms of work.

Danger and risk typify the work of the high-steel construction workers who erect the metal skeletons of modern high-rise buildings and bridges. They are called upon to negotiate narrow, 4- to 8-inch steel beams in all sorts of weather (Haas, 1972; 1974; 1977). There is the constant hazard of a fall from great heights caused by a gust of wind or by a misstep or miscalculation of their own. Such risks are compounded and intensified by the fact that the mistakes or foolishness of their coworkers can also endanger them. These workers confront a shared and collective risk daily. Consequently, it is imperative that they can depend upon and trust one another.

Dependence upon peers and shared physical risks are a routine attribute of the work of miners, lumberjacks, police, fire fighters, and military personnel, as well as the construction trades. In each, the question of trust occupies a central role in the everyday routine and is the dominant issue in the socialization process. Apprenticeships are carefully structured so as to provide a careful induction into situations that will reveal trustworthiness, and apprentices are subjected to an ongoing series of provocations designed to test their reliability. The career of the apprentice high-steel worker is organized into several well-defined stages.

Sponsorship.   In practice, questions of reliability and dependability are part of the process of selection and acceptance into the apprenticeship program. Access is greatly facilitated if the applicant is sponsored by a relative or current member of the trade. All groups benefit from this form of nepotism, albeit for different reasons. Contractors who employ high-steel workers are guaranteed a supply of interested and committed workers. The union is assured a stable and homogeneous group of recruits. Current members have an advantage in getting their children and relatives into the occupation. From an occupational perspective, sponsorship means that these members have already been screened; they are people who have had direct personal contact with representatives of the occupation, have an awareness of the problems and demands of the work, and have some sensitivity to the importance of trust.

The "punk."   The first phase of the actual apprenticeship program involves working as a "punk." During this stage recruits are taught, observed, and tested to determine their acceptability. In the very first days they act as "fire watchers." The professed object of this task is to survey the site from the ground and be alert for fires started by sparks from welding materials. The latent function of this job is to allow the new apprentices to familiarize themselves with the work tasks on a first-hand basis. They are expected to observe, to practice, and to learn. Soon the apprentice is called upon to punk for the journeymen high-steel workers. At first this involves no more than locating and distributing tools, equipment, and materials, but it does cause apprentices to walk the beams above ground. The testing begins in earnest at this point.

Fear is a normal part of the job. It is taken for granted, but the apprentices learn they must demonstrate the ability to overcome, or at least, control their feelings. Workers who allow fear to dominate them cannot be trusted for the simple reason that they may act rashly or irresponsibly or tentatively. Those who are fearful simply cannot be trusted because they endanger others who are dependent upon them. A high-steel worker speaks to this point:

> most of these guys know what they're doing, but you get some of the f————— apprentices, like that guy over there who's scared up here, and you really got to watch yourself, because you don't know what the hell they're liable to do. (Haas, 1977:154)

Apprentices learn they must prove themselves to be unafraid. Many seem to deliberately flaunt their courage by volunteering for the most dangerous work. Those apprentices who display fear are ridiculed and ostracized.

Controlling overt displays of fear is only one aspect of the testing that apprentices must endure. Workers must also know how newcomers will respond to crises. To gauge the apprentice's poise, self-control, and trustworthiness they are subjected to a persistent barrage of verbal abuse and provocation. There are obscenities and racial and ethnic slurs; their masculinity and sexual prowess are impugned. The senior workers are testing the apprentices' ability to maintain their self-control under pressure. It is assumed that if individuals lose control under verbal attack, they may also lose control in threatening situations on the steel beams where they could endanger the lives of others. Apprentices who show they can conquer their fears and endure the verbal pressures without breaking gradually win group acceptance. With approval comes the right to exchange verbal abuse with the journeymen high-steelers.

With group approval comes the freedom to assume more responsibility and undertake new tasks. The system allows apprentices to develop at their own pace and is a clear instance where the trainee with initiative can learn more and develop more rapidly. However, it is only after winning social approval that the apprentice begins to acquire the technical and mechanical tasks of the high-steel worker—bolting, welding, cutting.

Making scale.   The transition from "punk" to full-fledged ironworker is marked by "making scale," earning the same pay rate as journeymen. It is granted to any workers—whether or not they have completed the full 3 years of the formal apprenticeship—who have proved they can do the job. Doing the job involves both mastering the technical requirements and commanding the trust of coworkers.

The career of the apprentice high-steel worker illustrates the process of socialization among workers in dangerous occupations where personal risk can be increased by the inappropriate action of coworkers. In such jobs it is imperative that they be able to trust one another. As we have noted, trust is won by demonstrating the capacity to control personal fear and by maintaining poise in the face of verbal provocation, for these are the traits of persons who can be depended upon. Those who do not measure up do not win group acceptance. However, trust is a tenuous thing and can subsequently be destroyed at any time by some act that endangers others. The problem of loss of trust is manifested in the reactions of journeymen who have inadvertently done something such as dropping a tool or bolts which fall near those working below. They immediately leave the job site and never return! They understand they can no longer be trusted within this particular group and move on to some other location.

CONTROL AND COMPLIANCE

Police Work: An Ethos of Defensiveness

Occupational performance requires compliance with some established norms of behavior. Direct supervision by superiors can contribute to this, although it is impossible and inefficient to constantly monitor activity in all situations. All workers have periods of discretion when they are free from direct observation and accountability. Discretion is greatest in professional and managerial occupations. A significant degree of discretion is also available to people in occupations such as patrol police work, which takes place on the streets away from direct supervisory control of administrative officers. In discretionary situations, socialization may take the form of developing attitudes that encourage voluntary compliance.

Police work in a democratic society is an example of an occupation where compliance is especially crucial. The very nature of policing causes it to be highly susceptible to criticisms from the public and powerful groups. The most visible functions of police officers center on controlling criminal activity and mediating noncriminal conduct (crowd control, domestic disputes, traffic). In the process, any unwise use of their authority, the law, tactics, language, weapons, or physical force can generate media exposés, public complaints, political intervention, budget cutting, and other attacks upon the autonomy of the department. Police work is circumscribed by an elaborate set of procedures covering conduct in the field. There are rules for handling domestic quarrels, making routine auto checks, handling crowds, and making arrests. These procedures must thus be understood as a mechanism of limiting discretion to protect the individual officer and the department. Control and compliance is thus crucial to the continued functioning of the organization.

Intentionally or not, compliance is fostered by a socialization process—both in the academies and during field training—that inculcates the idea that the police must operate in an environment of hostility, suspicion, and distrust. This perspective has been described as an "ethos of defensiveness" (Harris, 1973). It is only by strict adherence to policy that street officers can protect themselves from physical danger and protect themselves and the department from public criticism, citizen complaints, civil suits, and criminal prosecution.

At the policy academy recruits are introduced to the dominant perspective, as in this address by a senior officer,

> You will gradually come to think in terms of two worlds, theirs (the general public's) and ours, and you will come to recognize and accept the bitter fact that the average law-abiding citizen views us with a certain distaste. He feels it is his constitutional right to abuse us verbally. But you, on the other hand, must not return that hostility. We set you up, in your blue uniform, as a target for every crackpot and nut around. You are identified, you are a public servant, and the public expects service from those on its payroll. Accept this as part of the price you must pay for the job you do. Accept it and the fact that you are alone when you are working and the only guy who will stick his neck out for you is another cop. Don't expect anything else from anyone else—it will not be forthcoming. (Uhnak, 1963:32)

Recruits are repeatedly warned of the risks and dangers of police work, the importance of conformity to procedure, and the threat posed by certain groups. Films and lectures single out the cases of police killed when unwary officers had failed to observe the correct procedure. They are admonished, "Walker (an officer shot and killed during a routine check of a driver's license and registration) made one mistake, and it cost him his life. You must make suspicion a condition of habit; it must be first nature" (Harris, 1973:44). Thus, the recruit is explicitly encouraged to approach the public with distrust.

Moreover, specific groups are singled out as posing special threats: politicians tend to infringe upon police prerogatives; the media tend to distort events to discredit police; female offenders present problems because lawyers tend to deliberately circumvent the law to protect clients; and judges tend to lack clear moral standards (Harris, 1973:47–102). These stereotypes further reinforce the positive value of treating outsiders with suspicion. Distrust of the media and the courts rise dramatically during academy training (Niederhoffer, 1967:234–35).

Departments monitor individual behavior by requiring detailed written reports. Each recruit must learn to keep a daily log; field reports are required for virtually every event: arrests, accidents, stolen cars, discharging weapons, missing persons, and so forth. It is a means of checking on compliance, and the instructions are explicit, as is the warning:

> Be legible; print if you have to. Don't abbreviate; avoid erasures in any form. Just draw a line through it. That's the way an auditor corrects his books. You show you haven't hidden anything. You wait till a defense lawyer sees an erasure. He'll make you feel so high, no matter what your intentions were.

It is not surprising that a recruit comments:

> You feel like you're not trusted all the way down the line. (Harris, 1973:35).

Thus, recruits leave the academy with a strong feeling for the need to follow procedures in order to protect themselves in a hostile environment.

Because police work occupies a highly visible and ambivalent position in American society it is frequently viewed with suspicion or outright hostility. The very symbols of the office—the uniform, shield, nightstick, gun, and summons book—are enough to stimulate confusing responses (Niederhoffer, 1967:1). The result of this is that the work is especially vulnerable to criticism. The collective response has been to standardize behavior and seek to limit individual discretion by establishing proscriptive rules of behavior, closely monitoring routine actions by maintaining close radio contact, and requiring written reports that permit retrospective identification of deviations from standard procedures. Compliance is encouraged by the threat of sanctions, and by emphasizing the hostility of the environment.

INSTITUTIONALIZED EVASIONS

Aircraft Assemblers and the Tap

Rules are part of every job. Some are introduced by the employing organization. Bureaucratic rules have many functions, one of which is to limit the areas of worker discretion in the interests of ideals of efficiency and productivity. In practice, such rules are destined to prove inadequate or inappropriate. They are inadequate because they typically define behavior in routine situations, although it is impossible to anticipate every contingency or make provisions for simple deviations from the conventional. And they are inappropriate because they may be unrealistic or unnecessary. Workers persistently confronted by problems with official work rules are likely to develop institutionalized adaptations or evasions that become part of the informal on-the-job socialization of new workers.

A common component of the industrial assembly process of any large product—whether an automobile, an aircraft, or a refrigerator—involves bolting parts together (this section draws upon the work of Bensman and Gerver, 1963). Engineering standards demand accurate alignment among the parts so that they fit snugly and are easily and neatly fastened together. However, mass production techniques sometimes result in deviations from perfect alignment—bolts do not exactly match with nuts. One response to this condition is to interrupt the assembly process to correct the alignment—which can be a lengthy and expensive solution. Another alternative is to employ a tool called a "tap," which can be used to cut new threads into a nut. This thus allows for the fastening of slightly misaligned parts. But this modification also means the product violates strict engineering specifications, and the use of taps is for that reason illegal. Yet in an aircraft factory in New York at least half the assemblers owned one, and initiation into the methods and norms of usage played a central role in the socialization of new workers.

The norms of tap use prescribe when it should be employed, when it is inappropriate, and the techniques of use. Workers learn that tapping is acceptable only when it is absolutely necessary to complete the task. Most new workers are introduced to the technique by senior workers only after all other legitimate attempts at alignment have failed. It is a last resort! Not to use the tap is unwise for it will limit the productivity of the workers, and ultimately threaten their jobs. On the other hand, indiscriminate use would seriously violate standards of production. The proper use of the tap is enforced by subjecting the offending worker to ridicule and reducing the worker's social standing in the work group. Frequent use suggests carelessness and incompetence and will result in being labeled a "botcher." In contrast, those workers who can get their work done with only infrequent use of the tap are referred to with respect as "mechanics."

The norms also prescribe that tapping be concealed from the inspectors, although inspectors are fully aware of what is going on. Technical instruction in the use of the tap by senior workers and foremen are accompanied by lectures and warnings which emphasize that the worker is doing something illegal and risks reprimand or dismissal if detected, despite the fact that it is common practice.

> The foreman warns the worker to make sure "not to get caught, to see that the coast is clear, to keep the tap well hidden when not in use, and to watch out for inspectors while using it." He always ends by cautioning the worker, "It's your own ass if you're caught." (Bensman and Gerver, 1963:591)

Even inspectors sometimes act to underscore the importance of the norm by taking a carelessly discarded tap and hiding it in a toolbox for a worker. Inspectors are willing to condone the use of taps so long as it is not done openly—which would mean trouble for them with their superiors since they are expected to prevent this practice. At various times this understanding between assemblers and inspectors is made explicit, as in this conversation:

> Now fellas, there's a big drive now on taps. The Air Force just issued a special memo. For God's sakes, don't use a tap when I'm around. If somebody sees it while I'm in the area, it'll be my ass. Look around first. Make sure I'm gone. (Bensman and Gerver, 1963:593)

It is apparent that the tap is seen as necessary for assemblers to accomplish their work within reasonable time limits considering the constraints imposed by less than perfect materials. It is imperative that newcomers be socialized to conform to a pair of norms that permit continued illegal use of taps. Workers must learn to use them sparingly and not to flaunt their behavior. It is only by adherence to these norms that workers can depend upon continued leniency by the inspectors who are in the position to strictly prohibit taps. Inspectors understand the assembler's problems and are willing to condone this institutionalized evasion so long as they can be reasonably sure that workers will maintain high production standards and not cause trouble for them with their superiors.

SOCIALIZATION IN NON-TRADITIONAL OCCUPATIONS

Women and men embarking upon careers in occupations not traditionally associated with their gender confront unique problems. Women in police work, and men in nursing, are examples of nontraditional work. Those who pioneer in nontraditional occupations are highly visible because their numbers are small. Kanter (1977:206–42) defines people in this situation as "tokens" and points out that being in the minority has important consequences. Highly visible because of their rarity, they are subjected to unusual scrutiny. This means that mistakes or errors are more likely to be noted and remembered. Their presence also emphasizes differences between themselves and members of the majority. Finally, responses to their behavior may be distorted by preexisting sterotypes. Consequently, "tokens" tend to feel that they are socially isolated (Spangler, Gordon, and Pipkin, 1978).

Pioneers may also encounter outright resentment from some, but not all, coworkers because of their sex. A sizable minority of women report various forms of harassment by male coworkers, ranging from practical jokes to threats of violence (Fox and Hesse-Biber, 1984:123). But it is important to note that research among women in nontraditional work has found that a majority of women feel at least some level of acceptance by most male colleagues (Jurick, 1982), and that some men prove to be especially helpful during the socialization process (O'Farrell, 1982). Coworker hostility is a major factor in producing job dissatisfaction (O'Farrell and Harlan, 1982). Generally, overt hostility declines over time, suggesting that the barriers are not insurmountable if people can endure resentment during the beginning of the career.

More complex difficulties arise from subtle assumptions and expectations that have evolved in response to the fact that the occupation has historically been the province of a single sex. Consequently, gender can produce barriers to socialization and hinder acceptance into the group. One of the most commonly encountered problems is that it is assumed (tacitly or explicitly) that nontraditional members will not possess the traits necessary to perform the roles. Women for example, have been in regular uniformed police roles (rather than administrative ones) since 1968, but many continue to confront resistance in specific departments. In one, strong opposition prevailed five years after women began doing patrol work (Martin, 1982). A major difficulty is that women in police work face the assumption that they do not have (and cannot develop) the one key trait necessary to win the *trust* of their male colleagues—physical strength. Male recruits enter academies observing and believing women are not as strong as men. Once there, they are exposed to socialization practices of emphasizing the hazardous aspects of police work, causing many male recruits to become preoccupied with danger (Charles, 1981). Moreover, they equate personal safety with physical prowess, despite the empirical fact that injury or death is seldom simply a matter of strength. Women experience and interpret the situation differently. They respond to the concern with danger by placing greater emphasis on interpersonal skills. Consequently, although women may score at least as well on tests, and may win the respect of their male counterparts for displaying courage and tenacity in physical contests, men leave the academy with an overwhelming preference for a male partner. And that preference is an expression of a subtle lack of trust, which continues out into the field (Remmington, 1981:168).

Thus, as individuals enter nontraditional occupations they experience problems not faced by others. They frequently report that they must work harder and perform better in order to be judged as an equal, and this is probably an accurate appraisal of their situation. In addition to acquiring the requisite skills and abilities they must confront either outright disbelief or the more invidious assumption that their gender experiences have placed them at a disadvantage in the more subtle and difficult to measure traits required of the work that are being tested during socialization.

CONCLUSION

The analysis of specific practices identifies some of the kinds of socialization involved in initiation into work roles. The saliency of undesirable or negative attributes of jobs can be neutralized by an occupational ideology offering a rationale providing legitimacy and allowing the individual to reconcile discrepancies between their self-image and public images. Commitment to the occupation is enhanced when competing loyalties can be reduced. Testing for trustworthiness allows members of the occupation to assess and anticipate the future reliability of recruits in stressful or dangerous situations. Compliance with group norms is encouraged by creating attitudes fostering conformity even in the absence of direct control. Finally, institutionalized evasions provide group-sanctioned methods of dealing with unusual problems.

THIRTEEN

Occupational Careers: Training and Testing

INTRODUCTION: CAREERS IN THE ORGANIZATIONAL CONTEXT

Work in organizations is typically arranged into formal careers in the form of a succession of roles demanding different tasks and responsibilities and graded in terms of increasing income and prestige. In some organizations careers form a definite and fixed sequence. The military, airline pilots, and academic careers are among those exhibiting well-established patterns. For example, at most American universities new faculty must progress from assistant professor, through associate professor to professor, completing their careers as professor emeritus. Promotion is determined by formal criteria, and standard timetables regulate progression from one role to another. Virtually every faculty member who embarks upon an academic career must follow this path. (Of course, a proportion opt for other occupations while some are involuntarily terminated; some others are stalled at a given level; and yet another group develop alternative careers in research or administration.) Not all careers are so neatly defined, graded, and structured. At the other extreme are indeterminate careers where the paths are loosely linked, criteria are vague, timetables uncertain, and opportunities for promotion severely limited or nonexistent.

Occupational careers can be examined from two different perspectives (Schein, 1971). A *subjective* approach focuses upon individuals as they move through these positions considering their experiences, expectations, perceptions, and attempts to cope with and control the process. In contrast, an *organizational* approach focuses upon the social structure of organizations as well as the objectives, perceptions, and expectations of decision makers (that is, people who hold formal and informal positions) that allow them to define these roles and manage movement through them. These two approaches complement each other, and both are necessary for an understanding of the structure and dynamics of occupational careers.

The Subjective Dimension

People embark upon occupational careers with a configuration of dreams, aspirations, and expectations forged from the interaction of their social origins, status characteristics, pre-occupational history, and socialization experiences. Each holds some vision of what the job entails and how to perform it. Most hope to be able to improve their position over time by earning increased income, prestige, and responsibility. Aspirations are realized or frustrated within the context of a preexisting and ongoing structure articulated by senior persons who control movement through the system. Subjective careers are thus to be understood as a process of behavioral and attitudinal adaptations to experiences and progress through administrative career paths.

Workers, of course, are not simply reactive, but are also actors seeking to impose order and meaning upon the uncertainty and ambiguity of work situations. There is room for negotiation and for worker control of the process for they are not without resources, having the ability to withhold cooperation or ultimately abandoning the organization. Thus, subjective careers are also to be understood as attempts to construct and manage careers within organizations.

The Organizational Enterprise

Organizations as ongoing human communities are confronted with a recurring complex of personnel problems that must be resolved if the organization is to function. (This section draws upon the ideas of Sofer, 1970: Ch. 2). The constant movement of people into, through, and out of the organization creates the need for structures and procedures for recruiting, selecting, socializing, appraising, motivating, rewarding, and promoting people. As Edgar H. Schein (1971:415) has put it, "Those individuals who are in the organization as managers take the 'organizational' point of view, build[ing] perspectives in terms of the development of human resources, allocation of the right people to the right slots, optimum rates of movement through departments and levels, and so on." Therefore, work roles and careers (and promotions, transfers, performance appraisals, demotions, and terminations) have meaning that extends beyond the technical tasks. Using this perspective, employees tend to become viewed as "resources to be deployed" as well as human beings with interests and hopes and dreams and aspirations (Sofer, 1970:14).

Formal authority for such tasks is diffused among various hierarchical levels in organizations. Formal policy decisions regarding tasks such as training programs may be formulated at the executive level, specific departments (such as Personnel) are called upon for administration of specific activities such as performance appraisal, and every supervisor is a participant in the process to the extent that they are involved in the evaluation and training of subordinates. Thus, the organizational perspective cannot be said to be limited to any specific group, but rather reflects the collective concerns, behavior, and expectations of those managers responsible for the careers of their subordinates. The organizational enterprise involves two fundamental issues.

Training, testing, and evaluation Organizations must develop a pool of trained personnel to fill positions of greater responsibility as they fall vacant. To this end people will need to be rotated through a variety of positions in order to gain skills and experience necessary for performance in subsequent positions. Organizations are also concerned with questions of commitment and loyalty. Therefore, more or less stable career paths are developed as a means of training, testing, and evaluating people for the higher-level positions. For example, American military personnel being groomed for the rank of general are given assignments as intelligence officers, military attaches, and congressional liaison officers (Janowitz, 1960:166). In this sense, the series of jobs that make up a career path are a deliberately structured set of roles in which individuals are able to demonstrate competence and acquire skills assumed to be necessary for subsequent positions. Promotions and demotions are announcements of success (or the lack of it), and suitability or unsuitability for further advancement.

Maintaining motivation and morale Managers must also be concerned with questions of motivation and morale, and the movement of specific persons and groups of persons through careers may also be guided by such criteria—although not usually at an explicit level. Organizations must, for example, be sensitive to the need to maintain motivation and loyalty of those qualified personnel passed over for promotion and to find jobs for long-time loyal employees unable to handle certain jobs. Failure to deal with such issues can produce organization-wide job dissatisfaction and high levels of turnover, and can make it difficult to recruit new people. Consequently, career paths may include positions specifically designed for people who have failed at some earlier point in their careers.

INSTITUTIONALIZED CAREER PATHS AND ROLES

An examination of the flow of people through organizations reveals that movement is more likely to be patterned than random (Sofer, 1970:36; Martin and Strauss, 1956). There are usually well-traveled routes that link certain positions and that account for much of the mobility, or lack of it, within organizations. These sequentially ordered roles may be labeled *institutionalized career paths.* Karen Gaertner's (1980) data from public school districts in Michigan between 1968 and 1972 displayed in Exhibit 13:1 is used for illustration. Institutionalized career paths are not unique to educational administration, but rather typify the structures and processes of careers in large industrial, education, and financial organizations. There-

EXHIBIT 13:1   Career Paths in Public School Administration

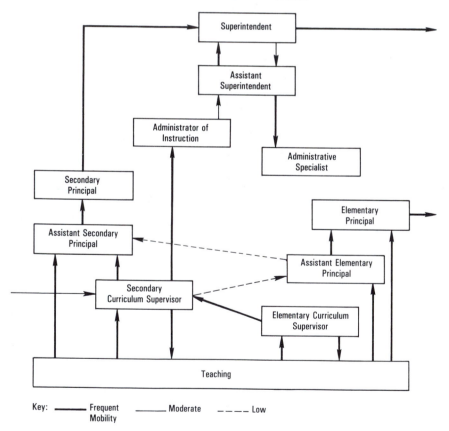

Source: Adapted from Karen N. Gaertner, "The Structure of Organizational Careers," *Sociology of Education* 53 (Jan. 1980), p. 17.

fore, it is an appropriate framework for the analysis of the career experiences of large numbers of workers.

Fast Tracks

Most organizations seem to have a *fast track*, a direct and rapid route to upper level positions reserved for people who have been identified early as having unusual potential and who are hence destined for continuous and rapid advancement. Colorful labels such as "officer material," "comers," "girl wonders," "high flyers," "fair-haired boys" or "water walkers" are applied to people who enjoy this designation. Kanter (1977:133) has estimated that approximately 10 percent of the managers in one corporation enjoyed this designation.

A fast track shows up on the left side of the exhibit. There is a direct, frequently traveled path from assistant principal (secondary school) to principal to superintendent. This pattern suggests that bright young teachers are identified as having administrative potential and moved into these positions where they can gain experience in administration, supervision of staff, budget management, and dealing with the public as well as having contacts with the superintendent and his or her staff. It is noteworthy that there is virtually no lateral or downward movement, suggesting that the only direction available is upward. Obviously not all administrators experience uninterrupted upward mobility, some people are stalled if for no other reason than there are fewer slots at each higher level.

Being placed on a fast track is a self-fulfilling prophesy. That is, these people are granted special experiences and opportunities and special treatment which guarantee their subsequent success. In one large industrial corporation (Kanter 1977:133–34), fast-trackers were given more frequent performance reviews (every year to 18 months compared to the usual 3 years), placed in positions with special experience or exposure, and were introduced into the network of senior, upper level decision makers. It also appears that location on the fast track resulted in greater tolerance of minor mistakes and errors in judgment. To use a sports analogy, "Super stars don't get as many fouls called against them." Fast-tracking also serves to reinforce attitudes that contribute to future success. Rapid mobility reinforces aspirations, work commitment, and organizational loyalty, which are major factors in future promotions.

Developmental Careers

The majority of people in organizations are on slower, more complex career paths involving a variety of training and assessment positions, plateaus and lateral movements, and even demotions. This pattern is illustrated in Exhibit 13:1 by focusing upon the only other successful route to the Superintendency. People who follow this route, like those on the fast track, start in teaching, and on the basis of expressed interest or some observed administrative ability, move first to curriculum supervisor (elementary school or secondary school). Either role usually combines teaching with administrative and supervisory tasks. It is an ideal situation for evaluating administrative potential among candidates with little or no previous practical experience. A few people become secondary curriculum supervisors on the basis of advanced degrees, with no practical experience. Competent performance in this role leads either to assistant principal (secondary) where they follow the same career path as those on the fast track, or to administrator of instruction, assistant superintendent, and then to Superintendent. Some people are also stalled in these lower level positions, never being promoted beyond administrator for instruction, suggesting that this is what will be called a plateau position.

Developmental careers also provide alternative options for those who do not demonstrate competence. Teachers recruited into the entry level position of curricular supervisor frequently return to the classrooms, either for reasons of poor performance or because they do not like administration. While it is, strictly speaking a demotion, the stigma is reduced by the administrative device of labeling curricular supervisor as a "temporary appointment" allowing a painless return to full-time teaching. A more clearly defined demotion is to the job of administrative specialist (including business, plant and facilities, personnel). Virtually all moves into this position are from assistant superintendent.

Low Ceiling Careers: Blocked Mobility

A third common form of career path found in organizations is characterized by an upper limit on advancement. The blocked mobility career path is found in elementary school administration. Teachers are able to achieve some upward mobility to the level of principal or assistant principal, but there is virtually no subsequent opportunity for advancement to any other position in the system. Those seeking advancement must achieve it by leaving the system for other opportunities. Similar situations are characteristic of secretarial careers and among nurses in hospitals.

CAREER PATHS AND TYPES OF ROLES

Work roles serve specific functions beyond the technical tasks involved. The actual work being done by a sales trainee, for example, may—from an organizational perspective—be much less important than the fact that the position gives supervisors the opportunity to train and evaluate the behavior of recruits. Virtually every organization utilizes *entry positions*, which are beginning level positions for new recruits where they may be trained and evaluated for future potential. In some ways this is the most important position in the career sequence. In Exhibit 13:1, curricular supervisor (elementary) serves this function. Aspiring administrators are recruited from the ranks of teaching or outside the system and given basic administrative responsibilities. Quite a few return to the classroom, but some are promoted to higher level positions.

Roles such as assistant secondary school principal function as *training positions*, providing candidates with the training, experiences, and social contacts considered desirable for performance in a subsequent position. A sports analogy is appropriate; training positions are the minor leagues of baseball or hockey, where athletes are "seasoned" by developing their skills on the way to the major leagues. After successfully functioning in training positions, candidates are deemed ready for more advanced positions.

Every position in a hierarchy offers the opportunity for evaluation by superiors, but certain positions seem to be more formally designated as *assessment positions*. Secondary curricular supervision is probably an assessment position where people are provided additional administrative responsibilities and evaluated for further advancement potential. Assessment positions also offer the opportunity for failure, and failures must be rotated somewhere out of assessment slots so that new cohorts of candidates will have the opportunity to demonstrate competence. The places they move to can be identified as *demotion positions*, and administrative specialist is one, representing a loss of income, prestige, and responsibility.

Plateau positions are reserved for persons who are disqualified from further advancement. The position of elementary principal is in this category, for it can be noted that there is virtually no upward mobility within the system, although some principals do move to other systems. Mobility may be blocked structurally by a lack of opportunity, by the mismanagement of people, or by personal incompetence.

Any given position may, of course, serve more than a single function. Assistant superintendent is one such role. For different candidates at different times it is: a training position for future superintendents; an assessment position for other candidates; a demotion position for unsuccessful administrators; or a plateau for the stalled. As will become evident, the ambiguity of certain roles has important positive consequences.

BREAKING IN: ENTRY POSITIONS
IN ORGANIZATIONAL CONTEXT

The first day of work in a new occupation—whether as raw recruit, participant in an on-the-job training program, or fresh from a professional school—begins a period which may be called the "breaking-in" stage of the career. Employers attempt to break-in new workers in the sense of molding them to the needs of the occupation through socialization into the social and technical requirements of the role. Breaking-in is considered accomplished when individuals demonstrate both a mastery of job skills and adoption of appropriate subcultural values and attitudes, which is measured by acceptance by coworkers and superiors.

The duration of the breaking-in stage tends to be counted in terms of days or weeks among the very narrow repetitive jobs characteristic of much blue-collar work. It is a much more lengthy process among occupations requiring experience, or the mastering of complex tasks, or those in which ability is difficult to assess. School teaching is such an occupation; it commonly involves a 3-year trial before a person can qualify for tenure. There is no clear timetable among occupations such as police and high-steel work, which demand something as ambiguous and hard to define as trustworthiness. Successful completion of this stage may be marked by some ceremony or ritual acceptance, such as bestowing "wings" on pilots, or it may merely be tacit to the acceptance of allowing the recruit to do the same work as a senior member.

From the vantage point of the organization entry positions are part of a training and probationary period. It is commonly assumed that newcomers have no real understanding of the role. This is perceived as especially true of those who come from some training school and must therefore "unlearn" some of what has gone before. Therefore, on-the-job experiences tend to be arranged to provide gradual introduction to the requirements of the job under the watchful eyes of more senior members who can observe their progress and judge their "suitability for admission." Those who can demonstrate their competence will be rewarded with expanded responsibility and pay, while those unable to meet these criteria are discouraged from continuing or are more directly terminated.

People in this position are called "rookies" or "punks" or "greenhorns." Each term connotes ignorance and lack of experience as well as emphasizing the fact that they have yet to achieve full membership status. A more neutral term might be *novice*. Novice roles are organized to provide opportunities for learning and for observation. Often, the novice period starts with a span of free time given over to observing senior people acting as role models. Railroaders are relegated to the caboose to watch others and to study training manuals, a task requiring the greater part of several months (Spier, 1959). High-steel workers are free to observe and learn during most of their duty (Haas, 1974). Machine operators and assembly line workers may have no more than a few minutes to understand the basic elements of a job before taking it over.

The more common strategy is to assign the novice to act as helper or assistant to the senior person. Management trainees, rookie cops, apprentices in the construction trades, are all initiated into their new jobs in this manner. These senior workers become the first role models for the novices.

In the case of the trades, these senior persons tend to be the most skilled and the most experienced—those with the greatest insight into the workings of the subculture and thus, those who have the most to offer. Yet, in the construction trades (which are typical) novices must "serve time" (as they put it) doing mostly hard, boring, dirty work. Novices run errands, carry the heavy materials, do the simple uninteresting jobs. Although mastering routine tasks is no guarantee of the ability to handle more complex tasks, ineptness is certainly cause for doubt about the capacity to assume greater responsibility.

While frustrating to the novice, it must be remembered that this is a probationary period, one that provides superiors with a structured opportunity to evaluate some important traits—traits that cannot be determined from resumes or in brief employment interviews. Although workers may not be fully sensitive to the implications of performance in entry positions, four traits are generally being evaluated. One is simply basic work habits (whether sloppy or neat, thorough or slipshod, meticulous or careless). A second is dependability—the ability to follow orders and work without supervision. Third is initiative, a willingness to learn and assume additional responsibility, but tempered by an awareness of inexperience. Finally, workers' social traits, such as the ability to relate to coworkers, are considered. The negative implications of not performing well on any of these traits should be obvious.

Entry positions can thus be decisive. Impressions created during the first few months on the job can determine both the direction and the kind of a career a person can anticipate. Images of a person as friendly, cooperative, or bright—or hostile or slow to learn—will influence and shape interaction with superiors and coworkers. Moreover, it is during the entry stage that preliminary decisions about fast tracking are made.

BREAKING IN: SUBJECTIVE RESPONSES

Reality Shock

People going to work for the first time are confronted with a bewildering array of unfamiliar demands and experiences—novel sights and sounds, new people, esoteric norms, strange jargon, and intricate social relationships. Those with a previous work history enjoy the advantage of experiences offering some preparation, but since each job has its unique features, even workers with experience encounter an unfamiliar situation. And since it is impossible to enter gradually, the change is dramatic and abrupt. This led Hughes (1958) to attach the term *reality shock* to this experience.

Recruits must assimilate, interpret, sort, and organize a vast array of new stimuli. They must "make sense" out of the situation, differentiate between the important and the irrelevant, reconcile reality with preconceived notions, and negotiate some attitudinal and behavioral framework enabling them to function in the job. The agenda ranges from the trivial (locating the rest rooms) through the practical (when to have lunch, the appropriate length of coffee breaks) and the social (how to deal with the boss, how to get along with coworkers) to the technical—the correct manner of doing the work (Van Maanen, 1977:16). It is a period demanding major behavioral and attitudinal adjustments, and for many, these adjustments cannot or will not be made; in some organizations the turnover rate during the first year approaches 50 percent (Kotter, 1973:91).

Demonstrating Competence and Social Acceptance

There are two immediate problems facing novices. One is the need to acquire the general competence necessary to perform the job, including not only the specific manual and mental skills, but also the formal and informal norms and values of the occupational group. The other is to gain acceptance into the subculture of coworkers, superiors, and subordinates by convincing them of the novices' ability, dependability and trustworthiness. It is a question of breaking into the job *and* the work group. The two processes are not independent, since senior persons are the source of information and insights that are absolutely essential to doing the job and ordinarily will be shared only with those who have earned social acceptance. For example, effective functioning as a nurse depends upon knowledge of the personal styles and idiosyncrasies of physicians; this information is only selectively passed on to those who have earned the trust of the senior staff (Kotter, 1973).

An important aspect of breaking in is learning to "look" and "act" like a member of the occupation. Part of becoming a dentist, executive, or electrician is having the appropriate tools, wearing the correct costume, and adopting the jargon of insiders. The evolution of an apprentice electrician is marked by the successive adoption of tools, speech, and attire (Riemer, 1977). Apprentice electricians typically begin by carrying many more hand tools than anyone else. Gradually, extraneous tools are discarded and those that are used tend to be the same brand name favored by journeymen. At the same time, ever greater numbers choose to wear bib overalls of dark blue denim. Color is a significant feature of the overalls: painters usually wear white, while carpenters select the blue and white striped version. Use of the technical jargon of the trade also evolves as the recruit begins to understand and use the technical dimensions of the trade.

Adoption of these external attributes are important for they are part of the criteria senior persons use in gauging the progress of the socialization process and in making judgments about the acceptability of rookies.

Acquisition of technical jargon is considered a prerequisite to participation in the group because individuals must be able to communicate with one another. The selection of tools is perceived as an emerging awareness of the superior quality of particular brands, which in turn reflects greater technical sophistication. Attire may have more symbolic than substantive meaning. Although bib overalls have some practical advantages as an insulator against inclement weather and providing pockets to carry tools, occupational clothing also serves to identify the occupation as suggested by the unusual significance attached to color. Clothing thus can be taken as an indication of increasing commitment to the group.

The symbolic importance of overt behavior and external appearance is frequently noted in managerial and professional occupations. It is no coincidence that virtually all aspiring young executives or lawyers tend to dress alike, because appearance is relied upon as an indication of being the "right sort of person" (that is, trustworthy, dependable, predictable) for advancement in the absence of any clear criteria (Kanter, 1977:48).

It appears that the quest for social acceptance dominates the first few months on the job. Research indicates that it takes an average of 3 months to "feel accepted" by coworkers (Feldman, 1976). Prior to that, an accounting clerk reports that she felt "like an orphan, hoping someone would take me in." A radiology technologist complains, "I've been here two months, and even now I don't feel accepted . . . I worry about my relationships with other workers all the time . . . This worry drives out concern for patients, for work, for everything" (Feldman, 1976:66). Being accepted by superiors and coworkers provides access to both the informal information necessary for effective performance and the emotional support and sense of self-esteem offered by social contacts.

Confronting Unmet Expectations

People enter careers with preconceived notions about the work. Expectations center on specific features such as pay, working conditions, and responsibilities as well as more general ideas about opportunities for personal achievement and advancement. Pre-entry expectations emerge from occupational stereotypes, experiences in the schools, and even the recruitment process. The reality of the job as it is perceived and experienced during the entry stage may not conform to expectations. Consequently, while some newcomers express satisfaction, it is not uncommon for people to suffer frustration, disillusionment, or a sense of anomie which can produce lasting attitudes and perspectives.

Occupational stereotypes.   Members of a society develop stereotypes or ideal models of occupations from a variety of different kinds of data. These grow out of media presentations of people at work. Everyday interaction brings people into contact with people in teaching or service occupations (waitresses, barbers, police, retail sales). Beginning sometime in the middle school years, youths are exposed to job descriptions created by vocational counselors, the government, and occupations themselves. The composite of information people have may be realistic and accurate, but it is just as likely to be a partial or distorted portrayal, seldom encompassing an awareness of the social and attitudinal dimensions of jobs. It may also involve grossly distorted expectations. Consequently, people may not be prepared for what they encounter. Police work is a good example.

Analysis of recruits to police work indicates it is viewed as an occupation offering the opportunity to do something that is important and meaningful in the community (Van Maanen, 1973). In addition, there is anticipation of adventure, drama, excitement, and even an element of danger. Many recruits have previously held other jobs and decided upon police work as an alternative to the routine of clerical or factory work. The shock of street reality confronted while training with senior officers frequently disappoints such expectations. There is always the chance of an exciting episode—"a good bust"—but the vast majority of time is devoted to paper work, routine patrol, traffic matters, settling domestic disputes, and handling crowds. Then, too, there is the "dirty work" of processing drunks and the victims of auto accidents and domestic violence. The public is often unappreciative or hostile. The discrepancy between expectations and reality must certainly contribute to the marked changes in attitudes that occur during the entry stage when a sense of cynicism toward the department develops (Niederhoffer, 1967:239) and there is a notable decrease in commitment to the organization (Van Maanen, 1975).

If there is any single major shortcoming of occupational stereotypes, it is that they are too simplistic and narrow. By focusing upon the technical operations and ignoring the social stereotypes, people are seldom prepared for the complex interpersonal dimensions of the work. Clerical workers in a hospital accounting department are a case in point (Feldman, 1976). Most people anticipated the work would entail simple information processing tasks (such as typing, billing, correspondence, key punching). In fact, the job—like most clerical jobs—had an interpersonal dimension for which most were unprepared. In this case it involved dealing with patients, lawyers, accountants trying to unravel payment problems or errors.

Schooling. The structure and experiences in schools, especially professional and technical schools, can unintentionally create expectations destined to be frustrated in practice. As students, people become accustomed to a clear, well-defined, unambiguous career path. Education is organized temporally around definite class periods, semesters, vacations, and academic years all neatly marked off in relatively short units of hours, days, and weeks. Student activities in each unit of time are likely to be limited to specific areas of responsibility defined by textbooks, lectures, and reading lists. The criterion of performance is the grade point average, and progress is measured by the accumulation of credits and specific courses. Graduates, accustomed to the school routine are usually unprepared for the ambiguity of the breaking-in process.

New workers frequently find it difficult to assess their progress, or even the criteria being used. This is because the early socialization process simply does not follow a rational and highly structured path with clear and unequivocal criteria. It is a more subtle process depending upon tacit evaluations that people have difficulty verbalizing. Most steel workers would be unable to indicate the basis of judgments of trustworthiness, just as most managers would be unable to explain the criteria for acceptable performance except in the most global terms. An exception is poor performance, which is quickly sanctioned simply because it is easier to identify, when a person makes a mistake or violates a norm. One of the most common complaints of new workers is that they only get feedback for poor performance, never for good performance (Feldman, 1976). The result is that new workers are often left without a clear indication of their progress toward acceptance. It is a much different situation than that experienced as a student, where the transcript is an unambiguous statement of how well one is doing, what one has accomplished, and what one has left to do.

The substance of pre-occupational training also produces unrealistic expectations. Managerial, technical, and professional personnel are usually unprepared for entry positions as administratively structured. Because entry positions are considered training and probationary roles, most recruits consider themselves technically overqualified for the tasks they are assigned. A bitter and frustrated MBA laments:

> My job is very boring. All I'm doing is routine financial analysis. This work could be done by a high-school graduate with a calculator. They didn't tell me in the MBA program that I'd be doing this routine work. We spent our time in the program discussing cases with important problems to be solved. (Dalton, et al., 1977:24)

This is a typical problem for business school graduates, because curricular emphasis is placed on topics such as the solution of executive level problems involving grand corporate strategy, leadership, and rational decision making. Business graduates develop expectations anticipating the utilization of such skills, but they obviously are not the kinds of assignments that management personnel assume upon entry. It is much more likely for them to be assigned to routine tasks until they can prove themselves. This has consistently been documented as a major problem in studies of recent graduates who report unrealized expectations about advancement, personal development, assuming responsibility, and the value of "theoretical" knowledge (Schein, 1964; Webber, 1976). In contrast, recruits are unprepared for organizational emphasis on conforming, taking on company values, and the ability to work in groups (Kotter, 1973). This mismatch can produce dissatisfaction and hinder the mutual accommodation of worker and organization. The more disillusioned are more likely to leave, contributing to the high turnover rate during the first year.

Recruitment.   The recruitment process itself can contribute to the creation of unrealistic expectaions about the occupation, at least among those embarking upon managerial and professional careers. Corporations, law firms, accounting agencies, all compete for graduates of professional schools. Students most likely to be recruited are those who already have high expectations as a result of their academic accomplishments and recommendations, and the nature of the recruitment ritual can unintentionally encourage even higher expectations about the kinds of work they can anticipate. For instance, when elite law firms execute their annual search for talent, they woo recruits with the illusion of immediate wealth, power, and success. Enticements include expensive gifts; entertainment at the best restaurants, hotels, and clubs; meetings with illustrious lawyers; and starting salaries approaching $50,000 per year. Impressions created about the job do not coincide with reality. New associates often spend the first year doing routine law library work and writing briefs and must usually wait 5 or 6 years for elevation to partner—and in the long run only one in ten can hope to become a partner in the firm.

Moreover, the role of "recruiter" encourages the creation of unrealistic expectations. Recruiters are employed to attract people and the dominant criteria for judging their success will be the number of persons placed. Pressure is placed on them to stress (or even exaggerate) advantages and ignore (or even conceal) the less desirable features of careers. Whether intentional or not they too can raise the aspirations of people entering the organization and contribute to the high attrition rate.

Summary

In some ways, entry level positions are the most difficult phase of the career. Previous experiences seldom prepare new workers for the situations they must confront. The physical and social environment itself is novel, producing a degree of reality shock. In addition, there are the demands on the entry-level worker to learn the job and the intricacies of the subculture while superiors and coworkers observe their behavior and demeanor using criteria and timetables which may not be clear to the novice. This can be compounded by the fact that novices may be disappointed when the job is not consistent with expectations formed prior to entry.

After approximately 6 months new workers begin to feel that they have mastered the technical aspects of the job and are competent to do the work (Feldman, 1976). It is, of course, a personal milestone, and not necessarily an evaluation shared by superiors. As a general rule newcomers are anxious to progress more rapidly than they actually do, to assume more responsibility than the organization is willing to grant, and to complete the informal "newcomer" phase of the career before this acceptance is achieved (Van Maanen, 1975).

Thus, the entry phase is fraught with the potential for dissatisfaction and frustration caused by a discrepancy between subjective and administrative careers. Workers seldom are prepared for, or apparently even understand, the largely informal expectations surrounding the entry position. Consequently, it is a period of high attrition and—for those who remain—a point at which some long-lasting negative impressions are formed.

PERFORMANCE APPRAISALS

Most organizations of any size depend upon some kind of regular performance appraisal to evaluate their employees. Mostly widely used is some variation of a 5- or 7- or 10-point rating scale, anchored at one end with "unsatisfactory" and at the other with "outstanding." Superiors are required to rate their subordinates on such generalized traits as effort, productivity, cooperation, and attitude. More elaborate techniques such as BARS (behaviorally anchored rating scales) translate the ratings into more specific tasks, and the choices for "effort" might range from "unlikely to complete tasks within a reasonable time," to "completes assignments on time." A still more sophisticated technique used for professional and managerial personnel emphasizes results rather than behavior. MBO (management by objective) calls for supervisors and subordinates to work out specific, agreed-upon goals, which can be measured at a subsequent evaluation session.

Despite their universality, there is widespread dissatisfaction with the instruments, the actual evaluation session, the outcomes—the whole process is, as one observer puts it, "a periodic agony thrust upon both bosses and subordinates" (Rice, 1985:31). Dissatisfactions and frustrations surrounding the performance appraisal have numerous sources. Participants often disagree over objectives or misunderstand the intent of the rating scale. The evaluation session is not an event many people enjoy, and many would prefer to avoid it. And, at the conclusion of it, there are residual feelings that neither party has accomplished what they had hoped for.

At an abstract level, it is easy to argue that an appraisal system should be able to meet the needs of both organization and employee. Ideally, they should be able to facilitate the organization's need to control and motivate, to encourage effective performance, and to utilize worker skills. At the same time, they should be able to address the individual's need to understand the official view of their work, their chances for advancement and rewards, and ways in which they might improve their performance (see Lawler, Mohrman, and Resnick, 1984). In practice, the structure of the situation mitigates against successful and meaningful evaluations.

The Performance Appraisal Session

Perhaps the most interesting observation that can be made about performance appraisal sessions is that frequently superior and subordinate cannot even agree on whether or not it has taken place! (Lawler, Mohrman, and Resnick, 1984). When appraisal sessions are more formalized, they tend to be announced on short notice, or subordinates report they are unlikely to cover what they had hoped and do not last as long as the subordinate would like. This may mean that supervisors are taking a casual, even cavalier, approach. Or it may suggest that it is an unpleasant encounter that they would much prefer to avoid, but because they cannot, rush through with a minimum of direct contact.

Neither party is generally satisfied with the process or the outcome. Exhibit 13:2 is the graphic presentation of evaluation sessions in a Fortune 500 firm, which asked appraiser and subordinates to indicate the items that should be covered and the extent to which they actually were. The data highlights the fact that the participants share goals, but also have different perspectives. It is agreed that the appraisal should do two things: document performance and suggest areas of development (items 1 and 3). However, subordinates place greater emphasis on the opportunity for input (item 2), the relationship between appraisal and pay (item 4), and mutual planning (item 5). Clearly, workers are expressing the desire for a more direct link between appraisal and salary and to use the sessions for more give-and-take about their roles. Considering the lack of agreement over some major objectives, it is not unexpected that neither party recalls the session as being particularly effective. It is only on the matter of documenting performance that they express any consensus. Subordinates are much more disappointed with the outcome than the supervisors (see also Mount, 1984).

There is also the potential for disagreement over the specific tasks to be evaluated. Consensus is more likely where work roles are clearly defined, usually in clerical and production work. As the amount of discretion increases, so too does the opportunity for uncertainty. For example, managers and their superiors in British factories, when asked to identify their areas of responsibility, could agree on only an average of 57 percent of the tasks, and there was even less concurrence on their relative priority (Dew and Gee, 1973:60–61). One pair of responses is illustrative:

EXHIBIT 13:2 Performance Appraisals: Desired Versus Perceived Outcomes

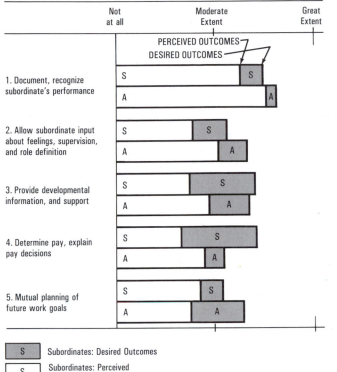

	S	Subordinates: Desired Outcomes
S		Subordinates: Perceived Outcomes
	A	Appraisers: Desired Outcomes
A		Appraisers: Perceived Outcomes

Source: Adapted from Edward E. Lawler III, Allan M. Mohrman, Jr., and Susan M. Resnick, "Performance appraisal revisited," *Organizational Dynamics* 13 (Summer 1984), figures 3 and 4.

Superior	**Subordinate**
1. Production schedules	1. Quality standards
2. Quality standards	2. Production schedules
3. Minimizing waste	3. Minimizing shut-downs
4. Budget control	4. Accident prevention
5. Minimizing overtime	5. Absenteeism; lateness
6. Absenteeism; lateness	
7. Accident prevention	

The manager responsible for performance appraisal used more tasks, several different tasks, and different priorities than the person being evaluated.

Discrepancies within Performance Evaluations

One consistent finding that emerges from research in this area is that subordinates tend to rate their own performance at a higher level than do appraisers (Ilgen, et al., 1981; Lawler, Mohrman, and Resnick, 1984). It is a perfectly understandable tendency for people to have a high opinion of their effort or even to inflate it somewhat. However, this finding is even more striking when it is noted that there is some evidence that superiors tend to inflate the scores of their subordinates, meaning that the "actual" discrepancy between appraisals is even greater than that recorded on the official forms. Apparently, appraisers are reluctant to cause the pain associated with low evaluations. They may also believe that inflated ratings will reduce the potential for conflict and confrontation among people they will have to continue to supervise. Then too, they may lack confidence in the rating scale and be sensitive to the legal implications of evaluations. The organizational position of the supervisor may also encourage inflated ratings; low performance ratings would reflect badly on their ability to manage and motivate.

There is no effective way to measure the gap between "actual" and recorded evaluation by superiors, but the observed gap between raters and workers remains to be explained. One of the most widely discussed is *attribution theory* (Green and Mitchell, 1979). This theory focuses upon the inferences people make about the causes of behavior. When confronted with poor performance, observers (in this case, appraisers) tend to attribute the cause to individual characteristics—lack of effort, ability, or motivation—while the people themselves look to structural causes—working conditions, equipment, and availability of resources. To the extent that this process operates, appraiser and subordinate will be unable to agree upon the sources and solutions to ineffective performance.

Performance appraisals are an integral part of organizational policy, but are handicapped by the context of evaluation and the social dynamics of the situation. It is clear that the participants often have different perspectives and objectives and that the nature of evaluation articulates problems that can produce questionable results. But the formal document remains, becomes part of the worker's record, and followers them as they progress through the organization.

TRANSFERS: TESTING ORGANIZATIONAL COMMITMENT

In many large organizations professionals and management-level personnel are transferred from place to place during the early part of their careers (Sell, 1983). One study of thirty-four middle-managers in a consumer products firm reveals that seventeen had been transferred five or more times. Most of the others reported somewhere between one and four moves with only five not ever having been relocated. (This data, and much of the analysis, is drawn from Margolis, 1979).

Transfers are an integral part of the overall career development of organizational managers. The military and corporations consciously and deliberately rotate personnel to achieve specific objectives. One is simply to move people around to meet the changing needs of the company. Another purpose is to evaluate the capabilities and potential of young managers on the basis of their ability to handle new situations, increased responsibilities, and a fresh set of coworkers. Successful performance in a new location will qualify an individual for promotion, while the lack of it can effectively limit future advancement. Transfers are also planned to provide an opportunity for people to acquire experiences that are necessary for movement up corporate ladders. Higher positions usually require familiarity with a number of specific operations. Thus, the transfer of personnel can be seen as part of an overall, long-term plan for screening and seasoning managers, as well as filling positions as needed.

However, it is important to note that transfers may serve other purposes and have latent consequences that may not be apparent to the people making such moves or even to their superiors in the organization. Whether it is recognized as such or not, the offer of a geographic transfer is simultaneously an opportunity and also a test of loyalty, commitment, priorities, and dedication. A move is a costly and disruptive challenge—not in monetary terms since organizations usually bear most of the financial burden—but in social costs. The manager faces the practical problems of selling a home and finding another in an unknown community; the manager also anticipates being separated from relatives, friends and neighbors, and coworkers. For many young managers, transfers mean leaving the community where they were born, grew up, and went to school. The strictly personal considerations are compounded by the costs imposed upon family members. Children must give up their friends and will have to start in new schools. Employed spouses are confronted with the need to terminate their careers and attempt to resume them elsewhere. Spouses not in the labor force will face a period of social isolation in a strange community until they can make new friends. A move thus imposes a heavy burden on managers and their families. Thus, accepting a transfer is used as an indication of managers' priorities, their willingness to make sacrifices for the company, and the depth of dedication to their careers.

Transfers can also contribute to the development of corporate loyalty and the adoption of corporate goals. Managers, because they share responsibility for the survival of the organization, are expected to internalize its goals and are depended upon to act to enhance them. This involves learning a new set of values and abandoning others. This process is usually facilitated by separating people from the people and places associated with former roles. A transfer is not unlike the experiences of military recruits sequestered in total institutions. The manager's first move severs ties with the family, friends, and community that formed and represented an older configuration of values and leaves the manager open to new ideas and values (Margolis, 1979:52).

Furthermore, since transfers are temporary assignments, managers are unlikely to be in new locations long enough to develop new extra-organizational relationships. Even the choice of home in the new locale can subtly contribute to the development of organizational involvement. It is not uncommon for managers to locate in neighborhoods dominated by other employees on temporary assignments. They are directed there by realtors and by tips from people at the new site. The result is that their neighbors—the people with whom they and their families will interact—will probably be members of the same organization. Many such families report having almost no social contacts with community members.

To refuse a transfer may be perceived as placing personal convenience above corporate needs. It implies divided loyalties, or it may be viewed as a sign that the employee lacks dedication to work, growth, new experiences. There is the risk of being labeled a "9 to 5" worker, one who does what is required, but no more. Any such typing will be a severe barrier to future career advancement.

Managers are seldom demoted or dismissed for refusing a transfer, but a refusal can be fatal to a career. As one corporate president puts it, "We wouldn't fire a man for refusing a transfer, but we would begin to watch him more closely" (Margolis, 1979:72). That may be merely a nice way of saying they will be looking for a reason for dismissal or at the least, a denial of a promotion. But, even if the statement is taken at face value, it confirms that the person's loyalty and dedication is suspect, and the employee will consequently be subjected to closer more careful supervision. Being labeled as such is a disadvantage and makes employees more vulnerable to failure since anyone's performance has weaknesses that will show up under close scrutiny.

Thus, transfers occupy an important place in the development of organizational careers. Experiences are accumulated and technical skills are expanded and sharpened. At the same time, in subtle and often unrecognized ways, transfers are opportunities for superiors to evaluate priorities and commitment. In addition, the process contributes to socialization for organizational roles.

Workers are not insensitive to the career and family implications of relocations, and for many it is a source of potential conflict. It appears that fewer people are today willing to accept disruptive geographic mobility than just a few years ago, and that at least some organizations are accommodating by altering career paths. Still, at least among managers where the transfers are more likely a part of institutionalized career paths, it is clear that a majority would move their families for a better-paying or more responsible job. In one study, only about one-quarter claimed that they would "definitely" or "probably" refuse to move (Schmidt and Posner, 1982).

In general, employed women express less willingness to move for promotions than men. Some of this overall difference is explained by structural factors; women are less likely to be the primary economic provider, tend to be at lower organizational levels and in careers where it is less obvious that relocation is a promotional advantage—all of which combine to reduce the potential work rewards they can anticipate. When such factors are taken into consideration, gender differences are reduced, but not entirely eliminated. It must be assumed that socialization experiences produce unequal levels of commitment to family versus career priorities, which show up in perspectives on geographic mobility. The dilemma is that the actual observed statistical reluctance, combined with sociocultural assumptions, may produce the *presumption* that a specific woman will be unwilling to relocate, thus reducing her career opportunities.

CONCLUSION: THE EARLY CAREER STAGE

Theorists have suggested that occupational careers typically progress through a number of predictable phases. Most models emphasize the importance of the first stage of career development where some crucial experiences occur, as shown in Exhibit 13:3. At each stage individuals are confronted with expectations and demands, experiences, and opportunities that differ from those later in the career. During the early months and years of the career the dominant concerns of the organization center upon testing, training, screening, indoctrination, and socialization (Schein, 1971:415). In countless subtle and direct ways the organization will evaluate employees' basic abilities and potential. Most desired traits are complex and vague and difficult to assess; judgment, initiative, responsibility, trust-

EXHIBIT 13:3 The Early Career

The Organizational Enterprise	Training	
	Testing	
	Screening	
	Indoctrination	
	Socialization	
	Reality Shock	
	Group Acceptance	
	Demonstrating Competence	The Subjective
	Long-term Career Development	Dimension

worthiness, and competence are among those most frequently mentioned. At the same time, the organization will attempt to place at least some individuals in roles that will allow them to develop and mature.

From the vantage point of individuals the first stage is usually identified as a period of exploration as they seek to accommodate to organizational demands, learning what is expected of them and seeking to become effective workers. There is also the task of negotiating a role within the structure of the organization by gaining peer and supervisory acceptance, creating a good impression, and assessing their mobility opportunities. For some the future holds the promise of promotion, but for others careers will be limited or blocked.

FOURTEEN

Occupational Careers: Mobility and Immobility

INTRODUCTION: PROMOTIONS—ORGANIZATIONAL REWARD SYSTEMS

Promotions are the major resource controlled by the organization, for as one administrator notes, "Money is not a motivator anyway. It's just a way for a company to cut its losses by ensuring that people do their job at all. The reward we really control is the ability to promote" (Kanter, 1977:129). Virtually all meaningful, tangible, and symbolic advances are based upon promotion. Income, prestige, responsibility, power, and future mobility opportunities are all intimately linked to upward movement in the hierarchy. Therefore, the immobile are effectively denied access to a whole constellation of meaningful advantages—which has implications for job satisfaction, self-concepts, aspirations, and commitment to the job.

Monetary rewards. Major increments in pay are dependent upon promotions because there are generally upper limits on the salary for a specific job. One obvious reason for such limits is that it is viewed as inappropriate for subordinates to earn more than their superiors. Certain other financial benefits may also be linked to promotions: stock options, expense accounts, insurance plans, and the like may be open only to executive positions.

Prestige.   Organizational positions are arranged in a hierarchy of prestige, and upgrading is obviously attainable only by promotion. Gradations of prestige are symbolized and announced by work space (the size of offices), physical amenities (the number of windows, furniture, carpets, and draperies), staff (private secretaries), privacy (for example, secretaries and technical personnel typically progress from open work spaces to shared offices and eventually to private offices), and physical locations (where corner offices are usually the most desirable) (Moore, 1962:101–2; Kanter, 1977:34–36).

Responsibility.   Opportunities for the expansion of responsibility, more challenging work, and personal autonomy are more likely to be a function of position than of experience or skill. For example, a corporate clerk earns the right to send out correspondence without the approval of a supervisor only by being promoted from Statistical Clerk I to Statistical Clerk II (Kanter, 1977:130).

Advancement.   The existence of institutionalized career paths means that long-term advancement depends upon intermediate promotions. In short, progress is measured by a series of promotions. Access to upper level positions is usually reserved for those who are first promoted into assessment and training positions where they can be groomed for subsequent jobs. This is most evident in military organizations where officers must pass through clearly graded ranks. In educational administration it is virtually impossible to reach the superintendency without having served first in minor administrative slots. Thus, a major advantage of being promoted is the opportunity for future promotions.

CAREER MOBILITY: SUBJECTIVE PERSPECTIVES

Career mobility could be expected to loom large in the overall perspective of workers simply because advancement articulates the organizational reward system. Workers understand the benefits attached to promotions, but there are also less obvious subjective, social, and symbolic meanings involved with advancement.

Promotion as personal and public recognition.   A job is a challenge, a test of personal ability and effectiveness, and there can be tremendous personal gratification in a job well done (Sofer, 1970:322). People derive great personal satisfaction from mastering the demands of their work. Even routine work and apparently unrewarding tasks can provide satisfaction; and yet within the organizational structure, a promotion is the only *external* verification of personal ability. Recognition of competent and effective performance in the form of salary increases, bonuses, affirmative appraisals by supervisors, are important; but they are only a personal and private confirmation, and workers prefer some more visible form of recognition. Promotions are a public and publicized form of social recognition. Promotions are announced in organizational publications and are sometimes accompanied by ritualized ceremonies. The military and some large corporations confer promotions at a gathering of functionaries. Acknowledgment of appointments in some organizations may reach the larger community via press releases, which are frequently printed in the local papers. Executive level positions in government, hospitals, or large industrial corporations may even qualify for a press conference.

Relative deprivation.   Individuals consistently evaluate their own progress not only in personal terms, but also relative to the achievements of reference groups both within the organization and outside it. There is strong interest in who is doing well, who is getting more pay, who is rising faster, who is given more authority, power, recognition, or status (Sofer, 1970:313). Such comparisons influence how people feel about their own careers and give added meaning to a promotion. Coworkers felt to have roughly similar ability and tenure and opportunities form the most immediate reference group. Any pattern of more rapid advancement among these cohorts can produce feelings of deprivation and frustration, elevating the salience of a promotion. Workers are also sensitive to what is happening to the careers of people in similar positions in organizations elsewhere. Professionals like to keep track of the careers of their former classmates. Even relatives and friends can be relevant. Their level of success, even though it may be in entirely different circumstances, can produce feelings of discontent (Chinoy, 1955). The presence of such reference groups means that career advancement can have meaning as a measure of keeping pace with the achievement of others.

Promotion and escape.   Advancement may be attractive more as a means of escaping from an undesirable job than because of the lure of additional rewards (Sofer, 1970:313–17). It is not uncommon for people to find themselves doing things they dislike, either because it is inconsistent with their interests, goals, and training or because it involves great personal sacrifice. This motivation is characteristic of newcomers experiencing the constraints of entry positions. It may also evolve over time as people tire of their positions. Apparently some scientific and technical personnel find management appealing as an alternative from technically oriented tasks.

Promotion, power, and influence   Promotions in large, hierarchically arranged organizations carry with them increasing opportunities to put one's ideas into action, have greater influence on decisions, mobilize resources, and to get things done—in short to carry out the work more effectively. Thus, promotions have meaning as a source of "power," that is, power in the sense of the enhanced ability to get things done, not as a personal need to dominate others.

PROMOTION SYSTEMS: FIXED VERSUS DISCRETIONARY SYSTEMS

Promotion implies effective performance and the potential for future advancement. Organizations employ any of a variety of criteria to make promotion decisions including: seniority, education, age, written and oral examinations, or performance ratings. There are two general types of criteria (Halaby, 1978). *Fixed criteria* are specific, objective, and standardized such as seniority, scores on paper and pencil tests, and age. Employment in the public sector in the United States has frequently included written exams since the Civil Service reforms of the nineteenth century. Such exams are widely used in large police and fire departments. Japanese industry uses age in making salary and promotion decisions. American labor unions have emphasized seniority, in part as a means of weakening the power of employers.

Fixed criteria tend to be employed whenever the prerequisites, skills, and qualifications can be defined in advance and measured with some degree of accuracy. An example would be the path leading to airline pilot (Roth, 1963:85–88). Promotions are heavily weighted toward the accumulation of fixed criteria—hours of flying time and schooling, because it is believed that these measure the skills required of a commercial pilot.

Seniority, to the extent that it is used as a measure of experience, is a criterion in situations requiring skills that can only be developed by practice. The premise being, all other things being equal, the greater the experience, the greater the skill. This line of reasoning underlies apprenticeship programs requiring that a specific number of years must be served prior to being promoted to journeyman. Educational institutions that insist upon a minimum number of years at one rank prior to promotion are acting on this same premise.

Discretionary criteria utilize subjective judgments of ability and potential. Exclusive use of discretionary criteria is apparent in such fields as the performing arts. Advancement in a symphony orchestra musician's world is measured by progress from the countless semiprofessional groups through a middle echelon of twenty-four orchestras located in large cities to the five major symphonies—Boston, Chicago, Cleveland, New York, and Philadelphia, and by moving up from one "chair" to another within an instrumental section (Faulkner, 1974). Promotions are based upon the subtle and strictly subjective judgments of performance.

EXHIBIT 14:1   Qualities Considered Important by Law Partners for Promotion of Associates

Quality	Percent Mentioning
Good lawyer; hard work	24.0%
Bring in business	14.3
Proper personality	10.5
Good client relations	9.0
Be lucky	9.0
Fulfill needs of firm	5.3
Social background	5.3
Sponsorship	4.5
Assume responsibility	3.0
Become indispensable	3.0
Leadership ability	2.3

Source: Abridged with permission of the Free Press, a Division of Macmillan, Inc., from *The Wall Street Lawyer* by Erwin O. Smigel. Copyright © 1964 by the Free Press.

Discretionary criteria involve some potential problems. Unless there are some rules, either formal or tacit, evaluators have the discretion to focus on any aspect of performance to the exclusion of others and to set their own standards. Even organizations that require formal performance appraisals may have numerous variations. One American-based multinational corporation has as many as fifty different evaluation forms in use by different supervisors (Lawler, Mohrman, and Resnick, 1984). The result can be an idiosyncratic and unstructured promotion system.

Lawyers aspiring to become partners in Wall Street firms have traditionally confronted this situation. The data (see Exhibit 14:1) reports responses of partners to the question, "What does the firm look for in a partner?" It is evident that there is no consensus among partners as to the relevant traits, since no one factor was mentioned by more than one person in four. Many of those that are mentioned seem logical enough, but certainly vague. A prospective partner should be a good lawyer, be hardworking, have a nice personality, get along well with clients, and be lucky! Consider the difficulties involved in objectively measuring such traits. Even the partners concede it is no easy task to evaluate these traits. They are, in effect, saying they know what they are looking for and confident in their judgment, even if unable to verbalize it (Smigel, 1964:109).

Uncertainty and Promotional Criteria

Exclusive use of any single criterion is rare. Most promotion systems utilize some combination of fixed and discretionary criteria. For example, a study of state, county, and municipal finance agencies showed that on the average, evaluations counted 40 percent, examinations 44 percent, and seniority 16 percent (Halaby, 1978:477). One major factor that helps to explain the particular configuration of criteria that prevail in a given organization or occupation is the perceived ability to formalize and accurately assess job qualifications (see Thompson, 1967).

The *uncertainty proposition* suggests discretionary criteria will be employed when job requirements are not subject to easy specification or assessment. James Thompson (1967:134–35) has identified three major sources of uncertainty, which can be illustrated using a common middle management position such as sales manager. One is lack of understanding of *cause-effect relationships.* Here, although a person may be expected to increase product sales, there is no clear understanding of what produces this outcome because consumer behavior is so extraordinarily complex and only partly rational. As one sales manager admits, "It's hard as a manager to know when you're doing well. You can't really take credit for improvements in sales." (Kanter, 1977:60). A second condition of uncertainty prevails when task outcomes are determined by *external agents and factors.* Product sales fluctuate in response to economic conditions, shifting consumer tastes, and the quality and price of competing products among others. All are external factors, and there is little control that can be exercised. Finally, uncertainty increases as job outcomes are dependent upon the *performance of other persons.* Actual customer contacts are the responsibility of field representatives and it is their collective efforts that determine monthly balances. Moreover, sales are also dependent upon the cooperation of other units—production, marketing, billing, and shipping.

Thus, it is evident that uncertainty characterizes many managerial and professional positions, with uncertainty generally increasing as one moves up professional and managerial ladders. Consequently, subjective criteria play an increasingly important role in promotion decisions at upper levels in the organization, producing informal, exclusive elites that have been so difficult for minorities and women to breach. For historical reasons these elites were dominated by white, male, Protestant, Western Europeans. Considering that there are no clear criteria for "good" decisions, that decision makers are in constant interaction, and that effective functioning depends upon cooperation and trust, recruitment into executive circles becomes limited to people who can be *assumed to* understand one another, get along well together, and be depended upon. Ease of communication and trust are facilitated by shared experiences, values, beliefs, and world views. Persons can, of course, demonstrate these traits, but certain categories of people start with an advantage. Individuals with the same social backgrounds, education, and circle of friends as the elite can be assumed to share the same value system. Thus, among a pool of equally qualified candidates, it has long been noted that factors such as similarities in religion, political affiliation, and family connections can be decisive (for example, see Dalton, 1959; Moore, 1962). Grooming and other attributes take on new meaning in a context of uncertainty, for they are used as clues to other attitudes and traits, just as they do in the application process (Chapter 11), creating strong social pressure for all dress in a similar manner.

CASE STUDY: WOMEN EXECUTIVES

For women executives, gender alone can immediately identify them as "different," and therefore possibly incomprehensible or unpredictable, but *certainly* lacking the same world view that men are assumed to have. The experiences of a group of 700 women executives reveal the subtle handicaps of being a female in the male-dominated executive subculture (Rogan, 1984):

Have you ever:

Been mistaken for a secretary at a business meeting?	61%
Had the impression that your views were not respected as much as a man's?	70%
Felt that you were being judged more on the basis of dress and appearance than a man in your position?	37%
Felt the presence of female executives made male executives more appearance-conscious?	33%
Felt cut off from social conversations or activities among your male colleagues?	60%

Half of the women in the study perceive being treated differently than men, sometimes in the feeling that their appearance is being more closely scrutinized, and sometimes in a deprecating or patronizing manner. Many of their experiences are negative. Even in the 1980s a majority complain of being mistaken for secretaries at business meetings and feel that their ideas win less respect than those of male colleagues. Such acts, while personally humiliating, have deeper implications for they reveal assumptions about the experiences and capabilities of women. But it is not the substance of responses that lies at the core of the matter; the essence of the problem is the fundamental fact that woman elicit a different response for no other reason than they are women. This response is strongly manifested in their feelings of being cut off from the social activities of their male colleagues. Social exclusion is a decisive handicap. As one woman notes, "When you get to a certain level within the organization, work isn't the issue anymore." It is a question of communicating and interacting with others, being included in the network of social relationships of other executives. It is matter of trust and ease of communication. In the absence of any better evidence, executives are selected for promotion on the basis of social characteristics that, even if not deliberately prejudiced, can discriminate on the bases of gender, religion, race, ethnicity, and social class.

Perceptions of the Promotion Process

Employees have a view of the promotion process based upon their own observations, interpretations, and experiences with the system operating upon them and those around them. The topic is not well researched, but what evidence there is suggests the existence of some general, organization-wide views of the promotion process as well as differences associated with organizational level and opportunity structure. Results from a study of nearly a thousand employees in a large midwestern manufacturing firm are instructive (Beehr et al., 1980). When asked to rate the relative importance of various criteria on a scale of 7 (very important) to 1 (no importance), the following ranking was produced:

Doing a good job	5.29
Seniority	5.29
Getting the right breaks	4.99
Good attendance	4.92
Educational level	4.62
How well supervisor likes you	4.36
Experience and ability	4.26
Having good ideas and initiative	4.22
Race	3.26
Gender	3.01

It is apparent that workers generally concede that performance ("Doing a good job") and seniority are believed to be of prime importance in career success—which is consistent with most administrative versions of the process. Noteworthy is the fact that nonperformance factors are high on the list. Simple "good luck"—being in the right place at the right time, unexpected vacancies, a chance meeting—occupies an important place. This perception is frequently associated with a belief in favoritism (how well a supervisor likes you; having an "in" with management; being a "fair-haired" boy or girl) as a basis of promotion (Beehr, et al., 1980). Among managers, favoritism is often construed as a decisive factor, with many believing that favoritism or the breaks make the difference in selection for advancement (Dalton, 1959:167). Ascribed characteristics of race and gender are at the bottom of the list. Interestingly, there are different perceptions of the process depending upon career opportunities. The immobile are more likely to see luck/favoritism and race/gender as a means for earning a promotion. In contrast, those having recently been upwardly mobile felt that performance and seniority had higher priority.

The promotion process receives a great deal of attention among those affected by it. A vacant position becomes a topic of office gossip, and there may be betting on the relative chances of competing candidates (Dalton, 1959:167). There is some indication among managers in British industry that some possess a fairly accurate evaluation of their own promotability

(Sofer, 1970:241–42). This suggests people are sensitive to the operation of a system in their organization, and that it combines factors over which they have control (performance, effort, education) as well as some they do not (luck, favoritism, ascribed characteristics, discrepant evaluations). At the same time we cannot overlook the possibility that perceptions are a means of rationalizing the consequences of their own ability.

WORK AND FAMILY ROLES

There are no clear boundaries between work and family roles, and they impinge upon one another at every point in the career. The relationship between work and family is interactive, with experiences in one area affecting the other in direct and subtle ways. The most direct and obvious linkages are found in multiperson careers, single-parent units, and in dual-career families.

Multiperson Careers

Hanna Papanek (1973) has pointed out that some occupations require the active participation of two persons—one of whom is technically outside the occupation—to achieve any significant degree of success. In the urban work force, the route to executive positions has more often than not required the collaboration of the wife in fostering the husband's rise in the corporate structure. The tasks of entertaining become important once men reach a certain level of middle management, leading to higher level positions in which the spouses's responsibilities extend to involvement in civic and community affairs.

Such arrangements were, and sometimes are, consistent with the historical gender-based division of labor, and some women have been willing to act to enhance an upwardly mobile husband. It would appear that fewer women today are willing to accept this role, and of course, more are pursuing independent careers. Then, too, there is the issue of recognition of such activities as a contribution to career success. Many observers predict the demise of the "corporate wife" multiperson career. The obverse of this is that the expansion of opportunities for women in management introduces a complex problem into the lives of wives and husbands. To be sure, some husbands have been able to slip into the male equivalent of the "corporate wife" role, but it does require more adjustment if only for the reason that there are no institutionalized expectations for the role. As with any new role, it may prove discomforting to both spouses and business associates to find a male giving dinner parties.

Spouses, usually wives, have also been able to facilitate careers simply by relieving their husbands of responsibilities that would normally fall on them. This is not limited to two-person careers, but also extends to many other types of occupations. The most evident examples are found in what have been called "greedy" or "absorbing" occupations—those demanding effort or hours beyond the ordinary work day. The profession of physician is a prime example; it is an occupation that can easily engulf the worker, leaving the spouse to handle home maintenance and other responsibilities usually performed by husbands.

Single-parent Families

Single-parent family units are on the increase as a result of rising divorce rates. There were over 9 million such families in the United States in 1983 (U.S. Department of Labor, 1984:2). In such cases all childrearing and home maintenance responsibilities fall to one person. Most are women, many are poor, but there are also an increasing number of single men in this situation. For example, in 1983, there were 600,000 single men raising children under the age of 18. The demands of childrearing can have serious consequences for careers. A study by Geoffrey Greif (1985) showed that approximately one-third missed work, were late, or had to reduce work-related travel as a result of family responsibilities. Some even lost their jobs or were forced to resign. In some ways the noneconomic problems facing men are greater than those facing single mothers. Male socialization experiences have been less likely to develop childrearing skills and generally result in a lessened ability to relate to other persons.

Dual-career Families

Large numbers of married women have always participated in the paid labor force, largely for economic reasons; but public recognition of the problems facing such families is more recent. There are many unanswered questions, but some issues and problems are worth considering.

Marital effects on occupational attainment. It is impossible to count the number of women who have foregone their own careers entirely in favor of their husbands, but the number must be formidable. When both continue to work, it is clear that women are much more likely to make accommodations in their own work in favor of fostering the husband's career (for example, see Duncan and Perrucci, 1976). When confronted, with the need to relocate geographically, the husbands' career will be likely to be given priority. Until recently, this was consistent with gender expectations, but also was often a quite rational decision for the male partner was more likely to have a job offering better long-term mobility potential. Relocation has become a much more complex issue as more couples are both in professional or managerial work. It is estimated that in 1985 22 percent of the largest American corporations assisted in relocating a spouse (Stone, 1986).

Although women are more likely to compromise their careers in favor of the husbands, there is some indication that husbands' career attainments are also limited when their wives are in managerial/professional careers (Sharda and Nangle, 1981). This may mean that dual-career couples accommodate to each other's work by limiting or restricting their own mobility.

Role conflict: Work and family roles. While the lure of full-time housewife is losing its appeal for American women, marriage and motherhood still play central roles in their lives. Seventy-two percent of the women who responded to a Gallup Poll (1985) viewed marriage and children as the "most satisfying way of life," but over half would prefer to combine it with a full-time job outside the home. The demands of work and parenthood create the potential for role conflict, and most research confirms that many workers do encounter some problems, and experience some stress. A recent survey revealed the following percentages of people able to report having "no problems" balancing work and family roles:

16% of single mothers
23% of single fathers
23% of married mothers
60% of married fathers (Johnson, 1985)

Not surprisingly, the burdens are heaviest for single parents of both sexes who must single-handedly manage a career and family responsibilities. However, the overwhelming majority of married mothers also experience a high level of conflict. For example, among a group of professional women in Philadelphia, 77 percent reported they "often" experienced strain between home and career roles (Gray, 1983). And it must be noted these women were in good-paying positions (law, medicine, academics), well able to afford paid child care, and operating in social environments in which spouses, parents, and colleagues were supportive of their careers.

In response to the pressures, they developed a number of different coping strategies, ranging from the pragmatic (hiring outside help) to the heroic (attempting to do everything everyone expected of them). Most (54 percent) were only "mildly satisfied" with the way they had been able to balance the conflicting demands. Thirty-one percent were "extremely satisfied" and the remaining 16 percent were "dissatisfied." Those who were most satisfied tended to have certain things in common. On a practical level they had become more sensitive to the need to organize and schedule their time and reduce their standards of performance; they were in families willing to share household tasks and were able to depend upon family members to help resolve conflicts that arose. Dissatisfaction was most likely among those who had no conscious strategies for dealing with role conflict and either attempted to meet all expectations or tried to separate work and family roles. The issues are complex, but it is possible to make satisfactory adjustments, especially with the aid of active social support within the family. Attempts to segregate roles or expand effort to meet all expectations are the least rewarding alternatives.

CONCLUSION: REORGANIZING SOCIAL SUPPORT SYSTEMS

The phenomenon of increasing numbers of women being in the paid work force for longer periods of time has begun to produce changes in the way in which employers structure careers as well as the forms of benefits they offer. For example, many large corporations are providing some form of child care benefits for their employees to relieve some of the problems emanating from single-parent and dual-career families. One hypothesis is that dual-earner couples are brought closer together by working (see Simpson and England, 1981). Work problems can more easily be understood, home tasks shared rather than divided, marital solidarity promoted. This would suggest that marital relations among dual-career couples will be improved. A different perspective raises the question of developing social support systems to replace the declining social division of labor in the larger society. While in no way depreciating the costs of a gender division of labor, which paired employed male workers with unpaid partners, it is suggested that women's work was vital to the well-being of both the worker and the family (Hunt and Hunt, 1977; Vandervelde, 1984). Their unrecognized and unrewarded tasks included the maintenance of social networks (to kin and work associates), childrearing and housework, and social and emotional support, creating a complementary role system. It is argued that single parents and dual-career couples are deprived of one source of social support, and until new forms emerge the psychic costs can be severe.

THE ROLE OF MENTORS

Successful career mobility depends upon a combination of personal and structural factors, but it is evident that many people benefit from the help and encouragement of an ally within the firm who acts as an informal sponsor or mentor. A *mentor* may be defined as a senior member of an occupation who takes an active role in developing the career of a junior person. The importance of mentors is well understood within the ranks of organizations; in fact, it is common for workers to have unofficial labels for the people who play this role. Terms such as "rabbi," "godfather," "office uncle," and "guardian angel" are used quite frequently. In fact, many people believe that it is impossible to succeed without the aid of a mentor (Roche, 1979:14). A rising young corporate executive manifests this perspective when he claims, "Everyone who does well has a sponsor . . . In my case, I had three managers. All of them have moved but continue to help me. A vice president likes me. I can count on getting any job up a level as long as he remains in favor" (Kanter, 1977:183). Research does not universally support this contention, but it is clear that mentors can and do play an influential role in career mobility. Reports by upper level managers consistently reveal that most enjoyed the assistance of at least one mentor at some point in their careers (Hennig and Jardin, 1977; Kanter, 1977; Roche, 1979). There is some evidence that women are more likely than men to have had a mentor, and to have had a greater number of mentors (Thompson, 1976; Roche, 1979). Their mentors are usually men (in part simply because there are so many more males in upper level positions), but it is apparently less common for a women to act as a mentor for a man (Kram, 1983). An overwhelming majority of women executives feel that they have an obligation to mentor younger female colleagues (Rogan, 1984).

Mentors apparently do make a difference in career success. Managers with mentors move up more rapidly, earn higher salaries, and exhibit greater satisfaction with their careers than those without mentors (Roche, 1979). In academic careers mentors can influence the level of productivity (Reskin, 1979) and the chance of winning research grants (Cameron and Blackburn, 1981). In addition, mentors have also been shown to be influential in the careers of military personnel (Janowitz, 1960), physicians (Hall, 1948), lawyers (Smigel, 1964), and recording industry musicians (Faulkner, 1971).

The relationship between mentors and the persons being aided (proteges) is complex and delicate, and not all that well understood at this point. It is not clear why or how a specific relationship emerges. One interpretation is that the single most important factor in attracting the attention of a potential mentor is outstanding performance or promise (Thompson, 1976). This does not mean that all promising candidates will develop sponsors, merely that merit is a prerequisite. Other investigators feel that it is ascribed characteristics (gender, race, social background) that are decisive and that place members of some groups at a distinct disadvantage. Others with a more psychological orientation have argued that senior people select a surrogate "son" or "daughter."

From the perspective of the protege, the relationship makes sense as a source of valuable information about the nature and functioning of the occupation. It offers the newcomer a chance to benefit from the mentor's accumulated knowledge, experience, and judgment and can be understood as a means of coping with the complexity and uncertainty of organizational life. No doubt some people are guided by the more calculating belief that anyone who hopes to be promoted must cultivate ties with one or more mentor. In fact, this is the explicit advice found in many books offering "rules" for aspiring young executives.

Although the origins of specific relationships is unclear, the process can have structural origins. Mentors may take on proteges as a test of their own ability and status. By successfully promoting the career of a protege they can demonstrate their own power and influence in the organization. A somewhat different goal may be to forge an exchange relationship. Sponsorship creates an obligation to repay such favors. It is seldom expressed explicitly, but is rather a tacit understanding which is a part of the occupational subculture. "I wanted them in positions where they could strengthen my own career," explains one corporate mentor (Thompson, 1976). The point is that as those being sponsored rise in the occupation they move into positions where they can help, protect, and defend their former mentors. And, "God help you if you are not grateful for the favors given," warns one executive (Kanter, 1977:183). All of these motives, plus others, may operate in any specific case. Thus, mentor-protege relationships are intricately linked to issues of organizational influence and advancement.

It must also be noted that there are occupations in which the sponsorship of an advocate has become a virtual prerequisite to career mobility. Musicians in the recording industry are in this situation (Faulkner, 1971:97–107). Access to the best paying studio jobs is generally open only to those who have the explicit recommendation of an insider. This endorsement is earned through an apprenticeship of rehearsal bands, dance bands, club performances, and pickup jobs where they can demonstrate their talent reliability and commitment. The system has evolved, in part, to restrain competition in a highly competitive and uncertain occupation.

Mentor Roles

Mentors can help proteges by playing any of four basic roles (or some combination of them). One role is that of unofficial *teacher*. By selectively sharing their technical expertise and work experiences they can help their proteges to function more effectively, thus giving them a competitive advantage over those without mentors. Many people also report they learned more quickly and avoided mistakes because of their mentors. Probably the most salient information that a teacher can pass along deals with the informal workings of the bureaucracy—how to circumvent the rules, what behavior is tolerated and what is not, and who has power—which contributes to effective performance.

Mentors also frequently function as *counselors*, offering advice, encouragement, and emotional support. They serve as a trusted confidant.

On the surface this might seem an indirect and passive form of help, but it is vital in the highly competitive and uncertain world of corporate management. In one study, women executives confirmed that this was the most important single function of their mentors (McLane, 1980). There is a large body of literature showing the value of social support in medicating against the effects of uncertain or stressful social situations, and this is a role played by mentors within organizations. Counselors would seem to be especially important during the uncertainty of the "breaking-in" phase of the career.

A third role is that of *facilitator.* Mentors use their positions and contacts to enhance either the opportunities or the visibility of proteges, thus offering them additional chances to prove themselves. Sometimes this requires nothing more than defining a specific person as a "promising candidate," thus bringing them to the attention of superiors responsible for promotions. This simple act of labeling can be decisive in the early stages of careers in large organizations where there are many competent candidates and anything that serves to isolate one from the others is a distinct advantage.

Among academics, careers can be facilitated by introducing proteges into the informal colleague networks in a discipline. These social networks extend between institutions and are a vital source of "insider" information about jobs, conferences, fellowships, research opportunities, and publications. Many eminent scholars have reported that this was the manner in which mentors contributed to their ultimate success (Zuckerman, 1977). Mentors who have some level of decision-making responsibility for work assignments can easily facilitate careers by selecting proteges for the most visible and advantageous projects. In academic careers senior scholars can increase the visibility of proteges by including them in ongoing research or by inviting them as co-authors. Each such opportunity is an advantage not available to those without mentors.

The final form of mentoring is to act as an *advocate.* In such cases mentors mobilize their own resources to help the career of a protege. Relevant resources are: formal position, reputation, and power or influence. Mentors may use their formal position to help others along. Scientists who occupy editorial positions with journals can tap their junior colleagues for positions on editorial boards, while those with positions in professional organizations can nominate proteges for offices. Mentors can stake their own prestige upon a candidate. They have, in effect, social credit with others based on their own ability and reputation. The most obvious forms are letters of reference and personal recommendations. Finally, they may employ whatever power or influence they may have to fight for favored candidates.

It must be noted that the mentor-protege relationship has symbolic value which may far outweigh the importance of any direct advocacy. The knowledge that individuals enjoy the backing of influential superiors can facilitate their success. It marks them as people of unusual promise—people who are on the "fast track." To be perceived as someone who is being groomed for an upper level position sets in motion a process that helps to ensure success. For example, these people are more likely to get the more desirable tasks such as projects that have visibility or higher probability of success, which will put them in contact with other senior management personnel. They are also given more frequent performance reviews, which in turn makes them more quickly eligible for promotions. In short, having a mentor is a signal to others in the organization that the person is "special"—which subtly contributes to their subsequent upward mobility.

The recipient also benefits from a special kind of power, which Kanter (1977:182) has called *reflected power*. The protege enjoys the potential threat of the use of mentor's power even if it is never tested. A threat may be enough, if it enables the protege to accomplish things others cannot. The potential intervention of a high-level mentor might for example persuade a superior to promote one individual over another equally qualified candidate.

The advocate-protege relationship is not without an element of risk for both parties. Proteges may find they may move at too rapid a rate without acquiring the experiences they need. They may also be faced with inflated and unrealistic performance expectations. Their label as "water walker" may be beyond their capabilities and invite frustration and premature failure. There is also the danger of becoming a pawn in other people's power struggles, or becoming too closely identified with a mentor who subsequently fails. In either case the young manager's career becomes inextricably entwined with the success or failure of the mentor.

Mentors, by publicly assuming the role of advocate, are also putting their own careers in jeopardy. Sponsorship involves making explicit or tacit claims about the capabilities and potential of their proteges. If they do develop as promised, the mentor's judgment is confirmed and position is strengthened. On the other hand, proteges' failure to live up to these claims can reflect badly upon sponsors in a number of subtle ways. Their judgment and ability to evaluate talent will inevitably be viewed as less reliable. In turn, they may be less successful as mentors for other candidates. There is also the possibility that the failure of the protege may be attributed to the manner in which the mentor handled the career. Thus, the stature and influence of mentors becomes linked to the success or failure of the people they sponsor.

Conclusion.   Mentor-protege relationships are a common feature of many occupations. Involvement in such relationships enhances the potential for career success by giving proteges access to resources not readily available to others. Counselors offer social support against the uncertainties of early career development. Teachers share expertise and experience that promotes effective performance. Facilitators supply visibility and contacts that allow proteges to prove themselves. Advocates utilize their positions, prestige, and power to directly assist the careers of selected proteges. Those who have mentors therefore enjoy a distinct advantage in some occupations, such as the recording industry in which these sponsorship systems have evolved to the point where they are a prerequisite to career movement.

Recognition of the consequences of sponsorship has frequently generated attempts to mandate their formation. J. C. Penney, the founder of the retail chain that bears his name, in 1901 directed his officers to select and direct managerial careers (Roche, 1979). More recently, a number of corporations have experimented with requiring senior executives to assume responsibility for specific young managers. These may be seen as attempts to institutionalize and standardize an informal system which in the past has worked to the disadvantage of women and minorities.

PROMOTION PATTERNS

Although reliable data on career mobility are not available for the full labor force, there are studies of specific organizations that can be instructive. In one such analysis James E. Rosenbaum (1979a) examined patterns of promotion between major hierarchical levels among white men in a large (10,000+) American corporation. Except during periods of rapid growth, somewhere between 11 percent and 14 percent of all employees were promoted in any given year. Promotion rates are displayed graphically in Exhibit 14.2.

These workers' experiences reveal a consistent relationship between age and the chances of promotion. One message is clear: Those not promoted early in the career face rapidly declining opportunities. A real threshold is reached by managerial and supervisory personnel in their early thirties, and a few years later by blue-collar/clerical people. By the time people reach their fifties their chances are negligible. This probably imposes a sense of urgency and anxiety upon workers who perceive that if they do not move upward early they run the risk of not ever being promoted.

This pattern is even more dramatic when college-educated men are compared to those without a degree. As would be expected, better educated workers enjoy a distinct advantage, having a much better chance of being promoted when they are young; but their opportunities decline precipitously to a point where by age 45 (supervisors) or 50 (for managers) there is *no upward mobility*. A small proportion of non-B.A. workers con-

EXHIBIT 14:2   Patterns of Promotion

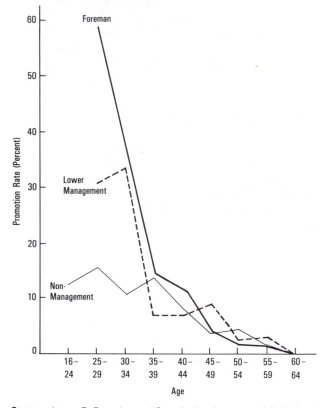

Source: James E. Rosenbaum, "Organizational career mobility," *American Journal of Sociology* 85 (July 1979), figure 1, p. 32.

tinue to be promoted well into their fifties. Hence the pressure on B.A.s for early promotion are extreme, and the implications for the immobile are dire.

BLOCKED MOBILITY: PLATEAUS AND DEMOTIONS

For all but a few individuals, career movement will eventually reach a *plateau*, a point at which upward mobility ceases for long periods of time. Plateaus are an inevitable attribute of pyramidal organizations where there are simply fewer positions at each higher level, and promotions become more competitive. Competent persons may also be blocked from further movement by slow turnover rates, which generate few vacancies.

Organizations can ill afford to ignore people stalled for structural reasons. In systems where promotions symbolize success and carry major rewards, immobility can easily be predicted to weaken commitment and undermine incentives to productivity. Research indicates corporations can employ financial incentives with some effectiveness. A study of over a hundred organizationally plateaued managers showed they earned salary increments well above the corporate average (Veiga, 1981). Although not pleased with their progress, they showed neither unusual dissatisfaction nor a special propensity to leave the organization. This appears to be a case where monetary rewards can signal effective performance and compensate for a lack of movement.

For others there is the failure and the risk demotion. Not all people moving along institutionalized career paths are able to fulfill the expectations of the job; the reasons may be personal, administrative, or organizational. Some are simply inept, lacking the social or technical abilities to perform satisfactorily. Other cases represent administrative miscalculations in the form of misjudgments of ability or premature assignments. In still others, organizational job requirements may change due to technological innovations, external competition, business cycles, or corporate policy shifts. Production and lower white-collar workers are likely to be considered expendable; organizations are generally reluctant to take such drastic action with their professional or managerial personnel. It is apparently much more likely for the inadequate to be retained, at least after they have been with the organization for a few years (for example, see Moore, 1962:175). Personnel are removed from positions where they have proved incompetent by being shifted into alternative jobs or by a structural reorganization of career paths. The term used to describe such strategies is demotion. *Demotions* may be formally defined as structural changes or career moves involving a reduction in some combination of rank, reward, or function.

Demotion must be understood, at least in part, as an organizational accommodation to the competing demands imposed by pressures for efficiency, justice, the protection of the integrity of individuals, and the need to maintain effective performance. On the one hand, there are practical pressures on members of the organization to deal with the inept and the incompetent decisively and directly. Since they are ineffective, they hamper the efficient functioning of the organization. Then, too, they clog career paths, limiting the ability to promote and foster the growth of the more competent. Finally, there is the question of perceptions of equity and opportunity among lower level participants. Feelings that upper positions are filled with entrenched incompetents can promote dissatisfaction and serve to reduce their level of effort.

However, it is not a simple matter, for such pressures must be balanced against other considerations that take into account the negative consequences of dismissal and demotion as organizational policy. First of all, there is the long-term implication for recruitment. Organizations that develop a reputation of high turnover are at a decided disadvantage in attracting new people. An atmosphere of competiveness also can have potentially negative consequences for performance within the organization. If the risk of dismissal or demotion becomes too great, people may be less willing to accept the added responsibility of promotion. Risk is also likely to foster conservative attitudes by reducing the willingness to be creative and innovative.

The validity of assessment criteria and procedures are still another consideration. Expectations tend to be vague and complex, especially as the level of responsibility increases. Judgments of effective performance are imprecise and not subject to easy quantification. Therefore, decision makers will have varying degrees of confidence in assessment techniques that further mediate against overly dramatic action.

To be defined as a failure has the potential of producing attitudes and behavior that are threatening to the individual and disruptive to the organization. Unless provided with some explanation or some consolation, individuals are likely to respond to the embarrassment of failure with hostility, withdrawal, and a loss of incentive (Goffman, 1952; 1956; Goldner, 1965). Hostility may manifest itself in deliberate attempts to sabotage the organization, and it contributes to strained interpersonal relations. Withdrawal isolates those perceived as failures from meaningful social contacts and interferes with the work process. A loss of incentive produces the ritualists, who put in their time, but derive no satisfaction from their work and make no significant contributions to the organization.

Still another set of considerations are the implications for the individual. The most obvious is that inadequacy in one role does not mean that a person cannot function effectively in some other position. This is an especially salient consideration when the failure is the fault of the organization rather than the individual. Previous performance considerations must also be factored in, even among those who have clearly demonstrated incompetence. Years of dedicated and loyal work cannot simply be forgotten. Nor can the humanitarian implications of failure be ignored. It is neither easy nor pleasant to have to invoke the destructive public label of failure. Therefore, if people are to remain in the organization and be expected to continue to function there, they must be allowed some protection from the disruptive consequences of a public announcement of failure.

These considerations combine to produce a general reluctance to dismiss the inadequate; they also result in the evolution of the elaborate and intricate patterns of demotion found in many large organizations. Demotion must thus be understood, at least in part, as an administrative attempt to achieve a balance among the competing demands for efficiency, morale, justice, and the protection of the integrity of the members of the organization (Sofer, 1970:23).

There are several common patterns of demotion involving either structural changes in career paths or the movement of personnel among existing jobs (Moore, 1962; Hall and Isabella, 1985). They differ in the ability to avoid the undesirable individual or organizational consequences. A key attribute of the demotion process is that it tends to be cloaked in ambiguity. Individuals, despite their understandable wish to know, are seldom fully appraised of the meaning and the reasoning behind organizational action. The ambiguity seems deliberate, and part of the process, for it permits individuals to interpret the demotion in the least destructive fashion.

Elimination of position and transfer. This situation qualifies as demotion only when it is done for the express purpose of relocating an unsatisfactory person. Since reorganizations are a common feature of bureaucracies in response to changing market conditions, mergers, efficiency studies, or shifts in managerial philosophy, it is not easy for participants to distinguish between the impelling motives. The ambiguity of this procedure serves both the organization and individuals by allowing inadequate personnel to be displaced without the personal or social stigma of failure.

Increasing the levels in the hierarchy. Reorganization may result in an increase in the number of intermediate positions between two jobs. Everyone below that is demoted in the sense of being further removed from access to the rewards of the higher position. This, too, is an ambiguous move since there may be reasons other than a deliberate attempt to prevent the advance of a particular person.

Same job with reduced functions. Demotions are frequently accomplished by restructuring the role in such a way as to reduce the incumbent's sphere of responsibility or influence. A common corporate strategy is to install an able "assistant" who assumes major role responsibilities. Another technique is to reallocate responsibilities among other positions in the hierarchy. The inadequate are allowed to retain their formal positions, titles, offices, and accompanying prerequisites, but are effectively removed from a position they were unable to function in. The advantages for both individual and organization are evident. Important functions are reallocated to more competent persons, but the individual is allowed to retain the formal trappings of rank and reward.

Same job with reduced salary. A quiet form of demotion is a reduction in the level of compensation without any alteration in the formal position. It may take the form of a direct reduction or an exclusion from a general organization-wide salary increment. The explanation usually starts, "Everybody is getting a raise this year, but . . ." This action indicates unsatisfactory performance, but it is apparent only to the individual and some superiors. It is unlikely to become common knowledge since victims will be reluctant to reveal this evidence of failure. Individuals are thus spared the social stigma, and they have the opportunity to reevaluate their performance and make private modifications in their aspirations and career plans or even consider "voluntary" movement to another organization.

Lower job at same level of compensation.   Reductions in rank are sometimes made without reducing salary levels. As such it is an ambivalent act, carrying the public stigma of a loss of responsibility, but softened by a continuation of previous rewards. Continuing economic rewards can deflect or neutralize immediate feelings of frustration and anger. Also implicit in the move is recognition of past efforts and contributions. Although salaries are typically a private matter, the employee has the opportunity to reveal this information as a means of coping with the stigma, thus making it evident that the organization does not abandon its people because of the inability to handle a single assignment.

Lower job with reduced salary.   In this situation, individuals suffer a reduction in both organizational rank and remuneration. Baseball players are "farmed out" to the minor leagues, military personnel are "broken," while a curriculum supervisor is sent back to teaching. This is the common-sense perception of the term demotion, but is apparently not the most common. Such a dramatic move is unequivocal; it is a clear indication of failure on the part of the individual and offers little in the way of protection for ego or image.

Although there is not much research on this subject, logic would suggest that the presence of certain conditions would produce this particular response. One would be that decision makers have a high level of confidence in the criteria and the assessment procedure. The consequences, being as dramatic as they are, would have to be supported by powerful evidence of failure. A case in point is sports, where a team's win-loss record is accepted as a useful indicator of a coach or manager's ability. Another situation producing this action would be the perception that deviant or inadequate performance has serious implications for organizational survival. The magnitude of the threat must then outweigh the psychic and motivational costs to individuals in the organization. The military uses this device, in part based on this reasoning. Finally, a third condition supporting the use of dramatic demotion would be the presence of a large pool of replacement personnel. A dependable supply of recruits would reduce the salience of worker motivation—since they could be replaced.

Thus, the handling of the inept and the incompetent reveals a general hesitancy to identify people as failures and a reluctance to exclude them or even restrict their areas of operation (Sofer, 1970:24). The reasons seem to include a concern with the devastating personal consequences; sensitivity to the social stigma of failure; a desire to reward loyalty; a lack of confidence in the assessment process; the need to maintain morale; and an awareness of the disruptive consequences of competition. Patterns of demotion function as a means of minimizing the costs of incompetence without disrupting the ongoing functioning of the system.

RESPONSES TO BLOCKED MOBILITY

Opportunities for advancement may be closed off for structural, managerial, or personal reasons. As noted earlier, there are four major sources of structural immobility: the diminishing number of positions at each higher level in bureaucratic organizations; a simple lack of vacancies; changing conditions requiring different abilities; and location on low ceiling career paths. Mismanaged careers result from failure to recognize and develop capabilities, channeling personnel onto inappropriate career paths, or advancing people too slowly or too rapidly. Personal immobility focuses upon limitations of individual ability. People react to blocked mobility in many personal and individual ways; but several common patterns of response can be observed among workers at all levels in the organization. Blue-collar production workers in assembly line jobs have always stood as the classic example of blocked mobility.

CASE STUDY: AUTO WORKERS AND THE AMERICAN DREAM

Career aspirations are frequently frustrated by the realities of the work situation and in turn produce attitudinal and behavioral adjustments over time. Chinoy (1955) in a study of production employees in the auto industry traced the evolution of aspirations and accommodations and provided a chronology that illustrates and summarizes the process among a group of workers having limited mobility opportunities as they come to grips with the inaccessibility of the American dream of upward mobility.

1. "Many young men who come to work in the factory define their jobs as temporary; they do not expect to remain in the ranks of factory labor." Some choose the work because of a lack of other opportunities, or are attracted by the money, but are aware of the dead-end character of the work: "You don't get advanced by going in the factory; there's no future here." Others hope to earn promotions within the organization. Either orientation supports the view of their current position as temporary.

2. "Workers are most likely to develop or sustain hope for promotion to supervision if while still relatively young they gain some form of advancement." Promotions are available, but usually from one job on the assem-

to another. Progress fosters mobility aspirations, but promotions rvisory positions are rare. Moreover, many vacancies are likely to d from the outside from the ranks of the college-educated. Other arch indicates that in any given year, only one blue-collar worker in n will be promoted (Rosenbaum, 1979a).

3. "The longer workers remain in the plant, the less likely they are to muster the initiative to leave," even if they continually talk of doing so." For these autoworkers their "American dream" is to have their own business and be their own boss. A few do strike out on their own—as small contractors, mechanics, service station operators—but the failure rate of such ventures is high and many return to the assembly line.

4. "As their seniority increases, workers can look forward to the possibility of individual wage increases and of transfer to more desirable jobs." The seniority system discourages the pursuit of their American dream since individuals must risk their seniority as well as their money in leaving, while seniority simultaneously offers advantages in horizontal mobility among shifts and jobs.

5. "Workers who do not gain promotion before the age of forty or thereabouts quickly lose hope because of management's preference for younger men." Despite the limited opportunity structure, aspirations persist until they reach an age perceived as a point where it is impossible to be promoted.

6. "After workers reach the low ceiling . . . they may be satisfied with what they have achieved or, alternatively, they may become bitter and frustrated because of their inability to advance farther."

For most workers the security, steady wages, horizontal progress are accepted as reasonable accomplishments and they turn to nonwork rewards, although some continue to harbor feelings of disappointment. There own aspirations are displaced upon their children who they hope will do better than they have been able to.

The experiences of these auto workers are not unusual and reveal that responses take many behavioral and attitudinal forms: quitting, hostility, cynicism, resignation, shifting attitudes toward the job and the organization, a redefinition of goals, and modified social relationships. They may be rational and calculating adaptations or may occur at a less conscious level. They must be understood as attempts to come to terms with frustration, protect self-images and social images, impute meaning to uncertain experiences, and find substitute forms of recognition.

Turnover

An obvious option available to those with limited opportunity is to leave the organization. Analysis of patterns of turnover among civil service employees reveals a quit rate of over 11 percent for men and women on low opportunity career paths compared to about 7 percent on high opportunity career paths (Smith, 1979:371). Perceptions of blocked mobility are hesitancy to identify people as failures and a reluctance to exclude them or even restrict their areas of operation (Sofer, 1970:24). The reasons seem to include a concern with the devastating personal consequences; sensitivity to the social stigma of failure; a desire to reward loyalty; a lack of confidence in the assessment process; the need to maintain morale; and an awareness of the disruptive consequences of competition. Patterns of demotion function as a means of minimizing the costs of incompetence without disrupting the ongoing functioning of the system.

RESPONSES TO BLOCKED MOBILITY

Opportunities for advancement may be closed off for structural, managerial, or personal reasons. As noted earlier, there are four major sources of structural immobility: the diminishing number of positions at each higher level in bureaucratic organizations; a simple lack of vacancies; changing conditions requiring different abilities; and location on low ceiling career paths. Mismanaged careers result from failure to recognize and develop capabilities, channeling personnel onto inappropriate career paths, or advancing people too slowly or too rapidly. Personal immobility focuses upon limitations of individual ability. People react to blocked mobility in many personal and individual ways; but several common patterns of response can be observed among workers at all levels in the organization. Blue-collar production workers in assembly line jobs have always stood as the classic example of blocked mobility.

CASE STUDY: AUTO WORKERS AND THE AMERICAN DREAM

Career aspirations are frequently frustrated by the realities of the work situation and in turn produce attitudinal and behavioral adjustments over time. Chinoy (1955) in a study of production employees in the auto industry traced the evolution of aspirations and accommodations and provided a chronology that illustrates and summarizes the process among a group of workers having limited mobility opportunities as they come to grips with the inaccessibility of the American dream of upward mobility.

1. "Many young men who come to work in the factory define their jobs as temporary; they do not expect to remain in the ranks of factory labor." Some choose the work because of a lack of other opportunities, or are attracted by the money, but are aware of the dead-end character of the work: "You don't get advanced by going in the factory; there's no future here." Others hope to earn promotions within the organization. Either orientation supports the view of their current position as temporary.

2. "Workers are most likely to develop or sustain hope for promotion to supervision if while still relatively young they gain some form of advancement." Promotions are available, but usually from one job on the assem-

---

bly line to another. Progress fosters mobility aspirations, but promotions to supervisory positions are rare. Moreover, many vacancies are likely to be filled from the outside from the ranks of the college-educated. Other research indicates that in any given year, only one blue-collar worker in ten will be promoted (Rosenbaum, 1979a).

3.   "The longer workers remain in the plant, the less likely they are to muster the initiative to leave, even if they continually talk of doing so." For these autoworkers their "American dream" is to have their own business and be their own boss. A few do strike out on their own—as small contractors, mechanics, service station operators—but the failure rate of such ventures is high and many return to the assembly line.

4.   "As their seniority increases, workers can look forward to the possibility of individual wage increases and of transfer to more desirable jobs." The seniority system discourages the pursuit of their American dream since individuals must risk their seniority as well as their money in leaving, while seniority simultaneously offers advantages in horizontal mobility among shifts and jobs.

5.   "Workers who do not gain promotion before the age of forty or thereabouts quickly lose hope because of management's preference for younger men." Despite the limited opportunity structure, aspirations persist until they reach an age perceived as a point where it is impossible to be promoted.

6.   "After workers reach the low ceiling . . . they may be satisfied with what they have achieved or, alternatively, they may become bitter and frustrated because of their inability to advance farther."

For most workers the security, steady wages, horizontal progress are accepted as reasonable accomplishments and they turn to nonwork rewards, although some continue to harbor feelings of disappointment. There own aspirations are displaced upon their children who they hope will do better than they have been able to.

The experiences of these auto workers are not unusual and reveal that responses take many behavioral and attitudinal forms: quitting, hostility, cynicism, resignation, shifting attitudes toward the job and the organization, a redefinition of goals, and modified social relationships. They may be rational and calculating adaptations or may occur at a less conscious level. They must be understood as attempts to come to terms with frustration, protect self-images and social images, impute meaning to uncertain experiences, and find substitute forms of recognition.

Turnover

An obvious option available to those with limited opportunity is to leave the organization. Analysis of patterns of turnover among civil service employees reveals a quit rate of over 11 percent for men and women on low opportunity career paths compared to about 7 percent on high opportunity career paths (Smith, 1979:371). Perceptions of blocked mobility are also cited as a major contributing factor in the high attrition from teaching (Bloland and Selby, 1980), and nursing (Price and Mueller, 1981).

Leaving the organization is a choice that declines rapidly with age (Mobley, et al., 1979). If people remain, they begin to accumulate advantages that can serve to neutralize the frustration of immobility. The most obvious advantage is seniority, which is a factor in salary and job security. Then, too, as workers gain experience, learn the subtleties of informal operation, and win acceptance into interpersonal networks, they are able to function more effectively. At the same time, family responsibilities increase and act as a deterrent to risk of departure when weighed against the relative security of a known job and seniority. Many other factors can also hold people in an organization: lack of other opportunities; commitment to the intrinsic features of the work; and the lingering belief in opportunity. Athletes who remain in the minor leagues even after it is apparent they will not be promoted to the major leagues exemplify the holding power of these forces (Faulkner:1974). These men tend to have few other marketable skills; they like playing the game; and they cling to the hope, "If the legs hold out, who knows. You're as good as your last season . . . I still might get a shot." Consequently, any organization will contain many blocked from future mobility, but who must make attitudinal and behavioral adaptations.

Hostility and Cynicism

Disappointment, embarrassment, frustration, even anger are human responses to blocked mobility. The intensity of such feelings depend upon many factors and seem to be the greatest among younger and more educated workers (with higher aspirations), men (as a result of traditional sex role socialization placing greater personal and social value upon occupational success), people stalled on a high-ceiling career path (having had the opportunity and "failed") (Kanter, 1977:139), and where opportunities are perceived as plentiful (Faulkner, 1974).

These personal emotions are often vented upon the organization or directed at superiors. It is common for the immobile to make claims of favoritism, politics, or unjust selection procedures. There may be an element of truth to such claims under conditions of "uncertainty" where promotion criteria are vague and administrative discretion is high. Under any circumstances such accusations permit the individual to displace responsibility for failure.

Discontent is strongest and most apparent for those who are demoted or passed over for promotion, while it evolves more slowly among those on low-ceiling career paths. Hostility and cynicism may be a prelude to some other form of adaptation or can become a permanent behavioral style of negativism producing what colleagues call the "chronic complainers" (Kanter, 1977:155–157). Criticism is directed at the organization and those in higher level positions, with new policies and initiatives being a favorite target. Innovations are resisted by reliance upon the contention that superiors fail to understand the situation or that similar policies had failed in the past. Criticism and resistance to change permits the immobile to carve out a role as wise and competent, but unappreciated, experts in the eyes of coworkers—they can be perceived as persons who are really smarter than those higher in the organization. By implication, this posture suggests that superiors have also erred in failing to recognize their ability by promoting them. Resistance may also be understood as a means of retaining some degree of influence since superiors must depend upon the cooperation of subordinates. The threat of failure to implement policies gives the resistant some power. Such power is obviously limited since outright opposition risks termination; it must be understood primarily as some small compensation for those who are effectively denied access to real power.

Ritualism

It is difficult to sustain enthusiasm in the face of limited opportunity; thus, over time, some workers evolve into ritualists, blindly following the rules. They are the people who have lost all real interest in their work, deriving no gratification from their work, and hence deriving no sense of accomplishment from doing it well. Activity is limited to the minimum acceptable level of performance, but without any personal involvement in it (Goffman, 1952).

Ritualism is a relatively rare and extreme response, but it is clear that blocked mobility is associated with a decline in the importance of work compared to other facets of life. Things like family, religion, community service, and recreation assume an ever greater place in their lives. This process occurs for almost everyone; the difference is the age of its onset. For managers on first tracks it emerges as people reach their fifties (and approach retirement), but for the immobile it is already evident among managers in their early thirties (Bray and Howard, 1982).

Depressed Aspirations

There is a pronounced relationship between a perceived lack of opportunity and weak mobility aspirations (see Pennings, 1970). The question of causation may be interpreted in different ways because there is virtually no data that traces the evolution of attitudes over long periods of time. One possibility is that less ambitious people are concentrated in dead-end positions because of their low motivation due either to self-selection or being channeled into such positions. The alternative interpretation is that a perceived lack of opportunity depresses aspirations. If mobility is unattainable, it becomes defined as an increasingly less desirable goal. Logic suggests this to be a rational and intelligent reaction, reducing the potential for future frustration.

Declining aspirations can set in motion a process further limiting opportunities for advancement. Depressed aspirations (combined with the lower importance of work) can reduce the probability of taking action that could improve the chances for promotion. Behaviors capable of influencing promotability range from the direct to the subtle and more invidious. Failure to request promotions, a lack of preparation for advancement in the form of additional training, refusing a transfer or promotion, and just the general impression of lacking "ambition" or "drive" can be destructive to a career. There can be no question that managers use this lack of drive as a criterion in making promotion decisions. Sometimes it surfaces among formal criteria, but more often than not, it is merely a commonly accepted factor.

Relative Definitions of Success

A lack of mobility need not be viewed as failure; it can also be defined as relative success. People may revise their expectations about the desirability of advancement while acquiring a new perspective emphasizing satisfaction with lesser accomplishments (Faulkner, 1974). A hockey player unable to make it to the majors reveals a scaling down of aspirations when he claims, "The National League is not the only league to play in. Believe me, I've given it a good shot . . . but it's a good life here (in the minors)- . . . where else can you make this kind of money and meet the people you do?"

A useful concept for understanding this process is *career anchorage* (Tausky and Dubin, 1965). Evaluating relative process involves locating one's current position on a career path extending from an entry position to the highest level of attainment. The point of reference can thus be "anchored" at either end of the career—upward toward ultimate possible attainment and thus emphasizing progress yet to be made or downward toward the point of origin emphasizing progress already made. Virtually all beginning hockey players anchor their careers upward to playing in the major leagues, but as the opportunities dwindle, the anchorage shifts downward to how far they have progressed from the minors and junior leagues. The same pattern appears among managerial occupations (Tausky and Dubin, 1965). It is not uncommon to find this process accompanied by an emphasis upon the costs of mobility—whether in terms of a professed unwillingness to make the sacrifices or by noting the problems suffered by those who have won promotion.

Horizontal Mobility

Teachers, nurses, secretaries, production workers, and others on low-ceiling career paths (and hence structurally denied access to rewards via promotion) frequently seek to maximize their situations by horizontal movement among jobs at the same level. Positions similar in rank, income, and prestige need not be identical in all other respects. Thus, while there are ordinarily no income differences or formal privileges associated with teaching positions within a school district, some jobs offer secondary rewards that assume great importance in the absence of the potential for upward mobility. As a result, career mobility for urban school teachers involves movement among schools in search of the most satisfactory place to work (Becker, 1952).

Becker (1952) argues that this reflects teachers' subjective ranking of jobs based on work relationships with four categories of people—students, parents, principals, and coworkers. Interaction with students involves both teaching and discipline, with teachers tending to believe there is more challenge and sense of personal accomplishment in dealing with brighter students, and that the potential for disruption is greater among lower class children and certain ethnic and racial groups. It is also assumed that parental support will be less likely among lower socioeconomic groups. Finally, it should be noted that larger schools are perceived as offering better facilities and greater resources. Over time this means that newer, less experienced teachers and principals will be concentrated in the schools perceived as less desirable, which contributes to making them even less desirable places to work, thus adding an additional incentive to transfer. Among clerical and secretarial personnel, horizontal mobility can be achieved by earning assignment to better bosses. The efforts of blue-collar workers focus on movement laterally among shifts (night work means a few cents an hour more, and less stringent supervision), foremen (who are ranked on style and closeness of supervision), different machinery (some equipment affords more free time than others), and work groups.

CONCLUSION

The concept of upward mobility is deeply imbedded in American culture and is strongly supported by organizational systems that link most salient tangible and symbolic rewards to career ladders. Personal hopes and dreams, ambitions and satisfactions, rewards and efforts are thus forged and frustrated in the context of occupational careers. For some fortunate few, careers unfold as a series of continuing promotions and rewards. However, for most workers, careers are limited by their own capabilities or structural opportunities. By the time most workers reach their forties they have made almost all the meaningful career moves they will ever make (Schein, 1980). Workers must reassess their careers and work out accommodations that will allow them to continue to function effectively with the reality of limited opportunities for future advancement.

Bibliography

ABC News. 1985. "Medical malpractice" (May 13).

Abrams, F. W. 1951 "Management's responsibilities in a complex world." *Harvard Business Review* 29: 29–30.

Adams, Larry T. 1985. "Changing employment patterns of organized workers." *Monthly Labor Review* 108: 25–31.

Agarawal, Naresh C. 1981. "Determinates of executive compensation." *Industrial Relations* 20: 36–46.

Albrecht, Sandra L. 1980. "Politics, bureaucracy, and worker participation: The Swedish case." *Journal of Applied Behavioral Science* 16: 299–315.

Alves, Wayne H., and Peter H. Rossi. 1978. "Who should get what? Fairness judgments of the distribution of earnings." *American Journal of Sociology* 84: 541–64.

Anderson, Harry, et al. 1982. "Jobs: Putting America back to work." *Newsweek* (Oct. 18): 78–84.

Anderson, John C., George T. Milkovich, and Anne Tsui. 1981. "A model of intra-organizational mobility." *Academy of Management Review* 6: 529–38.

Argyris, Chris. 1960. *Understanding Organizational Behavior.* Homewood, IL: Dorsey.

Armer, J. Michael. 1968. "Intersociety and intrasociety correlations of occupational prestige." *American Journal of Sociology* 74: 28–36.

Arnold, David O. 1970. *The Sociology of Subcultures.* Berkeley, CA: Glendessary Press.

Arnold, Erik. 1985. "The appliance of science: Technology and housework." *New Scientist* 28: 12–15.

Aronowitz, Stanley. 1973. *False Promises.* New York: McGraw-Hill.

Arvey, Richard D. 1979. "Unfair Discrimination in the Employment Interview: Legal and Psychological Aspects." *Psychological Bulletin* 86: 736–65.

———and James E. Campion. 1982. "The employment interview: a summary and review of recent research." *Personnel Psychology* 35:281–322.

Associated Press. 1985. "Fear of abuse charges keeps affection out of school, teachers say." *Wilmington News Journal* (May 31): 6B.

Associated Press. 1982. "Librarians say 'Go Ask Alice' is censored most in schools." *New York Times* (Nov. 28): 73.

Auerbach, Jerald S. 1976. *Unequal Justice.* New York: Oxford University Press.

BALL, DONALD W. 1976. "Failure in sport." *American Sociological Review* 41: 726–39.

BARNES, WILLIAM F., AND ETHEL B. JONES. 1974. "Differences in male and female quitting." *Journal of Human Resources* 9: 439–51.

BARON, AVA. 1982. "Women and the making of the American working class: a study of the proletarianization of printers." *Review of Radical Political Economics* 14: 23–42.

BARRERA, MARIO. 1979. *Race and Class in the Southwest.* Notre Dame, IN: University of Notre Dame Press.

BAUER, BETSY. 1985. "Health-test kits." *USA Today* (Dec. 24): 4B.

BEATTIE, CHRISTOPHER, AND BYRON G. SPENCER. 1971. "Career attainment in Canadian bureaucracies: Unscrambling the effects of age, seniority, education, and ethnolinguistic factors on salary." *American Journal of Sociology* 77: 472–90.

BECKER, EUGENE H. 1984. "Self-employed workers: an update to 1983." *Monthly Labor Review* 107: 14–18.

BECKER, GARY S. 1975. *Human Capital.* New York: Columbia University Press.

———— 1971. *The Economics of Discrimination.* Chicago: University of Chicago Press.

BECKER, HOWARD S. 1972. "A school is a lousy place to learn anything in." *American Behavioral Scientist* 16: 89–109.

BECKER, HOWARD S. 1963. *Outsiders: Studies in the Sociology of Deviance.* New York: Free Press.

———— 1952. "The career of the Chicago public school teacher." *American Journal of Sociology* 57: 470–77.

BEEHR, TERRY A., THOMAS D. TABER, AND JEFFREY T. WALSH. 1980. "Perceived mobility channels: criteria for intraorganizational job mobility." *Organizational Behavior and Human Performance* 26: 250–64.

BEGUN, JAMES W., AND ROGER D. FELDMAN. 1981. *A Social and Economic Analysis of Professional Regulation in Optometry.* Washington, D.C.: U.S. Department of Health and Human Services.

BELLACE, JANICE R. 1984. "Comparable worth: proving sex-based wage discrimination." *Iowa Law Review* 69: 655–704.

BELLAK, ALVIN O. 1984. "Comparable Worth: A Practitioner's View." In *Comparable Worth: Issue for the 80s.* Washington DC: U.S. Commission on Civil Rights.

BENET, MARY KATHLEEN. 1972. *The Secretarial Ghetto.* New York: McGraw-Hill.

BENSMAN, JOSEPH, AND ISRAEL GERVER. 1963. "Crime and punishment in the factory: the function of deviancy in maintaining the social system." *American Sociological Review* 28: 588–98.

BERK, SARAH FENSTERMAKER (ED.) 1980. *Women and Household Labor.* Beverly Hills, CA: Sage.

BERLANT, JEFFREY L. 1975. *Profession and Monopoly: A Study of Medicine in the United States and Great Britain.* Berkeley: University of California Press.

BEST, FRED. 1978. "Preferences on work-life scheduling and work-leisure tradeoffs." *Monthly Labor Review* 101: 31–37.

BIBB, ROBERT, AND WILLIAM H. FORM. 1977. "The effects of industrial, occupational, and sex stratification on wages in blue-collar markets." *Social Forces* 55: 974–96.

BIERSTEDT, ROBERT. 1950. "An analysis of social power." *American Sociological Review* 15: 730–38.

BIGGART, NICOLE W. 1983. "Rationality, meaning and self-management: Success manuals, 1950–1980." *Social Problems* 30: 298–311.

BIGUS, ODIA. 1972. "The milkman and his customer." *Urban Life and Culture* 1: 131–65.

BLACKBURN, ROBERT T., D. W. CHAPMAN, AND SUSAN W. CAMERON. 1980. "Cloning in academe: mentorship and academic careers." *Research in Higher Education.*

BLAINE, CHARLEY. 1985. "Union members now trail in wage gains." *USA Today* (May 7): 4B.

BLANK, JOSEPH P. 1975. *Migrants No More.* Pleasantville: Reader's Digest Association.

BLAU, PETER M. AND OTIS D. DUNCAN. 1967. *The American Occupational Structure.* New York: Wiley.

BLAU, PETER M. AND MARSHALL W. MEYER. 1971. *Bureaucracy in Modern Society.* New York: Random House.

BLAUNER, ROBERT. 1964. *Alienation and Freedom.* Chicago: University of Chicago Press.

BLOLAND, PAUL A., AND THOMAS J. SELBY. 1980. "Factors associated with career change among secondary school teachers: A review of the literature." *Educational Research Quarterly* 5: 13–24.

BLUMBERG, ABRAHAM. 1967. "The practice of law as confidence game: organizational co-optation of a profession." *Law and Society Review* 1: 15–39.

BLUMENFELD, RUTH. 1965. "Mohawks: Round trip to the high steel." *Transaction* 3: 19–21.

BOGDAN, ROBERT. 1972. "Learning to sell door to door." *American Behavioral Scientist* 16: 59–68.

BOLES, JACQUELINE AND A. P. GARBIN. 1974. "Stripping for a Living: An Occupational Study of the Night Club Stripper." In Clifton Bryant (ed.), *Deviant Behavior: Occupational and Organizational Bases.* Chicago: Rand-McNally.

BOND, RONALD S., ET AL. 1980. *Effects of Restrictions on Advertising and Commercial Practice in the Professions: The Case of Optometry.* Washington, D.C.: Federal Trade Commission.

BORGATTA, EMORY F., AND R. R. EVANS. 1967. "Behavioral and personality expectations associated with status positions." *Multivariate Behavioral Research* 2: 153–74.

BOSE, CHRISTINE E., AND PETER H. ROSSI. 1983. "Gender and jobs: prestige standings of occupations as affected by gender." *American Sociological Review* 48: 316–30.

BOULDING, ELISE. 1980. "The Labor of U.S. Farm Women: A Knowledge Gap." *Work and Occupations* 7: 261–90.

BOYD, JOHN A. 1979. "Research Management Stifles Innovation." *New York Times* (Mar. 11): 14F.

BRADLEY, KEITH AND STEPHEN HILL. 1983. "'After Japan:' The Quality Circle Transplant and Productive Efficiency," *British Journal of Industrial Relations* 21: 291–311.

BRAVERMAN, HARRY. 1974. *Labor and Monopoly Capitalism.* New York: Monthly Review Press.

BRAZIL, ERIC. 1985. "Women praise L. A. pay decision." *USA Today* (May 10): 3A.

BREEN, GEORGE E. 1983. *Middle Management Morale in the 80s.* New York: American Management Association.

BRENNER, M. HARVEY. 1973. *Mental Illness and the Economy.* Cambridge: Harvard University Press.

———. 1976. *Estimating the Social Costs of National Economic Policy.* Joint Economic Committee of the Congress. Washington: GPO.

———. 1980. "Industrialization and economic growth: estimates of their effects on the health of populations." In M. H. Brenner, et al, (eds.), *Assessing the Contributions of the Social Science to Health.* Washington: American Academy for the Advancement of Science.

BRODY, JANE E. 1976. "Experts seek ethical guidelines for sex research and therapy." *New York Times* (January 25): 39.

BROOKS, THOMAS R. 1971. *Toil and Trouble.* New York: Delacorte.

BROPHY, BETH. 1985a. "Two-tier pay plans stir debate." *USA Today* (June 12): 1–2B.

——— 1985b. "Time clocks keep more varied beats." *USA Today* (Sept. 3): 1–2B.

——— 1985c. "Obesity suit puts managers on notice." *USA Today* (May 28): 5B.

——— 1985d. "Job applicants might not be all they claim." *USA Today* (June 27): 7B.

BROWN, M. C. 1955. "The status of jobs and occupations as evaluated by an urban Negro sample." *American Sociological Review* 20: 561–66.

BROWNE, JOY. 1973. *The Used Car Game.* Lexington, MA: D. C. Heath.

BRUSH, LORELEI R. 1980. "The Significance of Students' Stereotype of a Mathematician for Their Career Planning." *The Personnel and Guidance Journal* 56: 231–35.

BRYAN, JAMES H. 1966. "Occupational ideologies and individual attitudes of call girls." *Social Problems* 13: 441–50.

BRYAN, JAMES H. 1965. "Apprenticeships in prostitution." *Social Problems* 12: 287–97.

BUROWAY, MICHAEL. 1983. "Between the labor process and the state: the changing face of factory regimes under advanced capitalism." *American Sociological Review* 48: 587–605.

——— 1976. "The Function and Reproduction of Migrant Labor." *American Journal of Sociology* 81: 1051–87.

BURRAGE, MICHAEL C., AND DAVID CORRY. 1981. "At sixes and sevens: occupational status in the city of London from the fourteenth to the seventeenth century." *American Sociological Review* 46: 375–93.

BUSINESS WEEK. 1978. "The rebellion against 'plain-English' law." (Jan. 23): 112.

BUSINESS WEEK. 1976. "The troubled professions." *Business Week* (Aug. 16): 126–38.

BUTLER, JOHN S. 1976 "Inequality in the military: an examination of promotion time for black and white enlisted men." *American Sociological Review* 41: 807–18.

BUTLER, SUELLEN, AND JAMES K. SKIPPER, JR. 1980. "Waitressing, vulnerability, and job autonomy." *Sociology of Work and Occupations* 7: 487–502.

BUTLER, SUELLEN R. AND WILLIAM E. SNIZEK. 1976. "The waitress-diner relationship: a multimethod approach to the study of subordinate influence." *Sociology of Work and Occupations* 3: 209–22.

CAMERON, SUSAN W., AND ROBERT T. BLACKBURN. 1981. "Sponsorship and academic career success." *Journal of Higher Education* 52: 369–77.

CAREY, JOHN. 1985. "Hospital hospitality." *Newsweek* 106 (Feb. 11): 78–79.

CAVANAUGH, R. C. AND D. L. RHODE. 1976. "The unauthorized practice of law and pro se divorce." *Yale Law Review* 86: 104–84.

CHAFETZ, JANET S. 1974. *Masculine/Feminine or Human?* Itasca, IL: F. E. Peacock.

CHAPMAN, WILLIAM. 1979. "Job-for-life myth exploding in Japan." *Wilmington News-Journal*, (Mar. 25): 1–2D.

CHARLES, MICHAEL T. 1981. "The performance and socialization of female recruits in the Michigan State Police Training Academy." *Journal of Police Science and Administration* 9: 209–23.

CHARNOFSKY, HAROLD. 1974. "Ballplayers, occupational image, and the maximization of profit." In Phyllis L. Stewart and Muriel G. Cantor (eds.). *Varieties of Work Experience*, pp. 262–73. Cambridge, MA: Schenkman.

CHERRY, MIKE. 1974. *On High Steel: the Education of an Ironworker*. New York: Ballantine.

CHI, KEON S. 1984. "Comparable worth: implications of the Washington case." *State Government* 57: 34–45.

CHINOY, ELY. 1955. *Automobile Workers and the American Dream*. Boston: Beacon Press.

CHIRA, SUSAN. 1985. "A tough ascent for Japanese women." *New York Times* (Feb. 24): 1–27F.

CHRISTENSEN, BARLOW F. 1980. "The unauthorized practice of law: Do good fences really make good neighbors—or even good sense." *American Bar Foundation Research Journal* 1980: 159–216.

CLAWSON, DAN. 1980. *Bureaucracy and the Labor Process: The Transformation of U.S. Industry, 1860–1920*. New York: Monthly Labor Review Press.

CLYMER, ADAM. 1985. "Low marks for executive honesty." *New York Times* (June 9): 1–6.

COHEN, HARRIS S. 1975. "Regulatory Politics and American Medicine." *American Behavioral Scientist* 19: 122–36.

———. 1980. "On professional power and conflict of interest: state licensing boards on trial." *Journal of Health Politics, Policy and Law* 5: 291–308.

———. 1973. "Professional licensure, organizational behavior, and the public interest." *Milbank Memorial Fund Quarterly* 51: 73–88.

COLE, ROBERT E. 1979. *Work, Mobility and Participation: A Comparative Study of American and Japanese Industry*. Berkeley, CA: University of California Press.

CONDRAN, JOHN G., AND JERRY G. BODE. 1982. "Rashomon, working wives and family division of labor." *Journal of Marriage and the Family* 44: 421–26.

COTGROVE, STEPHEN. 1972. "Alienation and automation." *British Journal of Sociology* 23: 437–51.

——— AND STEVEN BOX. 1970. *Science, Industry and Society*. New York: Barnes and Noble.

COUNTS, GEORGE S. 1925. "The social status of occupations: a problem in vocational guidance." *School Review* 33: 16–27.

COWAN, RUTH S. 1985. *More Work for Mother*. New York: Basic Books.

CRESPI, LEO P. 1968. "The implications of tipping in America." In Marcello Truzzi (ed.), *Sociology in Everyday Life*, pp. 75–86. Englewood Cliffs, NJ: Prentice-Hall.

CREWDSON, JOHN. 1979. "Alien workers exploited." *Wilmington News-Journal* (Nov. 22): 14E.

———. 1980. "Thousands of aliens held in virtual slavery in U.S." *New York Times* (Oct. 19): i–58.

CROWTHER, B., AND DOUGLAS M. MORE. 1972. "Occupational stereotyping on initial impressions." *Journal of Vocational Behavior* 2: 87–94.

CROZIER, MICHAEL. 1964. *The Bureaucratic Phenomena*. Chicago: University of Chicago Press.

CULLEN, FRANCIS T. AND BRUCE G. LINK. 1980. "Crime as an occupation." *Criminology* 18 (Nov.): 399–410.

CURRAN, BARBARA. 1984. "The legal profession in the 1980s." Paper presented at annual meeting of the Law and Society Association.

CURRY, ESTHER R. 1983. "The invisible worker." *Wilmington News-Journal* (Nov. 27): 1–10A.

DALTON, GENE W., PAUL H. THOMPSON, AND RAYMOND L. PRICE. 1977. "The four stages of professional careers: a new look at performance by professionals." *Organizational Dynamics* 8: 19–42.

DALTON, MELVILLE. 1974. "The ratebuster: The case of the saleswoman." In Phyllis L. Stewart and Muriel G. Cantor (eds.), *Varieties of Work Experience*, pp. 206–13. New York: Wiley.

———. 1959. *Men Who Manage*. New York: Wiley.

DALY, PATRICIA A. 1982. "Unpaid family workers: long-term decline continues." *Monthly Labor Review* 105: 3–5.

DANIELS, ARLENE K. 1985. *Invisible Careers: Women Civic Leaders in the Volunteer World*. Chicago: University of Chicago Press.

DANIELS, ARLENE K. 1969. "The captive professional: bureaucratic limitations in the practice of military psychiatry." *Journal of Health and Social Behavior* 10: 255–65.

DANZIGER, JAMES N. 1979. "The 'skill bureaucracy' and intraorganizational control." *Sociology of Work and Occupations* 6: 204–26.

DAVIES, MARGERY W. 1982. *Woman's Place Is at the Typewriter*. Philadelphia: Temple University Press.

DAVIS, FRED. 1959. "The cabdriver and his fare: Facets of a fleeting relationship." *American Journal of Sociology* 65: 158–65.

DAVIS, KINGSLEY, AND WILBERT MOORE. 1945. "Some principles of stratification." *American Sociological Review* 10: 242–49.

DAWKINS, MARVIN P. 1980. "Educational and occupational goals: male versus female black high school seniors." *Urban Education* 15: 231–42.

DEBOER, LARRY AND MICHAEL SEEBORG. 1984. "The female-male unemployment differential: effects of changes in industry employment." *Monthly Labor Review* 107: 8–15.

DEFLEUR, MELVIN L. 1964. "Occupational roles as presented on television." *Public Opinion Quarterly* 28: 57–74.

DE KADT, MAARTEN. 1979. "Insurance: a clerical work factory." In Andrew Zimbalist (ed.), *Case Studies on the Labor Process*, pp. 242–56. New York: Monthly Review Press.

DELLA FAVE, L. RICHARD, 1974. "Success values: are they universal or class-differentiated?" *American Journal of Sociology* 80: 153–69.

DENTZER, SUSAN. 1985. "Bitter harvest." *Newsweek* (Feb. 18): 52–60.

DENZIN, NORMAN K. 1968. "Incomplete professionalization: the case pharmacy." *Social Forces* 46: 375–81.

DEROSSI, FLAVIA. 1982. *The Technocratic Illusion.* Armonk, NY: M. E. Sharpe.

DEVENS, RICHARD M., JR., ET AL. 1985. "Employment and unemployment in 1984." *Monthly Labor Review* 108: 3–15.

DEW, R. BERESFORD AND KENNETH P. GEE. 1973. *Management Control and Information.* New York: Wiley.

DILL, BONNIE THORNTON. 1983. "Race, class and gender: prospects for an all inclusive sisterhood." *Feminist Studies* 9: 131–50.

DIPBOYLE, R. L., H. L. FROMKIN AND K. WIBACK. 1975. "Relative Importance of Applicant Sex, Attractiveness, and Scholastic Standing in Evaluation of Job Applicant Resumes." *Journal of Applied Psychology* 60: 39–43.

DIRKS, RAYMOND L., AND LEONARD GROSS. 1976. *The Great Wall Street Scandal.* New York: McGraw-Hill.

DORE, RONALD. 1973. *British Factory-Japanese Factory.* Berkeley, CA: University of California Press.

DOWD, MAUREEN. 1983. "Many women in poll value jobs as much as family life." *New York Times* (Dec. 4): 1–66.

DREHER, GEORGE F., AND THOMAS W. DOUGHERTY. 1980. "Turnover and competition for expected job openings: an exploratory analysis." *Academy of Management Journal* 23: 766–72.

DRUMMOND, DOUGLAS S. 1976. *Police Culture.* Beverly Hills, CA:Sage.

DUBIN, ROBERT. 1971. *Human Relations in Industry.* Englewood Cliffs, NJ: Prentice-Hall.

DUBIN, ROBERT. 1956. "Industrial workers' worlds: A study of the 'central life interests' of industrial workers." *Social Problems* 3: 131–42.

DUBOIS, JOHN. 1986. "Florida pharmacists unsure about prescribing drugs." *USA Today* (May 14): 5D.

DUDAR, HELEN. 1977. "The price of blowing the whistle." *New York Times Magazine* (Oct. 30): 41–54.

DUNCAN, E. PAUL AND CAROLYN PERRUCCI. 1976. "Dual occupation families and migration." *American Sociological Review* 41: 252–61.

DUNNE, FAITH. 1980. "Occupational sex-sterotyping among rural young women and men," *Rural Sociology* 45: 396–415.

DUNNETE, MARVIN D., RICHARD D. ARVEY, AND PAUL A. BANAS. 1973. "Why do they leave?" *Personnel* 50: 25–39.

DWORKIN, ROSALIND J. 1981. "Prestige ranking of the housewife occupation." *Sex Roles* 7: 59–63.

EASTO, PATRICK C., AND MARCELLO TRUZZI. 1974. "The carnival as a marginally legal work activity: a typological approach to work systems." In C. Bryant (ed.), *Deviant Behavior: Occupational and Organizational Bases*, pp. 336–53. Chicago: Rand McNally.

ECCLES, ROBERT G. 1981. "Bureaucratic versus craft administration: the relationship of the market structure to the construction firm." *Administrative Science Quarterly* 26: 449–69.

ECKLAND, BRUCE K. 1965. "Academic ability, higher education, and occupational mobility." *American Sociological Review* 30: 735–46.

EDWARDS, ALBA M. 1943. *Population: Comparative Occupational Statistics for the United States, 1870 to 1940.* Washington: Government Printing Office.

EDWARDS, RICHARD. 1979. *Contested Terrain: The Transformation of the Workplace in the Twentieth Century.* New York: Basic Books.

EHRENREICH, BARBARA, AND DEIRDRE ENGLISH. 1979. *For Her Own Good.* Garden City, NY: Anchor Press.

EISENSTEIN, JAMES. 1978. *Counsel for the United States: U.S. Attorneys in the Political and Legal Systems.* Baltimore: Johns Hopkins University Press.

ELDER, RICHARD. 1978. "My First Season on the Aisle." *New York Times Magazine* (July 16): 17–47.

EL NASSER, HAYA. 1986. "Video terminals watch workers." *USA Today* (July 7): 6B.

EMERSON, RICHARD M. 1962. "Power-dependence relations." *American Sociological Review* 27: 31–41.

ENGLAND, PAULA. 1979. "Women and occupational prestige: a case of vacuous sex equity." *Signs* 5: 252–65.

ESKEY, KENNETH. 1985. "Success in real estate might just be a figure of speech." *Wilmington News-Journal* (Oct. 12): 1C.

ETAUGH, CLAIRE AND S. ROSE. 1975. "Adolescent's sex bias in the evaluation of performance." *Developmental Psychology* 11: 663–64.

ETAUGH, CLAIRE AND ETHEL FORESMAN. 1983. "Evaluations of competence as a function of sex and marital status." *Sex Roles* 9: 759–65.

EVAN, WILLIAM M., AND EZRA G. LEVIN. 1966. "Status-set and role-set conflicts of the stockbroker." *Social Forces* 45: 73–83.

EWEN, ROBERT B., ET AL. 1966. "An emperical test of the Herzberg two-factor theory."*Journal of Applied Psychology* 50: 544–50.

FARBERMAN, HARVEY A. 1975. "A criminogenic market structure: the automobile industry." *The Sociological Quarterly* 16: 438–57.

FAULKNER, ROBERT R. 1974. "Making us sound bad: performer compliance and interaction in the symphony orchestra." In Phyllis L. Stewart and Muriel G. Cantor (eds.), *Varieties of Work Experience*, pp. 238–48. New York: Wiley.

FAULKNER, ROBERT R. 1974. "Coming of age in organizations: a comparative study of career contingencies and adult socialization." *Sociology of Work and Occupations* 1: 131–73.

FAULKNER, ROBERT R. 1971. *Hollywood Studio Musicians.* Chicago: Aldine-Atherton.

FEAGIN, JOE R. 1984. *Racial and Ethnic Relations.* Englewood Cliffs, NJ: Prentice-Hall.

FEDER, BARNABY J. 1981. "New twists in the foreman's world." *New York Times* (May 17): 3F.

FEIGELMAN, WILLIAM. 1974. "Peeping: the pattern of voyeurism among construction workers." *Urban Life and Culture* 3: 35–49.

FELDMAN, DANIEL C. 1976. "A contingency theory of socialization." *Administrative Science Quarterly* 21: 433–542.

————. 1981. "The multiple socialization of organization members." *Academy of Management Review* 6: 309–18.

FITZPATRICK, JOHN S. 1980. "Adapting to danger: a participant observation study of an underground mine." *Sociology of Work and Occupations* 7: 131–58.

FLAIM, PAUL O. 1984. "Discouraged workers: how strong are their links to the job market?" *Monthly Labor Review* 107: 8–11.

————, AND ELLEN SEHGAL. 1985. "Displaced workers of 1979–83: how well have they fared?" *Monthly Labor Review* 108: 3–16.

FOGEL, ROBERT W., AND STANLEY L. ENGERMAN. 1974. *Time on the Cross: The Economics of American Negro Slavery.* Boston: Little Brown.

FONER, PHILIP S. 1964. *History of the Labor Movement in the United States,* vol. III. New York: International Publishers.

FORM, WILLIAM. 1981. "Resolving ideological issues on the division of labor." In Hubert M. Blalock, Jr. (ed.), *Theory and Research in Sociology* pp. 140–55. New York: Free Press.

FORM, WILLIAM H. 1973. "Autoworkers and their machines." *Social Forces* 51 1–15.

FOX, LYNN H. 1981. *The Problem of Women and Mathematics.* New York: Ford Foundation.

FOX, MARY F. AND SHARLENE HESSE-BIBER. 1984. *Women at Work.* Palo Alto, CA: Mayfield.

FRANKLIN, BEN A. 1985."Dismissed nuclear worker awarded $70,000." *New York Times* (Aug. 4): 23.

FREIDSON, ELIOT. 1977. "The futures of professionalisation." In M. Stacey, et al, (eds), *Health and the Division of Labor,* pp. 14–38. London: Croom Helm.

FREIDSON, ELIOT. 1976. "The division of labor as social interaction." *Social Problems* 23: 304–13.

————. 1970. *Profession of Medicine.* New York: Dodd-Mead.

FREIDSON, ELIOT. 1960. "Client control and medical practice." *American Journal of Sociology* 65: 374–82.

FROMSON, DAVID. 1977. "Let's be realistic about specialization." *American Bar Association Journal* 63: 74–77.

FUCHS, VICTOR. 1971. "Differences in hourly earnings between men and women." *Monthly Labor Review* 94: 9–15.

GAERTNER, KAREN N. 1980. "The structure of organizational careers." *Sociology of Education* 53: 7–20.

GALANTE, MARY ANN. 1986. "California bar attorneys end strike." *The National Law Journal* (June 2): 8.

———. 1985. "Malpractice rates zoom." *The National Law Journal* (June 3): 1–26.

GALBRAITH, JOHN KENNETH. 1971. *The New Industrial State.* Boston: Houghton Mifflin.

GALLUCCIO, N. 1978. "The rise of the corporate lawyer." *Forbes* 122 (Sept. 18): 168–82.

GALLUP ORGANIZATION. 1981. *Americans Volunteer.* Princeton, NJ: Gallup Organization.

GALLUP ORGANIZATION. 1985. *Ideal Life-Style for Women.* Princeton, NJ: Gallup Organization.

GAME, ANNE, AND ROSEMARY PRINGLE. 1983. *Gender at Work.* Sydney (Australia): George Allen & Unwin.

GAMMONS, PETER. 1977. "Wild Willie gets a new lease on life." *Sports Illustrated* 47 (Nov. 28): 28–33.

GANS, HERBERT J. 1979. *Deciding What's News.* New York: Pantheon.

GARSON, BARBARA. 1975. *All the Livelong Day.* New York: Doubleday.

GERDES, EUGENIA P. AND DOUGLAS M. GARBER. 1983. "Sex bias in hiring: Effects of job demands and applicant competence." *Sex Roles* 9: 307–19.

GILLESPIE, CHARLES. 1974. "The open road for boys: meet Glen Young, master shuffleboard hustler." In Clifton D. Bryant (ed.), *Deviant Behavior: Occupational and Organizational Bases,* pp. 28–285. Chicago: Rand McNally.

GINZBERG, ELY. 1972. "Toward a theory of occupational choice: A restatement." *Vocational Guidance* 20: 169–76.

GLASER, EDWARD M. 1976. *Productivity Gains Through Worklife Improvements.* New York: Harcourt Brace.

GLENN, EVELYN N., AND ROSLYN L. FIELDBERG. 1977. "Degraded and deskilled: the proletarianization of clerical work." *Social Problems* 25: 52–63.

GLENN, NORVAL D. 1975. "The contribution of white collars to occupational prestige." *The Sociological Quarterly* 16: 184–97.

GOFFMAN, ERVING. 1961. *Asylums.* Garden City, NY: Doubleday Anchor Books.

———. 1956. "Embarrassment and social organization." *American Journal of Sociology* 62: 264–74.

———. 1952. "On cooling the mark out." *Psychiatry* 15: 451–63.

GOLD, RAYMOND L. 1964. "In the basement: the apartment building janitor." In P. Berger (ed.), *The Human Shape of Work,* pp. 1–49. New York: Crowell, Collier, and Macmillan.

———. 1952. "Janitors versus tenants: a status-income dilemma." *American Journal of Sociology* 57: 486–93.

GOLDIN, CLAUDIA AND KENNETH SOKOLOFF. 1982. "Women, children, and industrialization in the early republic." *Journal of Economic History* 42: 741–74.

GOLDNER, FRED H. 1965. "Demotion in industrial management." *American Sociological Review* 30: 714–24.

——— AND R. R. RITTI. 1967. "Professionalization as career immobility." *American Journal of Sociology* 72: 489–502.

GOLDSTEIN, BERNARD, AND JACK OLDHAM. 1979. *Children and Work: A Study of Socialization.* New York: New Brunswick, NJ: Transaction Books.

GOLDTHORPE, JOHN H., DAVID LOCKWOOD, FRANK BECHHOFER, AND JENNIFER PLATT. 1968. *The Affluent Worker: Industrial Attitudes and Behavior.* New York: Cambridge University Press.

GOODE, WILLIAM J. 1957. "Community within a community: the professions." *American Sociological Review* 22: 194–200.

———. 1960. "Encroachment, charlatanism, and the emerging profession: psychology, medicine and sociology." *American Sociological Review* 25: 902–13.

GOODE, WILLIAM J. 1961. "The librarian: from occupation to profession?" *The Library Quarterly* 31: 306–20.

———. 1969. "The theoretical limits of professionalism." In A. Etzioni (ed.), *The Semi-Professions and Their Organization,* pp. 266–313 New York: Free Press.

GOODSELL, CHARLES T. 1976. "Cross-cultural comparison of behavior of postal clerks towards clients." *Administrative Science Quarterly* 21: 140–50.

GOSS, MARY. 1961. "Influence and authority among physicians in an outpatient clinic." *American Sociological Review* 26: 39–50.

GOULDNER, ALVIN W. 1954. *Patterns of Industrial Bureaucracy.* New York: Free Press.

GRANDJEAN, BURKE D., AND PATRICIA A. TAYLOR. 1980. "Job satisfaction among female clerical workers." *Sociology of Work and Occupations* 7: 33–53.

GRAVES, BENNIE. 1958. "Breaking out: an apprenticeship system among pipeline construction workers." *Human Organization* 27: 9–13.

GRAY, DIANA. 1973. "Turning out: A study of teenage prostitution." *Urban Life and Culture* 1: 401–25.

GRAY, JANET D. 1983. "The married professional woman: An examination of her role conflicts and coping strategies." *Psychology of Women Quarterly* 7: 235–43.

GREEN, GLORIA P., ET AL. 1983. "Revisions in 'current population survey' beginning in January 1983." *Employment and Earnings* 30: 7–15.

GREEN, MARK. 1976. "The A.B.A. as Trade Association." In Ralph Nader and Mark Green (eds.), *Verdicts on Lawyers*. New York: T. Y. Crowell.

GREEN, S. AND T. R. MITCHELL. 1979. "Attributional processes of leaders in leader-member interactions." *Organization Behavior and Human Performance* 23: 429–58.

GREENWALD, HAROLD. 1969. "The social and professional life of the call-girl." In Simon Dinitz, et al., (eds.), *Deviance*. New York: Oxford.

GREIF, GEOFFREY. 1985. *Single Fathers*. Lexington, MA: Lexington Books.

GROSMAN, BRIAN A. 1969. *The Prosecutor*. Toronto: University of Toronto Press.

GROSS, NEAL, WARD S. MASON, AND ALEXANDER W. MCEACHERN. 1958. *Explorations in Role Analysis: Studies of the School Superintendency Role*. New York: Wiley.

GROSSMAN, ALLYSON, S. 1980. "Women in domestic work: yesterday and today." *Monthly Labor Review* 103: 17–21.

GUBRIUM, JABER F. 1980. "Patient exclusion in geriatric staffings." *The Sociological Quarterly* 21: 335–47.

GUERIN, DANIEL. 1976. *100 Years of Labor in the USA*. London: Ink Links Ltd.

GULLAHORN, JOHN T., AND JEANNE GULLAHORN. 1963. "Role conflict and its resolution." *The Sociological Quarterly* 4: 32–48.

GURNEY, ROSS M. 1980. "The effects of unemployment on the psycho-social development of school-leavers." *Journal of Occupational Psychology* 53:205–13.

GUSFIELD, JOSEPH R. AND MICHAEL SCHWARTZ. 1962. "The meanings of occupational prestige." *American Sociological Review* 28: 265–71.

GUSTAFSON, THANE. 1975. "The controversy over peer review." *Science* 190 (Dec. 12): 1060–66.

GUY, PAT. 1985. "Unemployed benefits hit fewer hands." *USA Today* (Nov. 6): 1B.

GUZDA, HENRY P. 1984. "Industrial democracy: made in the U.S.A." *Monthly Labor Review* 107: 26–33.

HAAS, AIN. 1983. "The aftermath of Sweden's codetermination law: Workers' experiences in Gothenburg, 1977–1980." *Economic and Industrial Democracy* 4: 19–46.

HAAS, JACK. 1972. "Binging: educational control among high steel ironworkers." *American Behavioral Scientist* 16: 27–34.

———. 1974. "The stages of the high steel ironworker apprentice career." *The Sociological Quarterly* 15: 93–108.

———. 1977. "Learning real feelings: a study of high steel ironworkers' reactions to fear and danger." *Sociology of Work and Occupations* 4: 147–70.

HAITCH, RICHARD. 1985. "Left-Hand Rights." *New York Times* (June 23): 39.

HALABY, CHARLES N. 1978. "Bureaucratic promotion criteria." *Administrative Science Quarterly* 23: 466–84.

HALE, ELLEN. 1983. "Middle-level managers losing faith in business, 30-year survey shows." *Wilmington News-Journal* (Sept. 6): 8C.

HALL, DOUGLAS T. AND LYNN A. ISABELLA. 1985. "Downward movement and career development." *Organizational Dynamics* 14: 5–23.

HALL, DOUGLAS T. 1972. "A model of coping with role conflict: the role behavior of college educated women." *Administrative Science Quarterly* 17: 471–86.

HALL, GAIL A. 1977. "Workshop for a ballerina: an exercise in professional socialization." *Urban Life* 6: 193–220.

HALL, OSWALD. 1946. "Informal organization of the medical profession." *Canadian Journal of Economics and Political Science* 12: 30–41.

———. 1948. "The stages of a medical career." *American Journal of Sociology* 53: 327–36.

———. 1949. "Types of medical careers." *American Journal of Sociology* 55: 243–53.

HALL, RICHARD H. 1986. *Dimensions of Work*. Beverly Hills, CA: Sage.

———. 1975. *Occupations and the Social Structure*. Englewood Cliffs, NJ: Prentice-Hall.

HALLER, ARCHIBALD O., DONALD B. HOLSINGER, AND HELCIO U. SARAIVA. 1972. "Variations in occupational prestige hierarchies: Brazilian data." *American Journal of Sociology* 77: 941–56.

HANDLER, JOEL F. 1967. *The Lawyer and His Community*. Madison, WI: University of Wisconsin Press.

HANSSON, ROBERT O., MARY E. CHERNOVITZ, AND WARREN H. JONES. 1977. "Maternal employment and androgeny." *Psychology of Women Quarterly* 2: 76–78.

HARGENS, LOWELL. 1967. "Sponsored and contest mobility of American academic scientists." *Sociology of Education* 4: 24–38.

HARRIS, LOUIS. 1975. "Malpractice insurance: doctors vs. lawyers." *The Harris Survey* (July 10).

————. 1978. "Occupational prestige." *The Harris Survey* (Jan. 12).

————. 1979. "Confidence in most institutions down." *ABC News-Harris Survey* 1 (Mar. 5).

HARRIS, RICHARD N. 1973. *The Police Academy.* New York: Wiley.

HARRIS, SARA, AND ROBERT F. ALLEN. 1978. *The Quiet Revolution.* New York: Rawson Associates.

HARTLEY, JEAN F. 1980. "The impact of unemployment upon the self-esteem of managers." *Journal of Occupational Psychology* 53: 147–55.

HARTMANN, HEIDI I. 1981. "The family as the locus of gender, class and political struggle: the example of housework." *Signs* 6: 366–94.

HAUG, MARIE R. 1977. "Computer technology and the obsolescence of the concept of profession." In M. R. Haug and J. Dofny (eds.), *Work and Technology*, pp. 215–28. Beverly Hills, CA: Sage.

————. 1973. "Deprofessionalization: An Alternative Hypothesis For the Future." *Sociological Review Monograph* 20: 195–212.

————. 1975. "The Deprofessionalization of Everyone?" *Sociological Focus* 8: 197–213.

————. AND MARVIN B. SUSSMAN. 1971. "Professionalization and Unionization." *American Behavioral Scientist* 14: 525–40.

————. AND MARVIN SUSSMAN. 1969. "Professional autonomy and the revolt of the client." *Social Problems* 27: 153–61.

HAUG, MARIE R., AND HAROLD A. WIDDISON. 1975. "Dimensions of occupational prestige." *Sociology of Work and Occupations* 2: 3–27.

HECHINGER, FRED M. 1984. "Censorship rises in the nation's public schools." *New York Times* (Jan. 7): 7C.

HEDGES, JANICE N., AND STEPHANIE BEMIS. 1974. "Sex stereotyping: its decline in skilled trades." *Monthly Labor Review* 97: 14–22.

HEILMAN, MADELINE E., AND LOIS R. SARUWATAI. 1979. "When beauty is beastly." *Organizational Behavior and Human Performance* 23: 360–72.

HEINZ, JOHN P., AND EDWARD O. LAUMANN. 1983. *Chicago Lawyers.* New York: Russell Sage.

HENNIG, MARGARET AND ANN JARDIM. 1977. *The Managerial Woman.* New York: Doubleday.

HENSLIN, JAMES M. 1967. "Dispatched orders and the cab driver: a study in locating activities." *Social Problems* 14: 424–43.

————. 1968. "Trust and the cabdriver." In M. Truzzi (ed.) *Sociology and Everyday Life*, pp. 138–58. Englewood Cliffs: Prentice-Hall.

HEPWORTH, SUE J. 1980. "Moderating factors of the psychological impact of unemployment." *Journal of Occupational Psychology* 53: 139–45.

HERSHEY, NATHAN. 1973. "The Defensive Practice of Medicine." In John B. McKinlay (ed.), *Economic Aspects of Health Care*, pp. 69–97. New York: Milbank.

HERZBERG, FREDERICK. 1966. *Work and the Nature of Man.* Cleveland: World.

————, BERNARD MAUSNER, AND B. SNYDERMAN. 1959. *The Motivation to Work.* New York: Wiley.

HERZOG, A. REGULA, JERALD G. BACHMAN AND LLOYD D. JOHNSTON. 1983. "Paid work, child care and housework." *Sex Roles* 9: 109–35.

HEYNS, BARBARA. 1974. "Social selection and stratification within schools." *American Journal of Sociology* 79: 1434–51.

HICKEY, MARY C. 1985. "Cleaning house loses its luster." *USA Today* (May 9): 1–2D.

HILL, ANN C. 1979. "Protection of women workers and the courts: a legal history." *Feminist Studies* 5: 247–73.

HILL, J. M. M. 1978. "The psychological impact of unemployment." *New Society* 43: 118–20.

HIRSHI, TRAVIS. 1962. "The professional prostitute." *Berkeley Journal of Sociology* 7: 33–49.

HOCHSCHILD, ARLIE RUSSELL. 1983. *The Managed Heart: Commercialization of Human Feeling.* Berkeley: University of California Press.

HODGE, ROBERT W., PAUL M. SIEGEL, AND PETER M. ROSSI. 1964. "Occupational prestige in the United States, 1925–1963." *American Journal of Sociology* 70: 386–402.

————. 1966. "Occupational prestige in the United States: 1925–1963." In R. Bendix and S. M. Lipset (eds.), *Class, Status and Power* (2nd ed.), pp. 322–34. New York: Free Press.

HODGE, ROBERT W., DONALD J. TREIMAN, AND PETER H. ROSSI. 1966. "A comparative study of occupational prestige." In R. Bendix and S. M. Lipset (eds.) *Class, Status and Power*, pp. 309–21. (2nd ed.) New York: Free Press.

HOLDEN, CONSTANCE. 1974. "Sex therapy: Making it as a science and an industry." *Science* 25: 330–34.

HOLUSHA, JOHN. 1984. "A race for greater auto profits." *New York Times* (Sept. 30): 1–13F.

————. 1983. "The new allure of manufacturing." *New York Times* (Dec. 18): 1–30F.

HOPPOCK, ROBERT. 1935. *Job Satisfaction.* New York: Harper & Brothers.

HORNUM, FINN. 1968. "The executioner: his role and status in Scandinavian society." In Marcello Truzzi (ed.), *Sociology and Everyday Life,* pp. 125–37. Englewood Cliffs, NJ: Prentice-Hall.

HORSFALL, A. B., AND CONRAD M. ARENSBERG. 1949. "Teamwork and Productivity in a Shoe Factory." *Human Organization* 8: 13–25.

HOULT, THOMAS. 1970. "Many are called; few want to be chosen." *Pacific Sociological Review* 13 (Winter): 17–18.

HOWE, LOUISE KAPP. 1977. *Pink Collar Workers.* New York: Avon.

HOWTON, F. WILLIAM, AND BERNARD ROSENBERG. 1965. "The salesman: ideology and self-image in a prototypic occupation." *Social Research* 32: 177–298.

HUBER, JOAN AND GLENNA SPRITZE. 1983. *Sex Stratification: Children, Housework and Jobs.* New York: Academic Press.

HUDIS, PAULA M. 1977. "Commitment to work and wages: earnings differences of black and white women." *Sociology of Work and Occupations* 4: 123–46.

HUNT, JANET AND LARRY HUNT. 1977. "Dilemmas and contradictions of status: The case of dual-career family." *Social Problems* 24: 407–16.

HUGHES, EVERETT C. 1962. "Good people and dirty work." *Social Problems* 10: 3–11.

————. 1963. "Professions." *Daedalus* 92: 655–68.

————. 1958. *Men and Their Work.* Glencoe: Free Press.

IACOCCA, LEE. 1984. *Iacocca: An Autobiography.* New York: Bantam

ILGEN, DANIEL R. ET AL. 1981. "Supervisor and subordinate reactions to performance appraisal sessions." *Organizational Behavior and Human Performance* 28: 311–30.

INCIARDI, JAMES A. 1975. *Careers in Crime.* Chicago: Rand McNally.

INKELES, ALEX, AND PETER H. ROSSI. 1956. "National comparisons of occupational prestige." *American Journal of Sociology* 66: 329–39.

JACOB, HERBERT. 1978. *Justice in America: Courts, Lawyers, and the Judicial Process.* Boston: Little, Brown.

JAHADA, MARIE, PAUL LAZARSFELD, AND HANS ZEISEL. 1971. *Marienthal: The Sociography of an Unemployed Community.* Chicago: Aldine-Atherton.

JANOWITZ, MORRIS. 1960. *The Professional Soldier.* Glencoe, IL: Free Press.

JASSO, GUILLERMINA, AND PETER H. ROSSI. 1977. "Distributive justice and earned income." *American Sociological Review* 42: 639–51.

JEFFRIES-FOX, SUZANNE, AND NANCY SIGNORIELLI. 1978. "Television and children's concepts of occupations." Paper presented at Telecommunications Policy Conference, Airlie House, Virginia.

JENSEN, JOAN M. 1980. "Cloth, butter, and boarders: women's household production for the market." *Review of Radical Political Economics* 12: 14–24.

JOHNSON, DOYLE P. 1974. "Social organization of an industrial work group: emergence and adaptation to environmental change." *The Sociological Quarterly* 15: 109–26.

JOHNSON, JANIS. 1985. "Career moms worry more than dads." *USA Today* (May 10): 1A.

JOHNSON, KIRK. 1986. "Courts rarely throw the book at lawyers." *New York Times* (June 29): 24E.

JORION, PAUL. 1982. "All-brother crews in the North Atlantic." *Canadian Review of Sociology and Anthropology* 19: 513–26.

JURIK, NANCY C. 1985. "An officer and a lady: Organizational barriers to women working as correctional officers in men's prisons. *Social Problems* 32: 375–88.

KAGAN, JULIA, AND JULIANNE MALVEAUX. 1986. "The uneasy alliance of the boss and the secretary." *Working Woman* 11: 105–38.

KAHN, ROBERT L. 1969 "Conflict, ambiguity and overload: Three elements in job stress." *Occupational Mental Health* 3: 2–9.

————, ET AL. 1964. *Organizational stress: Studies in role conflict and ambiguity.* New York: Wiley.

KANTER, ROSABETH M. 1977. *Men and Women of the Corporation.* New York: Basic Books.

————. 1982. "Power and entrepreneurship in action." In Phyllis L. Stewart and Muriel G. Cantor (eds.), *Varieties of Work,* pp. 153–71. Beverly Hills: Sage.

————. 1978. "Work in a new America." *Daedalus* 107: 47–78.

KAREN, ROBERT L. 1962. "Some factors affecting tipping behavior." *Sociology and Social Research* 47: 68–74.

KASL, S. V., ET AL. 1975. "The experience of losing a job." *Psychosomatic Medicine* 37: 106–22.

KATZMAN, DAVID M. 1977. *Seven Days a Week: Women and Domestic Service in Industrializing America* New York: Oxford University Press.

————. 1978. "Domestic service: woman's work." in Ann H. Stromberg and Shirley Harkess (eds.), *Women Working*, pp. 377–91. Palo Alto, CA: Mayfield.

KEMNITZER, LUIS S. 1973. "Language learning and socialization on the railroad." *Urban Life Culture* 1: 363–78.

KEMPER, THEODORE D. 1979. "Why are the streets so dirty?" *Social Forces* 58: 422–39.

KENDALL, PATRICIA L. 1963. "The learning environments of hospitals." In Eliot Freidson (ed.), *The Hospital in Modern Society*, pp. 195–230. New York: Free Press.

KERCKHOFF, ALAN. 1976. "The status attainment process: socialization or allocation?" *Social Forces* 55: 368–81.

KESSLER-HARRIS, ALICE. 1982. *Out to Work*. New York: Oxford University Press.

KHLEIF, BUD B. 1975. "Professionalization of school superintendents: a socio-cultural study of an elite program." *Human Organization* 34: 301–8.

KIESLER, SARA, LEE SPROULL, AND JACQUELYNNE S. ECCLES. 1983. "Second-class citizens?" *Psychology Today* 17: 40–48.

KIRKLAND, RICHARD I. 1985. "Are service jobs good jobs?" *Fortune* 111 (June 10): 38–43.

KLEINFIELD, N. R. 1985. "A squeeze on doctors' profits." New York Times (June 2): 1–7F.

KLEINMAN, DENA. 1979. "Medical School." *Wilmington News Journal* (Dec. 21): 45.

KOCHMAN, THOMAS. 1981. *Black and White Styles in Conflict*. Chicago:University of Chicago Press.

KOHLMEIER, LOUIS M. 1976. "Price-fixing in the professions." *New York Times* (April 18): 3F.

KOHN, MELVIN L. 1969. *Class and Conformity*. Homewood, IL: Dorsey.

KOMAROVSKY, MIRRA. 1962. *Blue Collar Marriage*. New York: Random House.

KONCEL, JEROME A. 1977. "Hospital labor relations struggles through its own revolution." *Hospitals* 51 (Apr. 1): 69–74.

KOSHIRO, KAZUTOSHI. 1984. "Lifetime employment in Japan: three models of the concept." *Monthly Labor Review* 107: 34–35.

KOTTER, JOHN P. 1982. *The General Managers*. New York: Free Press.

————. 1973. "The psychological contract: managing the joining-up process." *California Management Review* 15: 91–99.

KRAM, KATHY E. 1983. "Phases of the mentor relationship." *Academy of Management Journal* 26: 608–25.

KRAUSE, ELIOT. 1971. *The Sociology of Occupations*. Boston: Little, Brown.

KREMAN, BENNETT. 1979. "Lordstown: searching for a better way." In Rosabeth M. Kanter and Barry A. Stein (eds.), *Life in Organizations*, pp. 217–25. New York: Basic Books.

KROHN, ROGER B. 1972. "Patterns of Institutionalization of Research." In S. Z. Nagi and R. G. Corwin (eds.), *The Social Context of Research*, pp. 29–66. New York: Wiley.

Kronus, Carol L. 1976. "The evolution of occupational power: A historical study of task boundaries between physicians and pharmacists." *Sociology of Work and Occupations* 3: 3–37.

KURSH, HARRY. 1958. *Apprenticeships in America*. New York: W. W. Norton.

KURTZ, HARRY I. AND ALBERT ROBBINS. 1981. *Whistle Blowing*. New York: McGraw-Hill.

LANE, MICHAEL. 1970. "Publishing managers, publishing house organization and role conflict." *Sociology* 4: 366–83.

LANGER, ELINOR. 1970. "Inside the New York telephone company." *New York Review of Books* 14 (Mar. 12): 16–24.

LARSON, MAGALI S. 1977. *The Rise of Professionalism*. Berkeley: University of California Press.

LAW POLL. 1978. "The organized bar and public issues." *American Bar Association Journal* 64: 41–43.

LAWLER, EDWARD E., III AND J. RICHARD HACKMAN. 1971. "Corporate profits and employee satisfaction: Must they be in conflict?" *California Management Review* 17: 46–55.

LAWLER, EDWARD E., III, ALLAN M. MOHRMAN AND SUSAN M. RESNICK, 1984. "Performance appraisal revisited." *Organizational Dynamics* 13: 20–35.

LAWLER, EDWARD E., III, AND JOHN A. DREXLER, JR. 1978. "Dynamics of establishing cooperative quality-of-worklife projects." *Monthly Labor Review* 101: 23–28.

LAYTON, EDWIN. 1969. "Science, business, and the American engineer." In Robert Perrucci and Joel Gerstl (eds.), *The Engineers and The Social System*, pp. 51–72. New York: Wiley.

LEE, ROBERT E. 1983. "Flexitime and conjugal roles." *Journal of Occupational Behavior* 4: 297–315.

LeMasters, E. E. 1975. *Blue-Collar Aristocrats*. Madison: University of Wisconsin Press.

Leonard, W. N., and N. G. Weber. 1970. "Automakers and dealers: a study of criminogenic market forces." *Law and Society* 4: 407–24.

Lenski, Gerhard E. 1966. *Power and Privilege: A Theory of Social Stratification*. New York: McGraw-Hill.

Levi, Margaret. 1980. "Functional redundancy and the process of professionalization: the case of registered nurses in the United States." *Journal of Health Politics, Policy and Law* 5: 333–53.

Lewyn, Mark. 1985. "Write a will with software." *USA Today* (Dec. 19): 4B.

Lieberman, Jethro K. 1979. *Crisis at the Bar*. New York: Norton.

Linn, Erwin L. 1967. "Role behaviors in two dental clinics." *Human Organization* 26: 141–48.

Lipman-Bluman, Jean. 1972. "How ideology shapes women's lives." *Scientific American* 226: 34–42.

Lipset, Seymour M., Martin A. Trow, and James S. Coleman. 1956. *Union Democracy*. Glencoe: Free Press.

Little, Craig B. 1976. "Technical-professional unemployment: middle class adaptability to personal crisis." *Sociological Quarterly* 17: 262–74.

Lockwood, David. 1958. *The Blackcoated Worker*. London: Allen and Unwin.

Lo Piccolo, Joseph. 1977. "From psychotherapy to sex therapy." *Society* 14: 60–68.

Lorber, Judith. 1975. "Good patients and problem patients: Conformity and deviance in a general hospital." *Journal of Health and Social Behavior* 16: 213–25.

Louis, Meryl R. 1980. "Surprise and sense making: what newcomers experience in entering unfamiliar organizational settings." *Administrative Science Quarterly* 25: 226–51.

Mackenzie, Gavin. 1973. *The Aristocracy of Labor*. London: Cambridge University Press.

Magid, Alvin. 1976. *Men in the Middle: Leadership and Role Conflict in a Nigerian Society*. Manchester: Manchester University Press.

Mahigel, E. Louis, and Gregory P. Stone. 1971. "How card hustlers make the game." *Transaction* 8: 40–45.

Maniha, John K. 1974. "The standardization of elite careers in bureaucratizing organizations." *Social Forces* 53: 283–88.

———. 1975. "Universalism and particularism in bureaucratizing organizations." *Administrative Science Quarterly* 20: 177–90.

Maret, Elizabeth, and Barbara Findlay. 1984. "The distribution of household labor among women in dual-earner families." *Journal of Marriage and the Family* 46: 357–64.

Marglin, Stephen A. 1974. "What do bosses do? The origins and functions of hierarchy in capitalist production." *Review of Radical Political Economics* 6: 33–60.

Margolis, Diane Rothbard. 1979. *The Managers: Corporate Life in America*. New York: William Morrow.

Marks, F. Raymond and Darlene Cathcart. 1974. "Discipline within the legal profession: Is it self-regulation?" *Illinois Law Forum* 2: 193–236.

Marks, Stephen R. 1977. "Multiple roles and role strain: some notes on human energy, time and commitment." *American Sociological Review* 42: 921–36.

Marsh, Robert M. 1971. "The explanation of occupational prestige hierarchies." *Social Forces* 50: 214–22.

Marshall, Hanna Meara. 1972. "Structural constraints on learning: Butchers' apprentices." *American Behavioral Scientist* 16: 39–48.

Marshall, Ray. 1967. *The Negro Worker*. New York: Random House.

———, William Franklin, and Robert Glover. 1974. "Paths to construction journeyman." *Manpower* 6: 8–13.

Martin, D. L. 1980. "Will the sun set on occupational licensing?" *State Government* 53: 63–67.

Martin, Norman H., and Anselm L. Strauss. 1956. "Patterns of mobility within industrial organizations." *Journal of Business* 29: 101–10.

Martin, Susan Ehrlich. 1982. *Breaking and Entering: Policewomen on Patrol*. Berkeley, CA: University of California Press.

Martinez, Thomas M. 1968. "Why employment-agency counselors lower their client's self-esteem." *Transaction* 5: 20–25.

Maslow, Abraham. 1954. *Movtivation and Personality*. New York: Harper & Row.

Maurer, David W. 1981. *Language of the Underworld*. Lexington: University Press of Kentucky.

Mauro, Robert. 1984. "The constable's new clothes: effects of uniforms on perceptions and problems of police officers." *Journal of Applied Social Psychology* 14: 42–56.

May, Martha. 1982. "The historical problem of the family wage: the Ford Motor Company and the five dollar day." *Feminist Studies* 8: 399–424.

MEARA, HANNAH. 1974. "Honor in dirty work: the case of American meat cutters and Turkish butchers." *Sociology of Work and Occupations* 1: 259–83.

McCARL, ROBERT S., JR. 1976. "Smokejumper initiation: ritualized communication in a modern occupation." *Journal of American Folklore* 89: 49–66.

McGOVERN, T. V. AND E. A. HOWARD. 1978. "Interviewer evaluations of interviewee nonverbal behavior." *Journal of Vocational Behavior* 13: 163–71.

McKEE, J. P. AND A. C. SHERRIFFS. 1957. "The differential evaluation of males and females." *Journal of Personality* 25: 356–71.

McLANE, HELEN J. 1980. *Selecting, Developing and Retaining Women Executives.* New York: Van Nostrand.

MEER, JEFF. 1985. "Blue-collar stress worse for boys." *Psychology Today* 19: 15.

MEISSNER, MARTIN. 1969. *Technology and the Worker.* San Francisco, CA: Chandler.

MELLOR, EARL F. 1985. "Weekly earnings in 1983." *Monthly Labor Review* 108: 54–59.

MENNERICK, LEWIS A. 1974. "Client typologies: a method of coping with conflict in the service worker-client relationship." *Sociology of Work and Occupations* 1: 396–418.

MERTON, ROBERT K. 1957. "The role-set." *British Journal of Sociology* 8: 106–20.

————, GEORGE C. READER, AND PATRICIA KENDALL. 1957. *The Student Physician.* Cambridge, MA: Harvard University Press.

MILFORD, MAUREEN. 1984. "At the top, loyalty and hard work." *Wilmington News-Journal* (Apr. 2): 1–5C.

MILKMAN, RUTH. 1982. "Redefining 'women's work': the sexual division of labor in the auto industry during World War II." *Feminist Studies* 8: 337–72.

————. 1983. "Female factory labor and industrial structure: control and conflict over 'women's work' in auto and electrical manufacturing." *Politics and Society* 12: 159–203.

MILLARD, CHEEDLE W., DIANE L. LOCKWOOD AND FRED LUTHANS. 1980. "The Impact of a Four-Day Work-Week on Employees." *MSU Business Topics* 28: 31–37.

MILLER, DELBERT C. 1965. "Supervisors: evolution of an organizational role." In Robert Dubin, et al (eds.), *Leadership and Productivity,* pp. 104–22. San Francisco: Intext.

————. AND WILLIAM FORM. 1980. *Industrial Sociology.* New York: Harper and Row.

MILLER, STEPHEN J. 1964. "The social bases of sales behavior." *Social Problems* 12: 15–24.

MILLS, C. WRIGHT. 1951. *White Collar: The American Middle Class.* New York: Oxford University Press.

MINTON, MICHAEL H. 1983. "Female factory labor and industrial structure: control and conflict over 'women's work' in auto and electrical manufacturing." *Politics and Society* 12: 159–203.

MINTON, MICHAEL H., WITH JEAN LIBMAN BLOCK. 1983. *What is a Wife Worth?* New York: Morrow.

MINTZBERG, HENRY. 1973. *The Nature of Managerial Work.* New York: Harper and Row.

MIRE, JOSEPH. 1974. "Improving work life—The role of European unions." *Monthly Labor Review* 97: 3–11.

MITCHELL, JOSEPH. 1960. "The Mohawks in High Steel." In Edmund Wilson, *Apologies to the Iroquois,* pp. 3–38. New York: Farrar, Straus and Cudahy.

MITFORD, JESSICA. 1963. *The American Way of Death.* New York: Simon and Schuster.

MOBLEY, W. H., ET AL. 1979. "Review and conceptual analysis of the employee turnover process." *Psychological Bulletin* 86: 493–522.

MOLLOY, JOHN T. 1983. *Molloy's Live for Success.* Toronto: Perigord Press.

MOORE, WILBERT E. 1969. "Occupational socialization." In David Goslin (ed.). *Handbook of Socialization Theory and Research,* pp. 861–83. Chicago: Rand McNally.

————. 1962. *The Conduct of the Corporation.* New York: Vintage Books.

MORE, DOUGLAS M. 1962. "Demotion." *Social Problems* 9: 213–21.

————, AND ROBERT W. SUCHNER. 1976. "Occupational status, prestige, and stereotypes." *Sociology of Work and Occupations* 3: 169–86.

MORSE, NANCY C., AND ROBERT S. WEISS. 1955. "The function and meaning of work and the job." *American Sociological Review* 20: 191–98.

MORTIMER, JEYLAN T., AND ROBERTA G. SIMMONS. 1978. "Adult socialization." *Annual Review of Sociology* 4: 421–54.

MOTLEY, JAMES M. 1907. "Apprenticeship in American trade unions." *Johns Hopkins University Studies* 25: 482–604.

MOUNT, MICHAEL K. 1984. "Satisfaction with a performance appraisal system and appraisal discussion." *Journal of Occupational Behavior* 5: 271–79.

MULFORD, HAROLD A., AND WINFIELD W. SALISBURY. 1964. "Self-conceptions in a general population." *The Sociological Quarterly* 5: 35–46.

MURTAUGH, JOHN M. AND SARA HARRIS. 1958. *Cast The First Stone.* New York: McGraw-Hill.

NADER, RALPH. 1965. *Unsafe at Any Speed*. New York: Grossman.

———, ET AL. 1972. *Whistle Blowing*. New York: Grossman.

NEFF, WALTER S. 1977. *Work and Human Behavior*. Chicago: Aldine.

NELSON, JOEL I. 1972. "High school context and college plans: the impact of social structure on aspirations." *American Sociological Review* 37: 143–48.

NIEDERHOFFER, ARTHUR, 1969. *Behind the Shield: The Police in Urban Society*. Garden City: Anchor.

NILSON, LINDA B. AND MURRAY EDELMAN. 1979. "The symbolic evocation of occupational prestige." *Society* 16: 57–64.

NOEL, DONALD L. 1968. "How ethnic inequality begins." *Social Problems* 16: 157–172.

NORC (NATIONAL OPINION RESEARCH CENTER). 1947. "Jobs and occupations: a popular evaluation." *Opinion News* 9: 3–13.

NORDHEIMER, JON. 1983. "Europe's joblessness begets generation of despair." *New York Times* (April 17): 16.

OAKLEY, ANN. 1974. *The Sociology of Housework*. New York: Pantheon.

O'FARRELL, BRIGID. 1982. "Women and nontraditional blue collar jobs in the 1980s: An overview." In Phyllis A. Wallace, ed., *Women in the Workplace*. Boston: Auburn.

——— AND SHARON L. HARLAN. 1982. "Craftworkers and clerks: The effects of male co-worker hostility on women's satisfaction with non-traditional jobs." *Social Problems* 29: 252–65.

O'KELLY, HAROLD E. 1978. "How to motivate and manage engineers." *New York Times* (Nov. 26): 14F.

OLESEN, VIRGINIA, AND ELVI WHITTAKER. 1968. *The Silent Dialogue*. San Francisco: Jossey Bass.

O'TOOLE, JAMES (ED.). 1973. *Work In America*. Cambridge, MA: The MIT Press.

———. 1974. *Work and the Quality of Life: Resource Papers for "Work in America."* Cambridge: MIT Press.

O'TOOLE, PATRICIA. 1984. *Corporate Messiah*. New York: Morrow.

OTTO, LUTHER B., AND ARCHIBALD O. HALLER. 1979. "Evidence for a social-psychological view of the status attainment process: four studies compared." *Social Forces* 57: 887–914.

PAJAK, EDWARD F. 1983. "Teachers in bars: From professional to personnel self." *Sociology of Education* 57: 164–73.

PAPANEK, HANNA. 1973. "Men, women, and work: Reflections on the two-person career." *American Journal of Sociology* 78: 852–72.

PARMERLEE, MARCIA A., JANET P. NEAR, AND TAMILA C. JENSEN. 1982. "Correlates of whistle-blowers' perceptions of organizational retaliation." *Administrative Science Quarterly* 27: 17–34.

PARSONS, TALCOTT. 1970. "Equality and inequality in modern society, or social stratification revisited." *Sociological Inquiry* 40: 13–72.

PASCALE, RICHARD TANNER, AND ANTHONY G. ATHOS. 1981. *The Art of Japanese Management*. New York: Warner.

PAULY, DAVID. 1982. "The cream at the top." *Newsweek* (May 17): 76.

PAYNE, ROY, PETER WARR, AND JEAN HARTLEY. 1984. "Social class and psychological ill-health during unemployment." *Sociology of Health and Illness* 6: 152–74.

PENN, ROGER. 1975. "Occupational prestige hierarchies: a great empirical invariant?" *Social Forces* 54: 352–64.

PENNINGS, JOHANNES M. 1970. "Work value systems of white-collar workers." *Administrative Science Quarterly* 15: 397–408.

PERFETTI, LAWRENCE J., AND WILLIAM C. BINGHAM. 1983. "Unemployment and self-esteem in metal refinery workers." *Vocational Guidance Quarterly:* 195–201.

PERRUCCI, ROBERT, ET AL. 1980. "Whistle-blowing: professional resistance to organizational authority." *Social Problems* 28: 149–64.

PERSELL, CAROLINE HODGES. 1977. *Education and Inequality*. New York: Free Press.

PETERS, THOMAS J. AND NANCY AUSTIN. 1985. *A Passion for Excellence*. New York: Random House.

PETERSILIA, JOAN, PETER W. GREENWOOD AND MARVIN LAVIN. 1978. *Criminal Careers of Habitual Offenders*. Washington, D.C.: National Institute of Law Enforcement and Criminal Justice.

PIFER, ALICE. 1980–1. "Wanted: employment agencies that don't discriminate." *Perspectives: The Civil Rights Quarterly* 12: 16–23.

PILCHER, WILLIAM W. 1972. *The Portland Longshoremen*. New York: Holt, Rinehart and Winston.

PIRENNE, HENRI. 1962. "European guilds." In Sigmund Nosow and William H. Form (eds.), *Man, Work and Society*. New York: Basic Books.

POLANYI, MICHAEL. 1962. "Tacit knowing: Its bearing on some problems in philosophy." *Review of Modern Physics* 34: 601–06.

PONTELL, HENRY N., LAWRENCE SALINGER, AND GILBERT GEIS. 1983. "Assaults in the air: concerning attacks against flight attendants." *Deviant Behavior* 4: 297–311.

PORTER, JAMES N. 1974. "Race, socialization and mobility in educational and early occupational attainment: *American Sociological Review* 39: 303–16.

PORTER, LYMAN. 1964. *Organizational Patterns of Managerial Job Attitudes.* New York: American Foundation for Management Research.

PORTES, ALEJANDRO, AND KENNETH L. WILSON. 1976. "Black-white differences in educational attainment." *American Sociological Review* 41: 414–31.

POTHIER, DICK. 1974. "Down with niceness! Sell that insurance." *Philadelphia Inquirer* (October 1): 1C.

POUNDS, NORMAN J. G. 1974. *An Economic History of Medieval Europe.* London: Longman.

POWELL, BRIAN, AND JERRY A. JACOBS. 1984. "The prestige gap: differential evaluations of male and female workers." *Work and Occupations* 11: 283–308.

POWELL, DOUGLAS H., AND PAUL F. DRISCOLL. 1973. "Middle class professionals face unemployment." *Society* 10: 18–26.

PREVITS, GARY JOHN, AND BARBARA DUBIS MERINO. 1979. *A History of Accounting in America.* New York: Wiley.

PRICE, JAMES L., AND CHARLES W. MUELLER. 1981. "A causal model of turnover for nurses." *Academy of Management Journal* 24: 543–65.

PRIESTLY, PHILLIP. 1972. "The prison welfare officer—a case of role strain." *British Journal of Sociology* 23: 221–35.

PURDUM, TODD. 1985. "What's new in direct selling?" *New York Times* (Mar. 17): 21F.

QUARANTELLI, ENRICO L. 1961. "School-learned adjustments to negative self-images in high status occupational roles: the dental student experience." *Journal of Educational Sociology* 35: 165–71.

QUINN, ROBERT P., GRAHAM L. STAINS AND MARGARET R. McCULLOUGH. 1974. *Job Satisfaction: Is There a Trend?* Manpower Research Monograph No. 30. Washington: U.S. Department of Labor.

RADCLIFFE-BROWN, A. R. 1952. *Structure and Function in Primitive Society.* Glencoe: Free Press.

RAINEY, GLENN W., AND LAWRENCE WOLF. 1981. "Flex-time: short term benefits; long term . . . ?" *Public Administration Review* 41: 52–63.

RASMUSSEN, PAUL K., AND LAUREN L. KUHN. 1975. "The new masseuse: play for pay." *Urban Life* 5: 271–92.

RAYBACK, JOSEPH G. 1966. *A History of American Labor.* New York: Macmillan.

REED, JOHN P. 1969. "The lawyer-client: A managed relationship?" *Academy of Management Journal* 12: 67–80.

REGOLI, ROBERT M., ERIC D. POOLE, AND JEFFREY L. SCHRINK. 1979. "Occupational socialization: and career development: a look at cynicism among correctional institution workers." *Human Organization* 38: 183–87.

REMMINGTON, PATRICIA A. 1981. *Policing.* Lanham, MD: University Press.

RENARD, GEORGES F. 1918. *Guides in the Middle Ages.* London: G. Bell and Sons.

RENWICK, PATRICIA A., AND EDWARD E. LAWLER. 1978. "What you really want from your job." *Psychology Today* 11: 53–65, 118.

RESKIN, BARBARA F. 1979. "Academic sponsorship and scientists' careers." *Sociology of Education* 52: 139–46.

RICE, BERKELEY. 1985. "Performance review: The job nobody likes." *Psychology Today* 19: 31–36.

RIEMER, JEFFREY W. 1977. "Becoming a journeyman electrician." *Sociology of Work and Occupations* 4: 87–98.

———. 1979. *Hard Hats: The Work World of Construction Workers.* Beverly Hills, CA: Sage.

———. 1981. "Worker autonomy in the skilled building trades." In Phyllis L. Stewart and Muriel G. Cantor (eds.), *Varieties of Work,* pp. 225–34. Beverly Hills: Sage.

RIMER, SARA. 1984. "The airline that shook the industry." *New York Times Magazine* (Dec. 23): 18–29.

RIZZO, JOHN R., ROBERT J. HOUSE, AND SIDNEY LIRTZMAN. 1970. "Role conflict and ambiguity in complex organizations." *Administratives Science Quarterly* 15: 150–63.

ROBIN, GERALD D. 1964. "The executioner: his place in English society." *British Journal of Sociology* 15: 234–53.

ROCHE, R. GERALD. 1979. "Much ado about mentors." *Harvard Business Review* 57: 14–24.

RODGERS, DANIEL T. 1978. *The Work Ethic in Industrial America, 1850–1920.* Chicago: University of Chicago Press.

ROEDERER, DOUG, AND BENJAMIN SHIMBERG. 1980. *Occupational Licensing.* Lexington, KY: Council of State Governments.

ROETHLISBERGER, FRITZ AND WILLIAM J. DICKSON. 1939. *Management and the Worker* Cambridge, MA: Harvard University Press.

ROGAN, HELEN. 1984. "Women executives feel that men both aid and hinder their careers." *Wall Street Journal* (Oct. 29): 35.

RONEN, SIMCHA AND SOPHIA B. PRIMPS. 1981. "The compressed work week as organizational change: Behavioral and attitudinal outcomes." *Academy of Management Review* 6: 61–74.

ROOS, PATRICIA. 1981. "Sex stratification in the workplace: male-female differences in economic returns to occupation." *Social Science Research* 10: 195–224.

ROSENBAUM, JAMES E. 1975. "The stratification of socialization processes." *American Sociological Review* 40: 48–54.

_____. 1976. *Making Inequality: The Hidden Curriculum of High School Tracking.* New York: Wiley.

_____. 1979a. "Organizational career mobility: promotion chances in a corporation during periods of growth and contraction." *American Journal of Sociology* 85: 21–48.

_____. 1979b. "Tournament mobility: career patterns in a corporation." *Administrative Science Quarterly* 24: 220–41.

ROSENFELD, RACHEL A. 1986. "U.S. farm women: Their part in farm work and decision making." *Work and Occupations* 13: 179–202.

ROSENKRANTZ, P., ET AL. 1968. "Sex role stereotypes and self concepts in college students." *Journal of Consulting and Clinical Psychology* 32: 287–95.

ROSENSTEIN, DAVID I., ET AL. 1980. "Professional encroachment: a comparison of the emergence of denturists in Canada and Oregon." *American Journal of Public Health* 70: 614–18.

ROSENTHAL, DOUGLAS E. 1974. *Lawyer and Client: Who's in Charge?* New York: Russell Sage.

ROSENTHAL, HARRY F. 1978. "Apple growers outlast migrants." *Wilmington Morning News* (Oct. 2): 10.

ROTH, JULIUS A. 1963. *Timetables: Structuring the Passage of Time in Hospital Treatment and Other Careers.* Indianapolis: Bobbs-Merrill.

ROTHMAN, ROBERT A. 1979. "Occupational roles: power and negotiation in the division of labor." *The Sociological Quarterly* 20: 495–515.

_____. AND ROBERT PERRUCCI. 1971. "Vulnerability to knowledge obsolescence among professionals." *The Sociological Quarterly* 12: 147–58.

_____. AND ROBERT PERRUCCI. 1970. "Organizational careers and professional expertise." *Administrative Science Quarterly* 15: 282–93.

ROY, DONALD F. 1952. "Quota restriction and goldbricking in a machine shop." *American Journal of Sociology* 57: 427–42.

_____. 1954. "Efficiency and 'the fix' informal intergroup relations in a piecework machine shop." *American Journal of Sociology* 60: 255–66.

_____. 1960. "Banana time: job satisfaction and informal interaction." *Human Organization* 18: 158–69.

RUANE, JOSEPH W. 1975. "Controlling the pharmacist." *American Journal of Pharmacy* 147: 174–79.

RUBINSTEIN, JONATHAN. 1973. *City Police* New York: Farrar, Straus and Giroux.

RUNGE, THOMAS E., ET AL. 1981. "Masculine (instrumental) and feminine (expressive) traits." *Journal of Cross-Cultural Psychology* 12: 142–62.

RYNES, SARA L., HERBERT G. HENEMAN, AND DONALD P. SCHWAB. 1980. "Individual reactions to organizational recruiting: a review." *Personnel Psychology* 33: 529–42.

RYON, KATHY AND ANN ROSENBLUM. 1983. "Eyes right for success." Unpublished paper, University of Delaware.

RYTINA, JOAN H., WILLIAM H. FORM AND JOHN PEASE. 1970. "Income and stratification ideology." *American Journal of Sociology* 75: 702–16.

SALAMON, GRAEME. 1974. *Community and Occupation.* London: Cambridge University Press.

SALEH, S. D., AND J. HYDE. 1969. "Intrinsic vs. extrinsic orientation and job satisfaction." *Occupational Psychology* 43: 47–53.

SALES, STEVEN, AND JAMES S. HOUSE. 1971. "Job dissatisfaction as a possible risk factor in coronary heart disease." *Journal of Chronic Disease* 23: 862–73.

SAWHILL, I., G. PEABODY, C. JONES, AND S. CALDWELL. 1975. *Income Transfers and Family Structure.* Washington: The Urban Institute.

SAYLES, LEONARD. 1966. *Managerial Behavior and Administration in Complex Organizations.* Englewood Cliffs, NJ: Prentice-Hall.

SCHEIN, EDGAR H. 1980. *Occupational Psychology.* Englewood Cliffs, NJ: Prentice-Hall.

_____. 1977. "Career anchors and career paths: a panel study of management school graduates." In John Van Maanen (ed.), *Organizational Careers.* pp. 49–64. New York: Wiley.

————. 1971. "The individual, the organization, and the career: a conceptual scheme." *Journal of Applied Behavioral Science* 7: 401–26.

————. 1964. "How to break in the college graduate." *Harvard Business Review* 64: 68–76.

SCHEIN, VIRGINIA E. 1975. " Relationships between sex role stereotypes and requisite management characteristics among female managers." *Journal of Applied Psychology* 60: 340–44.

SCHENKER, JENNIFER. 1979. "Working the stroll." *Wilmington News Journal* (Oct. 21): 1H.

SCHILLER, BRADLEY R. 1976. *The Economics of Poverty and Discrimination.* Englewood Cliffs, NJ: Prentice-Hall.

SCHLESINGER, LEONARD A., AND BARRY OSHRY. 1984. "Quality of work life and the manager: muddle in the middle." *Organizational Dynamics* 13: 1–18.

SCHLOSSBERG, NANCY K., AND ZANDY LEIBOWITZ. 1980. "Organizational support systems as buffers to job loss." *Journal of Vocational Behavior* 17: 204–17.

SCHMIDT, WARREN H., AND BARRY Z. POSNER. 1982. *Managerial Values and Expectations.* New York: American Management Association.

SCHMITT, NEAL. 1976. "Social and situational determinants of interview decisions: implications for the employment interview." *Personnel Psychology* 29: 79–101.

SCHNEIDER, EUGENE. 1969. *Industrial Sociology.* New York: McGraw-Hill.

SCHONBERG, HAROLD C. 1978. "Elitism, in the arts, is good." *New York TImes* (Feb. 5): 23D.

SCIOLINO, ELAINE. 1985. "U.N. finds widespread inequality for women." *New York Times* (June 23): 10.

SELL, RALPH R. 1983. "Transferred Jobs: A neglected aspect of migration and occupational change." *Work and Occupations* 10: 179–206.

SENATRA, PHILLIP T. 1980. "Role conflict, role ambiguity, and organizational climate in a public accounting firm." *The Accounting Review* 55: 594–603.

SENNETT, RICHARD AND JONATHAN COBB. 1972. *The Hidden Injuries of Class.* New York: Random House.

SERRIN, WILLIAM. 1984. "The way that works at Lincoln." *New York Times* (Jan. 15): 4F.

SHEPARD, JON M. 1971. *Automation and Alienation: A Study of Office and Factory Workers.* Cambridge: MIT Press.

SHABECOFF, PHILIP. 1981. "March of the nine-to-five woman." *New York Times* (Mar. 29): 8F.

SHADE, BARBARA J. 1982. "Afro-American Cognitive Style." *Review of Educational Research* 52: 219–44.

SHAMIR, BOAS. 1980. "Between service and servility: role conflict in subordinate service roles." *Human Relations* 33: 741–56.

————. 1983. "A note on tipping and employee perceptions and attitudes." *Journal of Occupational Psychology* 56: 255–59.

SHANNON, DAN. 1982. "Productivity: Quality circles for supermarkets." *New York Times* (Apr. 18): 19F.

SHARDA, BAM DEV, AND BARRY E. NANGLE. 1981. "Marital effects on occupational attainment." *Journal of Family Issues* 2: 148–63.

SHAW, CLAYTON T. 1972. "Societal sanctioning: the pharmacist's tarnished image." *Social Science and Medicine* 6: 109–14.

SHENKEL, WILLIAM M. 1978. *The Real Estate Professional.* Homewood, IL: Dow Jones-Irwin.

SHEPPARD, HAROLD L. AND NEIL Q. HERRICK. 1972. *Where Have All the Robots Gone?* New York: Free Press.

SHERRILL, ROBERT. 1977. "Raising hell on the highways." *New York Times Magazine* (Nov. 27): 38–102.

————. 1973. "Unfortunately most workers don't have concave heads." *New York Times Book Review* (July 8): 2–3.

SHILLER, BRADLEY. 1976. *The Economics of Poverty and Discrimination.* Englewood Cliffs, NJ: Prentice-Hall.

SHORTER, EDWARD. 1973. *Work and Community in the West.* New York: Harper and Row.

SHOSTAK, ARTHUR B. 1969. *Blue Collar Life.* New York: Random House.

SHOVER, NEAL. 1973. "The social organization of burglary." *Social Problems* 20: 499–514.

SHRYOCK, RICHARD H. 1960. *Medicine and Society in America: 1660–1860.* Ithaca: Cornell University Press.

SIEBER, SAM. 1974. "Toward a theory of role accumulation." *American Sociological Review* 39: 567–78.

SIEGEL, BARRY. 1981. "Lawyer sues own firm: says fee in injury case was too high." *Wilmington News-Journal* (June 14): 11A.

SIEGEL, PAUL. 1965. "On the costs of being a Negro." *Sociological Inquiry* 35: 41–57.

SILVER, MARC L. 1982. "The structure of craft work: the construction industry." In Phyllis L. Stewart and Muriel G. Cantor (eds.), *Varieties of Work,* pp. 235–52. Beverly Hills, CA: Sage.

SIMMONS, JOHN AND WILLIAM MARES. 1983. *Working Together.* New York: Knopf.

SIMMONS, ROBERTA G., AND MORRIS ROSENBERG. 1971. "Functions of children's perception of the stratification system." *American Sociological Review* 36: 235–49.

SIMPSON, IDA H. AND PAULA ENGLAND. 1981. "Conjugal work roles and marital solidarity." *Journal of Family !ssues* 2: 180–204.

SLOSAR, JOHN A., JR. 1973. "Ogre, bandit, and operating employee: the problems and adaptations of the metropolitan bus driver." *Urban Life and Culture* 1: 339–62.

SLOTE, ALFRED. 1969. *Termination: The Closing at Baker Street.* Ann Arbor: Institute for Social Research.

SMART, R. G. 1979. "Drinking problems among employed, unemployed, and shift workers." *Journal of Occupational Medicine* 11: 731–36.

SMIGEL, ERWIN O. 1964. *The Wall Street Lawyer.* New York: Free Press.

SMITH, CATHERINE BEGNOCHE. 1979. "Influence of internal opportunity structure and sex of worker on turnover patterns." *Administrative Science Quarterly* 24: 362–81.

SMITH, JAMES P., AND MICHAEL P. WARD. 1984. *Women's Wages and Work in the Twentieth Century.* Santa Monica, CA: The Rand Corporation.

SMITH, MAPHEUS. 1943. "An empirical scale of prestige status of occupations." *American Sociological Review* 8: 185–92.

SOFER, CYRIL. 1970. *Men in Mid-career: a Study of British Managers and Technical Specialists.* London: Cambridge University Press.

SOUTH, SCOTT J., ET AL. 1982. "Sex and power in the federal bureaucracy." *Work and Occupations* 9: 233–54.

SPANGLER, EVE, MARSHA A. GORDON AND RONALD M. PIPKIN. 1978. "Token women: An empirical test of Kanter's hypothesis." *American Journal of Sociology* 84: 160–70.

SPIER, JOHN. 1959. "The railroad switchman." *Berkeley Journal of Sociology* 5: 40–62.

SPRADLEY, JAMES P., AND BRENDA J. MANN. 1975. *The Cocktail Waitress: Woman's Work in a Man's World.* New York: Wiley.

SPRUIT, INGEBORG P. 1982. "Unemployment and health in macro-social analysis." *Social Science and Medicine* 16: 1903–1917.

STAINES, GRAHAM L., AND ROBERT P. QUINN. 1979. "American workers evaluate the quality of their jobs." *Monthly Labor Review* 102: 3–12.

STANNARD, D. L. 1971. "White cabdrivers and black fares." *Transaction* 9: 44–46.

STARR, PAUL. 1982. *The Social Transformation of American Medicine.* New York: Basic Books.

STEINBERG, RONNIE J. 1984. "Identifying wage discrimination and implementing pay equity adjustments." *In Comparable Worth: Issue for the 80s.* Washington, D.C.: U.S. Commission on Civil Rights.

STELLMAN, JEANNE M. 1977. *Women's Work, Women's Health: Myths and Realities.* New York: Pantheon.

STERNGLANZ, SARA H. AND SHIRLEY LYBERGER-FICEK. 1977. "Sex differences in student-teacher interactions in the college classroom." *Sex Roles* 3: 345–52.

STEVENS, ROSEMARY. 1971. *American Medicine and the Public Interest.* New Haven: Yale University Press.

STEWART, LEA P. 1980. "'Whistle blowing': implications for organizational communication." *Journal of Communication* 30: 90–101.

STONE, ANDREA. 1986. "Workers on the Move." *USA Today* (Jan. 24): 8B.

STONE, KATHERINE. 1974. "The origins of job structures in the steel industry." *Review of Radical Political Economics* 6: 61–97.

STRAUSS, ANSELM, ET AL. 1963. "The hospital and its negotiated order." In Eliot Freidson (ed.). *The Hospital in Modern Society.* New York: Free Press.

SUDNOW, DAVID. 1965. "Normal crimes: sociological features of the penal code in a public defender office." *Social Problems* 12: 255–75.

———. 1967. *Passing On: The Social Organization of Dying.* Englewood Cliffs, NJ: Prentice-Hall.

SULLIVAN, TERESA A., AND DANIEL B. CORNFIELD. 1979. "Downgrading computer workers." *Sociology of Work and Occupations* 6: 184–203.

SWAFFORD, MICHAEL. 1978. "Sex differences in Soviet earnings." *American Sociological Review* 43: 657–73.

SYKES, A. J. M. 1966. "Joking relationships in an industrial setting." *American Anthropologist* 68: 188–93.

SYKES, GRESHAM M. AND DAVID MATZA. 1957. "Techniques of neutralization." *American Sociological Review* 22: 664–70.

SYLVESTER, KATHLEEN. 1984. "Women gaining, blacks fall back." *National Law Journal* 6 (May 21): 1–43.

TAMARKIN, BOB, AND LISA GROSS. 1980. "Starting over in Chicago." *Forbes* (Apr. 28): 74–76.

TATRO, CHARLOTTE. 1974. "Cross my palm with silver." In Clifton D. Bryant (ed.). *Deviant Behavior,* pp. 286–99. Chicago: Rand-McNally.

TAUSKY, CURT AND ROBERT DUBIN. 1965. "Career anchorage: Managerial mobility motivations." *American Sociological Review* 30: 725–35.

TAYLOR, FREDERICK W. 1911. *Principles of Scientific Management.* New York: Harper and Row.

TERKEL, STUDS. 1972. *Working*. New York: Random House.

TERPSTRA, DAVID E. AND JOHN M. LARSEN, JR. 1980. "A note on job type and applicant race as determinants of hiring decisions." *Journal of Occupational Psychology* 53: 117–19.

THOMPSON, JACQUELIN. 1976. "Patron, rabbis, mentors: whatever you call them, women need them too." *MBA* 17: 26–36.

THOMPSON, JAMES D. 1967. *Organizations in Action*. New York: McGraw-Hill.

THOMPSON, PAUL H., AND GENE W. DALTON. 1976. "Are R&D organizations obsolete?" *Harvard Business Review:* 105–16.

THUROW, LESTER C. 1981. "Where management fails." *Newsweek* (Dec. 7): 78.

TILSHER, ADRIANO. 1930. *Homo Faber: Work Through the Ages*. New York: Harcourt, Brace and World.

TIME. 1974. "New York goes modern." TIME (Aug. 12): 57–58.

TOREN, NINA A. 1973. "The bus driver: a study in role analysis." *Human Relations* 26: 102–12.

————. 1975. "Deprofessionalization and its sources." *Work and Occupations* 2: 323–37.

TREIMAN, DONALD J. 1977. *Occupational Prestige in Comparative Perspective*. New York: Academic Press.

TREIMAN, DONALD J. AND HEIDI HARTMANN. 1981. *Women, Work, and Wages: Equal Pay for Jobs of Equal Value*. Washington, D.C.: National Academy Press.

TREIMAN, DONALD J., AND KERMIT TERRELL. 1975. "Sex and the process of status attainment: a comparison of working women and men." *American Sociological Review* 40: 174–200.

TRICE, HARRISON M. AND PAUL M. ROMAN. 1972. *Spirits and Demons at Work*. Ithaca, NY: Cornell University Press.

TRIGOBOFF, DANIEL. 1986. "No-frills law clinics judged ok." *USA Today* (Jan. 13): 4B.

TUCHMAN, GAYE. 1972. "Objectivity as strategic ritual: an examination of newspapermen's notions of objectivity." *American Journal of Sociology* 77: 660–79.

TURNER, BARBARA F., AND CASTELLANO B. 1975. "Race, sex, and perception of the occupational opportunity structure among college students." *Sociological Quarterly* 16: 345–60.

TURNER, BARRY A. 1971. *Exploring the Industrial Subculture*. New York: Macmillan.

TURNER, CASTELLANO B., AND BARBARA F. 1981. "Racial discrimination in occupations: perceived and actual." *Phylon* 42: 322–34.

TUROW, SCOTT. 1977. *One L*. New York: G. P. Putnam's Sons.

TURVILLE, A. E. 1920. "Extreme view as to requirements for making optometry strictly professional." *Optical Journal and Review of Optometry* 46: 106–10.

TUTTLE, WILLIAM M., JR. 1970. "Labor conflict and racial violence: the black worker in Chicago, 1894–1919." In Milton Cantor (ed.), *Black Labor in America*, pp. 86–110. Westport, CT: Negro Universities Press.

UHNAK, DOROTHY. 1963. *Policewoman*. New York: Simon and Schuster.

U.S. BUREAU OF THE CENSUS. 1979a. *The Social and Economic Status of the Black Population in the U.S., 1790–1978*. Washington: Government Printing Office.

————. 1979b. *Lifetime Earnings Estimates for Men and Women in the United States*. Washington: Government Printing Office.

U.S. BUREAU OF LABOR STATISTICS. 1983. *Workers Without Jobs*. Washington, D.C.: Government Printing Office.

————. 1984a. *Families at Work: The Jobs and the Pay*. Bulletin 2209. Washington, DC: Government Printing Office.

————. 1984b. *Occupational Projects and Training Data*. Washington, DC: Government Printing Office.

————. 1985. *Handbook of Labor Statistics*. Washington, DC: Government Printing Office.

U.S. COMMISSION ON CIVIL RIGHTS. 1980. *Characters in Textbooks*. Washington: Government Printing Office.

U.S. DEPARTMENT OF LABOR. 1985. *Women and Office Automation*. Washington, D.C.: Government Printing Office.

————. 1984. *Families At Work*. Washington, D.C.: Government Printing Office.

————. 1982. *Employment and Training Report of the President*. Washington: Government Printing Office.

————. 1980. *Annual Construction Industry Report*. Washington, D.C.: Government Printing Office.

————. 1964. *Training of Workers in American Industry*. Washington, D.C.: Government Printing Office.

U.S. EMPLOYMENT AND TRAINING ADMINISTRATION. 1977. *Dictionary of Occupational Titles*. Washington: Government Printing Office.

USEEM, MICHAEL. 1976. "Government influence on the social science paradigm." *The Sociological Quarterly* 17: 146–61.

VANDEVELDE, MARYANNE. 1984. *Changing Life of the Corporate Wife.*

VANDIVIER, KERMIT. 1972. "Why should my conscience bother me?" In Robert Heilbroner, *In the Name of Profit*, pp. 3–31. New York: Doubleday.

VANEK, JOANN. 1974. "Time spent in housework." *Scientific American* 231: 116–20.

VAN GENNEP, ARNOLD 1960. *The Rites of Passage.* Chicago: University of Chicago Press.

VAN MAANEN, JOHN. 1973. "Observations on the making of policemen." *Human Organization* 4: 407–17.

———. 1975. "Breaking-in: socialization to work." In Robert Dubin (ed.). *Handbook of Work, Organization and Society*, pp. 32–103. Chicago: Rand McNally.

———. 1977. "Experiencing organization: notes on the meaning of careers and socialization." In John Van Maanen (ed.), *Organizational Careers*, pp. 15–48. New York: Wiley.

———. AND EDGAR H. SCHEIN. 1979. "Toward a theory of organizational socialization." *Research in Organizational Behavior* 1: 209–64.

VARCA, PHILIP E., GARNETT STOKES SHAFFER AND CYNTHIA D. MCCAULEY. 1983. "Sex differences in job satisfaction revisited." *Academy of Management Journal* 26: 348–53.

VARDI, YOAV. 1980. "Organizational career mobility: an integrative model." *Academy of Management Review* 5: 341–55.

VAUGHT, CHARLES, AND DAVID L. SMITH. 1980. "Incorporation and mechanical solidarity in an underground coal mine." *Sociology of Work and Occupations* 7: 159–87.

VEIGA, JOHN F. 1981. "Plateaued versus nonplateaued managers: career paths, attitudes and path potential." *Academy of Management Journal* 24: 566–78.

VELARDE, ALBERT J. 1975. "Becoming prostituted: the decline of the massage parlor profession and the masseuse." *British Journal of Criminology* 15: 251–62.

———, AND MARK WARLICK. 1973. "Massage parlors: the sensuality business." *Society* 11: 63–74.

VINEY, LINDA L. 1983. "Psychological reactions of young people to unemployment." *Youth and Society* 14: 457–74.

VINNICOMBE, SUSAN. 1980. *Secretaries, Management and Organizations.* London: Heinemann.

VON HIPPEL, FRANK. 1977. "Protecting the whistle-blowers." *Physics Today:* 9–13.

VOYDANOFF, PATRICIA. 1980. "Perceived job characteristics and job satisfaction among men and women." *Psychology of Women Quarterly* 5: 177–85.

VUKMAN-TENEBAUM, MIRJANA. 1981. "Organizing domestics in Ontario." *Resources for Feminist Research* 10: 32–33.

WALDMAN, H. BARRY. 1980. "The reaction of the dental profession to changes in the 1970s." *American Journal of Public Health* 70: 619–24.

WALDMAN, PETER. 1986. "More doctors and lawyers joining unions to fight large institutions." *Wall Street Journal* (May 23): 21.

WALKER, CHARLES R., AND ROBERT GUEST. 1952. *The Man on the Assembly Line.* Cambridge, MA: Harvard University Press.

WALKER, JON E., CURT TAUSKY AND DONNA OLIVER. 1982. "Men and women at work." *Journal of Vocational Behavior* 21: 17–36.

WALKER, K. E. 1973. "Household work time." *Journal of Home Economics* 65: 7–12.

WALLACE, MICHAEL, AND ARNE L. KALLEBERG. 1982. "Industrial transformation and the decline of craft: the decomposition of skill in the printing industry, 1931–1978." *American Sociological Review* 47: 307–24.

WALLICK, MERRITT. 1984. "Are bosses worth major league pay?" *Wilmington News-Journal* (June 10): 1–5C.

WALSH, DIANA CHAPMAN. 1984. "Is there a doctor in-house" *Harvard Business Review* (July-Aug.): 84–94.

WALSHOK, MARY L. 1981. *Blue Collar Women.* Garden City: Anchor.

WALTERS, KENNETH D. 1975. "Your employees' right to blow the whistle." *Harvard Business Review* 53: 26–162.

WALTON, RICHARD E. 1985. "From control to commitment in the workplace." *Harvard Business Review* 85: 77–84.

WAMSLEY, GARY L. 1972. "Contrasting institutions of air force socialization: happenstance or bellwether?" *American Journal of Sociology* 78: 399–417.

WANG, JOHN. 1979. "China's jobless youth: a mounting problem." *New York Times* (Sept. 30): 11F.

WANOUS, JOHN P. 1976. "Organizational entry: from naive expectations to realistic beliefs." *Journal of Applied Psychology* 61: 22–29.

———. 1977. "Organization entry: newcomers moving from outside to inside." *Psychological Bulletin* 84: 601–18.

WARNER, STEVEN. 1972. "A Conscientious Objector at Paris Island." *Atlantic* 229: 45–52.

WARR, PETER. 1984a. "Work and unemployment." In P. J. D. Drenth, et al. (eds.), *Handbook of Work and Organizational Psychology.* London: Wiley.

————. 1984b. "Reported behavioral changes after job loss." *British Journal of Social Psychology* 23: 271–75.

————. AND ROY PAYNE. 1983. "Social class and reported changes in behavior after job loss." *Journal of Applied Social Psychology* 13: 206–22.

WARREN, RICHARD L. 1975. "Context and isolation: the teaching experience in an elementary school." *Human Organization* 34: 139–48.

WATERS, L. K. AND D. ROACH. 1971. "The two-factor theories of job satisfaction." *Personnel Psychology* 24: 697–705.

WAYNE, LESLIE. 1982. "The year of the accountant." *New York Times* (Jan. 3): 1–15F.

WEAVER, CHARLES N. 1975. "Job preferences of white collar and blue collar workers." *Academy of Management Journal* 18: 167–75.

WEBBER, ROSS A. 1976. "Career problems of young managers." *California Management Review* 18: 11–33.

WEISS, MELFORD S. 1967. "Rebirth in the airborn." *Transaction* 4: 23–26.

WEST, CANDACE. 1982. "Why can't a woman be more like a man?" *Work and Occupations* 9: 5–29.

WESTCOTT, DIANE NILSEN. 1982. "Blacks in the 1970s: Did they scale the job ladder?" *Monthly Labor Review* 105: 29–38.

WHITE, KERR L. 1973. "Life and death in medicine." *Scientific American* 229: 3–13.

WHITE, LYNN K. AND DAVID B. BRINKERHOFF. 1981. "The sexual division of labor: Evidence from childhood." *Social Forces* 60: 170–81.

WHYTE, WILLIAM F. 1946. "When workers and customers meet." In William F. Whyte (ed.), *Industry and Society*, pp. 123–47. New York: McGraw-Hill.

WILCOCK, R. C. AND W. H. FRANKE. 1963. *Unwanted Workers.* Glencoe, IL: Free Press.

WILENSKY, HAROLD L. 1964. "The professionalization of everyone?" *American Journal of Sociology* 70: 137–58.

WILLIAMS, ROBERT E. 1984. "Comparable worth: Legal perspectives and precedents." *In Comparable Worth: Issue for the 80s.* Washington, D.C.: U.S. Commission on Civil Rights.

WILLIAMS, TREVOR. 1975. "Educational ambition: teachers and students." *Sociology of Education* 48: 432–56.

WOLKINSON, BENJAMIN W., GEDALIAHU H. HAREL AND DAFNA N. IZRAEL. 1982. "Employment discrimination against women: The Israeli experience." *Employee Relations Law Journal* 7: 466–89.

WOOD, ROBERT, FRANK HULL AND KOYA AZUMI. 1982. "Evaluating quality circles." Working paper, Center for the Study of Innovation, Entrepreneurship and Organizational Strategy, College Park, MD.

WOODWARD, KENNETH L., AND JANET HUCK. 1985. "Next, clergy malpractice." *Newsweek* (May 20): 90.

WOODS, CLYDE M. 1972. "Students without teachers." *American Behavioral Scientist* 16: 19–29.

WRIGHT, BENJAMIN D., AND SHIRLEY A. TUSKA. 1968. "Career dreams of teachers." *Transaction* 6: 43–47.

WRIGHT, ERIC O. 1978. "Race, class, and income inequality." *American Journal of Sociology* 83: 1368–97.

————, ET AL. 1982. "The American class structure." *American Sociological Review* 47: 709–26.

WRONG, MORRISON G. 1980. "Model students? teachers perceptions and expectations of their Asian and white students." *Sociology of Education* 53: 236–46.

ZEMANS, FRANCES KAHN AND VICTOR G. ROSENBLUM. 1980. *The Making of a Public Profession.* Chicago: American Bar Foundation.

ZIMBALIST, ANDREW. 1979. "Technology and the labor process in the printing industry." In Andrew Zimbalist (ed.), *Case Studies on the Labor Process*, pp. 103–26. New York: Monthly Review Press.

ZUCKERMAN, HARRIET. 1977. *Scientific Elite: Nobel Laureates in the United States.* New York: Free Press.

ZURCHER, LOUIS A., JR. 1965. "The sailor aboard ship: a study of role behavior in a total institution." *Social Forces* 43: 389–401.

————. 1967. "The Naval recruit training center: a study of role assimilation in a total institution." *Sociological Inquiry* 37: 85–98.

ZWERDLING, DANIEL. 1980. *Workplace Democracy.* New York: Harper and Row.

AUTHOR INDEX

SUBJECT INDEX

Mail carriers, 202
Malpractice, 25, 28
Managers, 12–13, 105–10
Meanings of work, 188–90, 200–203
Men:
    in clerical work, 124
    income, 190–93
    labor force participation, 8, 9
    subcultural rituals, 57
Mentors, 332–37
Mexican workers, 159–60
Military, 282–85
Mine workers, 49–50, 54–55
Multiperson careers, 19, 329–30

Nigerian prestige hierarchy, 217–18
Non-traditional work, 297–98
Norms, subcultural, 52–55
Nurses, 1, 72–74

Occupational choices, 253–74
Occupational sex typing, 256–60
Occupations, defined, 5
Operatives, 17, 150–55
Optometrists, 69
Organizational work systems, 3–4, 94–96
    professionals in, 110–21

Pay equity (see Comparable worth)
Performance appraisals, 313–16
Pharmacists, 62, 68–69, 113
Physicians, 26, 115
Police work, 24, 46, 47–48, 163, 293–95, 298
Power relations, 23–39
    managerial, 108–10
Prestige, 75–76, 189, 213–30
    achieved, 222–24
    ascribed, 220–22
    United States, 215–17
Printers, 140–43, 145–46
Professionalization process, 62–82
Professional work, 10–11, 16, 60–93
    autonomy, 16, 61, 90–91
    codes of ethics, 71–76, 118
    defined, 60
    deprofessionalization, 83–92
    employed in organizations, 110–21
    licensing, 70–71, 76–82
    monopoly, 16, 61, 91–92
    professional associations, 67–69
    self-regulation, 10, 67–68, 91
Proletarianization of clerical work, 124–29
Promotions:
    criteria, 324–29
    meanings, 321–24
    organizational patterns, 337–38
Prostitutes, 176, 225, 286–89
Public defenders, 53

Quality circles, 248–50
Quota restriction, 40, 59

Railroaders, 41, 45
Resocialization, 282–86
Rites of passage, 57–58
Rituals, subcultural, 55–58
Role conflicts, 37–39, 122–24, 331–32

Salespersons:
    insurance, 166
    real estate, 167

retail, 5
    used car, 167–68
Sales work, 17, 50, 163–68
    relations with customers, 163–65
    sales transactions, 165–68
Scientific Management (see Taylorism)
Scientists, 113–15
Secretaries, 129–32
Service work, 17–19, 162–87
    client typologies, 171–76
    service relationships, 169–71
Sex therapists, 65
Socialization:
    occupational, 275–98
    preoccupational, 253–66
Status dilemma, 169–70, 215
Stereotypes:
    customer, 50
    gender, 269–70
    occupational, 309–10
    occupational sex typing, 256–60
Subcultures, work and occupational, 40–59
    defined, 3, 40
    emergence, 40–42, 59
    functions, 42–43
Supervisors, first-line, 13, 121–24
Swedish:
    codetermination, 247–48

Taylorism (Scientific Management), 30, 121, 127,
    151–55, 183, 232, 251
Technical obsolescence, 113–14
Technicians, 14
Technostructure:
    defined, 14, 110
    emergence, 110–11
    organizational dilemmas, 111–21
Tipping, 173–75
Total institutions, 283–85
Transfers, 316–19
Trustworthiness, 290–93

Uncertainty, in executive roles, 101–2, 325–27
Unemployment, 203–12
    consequences, 206–8, 210–12
    discouraged workers, 204
    responses, 208–10
    vulnerability, 204–6
Uniforms, occupational, 48, 171
Unskilled work, 16, 155–60

Values, subcultural, 50–52
Volunteer work, 20

Waiters and waitresses, 1, 41, 169, 171–73
Whistle blowing, 117–20
White collar work, 15
Women:
    clerical workers, 124–29
    craft workers, 145–50
    family farm work, 19–20
    income, 191–95, 198–200
    labor force participation, 8–9
    unskilled work, 159
Work, defined, 5
    sociological perspectives, 2–5
    technical dimensions, 2, 53
    unpaid work, 20
    values, 188–90
Work and family roles, 127–28, 186–87, 329–32